Congress, Convention and
Exhibition Facilities

Architectural Press Planning and Design Series
Edited by Fred Lawson

Published books in the series:

Shopping Centres: Retail Development, Design and Management
Second edition – Nadine Beddington
Published 1991

Hotels and Resorts: Planning, Design and Refurbishment
Fred Lawson
Published 1995

Restaurants, Clubs and Bars: Planning and Design Investment for Food Service Facilities
Revised paperback edition – Fred Lawson
Published 1995

Airport Terminals
Second edition – Christopher J. Blow
Published 1996

Buildings for the Performing Arts
Ian Appleton
Published 1996

Tourism and Recreation Handbook of Planning and Design
Manuel Baud-Bovy and Fred Lawson
Published 1998

Congress, Convention and Exhibition Facilities
Fred Lawson
Published 2000

Credits for the front cover photos are as follows (from top left):

La Grande Motte
Architect: Jean Balladur
Photo: La Grande Motte Tourist Authority

Hong Kong Conference and Exhibition Centre
Architects: Wong & Ouyang with Skidmore, Owings & Merrill
Photo: Hong Kong Conference and Exhibition Centre

Telecom World, Hong Kong
Design: Met Studio

UNESCAP Hall
Architect: RMJM (Hong Kong)
Photo: UNESCAP

Edinburgh International Conference Centre
Architect: Terry Farrel & Partners
Photo: Edinburgh International Conference Centre

San Diego Convention Center
Architects: Arthur Erickson Architects, Deems/Lewis & Partners and
Loschky Marquardt & Nesholm
Photo: Hawkins Productions

Congress, Convention and Exhibition Facilities:
Planning, Design and Management

Fred Lawson

Architectural Press

OXFORD   AUCKLAND   BOSTON   JOHANNESBURG   MELBOURNE   NEW DELHI

Architectural Press is an imprint of Elsevier
Linacre House, Jordan Hill, Oxford OX2 8DP, UK
30 Corporate Drive, Suite 400, Burlington, MA 01803, USA

First edition 2000
Reprinted 2001, 2007

British Library Cataloguing in Publication Data
Lawson, Fred
  Congress, convention and exhibition facilities: planning,
  design and management. – New ed.
  1. Convention facilities – Design and Construction
  2. Convention facilities – Management   3. Exhibition buildings
  - Design and Construction   4. Congresses and conventions
  5. Meetings
  I. Title
  725.9′1

Library of Congress Cataloging-in-Publication Data
A catalog record for this book is available from the Library of Congress

ISBN: 978-0-7506-2790-0

For information on all Architectural Press publications
visit our website at www.architecturalpress.com

Printed and bound in *Great Britain*

07 08 09 10 10 9 8 7 6 5 4 3

Contents

Foreword

Union des Associations Internationales: Union of International Associations

Since its foundation in 1910, the Union of International Associations (UIA) has shown a permanent interest in the organization and venue of international meetings. Its conference calendar, originally seen as an information tool for NGOs, has become an important tool for the conference industry. The UIA helps its associate members (conference centres, congress interpreters, congress organizers) to raise the standards of international meetings quality. The Union is thus in a good position to observe the development of this important socio-logical phenomenon.

Much has been published on different aspects of the meeting industry. The present publication is unique in as much as it proposes a global approach, including the architecture and design of conference centres and their technological equipment, but also studies marketing and management aspects.

The constant growth of the number of international meetings held worldwide, and the ever growing development of the communication industry have largely influenced the increase in the number of purpose-built conference centres over the years. Centres recently opened – and/or to be inaugurated in the coming months – testify to the dynamism of the industry. As very clearly illustrated in this publication, infra-structures, facilities and technical equipment necessary for the meetings to be organized in the best possible manner, permanently have to adapt to new technologies. They must also be more and more flexible, to allow the optimization of the organization of different conference patterns, including virtual conferences using the Net facilities.

At the beginning of the new millennium, UIA welcomes the publication of a revised edition of this indispensable reference book for all those involved in planning, designing and managing conference centres worldwide, as well as for the users, namely international or local organizers of international meetings.

Anne-Marie Boutin,
President, Union of International Associations

By the President of the Convention Industry Council

CIC (Convention Industry Council), a U.S. based organization of twenty-six associations serving the meetings industry, is pleased to support and endorse the publishing of *Congress, Convention and Exhibition Facilities: Planning, Design and Management* by Professor Lawson. It is the desire of CIC that attention is drawn to both the importance of and the critical role in today's worldwide economy of the meeting, convention and exposition industry, and this book does it very well. We were pleased to work with Professor Lawson in providing some background information and material used in the book.

Garis F. Distelhorst, CAE, President

Preface

Meetings, incentive travel, conventions and exhibitions comprise a relatively new but rapidly growing industry which has wide ranging impacts on the economics of many countries. World wide, direct spending is expected to reach US$ 230 billion by the year 2000 (based on collected statistics). In the United States, the direct expenditure makes this industry the 22nd largest contributor to the gross domestic product (CLC Report in 'Convene' Magazine, 1995).

Conference, Convention and Exhibition Facilities, published in 1981, laid down the framework for the vast developments which have taken place over the last two decades. This new volume presents the latest information and examples as a guide for the new millennium, and has been prepared with a number of objectives in mind, namely to provide:

- a source of reference for organizers of events and managers of all types of venues covering, in particular, those technical aspects of management which are usually not included in books on general theory;
- a guide for owners, architects, planners, engineers and other consultants involved in new projects and the maintenance or refurbishment of existing facilities;
- a collection of the most interesting new examples and a summary of trends which are likely to influence the directions of the industry in the future.

To provide a comprehensive coverage of the Meetings, Incentives, Conventions, and Exhibitions (MICE) industry, this book summarizes key marketing and managerial aspects as well as details of requirements for congress, conference, training and exhibition centres, hotels, universities, galleries and visitor centres. Techncial subjects are explained together with examples of the latest systems and equipment.

As a busy practitioner, I am conscious of the need for compressed information backed by facts and figures and this is reflected in the style of presentation. However, it must be emphasized that the details are typical or illustrative, and may vary with particular circumstances and requirements.

The research and preparation of this extensive material has taken five years and involved contacts with numerous institutions, venues and architects world-wide. The response to my enquiries has been most gratifying, and I would like to thank, collectively, all those who contributed valuable information and examples. As far as possible, the names of organizations, architects and others are credited with the illustrations, and these represent the work of most of the leading international authorities in this field. Regretfully, space and reproduction difficulties limited the number of examples which could be included, and I sincerely apologize for omissions. Not least, I have been most encouraged by the interest shown and factual help given by international bodies like the UIA, CLC, ICCA, IACVB, IAPC, AIIC and IACC, as well as many individual and public authorities involved in this dynamic industry.

In particular, I would like to express my gratitude to Mme Ghislaine de Coninck, Director of the Congress and Services Department of the UIA for her positive support, as well as to Mrs Anne Marie Boutin, President of the Union of International Associations and Garis F. Distelshorst, President and Chief Executive Officer of the Convention Industry Council for kindly providing forewords to this book.

My greatest debt is to my long-suffering wife.

1 Influences on supply and demand

1.1 PROFILE AND TERMINOLOGY

1.1.1 Activities

The Meetings, Incentive travel, Conventions and Exhibitions (MICE) industry plays a vital role in tourism and economic development. It overlaps with business travel and events ranging from international expositions to individual product launches, and embraces meetings of all kinds, from international congresses to corporate training needs.

The boundaries in relation to facilities are also indistinct. Many premises used primarily for other purposes may serve as the occasional venue for a meeting or related event; equally, almost all purpose-designed congress/convention centres are also equipped to serve other cultural and entertainment needs.

Moreover, exhibitions extend over a wide spectrum of interests: they may be temporary, frequently changed or mainly permanent; attendance may be open to the public or limited to trade and professional viewers; and the venues may be halls set out with stands for each event or designed for more specific displays.

Range of activities

Purpose organization	Voluntary association (social, charitable, special interest)/voluntary professional association	Corporate	Government/public authority	Exhibitions
Types of activities	Annual general meetings, committee/board meetings, seminars/workshops, continued education/training, social/fund raising events	AGM/shareholders management meetings, sales conferences, presentations/external information, product launches, training programmes, incentive travel	Public enquiries, presentations/public information, sponsored events, training and work programmes	Major expositions, public exhibitions, agricultural shows, trade fairs[1], exhibitions with conventions[2], educational and cultural interests[3]

[1] Including specialized subject divisions and shows partly open to the public
[2] Also seminars run in parallel with exhibits
[3] Visitors centres, art galleries, museums, science and life centres.

Range of premises

	Meetings	Exhibits
Purpose designed	Executive conference centres, congress/convention/conference centres, multi-use auditoria	Visitor centres, art galleries, museums, science/life centres, exhibition centres, convention centres
Adaptable use[1]	Convention hotels, function rooms, theatres, concert halls, public halls[2], universities, colleges, arenas[3]	Sports halls, hotel ball rooms[4], public concourses, foyers[4]
Occasional use	Libraries, art galleries, museums[5], stadia[5]	Open air grounds[6]

[1] Designed and equipped for this use
[2] Equipped for plenary sessions
[3] With roof cover – for large conventions
[4] With appropriate access for exhibits, technical and support services
[5] May provide ancillary lecture/meeting rooms
[6] Associated with other premises/spill-over events/temporary marquees.

Singapore International Convention and Exhibition Centre

An integral part of the Suntech City complex, the SICEC covers 100 000 m² and is linked by overhead bridge to over 3000 hotel rooms and by underpass to the Mass Rapid Transit system and shopping malls. There are five functional levels:

* *Level 1 — lobby entrance with registration, information and service counters and offices;*
* *Level 2 — ballroom (2150 m²), with stage and prefunction areas, plus 10 meeting rooms;*
* *Level 3 — auditorium seating 596 plus 16 meeting rooms for 80–300 people;*
* *Level 4 — exhibition halls (12 000 m²) with pits and trenches for services;*
* *Level 6 — convention halls (seating up to 12 000).*

All the large halls are sub-divisible, with Levels 4 and 6 accessible for vehicles via a two-way spiral ramp. The basement provides a large car park.

Architect: Tsa & McKown, D.P. Architects
M&E Engineers: Parsons Brinkerhoff
Photographs: Richard Bryant. Arcaid. Singapore ICEC.

Singapore International Convention and Exhibition Centre

LEVEL 2

LEVEL 3

Singapore International Convention and Exhibition Centre

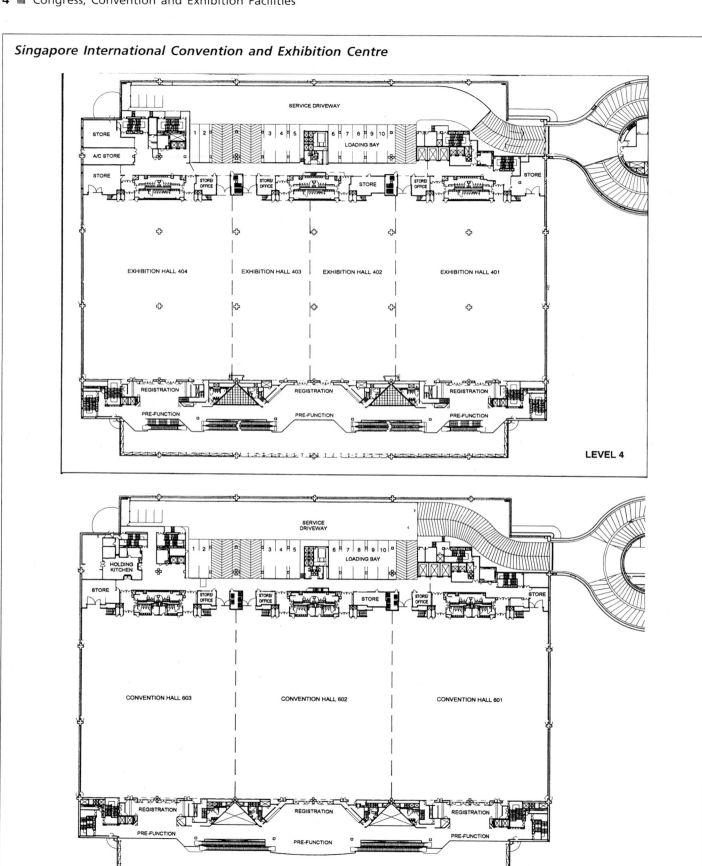

Whilst there are wide differences in character and scale, all these activities tend to have certain features in common. They involve:

- people sharing a common interest coming together, either as individuals or groups, for an organized meeting, exhibition and related events in a pre-arranged venue;
- the use of a venue that can provide the space and facilities required to satisfy the needs of the participants and the activities involved.

1.1.2 The need for meetings

The main drawing factor which generates a continuing demand for meetings is the need for communication at a personalized level; the opportunity for individuals, particularly in those activities which involve problem solving and innovation, to exchange ideas and views. Printed and electronic information, even with developments in video conferencing, cannot be a substitute for this personal contact. The importance of a congress or convention lies not only in what is said from the platform but also in the total atmosphere of the event and the stimulation provided as a result.

However, the enormous and continuing growth in meeting and convention business cannot be attributed to this motivating interest alone. Information needs to be shared for many reasons – education, training, team building, strategic planning, problem solving, sales promotion, new product introduction and reorganization – and these goals are most effectively achieved through group participation.

Conventions and incentive travel increasingly overlap, with international companies placing emphasis both on rewarding achievements and on creating a global family atmosphere amongst employees normally separated by considerable distances and, often, cultural differences.

Similar considerations apply to many international association meetings. Whilst Europe and America dominate in the choice of venue for practical reasons (location of headquarters, areas of concentrated membership, developed facilities and supporting interests), there is a tendency to stage some meetings in more remote centres, particularly in countries in receipt of development aid or where local associations are highly active.

Adding to this trend is the competitive development of outstanding convention facilities in exotic destinations like South East Asia (Hong Kong, Singapore, Thailand, Korea), Australia, Japan and the Middle East, and their strong promotion in world markets.

At a national level the choice of location for most total membership association events, such as annual conventions, invariably reflects a balance of considerations. Factors such as accessibility for the majority of members and the availability and suitability of facilities are over-riding considerations, but of considerable importance are the social and leisure attractions for delegates and those accompanying them (see 1.5.3). Staging related exhibitions is often seen as an important part of the information programme as well as a contribution towards the costs.

1.1.3 Exhibitions and trade fairs

In its broadest sense, an exhibition is a display, show or demonstration of something of beauty, value or particular interest to a targeted audience. Exhibits may be on permanent display or brought together temporarily for a particular event. Commercial exhibitions can be categorized as:

- trade shows and fairs, which bring sellers and buyers of products, goods and services together in particular industrial sectors;
- consumer shows or fairs, which are open to the general public;
- mixed trade-consumer shows or fairs, which admit the public on certain days only;
- private exhibitions, in which individual companies or agencies organize their own exhibitions to demonstrate their products to a selected or invited audience.
- product launches, which are to introduce new goods and services and may be featured in a trade fair, private exhibition or both.

The main advantages of trade and commercial exhibitions are that they provide a forum for sales leads (subsequent orders), contact with influencers (press, dealers, distributors), image building and market/competitor intelligence (enquiries, comments, responses, competition) (see 8.2.2).

Exhibitions provide an opportunity for sellers to explain and demonstrate their products and services directly to potential buyers gathered in one place, and are a cost-effective way of launching new products, penetrating new markets, reinforcing existing customer interest and maintaining or increasing market shares.

Like association meetings, exhibitions need careful planning and organization, involving long lead times and, initially, a high degree of risk (see 1.8.1). Once established, trade fairs and consumer exhibitions tend to continue to be held as a regular calendar event, invariably growing in size and hiving off more specialist exhibitions. Individual exhibitors may occupy stands exclusively or join together as an associated group in a larger assembly, and often need to reserve space well ahead to secure prime positions. The stands may be individually designed and built for the purpose, or use a basic shell scheme provided by the organizer.

Compared with meetings, established exhibitions usually generate operating profits both for the hall providers and organizers of the events. Exhibits and meetings are often held in parallel; large or specialized trade fairs commonly include optional seminars as an additional attraction and related source of information. Some 30–40 per cent of association conventions (see 1.8.2) include related exhibits, both to extend the value of attendance and contribute to costs of the meeting.

1.1.4 Incentive travel

This is defined by the Society of Incentive Travel Executives (SITE) as 'a global management tool that uses an exceptional travel experience to motivate and/or recognize participants for increased levels of performance in support of organizational goals' (SITE, 1998).

Travel to an attractive or/and uniquely interesting destination, with all expenses paid, is widely used as an incentive to:

* motivate and reward high-performing employees and sales representatives;
* provide an environment for team building, sharing of experiences and ideas;
* strengthen the loyalty of the participants to the company.

Activities often include a highly organized social programme, visits (including educational tours), elaborate presentation ceremonies, opportunities to meet top management and short conferences – including announcements of the company's plans, programmes and future targets.

Depending on the company's goals, the incentive programme is commonly aimed at identified groups of sales people, dealers, distributors, sales consultants or/and retailers. The programme is invariably framed around a theme to create a memorable experience for the participants, and is subsequently evaluated to measure the results (see 4.7.1–2).

Incentive travel is closely related to corporate hospitality and entertainment. The latter is concerned with strengthening the links within a company or between a company and its clients, and includes receptions, dinners or banquets (often with formal presentations) and opportunities to attend major cultural or sporting events or to take part in team building exercises.

1.1.5 Measurement of meetings

Whilst the meetings industry is concerned with communicating information, it is itself complicated by the lack of a universally accepted vocabulary to define and quantify the different types of meetings involved. Where surveys have been carried out each has had to determine its own criterion of measurement, and this lack of market intelligence often limits comparison of statistics and a true assessment of the scale and value of the industry.

Decisions on what constitutes a 'meeting' depend on the minimum number of attendees, the length of time involved, the subjects or activities included and, in some cases, the type of premises used. These dimensional limits are particularly

critical in the corporate sector, where the vast majority of meetings are small but, in aggregate, represent a sizeable proportion of the total attendance figures.

The Netherlands

Between 1989 and 1997, the number of international conferences in the Netherlands more than doubled and delegate days increased by 77 per cent.

Year	International conferences (1)	Delegate days
1989	328	514 291
1995	509	1 841 788 (2)
1996	542	788 645
1997	686	912 025
Main cities: 1997 (% of totals)		
Amsterdam	175 (25.5)	380 571 (41.7)
The Hague	88 (12.8)	122 383 (13.4)

(1) Those registered by the Netherlands Convention Bureau. Defined as lasting two days or more, with a minimum of 40 participants, at least one-third of whom come from abroad.
(2) Total boosted by several major conventions in Utrecht.

Source: Netherlands Convention Bureau.

Terms like conference, convention and congress are often used indiscriminately, and this also creates some difficulty in describing the types of facilities required. In the United Kingdom, conference centres are designed to accommodate large conventions and congresses; in the United States the conference centre is a self-contained property purposely designed for smaller meetings, especially for groups of between 20 and 50 people (Penner, 1991), and would be described elsewhere as an executive conference centre.

In drawing up a terminology that can be used in planning facilities, reference has been made to a number of authoritative sources. The following definitions are recommended in the *International Meetings Industry Glossary* of the American Convention Liaison Council and Joint Industry Council (CLC, 1998).

1.1.6 Meetings and conferences

Meeting:
> *A general term indicating the coming together of a number of people in one place, to confer or carry out a particular activity. Can be on an ad hoc basis or according to a set pattern.*

Conference:
> *An event used by any organization to meet and exchange views, convey a message, open a debate or give publicity to some area of opinion on a specific issue. No tradition, continuity or periodicity is required to convene a conference. Although not limited in time,*

Palais des Congrès de Lyon, France

This is one of a row of prestigious buildings that form the Cité International de Lyon along the edge of a large park fronting the River Rhone – the result of a joint planning initiative undertaken by the City and Urban Community of Lyon in partnership with the Lyon Chamber of Commerce, and Industry, regional and Rhone departmental councils and major financial institutions under the presidency of the Deputy Mayor Henry Chabert. Planned by Renzo Piano, the Cité is being extended in phases, with a new Hilton hotel, casino and forum to be completed in 1999.

The Palais des Congrès, opened in 1995, extends over four levels. The main level, above the entrance, accommodates a multi-use grand forum (3000 m²), which divides into three, and ancillary dining areas, whilst below are two auditoria (seating 872 and 300). The upper level and roof terrace provide 15 flexible conference rooms for 10–200 people.

In 1997 there were 281 events held in the centre, taking 404 event days, with a total of 274 000 visitors. Conferences and exhibitions accounted for 30 per cent of the annual turnover.

Operator: Palais des Congres City of Lyon
Architect: Renzo Piano Building Workshop
Photographs: M Denance, D.Fav., Nicholas Robin

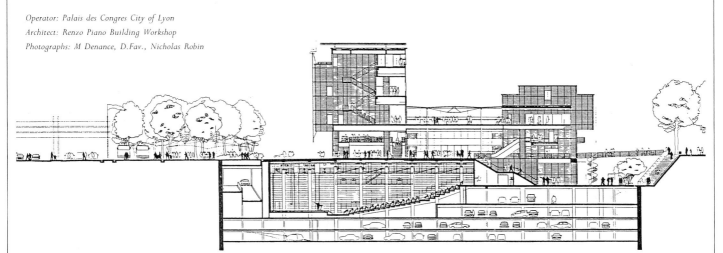

conferences are usually of short duration with specific objectives. Conferences are generally on a smaller scale than congresses.

Conferences are usually general sessions and face-to-face groups with a high participation primarily concerned with planning, obtaining facts and information or in solving organi-zational and operational problems. They are mainly confined to members of the same company, association or profession. The meetings are less formally organized, but encourage collective participation in reaching stated objectives and goals. Numbers of delegates attending a conference may range up to 150, but 30–50 is more typical.

Palacio Municipal de Congresos de Madrid, Spain

The Municipal Palace of Congresses is located in the Campo las Naciones – Madrid's new financial centre – near the trade fair and amongst business, entertainment and quality hotel facilities in a parkland setting with a golf course. Designed to express visual beauty and spaciousness, it has marble and glass facades extending 40 m high. Over 100 000 m² in size, it allows events of different types to be held simultaneously with two auditoria (2200 and 1500 persons), an all-purpose room for over 5000 persons, more than 100 meeting rooms and offices and a large exhibition area. The supporting facilities include a post office, shops, TV studio, press rooms and extensive food and beverage services.

Architect: Ricardo Bofill
Project Management: Architects and Engineers Group of the Municipality

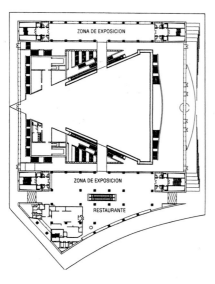

Características generales

- Montacargas (4) de acceso desde el muelle de carga, de 5.000 y 1.500 Kg.
- Megafonía ambiente y de avisos.
- Suministros eléctricos repartidos en tensiones de 380 v, cada 15m².
- Puntos de sujeción para estructuras de iluminación escenográfica.
- Sevicios Generales: climatización, iluminación y aseos.
- Acceso del público por ascensores y escaleras mecánicas.
- Luz natural.

Overall features

- *4 Service-elevators accessible from loading ramps with capacity for 5,000 and 1,500 Kg.*
- *Paging and background music loudspeaker system.*
- *Outlets for 380 v. available every 15 m².*
- *Anchor-points for stage-lighting structures.*
- *General services: air conditioning, lighting, rest-rooms.*
- *Public access via elevators and escalators.*
- *Day light.*

Características generales

- Megafonía general de la sala.
- Infraestructura de traducción simultánea por infrarrojos.
- Cabinas fijas de traducción simultánea normalizadas por la UNE1093: 1984 -UNE1094: 1984.
- Estructuras de sujeción para iluminación escenográfica.
- Suministro eléctrico 200 Kw, en RED y 100 Kw. en RED - GRUPO*.
- Capacidad 2.200 personas.
- Montacargas de accesos al escenario para 1.500 y 5.000 Kg.

* Para más información, consultar potencias eléctricas en Auditorios.

Overall features

- *Loudspeaker-system.*
- *Infrared simultaneous translation infrastructure.*
- *Simultaneous translation booths, standardized to UNE 1093:984 and UNE 1094: 1984.*
- *Anchor points for stage-lighting structures.*
- *Outles available for 200 Kw and standard electric-network and 100 Kw in group-network*.*
- *Capacity for 2,200 persons.*
- *1,500 and 5,000 Kg services-elevators with access to stage.*

* *For further information inquire about network loads in Auditoriums.*

Patio de butacas
Stalls

Configuración 'Exposición'
'Expo' shape

Configuración 'Stands'
'Stand' shape

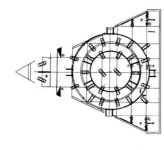

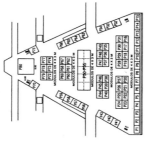

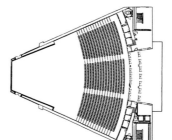

Anfiteatro
Amphitheatre

The characteristics of a conference influence the way the furniture is arranged. Tables are usually set out in a hollow square, circle, semicircle (senate style) or horseshoe shape whilst, for smaller groups, 'round the table' seating in board-room style is most often required.

1.1.7 Congress

Congress:

The regular coming together of large groups of individuals, generally to discuss a particular subject. A congress will often last several days and have several simultaneous sessions. The length of time between congresses is usually established in advance of the implementation stage and can be pluri-annual or annual. Most international or world congresses are of the former type whilst national congresses are more frequently held annually.

Palacio Municipal de Congresos de Madrid, Spain

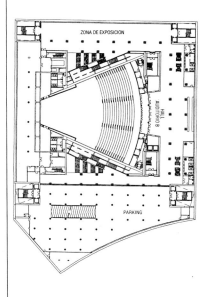

Características generales

- Megafonía general de la sala.
- Infraestructura de traducción simultánea por infrarrojos.
- Cabinas fijas de traducción simultánea normalizadas por la UNE1093: 1984 -UNE1094: 1984.
- Estructuras de sujección para iluminación escenográfica.
- Suministro eléctrico 200 Kw. en RED y 100 Kw. en RED - GRUPO*.
- Capacidad 800 / 1.500 personas.
- Montagargas de accesos al escenario para 1.500 y 5.000 Kg.

* Para más información, consultar potencias eléctricas en Auditorios.

Overall features

- Loudspeaker-system.
- Infrared simultaneous translation infrastructure.
- Simultaneous translation booths, standardized to UNE 1093:984 and UNE 1094: 1984.
- Anchor points for stage-lighting structures.
- Outles available for 200 Kw and standard electric-network and 100 Kw in group-network*.
- Capacity for 800 / 1.500 persons.
- 1.500 and 5.000 Kg services-elevators with access to stage.

* For further information inquire about network loads in Auditoriums.

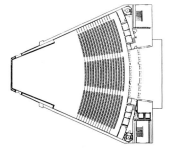

Congress halls are designed to accommodate large numbers of delegates, usually in close seated auditorium or theatre style grouping with or without inter-row writing ledges or tables. A number of flexible meeting rooms are also required for small group sessions.

An *assembly* may be described as a more specialized gathering of people for deliberation or discussion of some specific matter or a regular meeting of a deliberative body or legislative council. For this purpose the meeting room is usually arranged in a parliamentary style (semicircular, horseshoe or open rectangular layout), sometimes with double banks of chairs for the principals and their advisers. Facilities for microphone relay (with over-riding chairperson control), vote recording and simultaneous interpretation may be required.

Summit meetings of high level officials and heads of government require seating arranged round a table, with rows of seating grouped radially behind that of the principals, together with similar high quality services.

1.1.8 Convention

Convention:
A general and formal meeting of a legislative body, social or economic group in order to provide information on a particular situation and in order to deliberate and, consequently, establish consent on policies among the participants. Usually of limited duration with set objectives but no determined frequency.

The term convention is widely used, particularly by American associations, to describe the traditional form of total membership meetings. Conventions are usually general sessions, mostly information giving, often formed around a particular theme or subject matter of topical interest and increasingly accompanied by exhibits.

Over 80 per cent of associations hold an annual convention for their total membership and, in addition to public halls and convention centres, many 'convention hotels' offer extensive ballroom and banquet facilities for this purpose. In addition to the large halls and auditoriums required for the plenary sessions, most conventions break down into smaller groups to deliberate on particular matters of issue.

1.1.9 Other descriptions

Particular types of meetings (or subgroup meetings) may involve more specific requirements. The following are commonly accepted descriptions.

Seminar: usually one face-to-face group sharing experiences in a particular field under the guidance of an expert discussion leader. Meetings of this type are usually arranged for up to 30 persons.

Centre Salzburg, Austria

otracted debate, a decision was taken to construct the new congress centre on the site of the original building, necessitating a compact design on five main floors plus basement storage ng levels. Glass is used extensively in the facades, particularly over adjacent spa gardens. The main auditorium on the third floor, together with a balcony, has a variable stage (l) and seati. for 1320. The seats can be raised on tiered platforms or lowered to a flat floor for balls and presentations (m). Up to 12 meeting rooms can be formed by moveable partitions in the foyers on the ground and first floors (e), (h).

Innovative energy saving systems include an extensive roof area of voltaic cells and heat pumps extending 16 m in the ground to reduce heating and air-conditioning loads.

Client: City of Salzburg (Tourist Association)
Architects: Prof. Ernst Maurer, Friedrich Brandstatter
Technical services: Dick & Harner, Walter Hopferwieser, Klaus Hochschwarzer
Commencement of building: September 1998
Inauguration: 2000–2001
Estimated costs: AS510 million (US$36.8M)
Building footprint: 2500 m²
Total floor area: 15 700 m²
General accessible areas: foyers, 2470 m²; main hall, 1100 m², other event areas, 1200 m²; offices, 410 m²
Total capacity: 2500 persons (main hall, 1359 persons; meetings 60–500)
Encircled hall volume: 80 660 m³

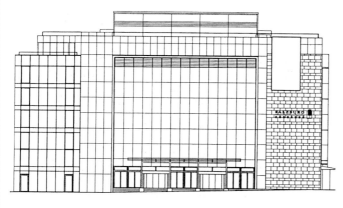

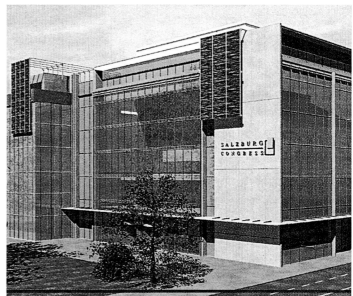

Workshop: typically comprises a general session together with face-to-face groups of participants training each other to gain new knowledge, skills or insights into problems. Attendance is generally no more than 30–35 participants.

Symposium: a panel discussion by experts in a given field before a large audience. Although some audience participation is involved, this is appreciably less than in a forum.

Forum: a panel discussion with opposite sides of an issue taken by experts in a given field and liberal opportunities for the audience to participate.

Panel: two or more speakers, each stating a viewpoint, with discussion between the speakers. The discussion is guided by a moderator.

Lecture: a formal presentation by an expert, followed by a question and answer period.

Institute: consists of general sessions and face-to-face groups discussing several facets of a subject. This is primarily to provide a substitute for formal education where in-house staff provide most of the training resources.

Colloquium: a programme in which the participants determine the matter to be discussed and the leaders then construct the programme around the most frequent problems. Meetings of this kind have equal emphasis on instruction and discussion, and are usually attended by up to 35 participants.

Poster sessions: accompanying meetings, poster sessions provide an opportunity for specialists, researchers, consultants and others working in the field to display information relating to their work or services and discuss aspects with interested delegates. The poster exhibits may be located in the concourse, foyer, a purpose-equipped exhibition area or a separate room.

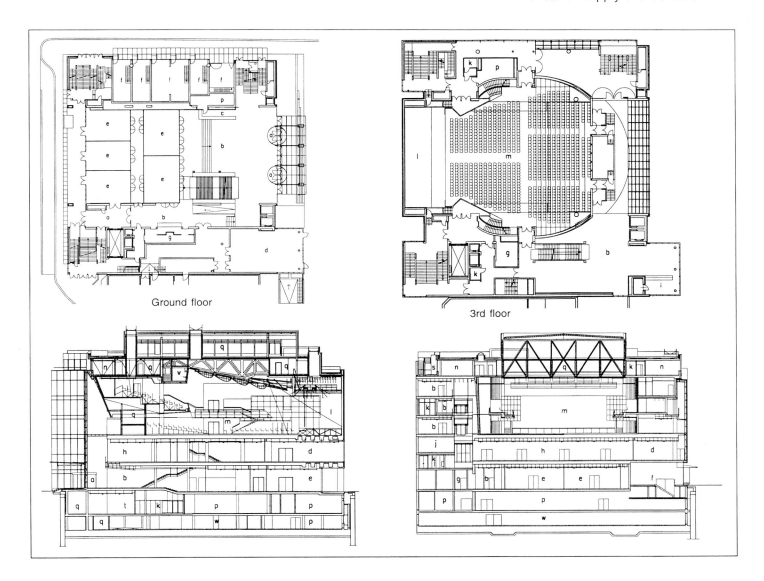

Ground floor

3rd floor

1.2 GROWTH, BENEFITS, RISKS

1.2.1 Growth

Although direct comparisons depend on the statistical criteria employed, the MICE industry has witnessed significant growth over recent years both at an international level and in most countries. The Union of International Associations (UIA), which has long reported consistent time series data, shows an increase of 90 per cent in the annual numbers of international meetings recorded over the 15 years between 1983 and 1997 (see 1.4.3) and progressive increases are stated in many national and venue reports.

This growth can be attributed to a number of factors. Some, like tourism in general, have arisen from increasing affluence and propensity to travel, aided by technological advances in air transportation and handling capabilities. Others are due more to specific needs associated with the development of international businesses and group interests.

General factors:
- Higher educational standards, an increasing propensity for people to travel and to take part in voluntary association activities;
- Growth in real per capita incomes with affluence spreading to new population groups – South East Asia, South America, Middle East;
- Increasing professionalism in tourism management applying a more precise knowledge of markets and motivations;
- Advances in transportation technology, airports, road and rail infrastructures and cruising coupled with economies in fuel, larger payloads and competitive costs.

Specific factors:
- Expansion of government and quasi-governmental organizations, together with an increasing need for meetings between the public and private sectors;

Tampere Hall, Finland

Tampere Hall is the leading congress centre in Finland and the civic and cultural focus of the City. With facades clad with soft grey granite and ceramic tiles, a spacious, glazed foyer and neat building outlines, the Hall epitomizes Finnish design. Granite extends into the lobby, but elsewhere floors are ash parquetry and the auditorium walls are lined with Finnish birch. Artwork is displayed throughout the public areas. A multi-use auditorium, with full stage facilities, seats 1806 (including balcony), a small auditorium 488, a studio 170 and meeting rooms 20–60 persons. There is a restaurant, cafeteria and Winter gardens and, in a linked hall, 2279 m² (gross) of exhibition space.

The hall is operated by a joint stock company owned by the City of Tampere. Convention and exhibition programmes are organized through the Congress Department. In 1997, the hall hosted 304 conference and business events (107 000 visitors) and 358 concerts and social activities (310 364 visitors).

Main building: 24 500 m² (155 800 m³)
Exhibition building: 2270 m² (18 700m³)

Operator: Tampere Hall
Architects: Sakari Aartela and Esa Piironen
Acoustics: Alpo Holme

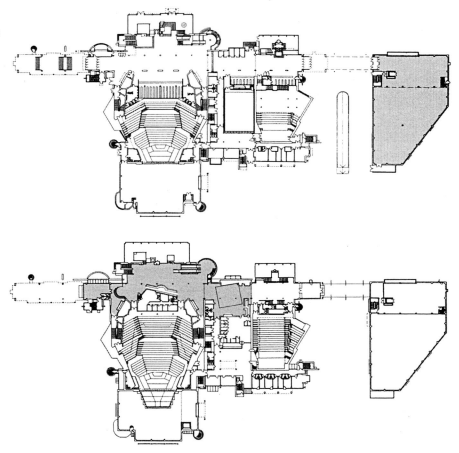

Istanbul Convention and Exhibition Centre, Turkey

Located in the heart of the city's business, commercial and cultural districts, the new ICEC is an elegant compact building with three storeys above ground plus a lower level of technical and kitchen services surrounded by restaurants and function rooms with a summer terrace adjacent. Above this, the auditorium, seating 2000, occupies the centre of the building with a total of 21 meeting and function rooms around the perimeter at each level. The 3000 m² main foyer can be used for product and service exhibitions, and a business centre and underground car park are provided. Technical facilities include moveable big screens, a 12–language simultaneous interpretation system, electronic voting and computer projectors.

Operators: International Congress Centre Inc. (88 management shareholders)

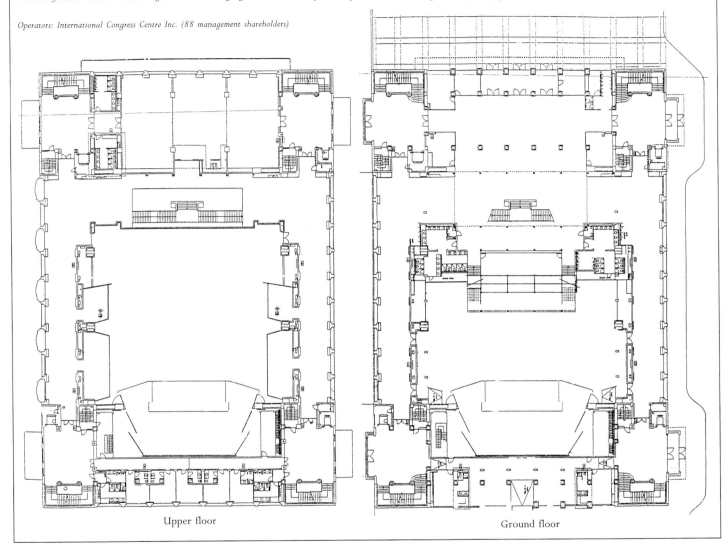

Upper floor   Ground floor

- Growth of multinational corporations and pan-national agencies, necessitating more interdepartmental and inter-regional meetings;
- Developments in association interests, co-operatives, professions and pressure groups;
- Changes in sales techniques, use of product-launch, specialist trade fair and sales promotion events;
- The need to up-date information and methods through in-company training, continuing professional development, attendance at *ad hoc* or scheduled meetings and exhibitions;
- Development of subject specialization – conferences enable an expert to pass on information to many others peripherally involved;
- Health insurance requirements – combining exercise and work programmes in off-site small group meetings (executive conference centres, hotels);
- Extension of incentive travel, hospitality and team building activities to promote better performance and loyalty.

1.2.2 Supply of services

On the supply side, the increasing market opportunities and apparent benefits of MICE business have resulted in a dynamic acceleration in the services offered, namely:

- specific promotion of conventions, meetings and other events, in most cases through the establishment of national and local convention bureaux and sales offices;

Le Grand Motte Palais des Congrès, France

The Mediterranean resort of Le Grand Motte has been planned with buildings of dominant architecture, adapted to sun and wind, rising out of a flat landscape. The congress centre also adapts form to function, using two cylindrical structures to accommodate the main halls (of 500 and 200 seats) superimposed over a base of supporting facilities. The interior of the Grand Salle is resplendent with wood and copper panels, whilst the smaller hall is simpler to allow for flexibility.

Architect: Jean Balladur
Structural engineer: Norbert Montalbett
Mechanical and electrical engineer: P. Soves
Landscape: Bernard Guillaumont
Photograph: Jean Balladur

Key: Plan
1 Foyer
2 500 seat main auditorium
3 Offices
4 200 seat multiuse hall
5 Committee/meeting rooms
6 Smoking area
7 Technical room
8 Exhibition hall
9 Office

Key: Section
1 Foyer
2 Main auditorium
3 Dressing rooms and storage
4 Cloakrooms
5 Control room-projection
6 Smoking area
7 200 seat multiuse hall
8 Restaurant
9 Control room-projection
10 Foldable seating

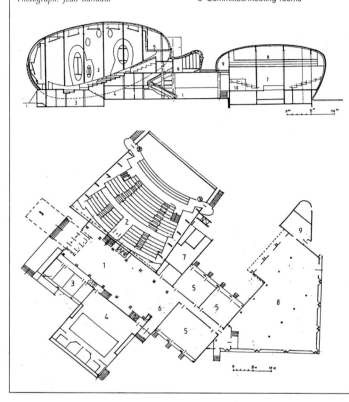

- provision of a wide range of services and assistance for convention, congress and exhibition organizers;
- construction of new, bigger and more sophisticated congress halls, conference centres, exhibition centres and convention facilities in hotels and other venues;
- self-generation of events, through the establishment of fairs and set programmes of meetings, as well as trade/public shows promoting venues to potential buyers;
- development of co-operative marketing by conference centres, hotels, universities and other groups offering meeting facilities;
- industry representation and co-ordination through international, regional and national associations.

1.2.3 Benefits

In economic terms, congresses, conventions, meetings and exhibitions offer many benefits to the host city and region when compared with other segments of tourism:

- *per capita* expenditure of conference visitors on a daily basis is higher than of tourists in general, both when comparing domestic and international visitors;
- main periods of demand occur in the intermediary and low seasons outside the peak times for leisure tourism;
- congress, convention and trade fair business is relatively stable, with arrangements for accommodation and travel fixed well in advance;
- organization is simplified and marketing is carried out through a relatively small number of intermediaries who are in direct contact with their members;
- transportation, accommodation and other services can be offered on a large-scale basis with a high degree of standardization;
- secondary business may be generated through exhibitions, displays, visits, trade delegations, and the host city or country has the opportunity to demonstrate its international standing in the subject;
- trade fairs and most meetings are generally indifferent to the

Sydney Harbour Casino

Providing an integrated entertainment and accommodation centre to add to the attractions of the area, the Aus$850 000 million (US$537 500 M) Sydney Harbour Casino opened in November 1997 and is one of the largest building projects undertaken in Australia. The huge complex incorporates a frontage of heritage buildings as well as a major traffic interchange and vast public areas. Views into and from the site and its special harbourside location strongly influenced the concept landscape design.

Amongst the facilities is a casino (145 000 m² in the main area) with public and private gaming rooms, a multi-use Lyric Theatre with 2000 seats on three levels, a cabaret theatre with 900 seats over five levels, a de luxe hotel providing 306 guestrooms and 44 suites, high-rise apartments and a roof-top health club.

Architects: Cox Richardson, Australia, with Hillier Group, USA.

(a)   Retained heritage frontage and main entrance on Pyrmont St with sinuous hotel and apartment towers rising above the podium.

(b)   Section (enlarged) from Pyrmont St to harbourside, through the hotel tower and pool deck over public and casino floors with traffic interchange and parking levels below.

(c)   Side elevation (enlarged) showing Lyric theatre flytower and drum feature with apartment tower behind.

(d)   Section (enlarged) through Lyric theatre with seating in intimate horseshoe plan.

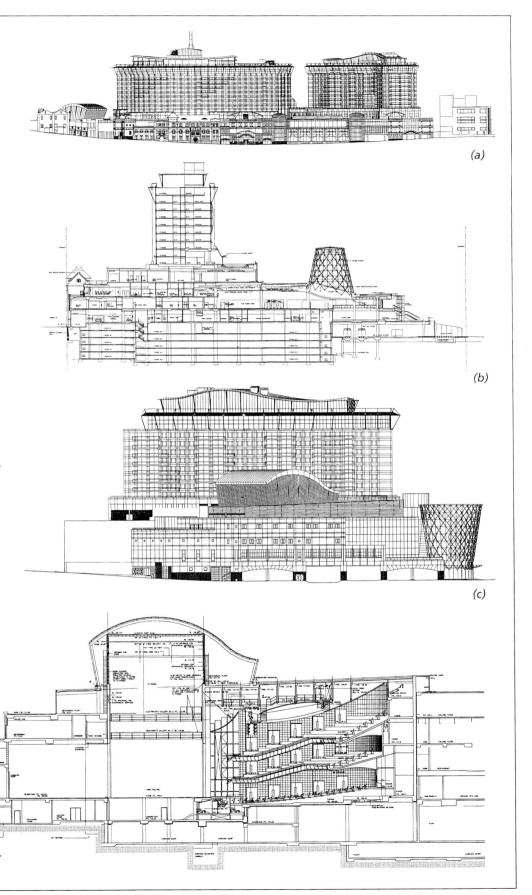

(a)

(b)

(c)

(d)

Hong Kong Convention and Exhibition Centre

The first phase of the Hong Kong Convention and Exhibition Centre, in 1988, included two hotels (1500 rooms), an office tower, apartment block and retail shops as well as a purpose-built convention hall for 1800 with meeting and exhibition facilities.

Extended over the waterfront, the new building of the second phase is characterized by its dynamic multiple arched roof, which is also expressed as the wave-like symbol for the Centre. The middle of the building is occupied by four large halls, which are superimposed on three main levels, surrounded by smaller meeting rooms and ancillary services. Vehicle access to the extension is through two underground roads to marshalling areas and circular ramps rising to each hall floor level. The three new exhibition halls provide an aggregate of 28 770 m² of sub-divisible floor space, and Hall 3, with a ceiling height of 10.5–15 m, is column-free. A Grand Hall (3880 m²) with tiered seating, a stage and foyer pre-function area giving panoramic views of the harbour is available for conventions. In the Centre as a whole there is a total of 52 meeting rooms and seven restaurants as well as a range of function rooms.

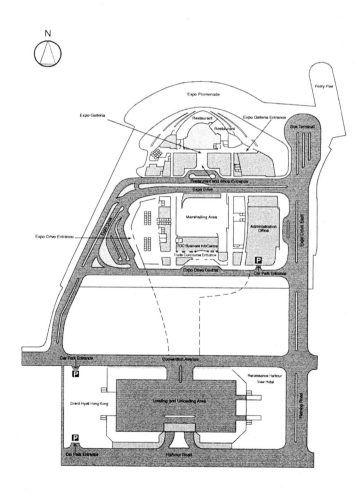

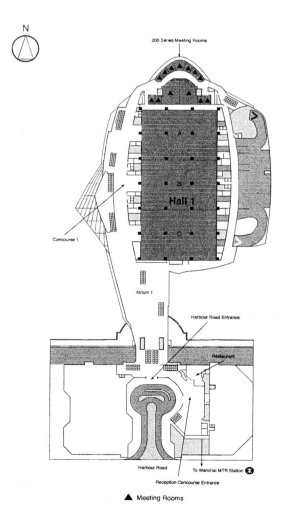

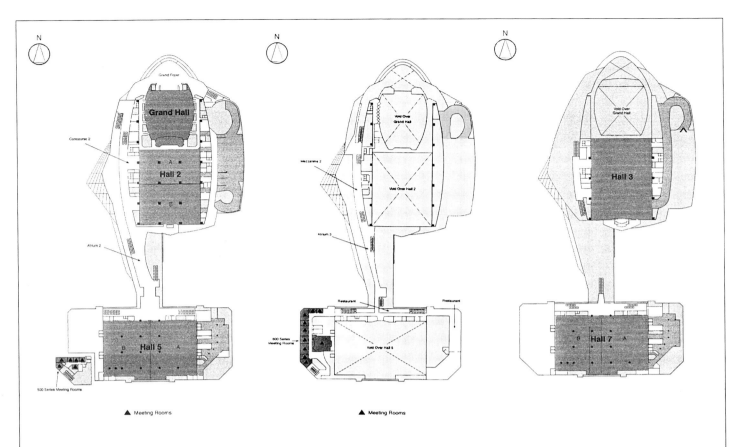

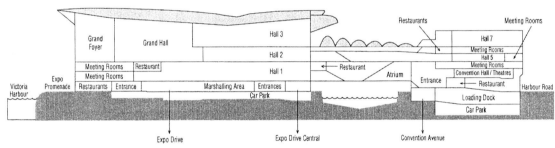

	Phase 1	Phase 2
Owner	Hong Kong Trade Development Council	Hong Kong Special Administrative Region Government (SARG)
Architects	Ng Chun	Wong & Ouyang in association with Skidmore, Owings & Merrill
Completed	1988	1997
Costs (adjusted to equivalent 2000 prices)		
Construction	US$ 320 million	US$ 460 million
Total costs	US$ 980 million	US$ 660 million
	(including hotels, etc)	
Site area	10 ha (25 acres)	
Total HKCEC covered area	250 800 m² (2.7 million sq ft)	
Rentable space	64 100 m² (690 000 sq ft)	

The Centre is operated by Hong Kong Convention and Exhibition Centre (Management) Ltd and is marketed by a private company and the Hong Kong Tourist Association. In order of priority, the primary users in 2000 were:

- Exhibitions (66 recurrent major shows annually)
- Conventions with trade shows
- Major conventions/conferences/meetings
- Consumer shows
- Major banquets/F & B events
- Entertainment events (concerts, family shows)
- Meetings, receptions, local events

The new Munich Trade Fair

The new Munich Trade Fair (moved from previous fairgrounds, 1998–2000) is being developed on the site of a former airport with major highway, rail and bus services. Up to 1998, the Fair hosted an average of 20 international events per year attended by 27 000 exhibitors from 90 countries with two million visitors from over 140 countries. The estimated total turnover generated by the Fair for Munich and Bavaria is 3600 million DM (US$1830 million), generating 160 million DM (US$81 million) of fiscal income and 20 000 jobs directly or indirectly dependent.

---

lack of tourism attractions in a destination; other features and interests (social, technical, cultural, etc.) may be traded off;
- no particular destination or venue is compulsory for the large majority of meetings, and there is a relatively free field for competition;
- facilities normally used for other purposes (municipal halls, universities, theatres, sports stadia) can also be used for meetings, generating additional revenue.

For these reasons, as well as for the benefits of tourism generally, MICE business is highly competitive, demanding a high degree of professionalism from tourism authorities, organizers and 'suppliers'. The 'buyers' of congress and meeting facilities are increasingly selective in demanding the type of accommodation and services they require.

1.2.4 Investment in congress centres

Whilst buffered to some extent from the seasonality and rapid changes in market take-up liable to affect leisure segments of tourism, the MICE business is not without its own drawbacks. As with leisure tourism, the vast capital required in the infrastructure of premises and equipment creates a long-term commitment made years in advance of operation.

The arguments for and against public investment and the formalities of public enquiries, as well as the planning processes, site acquisition and other procedures, have delayed the start of many major projects by up to 4 years or more. A further 2–3 years is typically required for the building and fitting out programme of most large complexes.

As a rule, investment in a purpose-designed congress or convention centre cannot be based on a project-cost feasibility analysis alone. The direct revenue generated is often inadequate to meet operational costs, let alone service the debt. Wider economic issues are involved, such as the benefits of broadening tourist markets or extending tourism over a longer period of the year. Other specific objectives may be to:

- provide a catalyst for regeneration of run-down city centre areas, leading to private investment in hotels, restaurants and other commercial developments;
- revitalize traditional resorts by extending market opportunities and encouraging investment in upgrading hotels and other facilities;
- contribute to the image and prestige of the city as a leading cultural and commercial capital;
- support the role of the city or area as a focus for business, trade, technology and/or research;
- emphasize the independence and maturity of the country as a meeting place for nations.

The vast majority of purpose-built centres are municipally owned, and some have been financed in part with state, federal or European Union grants (see 7.1.6). Private investment may be encouraged through the granting of planning consent for associated commercial development or the leasing of part of the site for this purpose.

In most cases a loss is experienced on the operating costs and/or debt charges, which has to be borne by local tax contributions or levies on other properties (hotels, restaurants, etc.). Against this must be measured the direct economic benefits to the area in attracting more visitors, higher tourist expenditures and greater room occupancies in hotels together with the resultant multiplier effects (see 1.6 and 7.1.3).

1.2.5 Multipurpose centres

No congress centre is planned for one purpose alone. The majority of them are designed to cater for the entertainment and cultural needs of the area and, in many cases, to add to the tourist attractions. Most purpose-built centres are linked to exhibition complexes, thus extending their coverage into the promotional orbit of trade fairs.

The main auditoriums are adaptable for concerts (classical or/and popular) or other theatrical performances; flat-floored halls are invariably equipped to be used for meetings, exhibits and/or functions (receptions, dinners, banquets). In some cases, tiered seating can be removed to leave a flat floor for alternative requirements (see 2.4.7).

Conversely, many theatres and concert halls have been planned or adapted for congress use with a view to generating new forms of revenue to cover rising costs. Other multipurpose arts centres have been designed to allow rearrangement of flexible seating to suit spectator sports, staged performances, conferences and exhibitions.

It makes economic sense to provide for dual or alternative use. Congresses and conventions tend to be held outside the peak tourist seasons, which can then benefit from the entertainment attractions. Meetings mainly occur on weekdays whilst weekends and the evenings are times for leisure and entertainment; this increases the utilization of facilities, infrastructures, car parks and services.

1.3 INFLUENCES ON DEMAND

1.3.1 Elasticity of demand

As with discretionary spending on tourism, the demand for conventions and meetings is generally affected by risks (political unrest, terrorism) and economic conditions (recession, currency fluctuations) as well as by individual purchasing decisions on the part of the organization and participants. Some degree of substitution can be applied affecting, for example, the budgets allocated by companies.

Unlike leisure tourism, most decisions affecting large international meetings have to be made 2–4 years in advance and are largely based on the conditions prevailing at that time.

Corporate meetings generally have a much shorter lead time (1–6 months) but, for major trade fairs, reservations may need to be made years ahead to secure prime locations and ensure additional facilities are available (see 3.1.5).

Factors such as relative costs of travel and accommodation can have a bearing on choice and have tended to lead to intensive sales efforts and cost discounting, particularly when large, prestigious events are concerned. To attract off-season meetings and trade shows many cities and resorts will offer a package of free services, and this degree of competitiveness extends to airlines and hotel groups. Invariably a 'flat rate' of inclusive costs is negotiated.

Effects of economic uncertainties tend to be reflected in late bookings and the fall-off in attendance at association conventions. In general the corporate market is less sensitive to costs than associations, particularly when national sales promotions and product launches are involved.

1.3.2 Scope for international competition

Many association congresses and other meetings are, by their nature, geographically limited in their choice of venue. The 1997 statistics reported by the International Congress and Convention Association indicated that 55 per cent of international meetings rotated world-wide, 27 per cent rotated on a European scale and the remainder in other regions.

Most of the decisions affecting the choice of venue for international associations stem from invitations made through their national branches or chapters. In some cases, particularly those associations with a medical, agricultural or political subject orientation, the rotation of venues is done deliberately to provide opportunities for a wider membership to participate – for example, those from developing countries.

Corporate meetings form a significant – but less reported – part of the international market. Most of the international demand can be attributed to conventions held abroad by companies (including incentive travel) and meetings of multinational corporations. The former are strongly influenced by destination images/attractions and the latter by company objectives/marketing.

1.3.3 Market geography

The geographical distribution of a market in terms of size and accessibility exerts a considerable influence on the choice of congress or convention destinations, and even more so when exhibitions and trade fairs are involved. An evaluation of time-distance and cost-distance catchment areas, the numbers of potential attendees and other visitors, revenue generation and organizational costs usually has to be made before the venue of a meeting is decided.

Geographical factors may, in themselves, contribute to marketing and promotion, for example:

- convenience of travel (time–distance to international airport, transport services to venue and city, high-speed rail station, junctions of major highways);
- tourist attractiveness of the location, choice of local places to visit (cultural events, social programmes, pre- or post-convention tours);
- quality, range and proximity of accommodation, restaurants, shops and other services;
- links with related institutions, universities, research establishments, teaching hospitals in the area.

More distant destinations may collaborate in regional promotion of joint programmes and packages of extended tours or stop-overs *en route*.

1.3.4 Accessibility

Most major conventions take place in 'gateway cities', which have large international airports and good highway and rail connections. Airport hotels often provide extensive facilities for meetings (of airport administrators and operators, travellers and local groups); some airports (Schipol) have a conference centre linked to the terminal buildings, others have large exhibition centres nearby (Palexo – Geneva, McCormick – Chicago).

Difficulties in access and the additional time, transfer and travel costs of attendance invariably restrict large-scale developments. However, executive conference centres for high quality residential courses, and 'hide-away' resorts offering exclusive attractions, can gain from some isolation. Cruise ships and ferries have been chartered for special conventions and floating exhibitions.

1.3.5 Developments in trade fairs and exhibitions

Amongst the thousands of trade fairs and consumer exhibitions held world-wide, some 1500 may be characterized as being of major international interest. They are located in 200 cities, about two-thirds of which are in Europe. The word 'international' may be included in the title only if it is intended to undertake considerable overseas promotion or if the foreign displays account for at least 10 per cent of the stand space (see 8.3).

The trend in trade shows and exhibitions is not only to create sales, contact and market orientation, but also to exchange ideas and information between experts, exhibitors and visitors. Exhibitions are becoming more specialized, integrated with conventions and aimed at distinct target markets.

Horizontal integration has led to the creation of large exhibition organizer groups — often with interests in publishing and other media — and established venues increasingly offer their management and organizational expertise, market intelligence and other services to newly created centres.

Self-sponsorship of exhibitions by the venues, including the choice of 'tied' or optional contracted services, has extended to staging other events (popular concerts, spectator sports and entertainment, functions) in order to increase space utilization and publicity, and this has implications in design or renovation programmes.

In parallel, the demand for representation offices, showrooms and sophisticated but adaptable display facilities has stimulated the development of World Trade Centres, permanent trade marts and collective business centres.

Fairs, whether for trade or consumer interests, are generally run as regular calendar programmes, facilitating future reservations and organization. *Ad hoc* exhibitions may range from large-scale expositions (see 1.6.4) to promote trade, business and tourism with a city or country — which often leaves the infrastructure for permanent exhibition and convention facilities — to specific promotions directed at target markets (product launches, publicity campaigns, in-store promotions) and temporary/touring exhibits of art or artefacts (see 3.3.2) to supplement permanent displays in galleries, museums, libraries and visitor centres etc.

1.3.6 Locational considerations

Trade fair and exhibition complexes have traditionally developed in city centres and industrial conurbations, facilitating public access for large numbers of visitors. Expansion of hall space and changes in modes of transport can give rise to difficulties due to:

- the high cost of urban land and relatively low floor space : site area ratios;
- the utilitarian appearance of large span 'shed design' buildings;

Category	Examples	Characteristics
International governmental organizations and agencies	The UN, EU, OECD, WTO, IBRD, IMF	Meetings are mainly held in the country hosting the headquarters of the organization and selection of venue is generally made on diplomatic grounds
International associations	Some 80 groups classified into trade associations, learned societies, scientific bodies, social and charitable groups, etc.	Meetings may be restricted or held in many countries — usually at the request of their national branch members. Total membership meetings are often large and, on average, about 20 per cent of delegates bring accompanying persons
Federal, state and national government bodies, regional and local authorities; *quasi* non-government organizations	Government departments, national boards and agencies, local authorities, statutory undertakings, educational bodies, health services	These bodies generally hold their meetings in government offices, town halls, municipal buildings and universities. They also represent a large faction attending meetings of other associations
National associations, regional and local voluntary groups and associations	Voluntary associations of a professional, scientific, educational, trade, social, charitable or special interest nature which are made up of individual members	Associations are a major source of demand for meeting facilities. Most have a total membership meeting once a year in addition to regional, committee and special subject meetings. Most large association have a permanent secretary. Over half of American associations have a convention or meetings manager
Corporate bodies, international, national and local companies	All types of commercial companies involved in manufacturing and service sectors	Corporate meetings are the most numerous but tend to be relatively small. They include board and executive meetings, management seminars, training courses, sales meetings and product launches. Many companies also hold an annual shareholders meeting. Meetings and incentive travel events may be held in other countries.

- traffic congestion during delivery/removal of exhibits and extensive car and truck parking requirements.

New exhibition centres may be sited in the city, using redundant railway stations and sidings or in disused industrial or docklands ('brown' land sites), or on low value agricultural land, disused airports or exhausted mineral workings. In every case, however, this must be part of a regional development plan with provision for easy access from the international airport and city, junctions to the main highway network and an integrated system of frequent and fast public transport designed to carry the large numbers of public likely to attend.

Good landscaping and associated development (business, research and/or science parks, hotels, shops, institutional and commercial buildings, recreation facilities) are important in generating an attractive image and viable services.

In contrast, congress centres are often better sited near the heart of the city, convenient for hotels, shops and entertainment, and serving as a stimulus for private sector investment in commercial services and related development.

1.4 MARKET INTELLIGENCE: INTERNATIONAL MEETINGS

1.4.1 Types of organizations and characteristics

Markets for meetings are usually categorized into international, national/regional and local tiers, each having particular requirements in terms of marketing and operations and different economic impacts. There are also significant differences in the meeting requirements of associations, companies and public agencies.

1.4.2 International association meetings: main sources of data

Time series data on international meetings are published by the Union of International Associations (UIA, 1997) and International Congress and Convention Association (ICCA, 1997).

UIA figures are based on the meetings organized and/or sponsored by the international organizations that appear in the *Yearbook of International Associations and International Congress Calendar*, together with some national meetings having international participation organized by national branches of international associations. This latter category includes meetings that are not collected systematically but which meet the following criteria: minimum number of participants, 300; minimum proportion of foreigners, 40 per cent; minimum number of nationalities, five; minimum duration, 3 days.

Excluded from the UIA data are purely national meetings and those of an essentially religious, didactic, political, commercial or sporting nature (religious gatherings, courses, party conferences, fairs, sales meetings, sports contests etc.). Also excluded are meetings that are strictly limited in participation, such as committees and groups of experts, most of which take place in headquarters of the large International Government Offices.

The UIA data enables comparisons to be made over a long time, and are indicative of trends and changes in market shares.

ICCA data is based on the meetings of international associations that have at least 50 participants, are organized on a regular basis and move between at least four different countries. The figures are therefore not directly comparable with those of the UIA, but confirm the progressive fall in the percentage of meetings held in Europe (to 58 per cent in 1997) and large increases in Asia and Australasia.

1.4.3 Growth in international association meetings

Year	1977	1982	1987	1992	1997
Total meetings held	3727	4376	7370	8307	9273
Average increase per year (%)		3.48	13.68	2.54	2.33

Regional distribution of meetings (%)

Africa	3.57	4.35	5.41
America	20.87	20.40	20.20
Asia	10.12	12.83	14.07
Australasia	1.69	2.19	3.81
Europe	63.75	60.23	56.51

Source: UIA comparative tables 1977, 1982, 1987, 1992 and 1997.

Over the last 10 years, the market share of international association meetings held in Europe has increased by only 18.1 per cent compared with growths of 118.8 per cent in Australasia, 38.1 per cent in Asia and 56.6 per cent in Africa (due mainly to changes in South Africa). This long-term trend is significant in light of the considerable investment in new facilities in Australia and Asia.

1.4.4 Locations of international association meetings

At destination level there are also shifts in the market shares attracted by competing countries and cities, together with consequential changes in the benefits derived from participant expenditure and currency exchange.

Countries and cities holding the highest numbers of international association meetings in 1987 and 1997

Country	1987	1997	City	1987	1997
USA	776	1054	Paris	356	249
France	579	647	London	265	205
UK	701	593	Brussels	160	182
Germany	496	519	Vienna	88	178
Italy	331	379	Geneva	150	146
Netherlands	305	341	Singapore	91	138
Spain	274	300	Amsterdam	93	112
Belgium	262	295	Copenhagen	62	106
Australia	107	294	Washington	66	100
Switzerland	267	260	Berlin	144	97
Austria	164	260	Barcelona	64	93
Japan	178	250	New York	79	89

Source: UIA comparative tables, 1987 and 1997.

Europe, as the headquarters of over two-thirds of international organizations, has long attracted the majority of international congresses and meetings. However, the distribution of UIA meetings between cities has changed, with significant reductions in Paris and London and large increases in Vienna, Copenhagen and Barcelona – the last being influenced by huge investments in the Olympic Games and other attractions. The administration of the European Union has also contributed to the growth of meetings in Brussels, Strasbourg and other centres.

At national level, larger than average increases between 1987 and 1997 have been reported by the UIA in the USA (+35 per cent), Australia (+75 per cent) and Japan (+40 per cent), whilst the number of meetings held in the UK has reduced by over 15 per cent. Against this, although not directly comparable, ICCA data for the 3 years to 1997 show consistent falls in the market shares of the USA, France and Japan, whilst Australia has increased to rank third. The large-scale developments in Sydney for the Olympic Games, as well as in other cities in Australia, are likely to reinforce this trend.

1.4.5 Frequency and sizes of international association meetings

Some 88 per cent of UIA international associations hold regular congresses and statutory meetings. Over 45 per cent of these are annual, 24.7 per cent are held every 2 years, 13.8 per cent every 3 years, and others vary from 4–6 years apart.

The vast majority of meetings tend to be small, with attendances of less than 500.

Le Palais de la Musique et des Congrès, Strasbourg, France

Strasbourg has been the setting for over 3200 conferences over 20 years, including the summit meeting of Heads of State. Over 400 events are organized at the centre each year. Progressively updated, the Centre has a surface area of 50 000 m² spread over two floors, allowing several events to take place at the same time. Designed around two auditoria (seating 2000 and 1100), the facilities include 22 meetings rooms, reception lounges, organizers' offices, six bars, two restaurants (seating 80–1600 diners) and 2100 m² exhibition area.

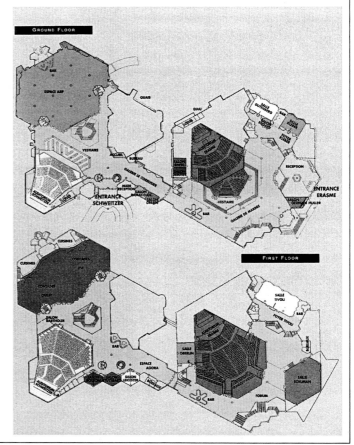

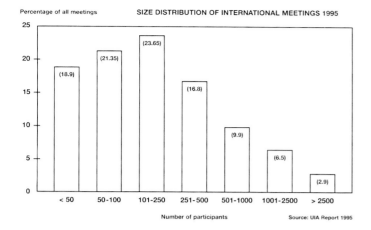

The sizes of meetings recorded in ICCA data has shown a progressive increase in the 5 years to 1997; average sizes vary with the region, from 1038 in North America, 801 in South/Central America, 780 in Australia/Pacific region, 737 in Asia, 639 in Europe to 475 in Africa.

Over two-thirds (72 per cent) of UIA meetings include accompanying persons, the majority (52 per cent) having between and 10–50 per cent of delegates accompanied, 11 per cent of meetings having fewer than 10 per cent accompanied and 9 per cent of meetings have more than 50 per cent of delegates accompanied.

1.4.6 Time of year and duration of meetings

Both UIA and ICCA data show similar patterns in seasonality of meetings, with the peak months being May, June, September and October.

Only 9 per cent of meetings reported by the UIA are limited to 1 day. The largest number (42 per cent) extended over 4–5 days, almost as many (39 per cent) over 2–3 days and 10 per cent of the meetings lasted 6 days or more. Records of the ICCA show the average length of meetings varies somewhat with the region, being shorter in Europe (4.4 days) and longer

in more remote regions like Africa (5.5 days) and South/Central America (5.2 days). The general tendency is for meetings to be shorter and more specific.

1.4.7 Subjects

Over a quarter of ICCA recorded meetings in 1997 were concerned with medical sciences, and this percentage has progressively increased with the rapid advances in this subject world-wide. There are also more meetings concerned with technology, transport and communication, these subjects invariably involving associated exhibitions.

Types of international association meetings	Percentage of total meetings held in 1997
Medical sciences	27.0
Science, technology, industry, transport and communication, safety and security	32.0
Commerce, economics, management, law	13.0
Agriculture, ecology and environment, sports and leisure	8.3
Culture and ideas, arts, architecture	5.7
Education, linguistics, literature, history, geography, mathematics and statistics, library and information	9.6
Social sciences, other subjects	4.4

Source: ICCA data, 1998

1.4.8 Venues and facilities used

The preferred choice of venue for most international association meetings is a conference centre. More than one-third (36 per cent) of UIA meetings in 1995 were accompanied by an exhibition.

	Percentages of all meetings		
Venues used	UIA meetings 1995 (with exhibits)	ICCA recorded meetings	
		1995	1997
Conference centres	36 (46.5)	52	51
Hotels	34 (26.6)	24	22
University facilities	19 (21.0)	20	18
Other premises	11 (5.9)	4	9

(All figures rounded).

In 1995 over half of the major meetings reported by the UIA used only one language, and this trend has increased significantly over the previous 10 years.

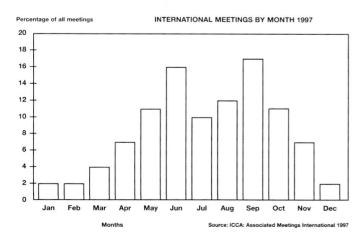

Languages used	Percentages of meetings involved				
	1	2	3	4	5+
For oral communication	52	22	16.5	6	3.5
For written communication	57.7	21.4	14.7	3.75	2.45

Source: UIA report, 1995.

1.4.9 Other meetings of international associations

In addition to their major congress and statutory meetings, the majority of international associations of the UIA held an average of 1.8 other meetings in 1995. More than half of the secondary meetings were yearly or half-yearly and most were relatively small, two-thirds having less than 50 participants and practically all fewer than 500 participants.

1.5 NATIONAL, REGIONAL AND LOCAL MEETINGS

1.5.1 Data sources

Details of meetings and other related events are compiled by many organizations and associations involved in these activities at international, national and local levels and in the roles of 'buyers' or 'suppliers'. Further information about some of the main representative bodies is given in Chapter 8, section 8.3.

Most organizations have individual databases of the events with which they are directly concerned. Inevitably, because of the fluid nature of meetings, historical details provide only a guide to future requirements, and competition within the industry generally results in a dearth of comprehensive statistics. Trade fairs and consumer exhibitions are somewhat different since they tend to be calendar events fixed many years ahead (see 3.1.5).

1.5.2 Differences in requirements

Meetings can be broadly grouped into three main markets, each having different requirements. The full membership meetings of associations tend to be well publicized, large, and flexible in their choice of destination. Corporate meetings, by contrast, are generally smaller, regular but less reported. However, there are many exceptions, as indicated in the summary.

1.5.3 Association markets

Associations broadly fall into three groups:

Germany

In 1994, Germany attracted a total of 610 000 registered conventions and meetings attended by 50 million participants over 1.4 million event days. Only 23 per cent of the events were for 50 or more participants, but these yielded 62 per cent of the entire revenue.

Expenditure analysis	DM million	US$ million
Transport costs	*8*	*4.06*
Venues — hotels	*8*	*4.06*
Congress halls	*2*	*1.0*
Restaurants, shops, taxis etc.	*25*	*12.69*
Total	*43*	*21.83*

Average daily expenditure/participant[1]		
Day meetings	*DM 180*	*$91.4*
Longer events[2]	*DM 340*	*$172.6*

[1] Rent, accommodation, food, entertainment (excluding transport to destination).
[2] Involving overnight stays.

Eight per cent of meetings and conventions were accompanied by exhibits. Nine per cent of participants had accompanying persons, and 4 per cent (13 per cent of foreigners) attached a few vacation days to their visit. The average duration of an event was 2.3 days.

Overall, German venues provide 6800 meeting places, with over 20 000 rooms and nearly 2 million seats.

	Total (in new states)
Hotels	*6300 (1000)*
Congress centres	*350 (30)*
Universities/polytechnics	*160*

Capacity boomed between 1986 and 1996, the number of congress centres and halls increasing by 10 per cent and hotels and meeting places by 56 per cent (source: German Convention Bureau, Infratset Study (1994/5). The German Meetings Market).

- voluntary associations;
- voluntary professional associations;
- other organizations.

Voluntary associations include those involved in social and/or charitable activities, and special interest groups. These cover a very wide range of activities, and the membership may be very local or extend to numerous branches world-wide. Local meetings and functions are often held regularly, and most national associations have large annual congresses or conventions.

Voluntary professional associations cover the societies, institutions and associations whose members share a common interest in trade, profession or business. Technical and managerial expertise is extending rapidly, and associations are continuously increasing as subject areas split up into more tightly defined specialities.

The majority of professional associations hold at least one full-membership meeting a year, and this may be the only opportunity for all members to come together. In addition, larger associations have regular regional and special committee meetings. Scientific, professional and medical associations, in particular, will often run several seminars and special subject

Features	Association (full membership)	Corporate meetings	Government and public authorities
Notification	Usually well publicized in advance. Long lead times (several months to years)	Arranged privately and directly with venues, usually at short notice (weeks)	Usually arranged internally. Inter-sector and public meetings require formal notice
Contacts	Details of meetings and contacts easily obtainable. Committee organized	Often difficult to identify – meetings organized internally by many individuals	Difficult to identify unless external attendance is involved
Attendance	Delegates choose to attend. Two-thirds of meetings have accompanying persons	Compulsory for selected participants. Rarely with accompanying persons – except incentive travel	Compulsory for selected delegates. Public may be invited to consultations and enquiries
Charges	Participants normally pay their own expenses and conference fees	Costs met by the employers	Expenses normally reimbursed
Pattern	Regular cycles. Major events mainly in spring and autumn, sometimes summer	Held as the need arises, year round but few in the peak holiday season	Both *ad hoc* and regular meetings
Destination	Generally flexible in choice of destination and venue	Often restricted to business locations or sales area. Tend to be repeat business	Usually limited to area of administration or locality involved
Influences	Choice of destination for conventions influenced by tourist attractions	Depends on accessibility and specific needs. Attractions important only for incentives	Convenient location for delegates. Public meetings held centrally to allow easy access
Group sizes	Often more than 100 participate in full membership events, sometimes thousands	Meetings mainly involve small groups of less than 100	Most departmental meetings are very small. Public meetings may involve large numbers
Number of meetings	Fewer meetings held: full membership meetings are usually annual	More numerous meetings	Numerous meetings are involved and are rarely included in published statistics
Exhibits	Major conventions often include a range of companies exhibiting their products	Sales meetings may include company sample displays, demonstrations or product launches	Exhibits are not required other than information displays and visual aids
Duration	Generally 3–5 days for conventions	Mainly 1–2 days. Training programmes and incentive travel, 3–5 days or longer	Invariably less than one day except for complex public enquiries
Accommodation	Wide range of accommodation required, including budget options	Usually accommodated in hotels (3 or 4 star)	Overnight stays mainly in mid-grade hotels. Residential courses often held in universities
Venue and facilities	Wide range, including convention centres and universities. Several rooms required	Mainly in good standard hotels with meeting facilities	Held in government offices, town halls, municipal centres, occasionally universities
Main exceptions (1–day events)	Associations also include small committee and working group meetings	Companies also hold large annual shareholders' meetings (attendees pay own costs) Product launches attract large invited audiences and publicity	Meetings with the press are often large and may require special interview rooms International meetings involve special consideration (see 1.6.5)

meetings during the course of the year as part of a programme of continuing professional development.

Other organizations that exist to provide a service to their members and to the community at large, such as trades unions, political parties and religious institutions, also fall into this grouping but may be classified separately.

Association markets have the great advantage in having a permanent secretary for information, and details of meetings are invariably published in advance. The meetings can be categorized as major conventions/congresses with or without exhibitions, and other off-premises meetings (committee meetings, professional/teaching meetings and educational seminars).

Congress Hall Complex, Sirt, Libya

The Congress Hall Complex, completed in 1997, forms the key building of Libya's new administrative centre in the City of Sirt. It provides multipurpose integrated facilities for large numbers of people and grand occasions, but also for conferences on a smaller scale. The complex is planned as an elongated building with the axis forming a 'spine' rising from the building mass and separating the spaces functionally into two zones. Congress facilities , located on the Main Square and entrance side, include the main congress hall (4500 seats in a semi-circle), four 750–seat conference halls, the Presidential meeting room for 150–300, foyers, waiting rooms and visitor areas. On the opposite side are the smaller conference rooms, offices, cafe, restaurant, rooms for prayer and other areas. Below the 'spine' runs a 300–m long indoor street connecting all the parts and widening into foyers and cafes.

The design concept captures the essence of Libyan-Arab architecture, though the building is stylistically modern. The closed-in, wall-like character of the elevations is representative of traditional buildings, whilst glass walls to the foyers form openings to the outdoor spaces and water features. The elevations of public congress and conference halls are distinguished with green and white horizontal marble banding, whilst the Presidential meeting hall is in red and white marble under a gilded dome. The same colours, in marble, are repeated inside.

Floor area: 40 000 m²
Volume: 300 000 m³
Presidential meeting hall 1300 m²

Architects: CNJ Architects, Finland (selected by architectural competition), Devecon Oy Engineers & Architects
Clients and project co-ordinators: National Consulting Board and Organization for Development of Administrative Centres (ODAC), Libya

1. FOYER
2. BALCONY FOYER
3. FOYER VOID
4. CONGRESS HALL 700 SEATS
5. PRAYING ROOM VOID
6. PRESS CENTER
7. RESTAURANT
8. MAIN CONGRESS HALL 3500 SEATS
9. PRESIDENTIAL MEETING HALL VOID
10. EXECUTIVE MEETING ROOM
11. VIP MEETING ROOM VOID
12. OFFICES
13. MEETING ROOM

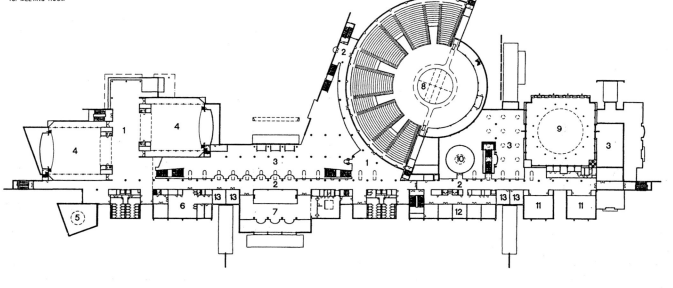

The UK Conference Market Survey, 1995–1996

Surveys of 500 corporate conference organizers representing a sample of leading companies in the UK commissioned by the Meetings Industry Association indicated the following data (averaged for 1995 and 1996).

Types of meetings	%	All meetings – average size	%
Management	28	<25	19.5
Sales	17	26–50	21.5
Training	15	51–100	32.0
Presentations	15	101–200	12.5
Product launches	10	201–300	6.0
Annual General Meeting	6	301–400	3.25
Other	9	>400	5.23

Length of meetings	%	Lead times (bookings)	%[1]
<1 day	33	Within 1 month	9
1–2 days	39	1–3 months	27
2–3 days	18	4–6 months	34
3–4 days	5	6–12 months	22
4–5 days and over	5	1 year and longer	8

[1] *1996 survey.*

Key factors influencing venue selection:
- *Availability*
- *Good standard meeting facilities*
- *Efficient/attentive service*
- *Convenient location*
- *Good catering standards*
- *Clear terms and conditions*
- *Competitive rates/price*
- *Flexible food/choice of menus*
- *Good standard sleeping accommodation*
- *Car parking on site.*

Source: MIA (1995/1996) The Right Solution Reports 1995/1996. Meeting Industry Association.

Decisions on the choice of location for major conventions are invariably made by committee, following invitations and bid proposals from competing destinations (see 8.1). The lead time required to organize reservations, activities, facilities and services, to arrange speakers and programmes and to publicize and set up the convention is typically 3–4 years, average 3.9 years in USA (ASAE, 1992), but may extend to 10 years or more if there is a limited number of cities or resorts able to accommodate the requirements.

The take-up of potential attendance is dependent on individual choice, and in many cases is influenced by the image and attractions of the destination for both the participants and those accompanying them. Accessibility, cost, dates (other events, commitments) and professional goals (quality of speakers, contacts, value) also affect attendance.

About one-third of major association meetings are held in conjunction with an exhibition, which provides a significant contribution to revenues.

1.5.4 Corporate markets

Whilst this is the largest single market segment – over 65 per cent of all meetings and some 35 per cent of the revenue generated – the corporate market is the most difficult to identify. The executive responsible for venue selection and other decisions affecting meetings often does this as a subordinate function to some other role. Some 70 per cent of bookings are for less than 6 months ahead (Meetings Industry Association, 1997).

Corporate meetings also tend to be small; in the UK, some 61 per cent of non-residential meetings were for fewer than 50, and only 13 per cent had more than 200 participants in 1998 (Shawcross, 1998). Residential meetings were generally much smaller, 77 per cent being for up to 50 participants. Exceptions apply to product launches, sales conferences and presentations, which may attract up to 1000 or more attendees.

Key factors influencing the selection of venues are typically location/access, size and standards of conference facilities, price/cost, quality of venue and service and, not least, availability. The majority (over 60 per cent) of corporate meetings are held in good standard hotels (3 star or higher). Other venues include own company facilities, purpose-built conference centres, residential conference centres, universities and unusual meeting places (Meetings Industry Association, 1997).

Changes have taken place in the structure of company meetings, with emphasis on rationalization and effective work purpose reflecting the need to maximize benefits to balance costs of travel and participants' time. At the other extreme, the need to provide incentives and performance awards, perhaps also to engender company loyalty, has created a demand for company conventions which bring together work, social and leisure objectives in an attractive venue.

1.5.5 Classification of corporate meetings

Types	Characteristics
Management meetings, including professional/technical meetings	These tend to occur frequently and normally involve fewer than 100 participants (most less than 50). The venue is often dependent on convenience (e.g. near headquarters), and hotels of good standard are invariably used. Meetings are informal and arranged conference style with the addition of projection and chart display facilities for presentation of data
Sales conferences	The size range is mainly 25–200. Regional sales force meetings are in the lower range, whilst those at national level are larger (100–200 or more) and often extend over 2 days or longer. Sales conferences usually require both informal and congress-style layouts, with good audio-visual aid facilities (usually company provided) for presentations,

Product launches	Exhibition and demonstration areas and separate syndicate/discussion rooms may be required
	These are generally for invited representatives, mostly with attendances ranging from 50–300 or more. Good access, handling and display equipment is essential, including special lighting and sound effects, reception, meeting, filming and reporting facilities, security and support services. Venues used include high-grade hotels and purpose-built exhibition and conference centres. The main events may be over 1 or more days, and additional time is required to set up and dismantle the displays.
Presentations, including promotion and shareholders' meetings	Presentations also involve larger numbers (mainly 100–300, sometimes up to 1000), and are usually day events. A large stage with video projection and other sophisticated audio-visual equipment (often hired) with theatre-style seating, a reception area (buffet meal) and hospitality rooms may be specified.
Training seminars and courses	Executive training programmes are increasingly needed to introduce new entrants to company policies/procedures and to keep abreast of changes in management, technology, law and economic factors. Unlike employee work training, executive courses are usually off-site, for small groups (less than 50) and commonly over 3 days (mid-week or weekends). Meeting rooms must be flexible to allow re-arrangement for classroom presentations or discussion groups. Venues may be mid-grade hotels, residential conference centres or universities, combining work with sport and recreation.
International meetings, incentive travel	Company conventions may be held abroad, or used as performance awards and incentives for their own employees, dealers, agents or retailers. Destinations are invariably chosen for their images and attractions. Detailed recreation and programmes must be organized, together with elaborate presentations and functions, for participants and accompanying persons. Meetings generally extend over a week, with travelling at the weekend (see 4.7.1–2)

1.6 ECONOMIC IMPACTS

1.6.1 Measurement

Economic benefits from meetings, conventions and incentive travel can be measured in terms of:

Overseas visitors to the UK

Purpose	1996		1986	
	Total number 000's	%	Total number 000's	%
Total visitors	25 293		13 644	
Business visitors	6133	24.2	3286	23.6
Conference visitors	720	2.8	213	1.5
Trade fair/exhibition visitors	250	1.0	168	1.1

Expenditure: Ratios compared with total visitors:

	1996				1986			
	Average expenditures (£)				Average expenditures (£)			
	per day	ratio	per visit	ratio	per day	ratio	per visit	ratio
Total visitors	55.1	1.00	488	1.00	34.8	1.00	396	1.00
Business visitors	119.1	2.16	535	1.10	80.0	2.30	472	1.19
Conference visitors	151.1	2.74	656	1.34	85.2	2.45	510	1.29
Trade fair/exhibition visitors	170.7	3.09	610	1.14	98.8	2.84	513	1.30

Average length of stay in 1996 (nights): total visitors, 8.7; business visitors, 4.6; conference visitors, 4.3; trade fair/exhibition visitors, 3.6.

The length of stay for conference and trade fair/exhibition visitors depended to a large extent on their origin. Visitors from North America and the rest of the world stayed about twice as long as those from the European Union. Over 50 per cent of these visitors stayed in London.

Source: British Tourist Authority/English Tourist Board (1997). International Passenger Survey.

- direct expenditure by incoming participants, together with the number of jobs directly created and the local taxes generated;
- indirect and induced expenditure resulting from the additional revenues generated within the area, calculated by the use of appropriate income, employment and government revenue multipliers;
- leakages of expenditure out of the local economy and other negative costs – such as the opportunity costs of alternative investments.

The extra revenue coming into an area is not the only consideration; the all-year round activity is often crucial in utilizing out-of-season tourist accommodation and services, thereby contributing to the feasibility of investment in new and upgraded facilities as well as stimulating other developments (see 1.2.3/1.2.4).

Beneficiaries include not only the venues used by meetings, but also other accommodation, air and ground transportation, the restaurant and retail trade, entertainment, advertising, equipment rentals, and specialist services used by organizers, participants and accompanying persons.

1.6.2 Factors affecting expenditure

Levels of expenditure by delegates attending conventions and

Value of convention and meeting business in the USA

The Convention Liaison Council, comprised of 25 leading member organizations in the USA, reported the value of the convention, meetings, expositions and incentive travel market in the United States to be worth US$82.8 billion in 1994, providing direct employment for 1.57 million people and generating US$12.3 million in direct taxes.

Industry segment	Direct spend ($billions)	%	Direct employment (no. of jobs)
Conventions and expositions	52.20	63.1	993 100
Meetings	27.04	32.6	513 700
Incentive travel	3.51	4.2	66 700
Totals	82.80 (1)	100.0	1 573 500
% increase since 1991	+9.5%		+2.0%
(figures rounded)			

Market segment	Direct spend ($billions)	%
Association sponsored	56.1	67.8
Corporate sponsored	26.7	32.2

Volume	Numbers (millions)
Out-of-town delegates	57.46
In-town delegates	15.64
Room nights purchased	143.64

The direct tax impact was estimated at US$12.31 billion, divided into federal (57.6 per cent), state (26.8 per cent) and local (15.5 per cent) segments.

Main recipients of direct spending (1)	$	%
Hotels and other meeting places	26.9	32.5
Air transportation	19.3	23.3
Restaurants	9.9	12.1
Ground transportation	7.2	8.7
Retail trade	5.6	6.7
Business services	5.5	6.6
Entertaining	3.8	4.5
Equipment rentals	0.5	0.6
Cruises	0.3	0.4
Other	3.8	4.6
Total	82.8	100.0

(1) (figures rounded)

Industry spending in hotels was US$23.8 billion, representing 36 per cent of total hotel operating revenues and 25 per cent of hotel occupancy plus a higher ratio of food and beverage revenue.

Source: Convention Liaison Council (1995). Data reported in Convene Magazine

---

Vienna, Austria

Types of events, 1997	Conferences	Delegate nights	Per conference average
International conferences	226	434 000	1920
Domestic conferences	75	54 100	721
Corporate meetings and incentives	1000	126 000	126
Total	1301	614 000	

International conferences were fewer than in 1996, but larger and of longer duration. September was the most popular month, followed by April and May.
Thirty-one per cent of conferences were held in hotels, 21 per cent in universities, 17 per cent in congress centres and the rest in palaces and other venues. Viennese international conferences contributed AS2.4 billion (US$173 million) to GDP and supported 4300 full-time equivalent jobs.
Source: Vienna Convention Bureau

---

the longer the overall stay. Often the trip will include pre- or post-convention tours, and sometimes multi-destination visits.

- **Non-participants.** The percentage of accompanying persons depends largely on the nature and length of meetings and the tourist attractiveness of the destination. Full membership conventions with interesting programmes and incentive travel to exotic locations attract high ratios of accompanying persons.
- **Relative costs.** Levels and percentages of visitor spend are affected by comparative levels of prices, currency exchange rates, type of accommodation, width of choice (entertainment, shopping), local transportation and admission costs.
- **Metropolitan areas.** A higher level of spend is usually incurred in capital cities and large metropolitan areas with high costs of living and higher prices. These also attract larger conventions and congresses, with delegates from a wider geographic area, and longer than average stays.
- **Subject matter and venue.** University-based meetings tend to have lower daily charges, but extend over a longer time than those held in hotels and other venues.

Sensitivity to cost, travel distance and other factors depends on the market segment:

Washington DC, USA

In 1997, out-of-town delegates to conventions and meetings represented 6.7 per cent (5.5 per cent in 1994) of the total domestic visitors to the city.

	Number	Delegates	Average no./event	Change 1993–1997 (%)
Conventions	21	293 150	13 960	+34
Meetings	1276	1 088 800	853	+6

Hotel nights used: 3.776 million (2.73 per delegate; down 11%)
Revenues generated: US$1934 million ($1400 per delegate).

Source: Washington DC Convention & Visitors Association Annual Report, 1997

---

other meetings and the proportions of spend depend on several variables:

- **Markets.** The highest expenditure per head is invariably by international participants, both in transportation and at the destination itself. National and regional participants spend significantly more than local attendees, and stay for more nights.
- **Distance and frequency of visits.** As a rule, the greater the distance from the countries or home location of delegates and the less familiar they are with the destination,

Considerations deemed important by various groups

Market segment	Travel distance (cost)	Time spent away from work	Overall attendance cost	Attractive venue	Social purpose, innovative motivation	Good hospitality/accommodation	High quality named speakers	Exhibits	Sophisticated AVA equipment, presentations	Accompanying persons' programmes
Traditional professions	U	I	U	I	I	I	I	N	I	I
Pure sciences	I	I	I	U	I	U	I	N	I	u
Behavioural sciences	N	N	I	I	N	N	u	u	N	u
Social sciences	I	I	I	U	N	N	u	u	u	u
Industry and commerce	U	I	U	I	U	I	u	u	u	I
Travel and tourism	U	I	U	I	U	I	u	N	u	I

U, unimportant or not applicable; I, important criterion, N, neutral impact.
Source: US Travel Service (1975). *The Market for International Congresses*, Washington.

Greater Vancouver, Canada – economic impacts of conventions

Comparisons 1997	Convention delegates	Comparisons with all overnight visitors
Number of conventions (1)	355	
Number of delegates	252 410	3.25% of all visitors
Average delegates/convention	711	
Delegate spending per day	C$355	377% higher than all visitors
Average length of stay (days)	3.48	3.53
Total spending by delegates	C$311.83 million	12.10% of all visitor spending
Industry output (2)	C$554.98 million	12.80% of all visitor impact
Wages and salaries	C$202.58 million	13.31% of all visitor impact
Taxes	C$108.95 million	13.49% of all visitor impact
Employment (jobs)	10 291	14.32% of all visitor impact

Sources:
(1) Tourism Vancouver: MOST (Marketing Operations Systems Technology) system
(2) Tourism Vancouver: TEAM (Tourism Economic Assessment Model).

Overseas visitors to London, 1997

There were 12.28 million total overseas visits to London in 1997, of which 0.16 million (1.3 per cent) were to attend trade fairs and 0.41 million (3.3 per cent) were for conferences. London attracts more than 50 per cent of all foreign visitors attending conferences and trade fairs in the UK. The ratio of spend/day for trade fair visits was 2.37 times, and for conference visits 2.58 times, that of the total foreign visits, although the trips were on average much shorter:

Comparisons	Total visits	%	Trade fairs	%	Conferences	%	Other business	%
Number (million)	12.28	100	0.16	1.28	0.41	3.33	1.98	16.11
Nights (million)	79.11	100	0.59	0.74	1.46	1.84	8.77	11.09
Average stay per visit (nights)	6.4		3.8		3.6		4.4	
Expenditure	£	ratio	£	ratio	£	ratio	£	ratio
Spend per trip	488	1.00	677	1.39	699	1.43	690	1.41
Spend per day	76	1.00	180	2.37	196	2.58	156	2.05

Source: London Visitor and Convention Bureau (1998). *International Passenger Survey*

1.6.3 Expenditure breakdown of conference delegates, associations and trade fairs

Discounting travel to the destination, nearly half of all delegate spending goes on the accommodation and another quarter is spent on food and beverage (about 13 per cent in hotels and 12 per cent on meals out). Shopping is also a significant attraction; in most cases this accounts for 10–14 per cent of the expenditure, but rises to twice this proportion in destinations like Singapore.

Singapore: foreign convention and exhibition expenditures

	Foreign convention delegates	Foreign exhibitors	Foreign exhibition visitors
Ratios to convention delegates			
Average per capita expenditure (1)	1.00	1.36	0.84
Average expenditure per day	1.00	1.16	1.30
Average number of nights (1)	4.26	4.99	2.74
Breakdown of major spending (%)			
Accommodation	43.6	49.9	37.9
Shopping	28.7	16.5	32.4
Food and beverage	13.6	17.6	15.2
Sightseeing	4.6	1.9	2.3
Local transportation	3.3	4.0	5.5
Entertainment and recreation	3.7	6.3	4.4
Miscellaneous	2.5	3.8	2.4
Total	100.0	100.0	100.0

(1) Per trip.
Source: Singapore Tourist Office

Expenditure breakdowns are necessary to estimate the distribution of benefits and the overall impact on employment and the economy of the area. They are also used to justify local taxation levies on segments of the tourist industry. Most destinations in North America take the International Association of Convention and Visitor Bureaux data (IAVCB, 1999) as the basis for comparison.

Delegate expenditure is only one part of the total spend in the destination. The association organizing the event normally charges registration fees and incurs expenses on hall hire, organization and administration (see 8.1.2). Association expenditure typically ranges from 8–12 per cent of the total spend in the destination, but in larger conventions this is offset by charges for exhibits.

The expenditure incurred in trade fairs and exhibitions is much more complex. Pre-financing costs are incurred by the exhibition venues, organizers and exhibitors, in addition to the expenses of attending an exhibition. As a rule, the benefits gained are more valuable and more widely dispersed through the economy (see section 1.8).

1.6.4 World expositions

World expositions and other major international events (games, festivals) have a major impact on tourism to a destination, and often leave the infrastructure for continued attractions and economic development. Expositions are staged to promote commercial and trading links and proclaim the status of the city and region. The award of a World Exposition is made by the Bureau International des Expositions (BIE) on the basis

Analysis of delegate expenditures: International Association of Convention and Visitor Bureaux

The IACVB Convention Income Survey, based on a sample of 99 bureaux in the United States and Canada, is the most reliable source of data on convention expenditure in North America as well as a model for comparison elsewhere.

All events: 1998 Expenditure per delegate	Average expenditure Daily ($)	Total ($)	%
Accommodation and incidentals	113.79	342.52	49.2
Hotel food and beverage	31.04	93.44	13.4
Other food and beverage	28.69	86.35	12.4
Tours/sightseeing	4.66	14.04	2.0
Museum/theatre admissions	2.51	7.55	1.1
Recreation/sporting events	3.28	9.89	1.5
Shopping	24.48	73.67	10.6
Local transport, auto-rental, parking	15.17	45.66	6.6
Other (gambling, gratuities, etc.)	7.50	22.58	3.2
Totals	231.13	695.70	100.0
Out-of-town delegate expenditures	245.62	739.31	751.7[1]
In-town delegate expenditures	32.67	98.35	13.3[1]
Average number of nights/delegate		3.01	

Source: IACVB, 1999.

Total expenditures per delegate per event : IACVB data:

Spending per delegate 1998	Average expenditure Daily ($)	Total ($)	Conventions %	Trade shows %
International, national and regional events				
Delegate expenditures	239.87	839.53	92.4	69.8
Association expenditures	17.29	69.25	7.6	5.8
Exhibitor expenditures (trade shows)	76.07	294.36		24.4
State and local events				
Delegate expenditures	198.72	405.39	87.5	55.8
Association expenditures	17.49	57.70	12.5	8.0
Exhibitor expenditures (trade shows)	97.83	263.15		36.2

Source: IACVB, 1999

of competitive bids and, after the year 2000, will fall into two categories:

• 'registered' – these will be held every 5 years and run for a maximum of 6 months; pavilions can be built by the participating countries themselves;
• 'recognized' – these will be held in intervening years and run for a maximum of 3 months; the pavilions will be provided by the organizing country.

Current and future World Expositions include EXPO 98 in Lisbon, EXPO 2000 in Hannover, EXPO 2002 in Manila, The Philippines ('recognized'), EXPO 2005 in Seto, Japan ('registered').

Roles in marketing

Level	Type of organization involved	Marketing objectives
National or regional	National Tourist Board Associations of congress centres, resorts, towns	International promotion of country as a tourist/congress and convention destination
City, town or local district	Visitor and convention bureaux, local tourist office, local trade associations representing facilities, airlines	General and specific promotion of a particular area aimed at congress and convention organizers, large associations and companies of international and national status
Individual units	Congress centres, hotels, exhibition centres, universities	Direct marketing and sales promotion aimed at potential 'buyers of facilities, i.e. associations and companies
Individual events	Congress and convention organizers, meeting planners, exhibition promoters	Association membership, company representatives and their sales contacts, potential exhibitors for sale of exhibition space, markets for visitors and attendees

The planning of a World Exposition park involves decisions on land and funding allocations, a main theme with sub-theme areas, the siting, design and financing of pavilions and projects by the host and participating countries, public and private sector partnerships, logistics and visitor flows, technical and support infrastructures, and co-ordination and quality control.

1.6.5 Prestigious international meetings

Inter-governmental meetings of Heads of State, ministers, senior representatives and other high ranking officials, and the prestigious meetings of international agencies, involve much more organization. Questions of protocol and sensitivies have to be addressed in addition to the practical requirements of hosting a large, publicized event, for example:

- numbers of principals, personal staff and other attendees;
- consultations on protocol, procedures, individual requirements (medical, dietary, etc.);
- accommodation, service and support requirements at all levels;
- formats and procedures for the meetings and events;
- arrangements for transportation and reception;
- provisions for security and safety, confidentiality of contacts and exchanges;
- simultaneous interpretation, voting and technical systems;
- press offices and communication networks;
- parallel programmes of meetings, events and visits;
- risk assessment, procedures for action and alternatives;
- organization and administrative arrangements and performance standards;
- vetting and training of personnel and service providers;
- monitoring of programme, liaison with delegates and representatives.

1.7 PROMOTION AND ORGANIZATION

1.7.1 Levels of promotion

Like tourism, promotion of congress, convention and meeting facilities takes place at various levels, each having different immediate objectives.

The involvement of public sector authorities (state and municipal level) can be justified on several grounds. Conventions and meetings make an important contribution to tourism and the extended use of tourism facilities in the area as well as to the promotion of commerce and trade. Convention facilities are often combined with local requirements for the arts, entertainment or recreation needs of the community. The local authority may also have a direct involvement through its ownership of premises (civic halls, congress-arts centres, coliseums) that can be leased for meetings.

1.7.2 National and local tourist organizations

The role and funding of national tourist organizations varies from one country to the next. In every case it is concerned with promoting interest in the country as a tourist destination. In promoting congresses and conventions the national organization will generally work in liaison with other bodies, and may have a business travel section concerned specifically with developing this segment of tourism. In addition, the national office provides overseas representation in the main market areas as an initial point of contact and information.

Specific promotion of congress, convention and meeting facilities is the role of the regional or municipal authority. Most major cities have their own visitor and convention bureaux and this service is usually sponsored partly by the authorities themselves, partly by trade and industry. Funding of the congress bureau's activities is generally through subscriptions (hotels, restaurants, retail groups, etc), advertising and fees, together with local government and/or state appropriations.

Both national and local organizations must define their missions, agree strategies and set goals for their activities. The main services include marketing and promotion, statistical surveys and product improvement.

Marketing and promotion:

- Information services and visitor centres (local and overseas);
- Promotional and information literature (guide and leaflet distribution);
- Direct mail and response to enquiries (databases);
- Selective advertising (trade and consumer press, television);
- Trade fairs and consumer exhibitions;
- Major promotions (in high yield, high growth markets);
- Educating and up-dating (sales missions, workshops);
- Internet marketing (web sites, information);
- Market support, image building (journalist/travel visits, press releases);
- Joint promotions and participation (regional, airlines, international bodies).

Statistical surveys:

- Regular visitor surveys (demography, activities, spending patterns);
- Data collection (visitor statistics, hotel occupancies, employment);
- In-depth research (market intelligence, competition, trends).

Product improvement:

- Investment in venues (municipal ownership);
- Product enhancement (training, seminars, planning trends);
- Collaboration in events (festivals, special events);
- Civic hospitality and support (conventions, social programmes).

1.7.3 Product and service providers

Airlines

The business travel market is an important segment in airline operations, both for individual and group travel needs. Whilst business travel is generally non-discretionary in destination and programme, competition between carriers and the need to engender customer loyalty has led to airline involvement in group travel services at several levels:

- research into forthcoming events and liaison with other ground services;
- special fare rates, stop-over, extended travel and other incentives;

- inclusive packages with travel, transfers, accommodation and special programmes;
- assistance and advice (planning, travel, hotels, pre- or post-convention tours);
- arrangements for study tours, fact-finding packages, trade missions.

Hotels

Most city and airport hotels and many in resort areas depend on business travel markets. The convention, meetings and incentive travel segment generates a high yield and justifies specific marketing attention. Median daily expenditure of a conference/meeting resident is commonly 2.4 times that of a rack-rate guest, nearly twice that of a travel agent or corporate booking, and often three times that of a tour group contact (Lawson, 1982).

Chain and group hotels and market consortia invariably publish lists and details of their own hotel products and target organizers, business companies and associations. Marketing channels include tourist brochures, trade journals and fairs, direct mailing, the Internet, e-commerce, hospitality visits and participation in joint activities.

Congress/convention venues

Venues also produce their own brochures describing and illustrating the facilities and services available (with separate price lists) and the attractions of the area. Large venues also undertake similar marketing activities to those of hotels. The long lead time (4 years or more) involved in organizing major conventions makes it imperative to start promotion well in advance of completion and preferably at the commencement of a construction or refurbishment programme (see 7.1.3). In the interim stage, this may include drawings, models, artists' sketches and computer disks to illustrate the main features.

Other venues

Most executive and residential conference centres operate in a similar way to hotels targeting, in particular, the corporate markets. They may be unrestricted, geared to particular client companies or operated for one client body. In addition to their own promotion, most conference centres belong to representative associations.

Universities also operate independently and through co-operative marketing associations. In the main, their objectives are to utilize the accommodation, lecture theatres and other facilities in the vacation periods, although several institutions have dedicated conference centres available all year round.

1.7.4 Ground services

Organizing large-scale international meetings and conventions calls for extensive ground services to complement the air handling arrangements, for example:

- transfers – on arrival, departure, to and from the hotel, meeting venues, exhibit venues, reception, banquet, entertainment, etc.;
- accommodation to suit specific requirements;
- meals and banquets;
- social programmes;
- accompanying persons programme;
- hospitality desk services;
- study visits;
- pre- or post-convention tours.

In addition, the agencies involved may provide:

- creativity in planning;
- advice on administration procedures;
- communication facilities;
- packaging arrangements for meetings abroad;
- contacts with potential sponsors, partners, etc.

1.7.5 Organizers

Organization of meetings, conventions and related events may be carried out by the association or company itself, or by professional organizers acting on their behalf. In the case of companies the responsibility for arranging particular meetings is often secondary to some other function, for example the managing director or secretary (board meetings), sales/marketing director (sales, product launches), personnel manager/technical director (seminars, training).

Associations invariably have a permanent secretary with overall responsibility, although larger bodies often have a convention office. Programmes, venues and other matters pertaining to conventions are normally decided by committees.

Professional organizers often specialize in incentive travel management and meeting planning or exhibition organization, and most belong to associations which collectively represent their interests and lay down guidelines and standards (see 8.3). The services vary with client instructions and may include all aspects from identifying objectives and goals, arranging all activities and requirements, to post-convention evaluation.

The borderline between a successful meeting and one that gives rise to complaint or disappointment is often very fine. Furthermore, different weightings of importance will be attached to the various components that go to make up a 'meetings' package, depending largely on the group interests and attitudes. What may be highly attractive to one group could be equally unsuited to another. Various surveys of American associations considered the four most important factors, in general, to be:

- importance of subjects;
- good facilities;
- opportunities to exchange ideas with peers;
- attractive location.

1.7.6 Budgeting

In budgeting for an association congress or convention there are two types of expenditure to be considered: the conference programme and the extra or optional expenses.

Programme costs should cover:

- financing the congress business sessions (rents, charges);
- administrative arrangements;
- fees, travelling and incidental expenses of speakers;
- hire or purchase of any special equipment and extra services;
- transporting equipment and stationery and staffing a congress office;
- printed material (invitations, programmes, registration forms);
- advertisements and direct mail to potential delegates;
- preparing, printing and distributing papers and account of proceedings;
- exhibits and stage decorations required for the congress;
- miscellaneous items (badges, special forms, mementos).

These costs may recouped in several ways; by including expenses as part of the registration fee, calling on special funds allowed by the association or company for meeting expenses, selling space in programmes and other publications and leasing space for other exhibits.

Optional extra expenses may be underwritten by the organization, included in the registration fee or charged directly to the delegates. Specific events (entertainment, meals) may also be sponsored by associated companies. Amongst the expenses likely to be incurred are:

- costs of entertainment for relaxation after work sessions;
- occasions such as special lunches, dinners, gatherings;
- tours or technical visits;
- programmes for accompanying persons.

Usually separate rates of fees are charged for delegates and accompanying persons.

Accommodation and meals are usually included in the registration fees in order to simplify the agreement and settling of contracts with hotels and other establishments – estimates of numbers and costs will have to be prepared well in advance.

1.7.7 Resources

In considering the financial and practical commitments involved in mounting a large congress or convention, a local association will need to consider:

- the local association resources (financial outlay, staff, support);

- local supply of hotels, meeting rooms, food services, transport to and within the area, entertainment and visits (availability, standards, costs).

Corporate meetings follow a similar pattern. Whilst charges may not be levied on individuals, the company will have to account for the costs incurred and evaluate this expenditure in terms of performance and corporate benefits. Incentive travel also requires an evaluation of the goals, costs and subsequent results.

1.7.8 Agreements

Competition to win major congresses is often very keen, with lobbying and sales promotion at both national and local levels. Initial discussions will usually need to be followed by a series of formal steps, as illustrated for a hotel using the format recommended by the Convention Liaison Committee (Wilkie, 1987):

- **Formal proposal or presentation** – a letter from the hotel outlining the understanding between the buyer and hotel;
- **Option dates** – the agreed date when a tentative agreement becomes a definite commitment between the buyer and seller;
- **Letter of agreement** – letter from the buyer accepting the hotel proposal, this exchange forming the legal basis of agreement;
- **Cut-off date** – the designated day when the buyer must release or add to the function room or bedroom commitment;
- **Rooming lists** – lists of names to occupy the reserved accommodation;
- **Commitment** – detailed arrangements as agreed.

1.8 TRADE FAIR AND EXHIBITION ORGANIZATION

1.8.1 Roles and motivations

For an organization selling products or services, exhibitions are one of several marketing activities that will also cover advertising, direct mail, point of sale promotion and other sales team activities. Trade shows and consumer exhibitions involve exhibition venues, exhibition organizers, visitors, exhibitors, contractors and service suppliers as well as many peripheral agencies. The costs of staging trade exhibitions largely fall on the exhibitors and the organizer and/or venue can also generate revenues from other sales, including admission charges for public open days and consumer exhibitions.

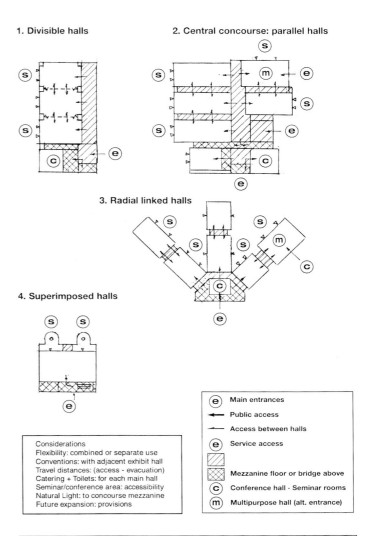

1. Divisible halls 2. Central concourse: parallel halls 3. Radial linked halls 4. Superimposed halls

Considerations
Flexibility: combined or separate use
Conventions: with adjacent exhibit hall
Travel distances: (access - evacuation)
Catering + Toilets: for each main hall
Seminar/conference area: accessibility
Natural Light: to concourse mezzanine
Future expansion: provisions

(e) Main entrances
← Public access
← Access between halls
(e) Service access
▨ Mezzanine floor or bridge above
(c) Conference hall · Seminar rooms
(m) Multipurpose hall (alt. entrance)

Feria de Madrid, Spain

The Trade Fair Centre of Madrid is located on the outskirts of the city with good access and en route to the airport. The complex includes eight modular halls, giving a total 972 000 m² of exhibition space, radiating from a central reception building which also provides a convention centre with an auditorium (for 600), banqueting and meeting rooms. Each hall has self-contained facilities for flexible use, and one hall (10 800 m², 15 m clear height) is also designed for spectator events. There is a 30 000 m² outdoor exhibit area, and parking for 14 000 cars, 78 buses and 60 trucks.

In 1996, the Trade Fair Centre of Madrid hosted 50 trade shows and consumer exhibitions: 12 651 companies participated directly, occupying a total of 613 610 m² hall exhibition space and attracting 2.964 million visitors. The turnover rate for space (number of times fully occupied if dimensions for all events were added together) was 14.3, compared with a normal optimum figure of 13. Forty-one of the events were organized by the managing company, IFEMA.

Income	%	Expenses	%
From exhibitions	80.84	*Promotion, advertising, PR*	19.71
From visitors	4.01	*Service costs*	21.85
Other income	8.35	*Personnel*	30.99
Convention centre activities	6.80	*Overheads, maintenance*	14.11
Other expenses	13.34		
Surplus of income over expenses	33.37		

Source: IFEMA Annual Report, 1997.

German trade fair industry

Germany is the major trade fair and exhibition destination in Europe. In 1998 total hall space amounted to 2.33 million m², and further large investments planned to 2000 will add 130 000 m² (over 5.5 per cent) to this capacity.

Leading locations	*Hall space (m²)*	*Outdoor (m²)*	
Hannover	*484 130*	*168 420*	
Frankfurt	*290 280*	*75 762*	
Cologne	*275 000*	*52 000*	
Dusseldorf	*203 925*	*30 500*	
Munich	*177 400*	*280 000 (in two venues)*	
Nurnberg	*133 000*	*76 000*	
Berlin	*130 000*	*10 000*	
Leipzig	*101 200*	*33 000*	

Profile of trade fairs	*1993*	*1997*	*% increase*
Number of events	*103*	*128*	*24.3*
Total number of exhibitors	*131 015*	*151 402*	*15.6*
Foreign exhibitors	*57 668*	*70 140*	*21.6*
% of total exhibitors	*44.0*	*46.3*	
Total visitors (millions)	*8.968*	*9.755*	*8.8*
Foreign visitors (millions)	*1.50*	*1.78*	*18.6*
% of total visitors	*16.7*	*18.2*	
Total rented space (million m²)	*5.865*	*6.337*	*8.0*

Of the foreign visitors in 1997, 61 per cent came from the European Union, 21 per cent from the rest of Europe and 18 per cent from overseas. German industry also participated in 163 foreign trade fairs in programmes promoted by the Federal Ministry of Economics, and a number of the venue operators are also involved in the organization or joint management of projects overseas.

Source: Association of the German Fair Industry AUMA

1.8.2 Exhibition venues

Venues vary widely, from purpose-built highly sophisticated complexes to hotels with display facilities or improvised halls and arenas into which all the necessary technical services must be temporarily installed. The venue may be privately owned or publicly or jointly owned by the city or state in which it is located. Joint ownership may also involve other participating organizations (chambers of commerce or trade) and public/private ventures.

Ownership of a venue may affect the type of returns expected from exhibition use, public venues taking into account the wider economic and social needs of the community. However, the large purpose-built venues are invariably operated on a commercial basis by a management company set up or contracted for this purpose.

Exhibitions may be organized directly by the venue operators, or the halls rented to other commercial exhibition organizers. Often both types of arrangement are used to maximize the annual take-up of space and facilities. Factors influencing the success of a venue in attracting exhibitions include:

- location relative to market areas and access for visitors and exhibitors;
- space, hall size, flexibility and quality of facilities and services;
- availability for the optimum dates required (calendar programmes);
- costs and conditions of space hire, including 'tied' services and charges.

Trade shows must attract buyers and consumer exhibits need a large public attendance to justify the costs of exhibiting. In both cases, convenient location (near airport, near town) and easy access for trucks and visitors (near major road junctions and rail stations), together with adequate space, are crucial considerations in planning new centres (see 3.2.1).

Exhibits are also used to support association conventions and for launching company products. Often this space is multipurpose and is, on other occasions, used for banquets, functions or large group meetings. In hotels, benefits arise from increased room occupancies as well as the hire of convention halls and ballrooms.

Evaluation of venue investment usually takes account of the following.

Revenues	Costs	Economic benefits
Hall and office rentals	Debt service charges	Visitor and exhibitor spending
Food and beverage sales	Property operations, maintenance/ replacements	Attracted investment (hotels, contractor services, warehousing)
Secretarial services	Energy and utility costs	Employment (direct and indirect)
Equipment hire	Insurance, security	Industrial/commercial stimulation
Technical services	Administration, marketing	Introduction of new attractions (public shows, entertainment)
Seminar rooms	Promotion, hospitality	
Hospitality suites	Employees, benefits	
	Transport, training	

1.8.3 Exhibition organization

Exhibition organizers may be independent commercial companies (often with publishing interests), associations or the hall/venue management. The organizer pre-finances the shows with costs of market research, hall rental, stand construction, promotion, and other services.

The expenditure is normally in stages over 1–2 years (see 8.2.6). These costs are later recouped by sales of stand space (with or without shell scheme construction), entrance charges (public events), sale of catalogues, advertising, sponsorships and commissions. Often free concessions are negotiated (site offices, hotel rooms).

1.8.4 Exhibitors

Trade fairs and exhibitions are classified by the Union des Foires International (UFI) into multi-branch fairs (technical, consumer goods), specialized fairs (ten trade categories) and consumer exhibitions (art and antiques, general local exhibitions).

In each case, costs met by the exhibitors include the following.

Requirement	Main costs incurred
Space rental	Rates per m^2 depending on location, shell or free-standing schemes
Stands	Design, construction, graphics, technical installations, furniture
Stand services	Cleaning, security, connected technical services, catering, listings
Transport	Freight forwarding, handling, customs, storage, insurance
Staff	Stand personnel, expenses, accommodation, hired extras
Public relations	Literature, press interviews, hospitality, entertainment, advertising
Miscellaneous	Equipment written off, overheads, opportunity costs of alternatives

Although these costs vary with the type of exhibits, the nature and length of show and location, surveys (Lawson, 1985) indicate proportionate costs in the UK averaged:

- space rental and services, 30–33 per cent;
- stand design, construction, exhibit handling, 50–55 per cent;
- staff and hospitality expenses, 15–17 per cent.

1.9 TRENDS IN MARKETING AND ORGANIZATION

From evidence of changes that are taking place and comments by the representative organizations involved, a number of trends can be identified towards:

- more working congresses and smaller meetings in which delegates take an active part in the discussions and seminars;

- more substantive programmes justifying the time and opportunity costs of attendance;
- meetings combined with exhibits or/and visits to related facilities (research laboratories, hospitals, plants, new developments, etc.);
- opportunities for pre- or post-convention tours and professional visits;
- shorter meetings with a more specific purpose and theme;
- greater use of convention bureaux and other professional services in organizing events and associated visits;
- demand for better meeting facilities and more responsive services in hotels and other venues;
- greater use of 'state of the art' facilities in presenting information, communications, environmental control and management.

Trade fairs and consumer exhibitions are also experiencing many changes. In particular, older traditional industries are tending to concentrate and consolidate activities. The industrial revolution has shifted towards the emerging countries of South East Asia, whilst Europe and the urban centres of North America have witnessed partial de-industrialization and a transformation towards a more service-orientated society. Market maturation and increased competition are reshaping the traditional show format in several ways:

- rationalization of consumer and trade shows with more specific marketing and targeting of exhibitors and identified markets at specific locations and at varying appropriate intervals;
- verticalization or division of large marketplace shows to provide more specialized events or sub-sections;
- continuation of regionalized and rotating shows to extend market representation and creation of 'niche' events for specialist interests;
- combination of trade shows with parallel seminars for professional interest and marketing/research intelligence;
- extension of consumer shows into the services sector, employment, careers, science/technology and entertainment;
- further development of high technology in displays, communications and management of events.

2 Congress and convention centres

2.1 CHARACTERISTICS: MAIN FEATURES

2.1.1 Range of premises

A wide range of premises is provided to cater for the various needs of meetings and to generate revenue from this potential market. Some, like congress/convention centres and executive conference centres, are designed specifically for this purpose; others, such as hotel ballrooms, are often more secondary to the letting of bedrooms and need to provide for a variety of functions.

In universities, on the other hand, whilst the lecture theatres and seminar rooms are well equipped, the accommodation services may be less suitable for conference users. Theatres, concert halls and municipal halls may also be used on occasions for large congresses or conventions, but often lack adequate supporting facilities.

Range	Features
Multi-use halls	Flat floors with flexibility for a wide range of activities. Loose (or telescopic tiered) seating. Set up for each event. Municipal halls, arenas, hotel ballrooms.
Secondary use auditoria	Permanent tiered seating with good sight-lines, foyers and stage facilities. Acoustics and AVA may need attention. Theatres, concert halls, lecture theatres.
Primary use centres	Auditoria for large groups combined with smaller meeting rooms and flat-floored halls for accompanying exhibits and functions. Equipped with audio-visual aid facilities and supporting services.

Although congress/convention centres are equipped for this purpose, they are invariably designed to also meet other needs. Congresses and conventions are seasonal, and the competition between venues for the large group meetings often results in long and predictable gaps in the conference calendar (see 1.4.5, 1.4.6). The justification for the large public investment required can be reinforced by the added benefit of an amenity (theatre, concert hall, popular entertainment venue) which can be used by the local community and tourists during the peak holiday season and at other times.

2.1.2 Feasibility

The type and capacity of facilities appropriate for a particular town, resort or region will depend on many factors. A realistic appraisal must be carried out of the market demand in terms of the numbers, sizes and frequencies of meetings likely to be attracted. This must take into account the available hotel and other accommodation (standards, numbers of rooms), amenities and tourism services in the area. Requirements for alternative community uses must also be considered, and this may determine the optimum size and design of the main auditorium and supporting facilities.

A wide-ranging feasibility review is also required when major improvements or extensions to existing premises are required. This should examine the limitations of the site and options for relocation or redevelopment.

A comprehensive feasibility study should cover the following aspects, although this is usually carried out in stages with decisions taken at each stage (see 2.1.3).

- **Market research** (pertinent to the destination area): Statistics of meetings, origins, sizes, frequencies, freedom to travel to the preferred destinations, facility requirements, lead times, services, influencing factors, contact details (see Chapter 1).
- **Existing facilities** (conditions): premises used for meetings and/or exhibitions/trade fairs in the region: nature of use, suitability and limitations, options for redevelopment, extension or relocation.
- **Locational factors** (potential sites): site requirements: accessibility (time distance) to airport (airlines, destinations served, frequencies of flights), to town centre amenities and major highways; public transport services.
- **Tourism image and attractions:** characteristics of the town and surroundings, general features of attraction (environment, history, culture, administrative centre), particular interests (research, university, hospital developments).
- **Tourism infrastructure** (in the area): capacity, quality and availability (at times of the year) of hotels, guest houses and other accommodation, restaurants and places for entertainment; organized ground services and supporting agencies.
- **Catchment area** (locality): population, socio-economic analysis, main streams of employment, businesses, company headquarters, development and investment plans; organizations and social group activities; existing amenities and the need for additional community/tourism facilities.

International Convention Centre, Birmingham, UK

The ICC in the centre of Birmingham is a vast complex of 11 main halls and 10 executive rooms grouped around a landscaped mall extending the full height of the building. It includes the Birmingham Symphony Hall (Hall 2), which is a rectangular hall with curved ends based on the classic concert shape but which also incorporates openable reverberation chambers, acoustic curtains and an acoustic canopy to vary the acoustic environment. This seats 2200 and can be used for plenary sessions and hospitality. The nearby National Indoor Arena provides a spacious clear-span interior, which can seat up to 12 000 delegates.

Main facilities include:

- *Hall 1 – 1500 tiered seats which have individual fold-away tables or can provide adjustable desks (with reading lamps) in each alternate row. The large adaptable stage has full AVA and theatre lighting facilities, with street access for product displays and presentations. Twelve simultaneous interpretion lines are installed and there are 300 computer/telephone lines in an adjacent media suite.*
- *Hall 3 – flat-floored room of 3000 m² with underfloor ducted services for exhibitions, banquets (2000) or conventions (2900).*
- *Hall 4 – 800 m² for banquets (600), conventions (800) or additional exhibition space.*
- *Hall 5 – auditorium seating 300, with convertible desks and three interpreters' booths*
- *Halls 6 to 11 – sub-divisible meeting rooms seating 30–300 in self-contained suites.*

Architects: Renton Howard Wood Levin (RHWL)
  Percy Thomas Partnership (PTP)
Engineers for all services: Ove Arup Partnership
Theatre and acoustic consultants: Artec Incorporated
Photographs: ICC

International Convention Centre, Birmingham, UK

- **Competition for identified markets:** locations of other facilities available or planned, competitor strengths and weaknesses, opportunities for development (niche markets, growth areas, larger facilities) and optimum requirements.
- **Local planning strategy:** planning objectives, area redevelopment plans, catalyst for other investment, stimulus for tourism regeneration and visitor attractions.
- **Initial design concept:** outline of facility requirements, spaces, relationships, circulations and layouts; particular design features; alternative options; preliminary cost estimates.
- **Economic appraisal:** delegate expenditure analyses; operating revenue and cost projections, jobs generated,

direct and indirect benefits in the town and region; comparisons of opportunity costs and risks.
- **Financial and other resources:** levels of investment required; resources of the municipality and regional/state authority; sources and conditions for grant aid; possible joint public/private ventures, other commercial revenues (hotel leases, concessions); sale of land released by relocation; bond issues and special taxes.
- **Organizational structure and financial plan:** management of centre, company framework and representation, management contracts; financial planning, provisions for deficit funding and use of surpluses; business plan.

Cairns Convention Centre, Australia

The first stage (1996) of the Cairns Convention Centre, designed with a striking curved fluted roof (used as a symbol), has a multi-use Great Hall of 1720 m², which can be partitioned into four quadrants and has moveable tiered seating over a flat floor. A business centre and restaurant/bar are located off the foyer at ground level, with seven meeting rooms at mezzanine level. Within 3 years of opening, a 1470 m² multipurpose exhibition/entertainment hall was added. This can convert to a 5800-seat sports stadium, 5000-seat plenary or concert hall, 1080 banquet hall (tables of 10) or 88 exhibition booths (3 m × 3 m).

Developer: A Queensland Government initiative
Operator: Ogden IFC (Cairns) Pty Ltd
Architect: Cox Rayner

2.1.3 Procedures

Local government administration

Mission statement
Goals and strategies
for development
Managing Committee/Board
terms of reference

Consultation

State/regional authorities
Commercial investors, tourism
organizations
Community representatives

Marketing ⟷	Development ⟷	Resources
Markets for meetings, community needs	Existing facilities	Tourism infrastructure
▼	▼	▼
Potential for growth, amenity requirements	Redevelopment options, alternative sites	Planning framework, economic goals
▼	▼	▼
Project recommendations	Site selection	Decisions in principle
▼	▼	▼
Facility programme, specifications	Site acquisition, design concept	Management structure
Financial appraisal	Initial cost estimates	Financial resources
▼		▼
Economic analysis	Design development	Financial planning
	▼	
	Project definition	

(data exchange/consultation ⟷, progressive stages ▼)

2.1.4 General facilities

Modern congress centres provide a range of facilities to accommodate both large and small groups. Invariably, they include exhibition halls for exhibits running in parallel with conventions or organized independently, and at least one large multi-use hall for banquets, receptions and large gatherings. Although each project is different, depending on marketing and other factors (see 2.1.2), congress centres generally fall into three categories of provision.

2.1.5 Large purpose-built congress/convention centres

Centres serving the largest resorts and capital cities of countries or states invariably provide two auditoria, each with stage facilities. In some cases, a dedicated concert hall may be included as part of the complex. There is also a range of multi-use halls for meetings, banquets, functions and exhibits associated with conventions, and numerous meeting or break-out rooms for smaller groups.

Larger exhibitions and trade shows are accommodated in a range of halls, having vehicle access through loading docks and

Kunibiki Messe, Japan

Completed in 1993, the Kunibiki Messe (Shimane Prefecture Industrial Exchange Hall) is representative of the many convention centres built recently in Japan. Clad in shining metal, it has a built area of 8733 m² on a site of 15 717 m². On the waterfront there is a circular international conference hall (seating 510) over a lower exhibition floor. Another circular extension provides a multi-use hall (686 m²), and along the rear is a 90 m × 45 m exhibition/convention/events hall (divisible into one-third and two-third areas). The central building accommodates offices promoting local professional, enterprise and technological development, as well as 19 individually designed conference rooms — including special rooms with cylindrical walls and ceilings to lift the spirits of participants. The role of the Messe (reception, transmission, exchange and harmonization) is represented in a monument at the entrance, which also serves as the symbol for promotion.

Operators: Shimane Prefecture Industrial Exchange Hall
Architect/designer: Shin Takamatsu

Tokyo International Forum, Japan

Designed by Rafael Vinoly, winner of an International Design Competition, the Tokyo International Forum accommodates the performing arts, exhibitions, meetings and various ceremonies. It is symbolized by a huge Glass Hall shaped like a ship, 207 m long and 60 m high[1], serving as the main lobby to all the areas[2] and linked to subways and stations.[3]

The facilities include three theatre-type halls: the vast Hall A has seats for 5012 on two levels, the walls flanking the seating being illuminated internally to serve as house lights[4]. Hall C seats 1502 on three levels for concerts, music and theatre. Hall D (340 m²) provides roll-back tiered seating for 600, and is designed for versatile use for experimental theatre and as a conference/audio-visual room.[5]

Hall B (1400 m²) and the Reception Hall (600 m²) can both be subdivided into two, and a separate Exhibition Hall (5000 m²) is also divisible[6]. There is a total of 34 conference and meeting rooms seating 26 to 285.

Each of the halls was constructed with 'box in box' soundproofing to prevent penetration of noise and vibration. Halls C and D also have acoustic control systems to adjust reverberation time. All the halls have simultaneous interpretation facilities (eight languages), audio, lighting and projection rooms and broadcasting equipment.

Within the complex are 11 restaurants and coffee shops, an information centre, shops and other services.

Completed in 1996, the complex includes many innovative arrangements for energy saving, including 594 m² of crystallized solar cells and 410 m² of vacuum glass solar heat collectors on the roof.

Land area, 27 000 m²; building area, 21 000 m²; total floor area, 145 000 m²
Number of floors: 11 plus three basements
Height: 60 m
Cost: US$1.6 billion

Operator: The Tokyo International Foundation
Architect: Rafael Vinoly
M & E consulting engineer: PT Morimura & Associates
Structural engineer: Watanabe Structural Engineers
Photographs: Tokyo International Forum

1. Glass Hall

2. Lobby

3. External Linkages

4. hall A

5. Hall D

6. Exhibition Hall

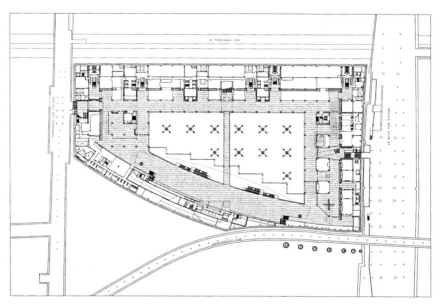

Concourse plan

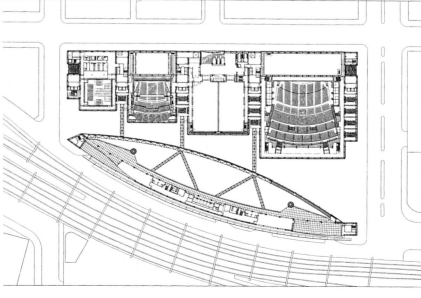

Theatre plan

Europarque Convention Centre, Portugal

The Europarque is an integrated economic and cultural complex located outside Porto, 30 km from the airport with major road and rail links. It encompasses new scientific, technological and business facilities combined with sport and recreation in a landscaped environment. The Convention Centre is a key component, and provides a range of flexible meeting rooms of 35–1000 m², a multipurpose exhibition hall and an auditorium for 1500 people, which can also be used for concerts, ballet and artistic events.

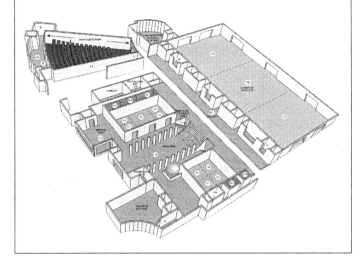

equipped with technical services for connections to the display stands. In every case, the layout is planned to accommodate different group sizes and requirements, and spaces may be changed by division or extension.

Typical provisions:

- Main auditorium seating (1200–2000, exceptionally up to 3000) with equipped stage and support facilities;
- Secondary auditorium (500–800 seats), where alternate rows of seats may convert to tables, also with stage and support facilities;
- Studio theatre (200–350 seats) with tiered seating (telescopic or permanent);
- Grand hall (ballroom) for conventions (1000–2500; in the USA, ballrooms may hold up to 5000), banquets, receptions, exhibits;
- Three or more multi-use halls (400, 300, 250 seats) suitable for functions and meetings;
- Twenty (range usually 15–25) meeting/seminar rooms for 25–200 persons (divisible spaces);
- Ten or more offices and board rooms for 10–20 participants;
- Two to four exhibition halls with 2000–4000 m² of serviced floor space (may be much larger for trade show requirements);
- Registration halls, foyers, lounges, restaurant, cafeteria, information centres;
- One or two shops, a bank and tour agency, organizers' offices, supporting services;
- Hotel accommodation (4*) linked to the centre or nearby;

- Total built floor area (excluding hotel): 25 000–40 000 m² (rising to 140 000 m² for very large complexes such as the Tokyo Forum).

2.1.6 Large convention centres, trade fair complexes

Many of the largest centres in the United States and Germany are combined with, or linked to, trade fair and exhibition grounds. This is also the trend in Australia and South East Asia (Singapore, Hong Kong, Korea). The purpose-designed facilities are generally the same as in the above section, but halls seating up to 5000 may be provided to accommodate the larger convention plenary sessions. Exhibition halls range from 50 000–150 000 m² (Frankfurt 230 000m²), and may be part of the centre or joined by bridging or linking.

Even larger gatherings can be temporarily accommodated in arenas, coliseums and stadia, and these centres usually have small permanent rooms for meetings and events.

2.1.7 Medium-sized centres

Sizeable provincial cities and most large resorts also have opportunities to attract congresses and conventions, particularly if there are historical attractions or/and universities, large teaching hospitals, major commercial offices and other market generators. The facilities are usually rationalized, but the size may be dictated by the need for a viable theatre or concert hall with adequate audience numbers. Flexibility to accommodate different sizes of meetings and functions can be provided by division or extension of the room areas.

Typical provisions:

- One large auditorium seating 2000–2500 with stage and support facilities;
- Two medium-sized halls with 200–350 seats for meetings or functions;
- Ten or more meeting/seminar rooms for 25–150 (divisible);
- Exhibition halls, 1000–2000 m² floor area, one hall being multi-use for banquets, etc.;
- Registration hall, foyers, lounge areas, one or two restaurants, information centre;
- Total built floor area 8000–10 000 m²

2.1.8 Secondary use venues

Buildings designed for the performing arts may be used, on occasions, as venues for large congresses or conventions. Plenary sessions and other full group meetings usually require theatre style seating together with good stage and projection services, and this can supplement other seminar/syndicate and function rooms available in the hotels.

Sydney Convention and Exhibition Centre, Darling Harbour, Australia

Sited on the redeveloped waterfront of Darling Harbour, the original SCEC has a three storey circular Convention Centre (North) linked to five single storey exhibition halls. The convention centre includes a 3500–seat auditorium, which can be divided into one-third and two-thirds areas, on two levels over a banquet hall. There are 14 other rooms (seating 20–600) all grouped around a central foyer, with wheelchair access to all levels.

A new Conference Centre South, added in late 1999, provides the main central entrance plus another auditorium (seating 1000), banquet hall, meeting rooms and flexible exhibition space.

Five main exhibition halls, with 80 m cable supported spans, provide a total of 25 000 m² column-free space with 14 m high ceilings (10.4 m below ducts). Technical services are provided in underfloor pits, and the floors are designed for large, heavy loads (2000 kg/m² distributed). Each hall has its own café and restaurant and can accommodate up to 1800 for a banquet. There is parking for 900 cars below the exhibition centre.

Architects: Original building (1988): John Andrews; Convention Centre South extension (1999): Anchor Mortloch & Wooley
Engineers: Connell Wagner
Builders: Department of Public Works, NSW

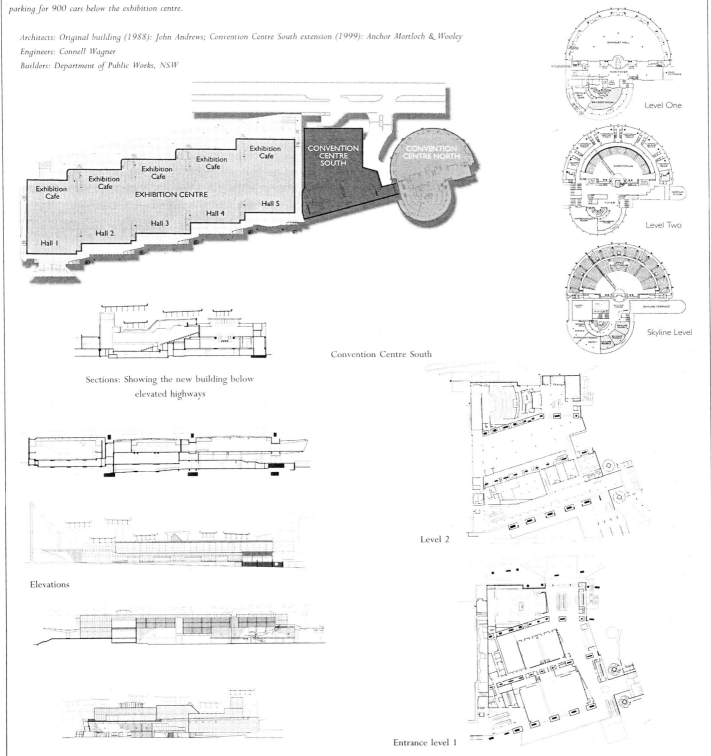

Level One

Level Two

Skyline Level

Sections: Showing the new building below elevated highways

Convention Centre South

Elevations

Level 2

Entrance level 1

Bridgewater Hall, Manchester, UK

Opened in 1996, the Bridgewater Hall is a new international concert hall; the home of the Halle Orchestra and the main performance base for the other famous ensembles in Manchester. The 2335—seat auditorium is carefully related to the large concert platform, with sculptured tiers focusing on the performance within a generally parallel-sided form and continuing around the platform to provide choir seating with the organ rising above.

The hall is also available as a conference venue and can be used in conjunction with the adjacent G-Mex Exhibition complex. In addition to the auditorium, there are two small conference/banqueting rooms. The Hall's extensive glazed foyers overlook an attractive piazza and new canal waterfront for seminars, product launches and other corporate functions.

Client: Manchester City Council & Central Manchester Development Corporation:
Architect: Renton Howard Wood Levin (RHWL) Partnership
Building engineers: Ove Arup & Partners
Theatre equipment: Technical Planning International

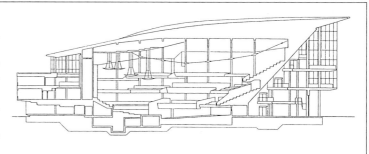

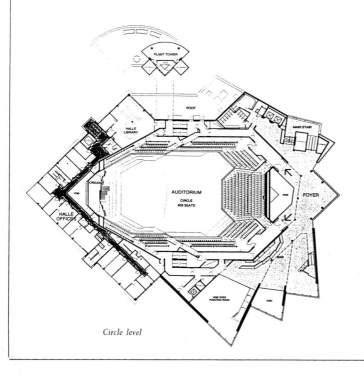

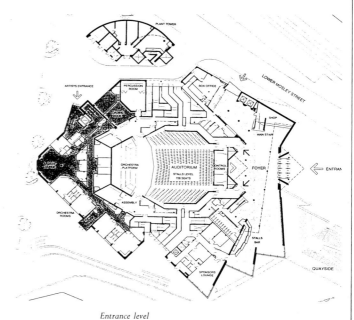

Entrance level

Circle level

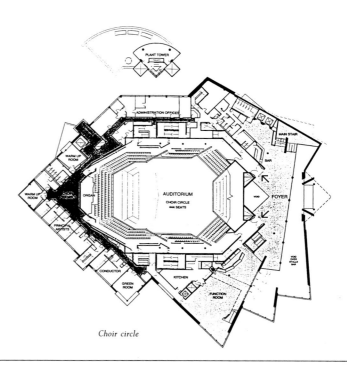

Choir circle

Waterfront Hall, Belfast, Northern Ireland

Designed for symphony concerts, the Waterfront Hall was also required to accommodate alternative uses for economic viability. The main element of the building, the 2250-seat auditorium, incorporates moveable stall seating to provide a 20 m × 30 m arena floor, conference facilities, a stage theatre grid with scenery hoisting gear, and cinema projection. Terraced seating is cantilevered in a series of profiled stepped levels from the rear down the sides in self-contained blocks of 35–80 seats, creating a sense of intimacy. Extensive glass curtain walling has been used in the three levels of foyers, providing spaciousness and wide views over the river and city. There is a separate studio theatre with bleacher-style tiered seating and a gallery for up to 380 people, and 16 multi-use meeting rooms around the perimeter.

Total cost: £32 million (US$50.8 million)
Total floor area: 14 000 m²

Cost analysis (excluding client-supplied items)	%
Substructure	7.62
Superstructure	29.23
Internal finishes	8.17
Furniture and fittings	4.40
Services	40.81
Preliminaries and insurance	9.77

Client and operator: Belfast City Council
Architect: Robinson & McIlwaine
Structural engineer: Kirk McClure & Morton
M & E engineer: Mott MacDonald
Theatre consultant: Carr & Angier
Quantity surveyor: V. B. Evans

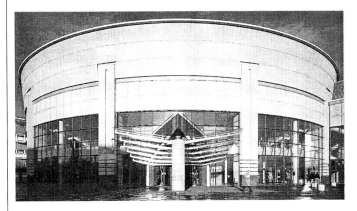

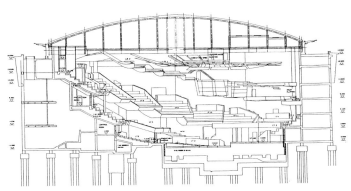

Section: auditorium

Bali International Convention Centre, Indonesia

Within 10 km of the international airport, the Bali Centre is located on the famous Nusa Dua beach adjoining two luxury Sheraton resorts. There are over 3000 first-class hotel rooms in the immediate vicinity as well as entertainment, shopping and a championship golf course. Designed as a series of linked pavilions, in keeping with the local architecture, the centre provides 3500 m² of meeting space and 5000 m² for exhibitions. The main hall, equipped with a stage and full technical services (a), seats 2500 theatre-style (b) or 1500 for a banquet; an auditorium has 506 seats and there are eight smaller flexible meeting/function rooms (c).

Photographs: Bali International Convention Centre

(a)

(b)

(c)

The main limitations in theatre or concert hall buildings arise because:

- delegates are seated in the main auditorium area (balconies may be closed off);
- there is inadequate space and facilities for banquets and exhibits (often in the foyer);
- there are few rooms for supporting group sessions (transport to hotels);
- availability is limited during the shoulder seasons (peak convention months);
- acoustic characteristics usually need to be modified.

2.1.9 Multi-use halls

A wide variety of halls are used for conventions, including those in municipal and other public buildings, church halls, sports centres and trade centres. Very large gatherings may hold events in covered stadia and arenas. In most cases this will involve prior adaptation to meet the needs of the sessions (reception desks, furniture, stage fittings) and the installation of projectors, screens and audio-visual aid equipment (usually hired).

Difficulties may arise from inadequate technical services and the lack of space and flexibility for other functions, including break-out sessions.

Special events, such as banquets and meetings combined with dinners, are sometimes held in unusual venues (museums, historic/cultural centres, mansions) to create the desired prestigious or memorable atmosphere. The food service may be supplied 'in-house' or by contract caterers, and technical equipment is usually hired.

2.2 SITE AND SPACE REQUIREMENTS

2.2.1 Location

As indicated in section 1.3.4, the location of a new purpose-built congress/convention centre involves wider issues than the

City centre siting: planning merits	Potential difficulties
Proximity to commercial, tourism and entertainment districts	High land and development costs and restrictions
Enlivened urban environment: day and evening activities	Integration with surroundings
Links with public transport systems, dual use of car parks	Congestion from generated visitor and service traffic
Stimulus for other investment and regeneration	Future expansion will be difficult, limited and expensive

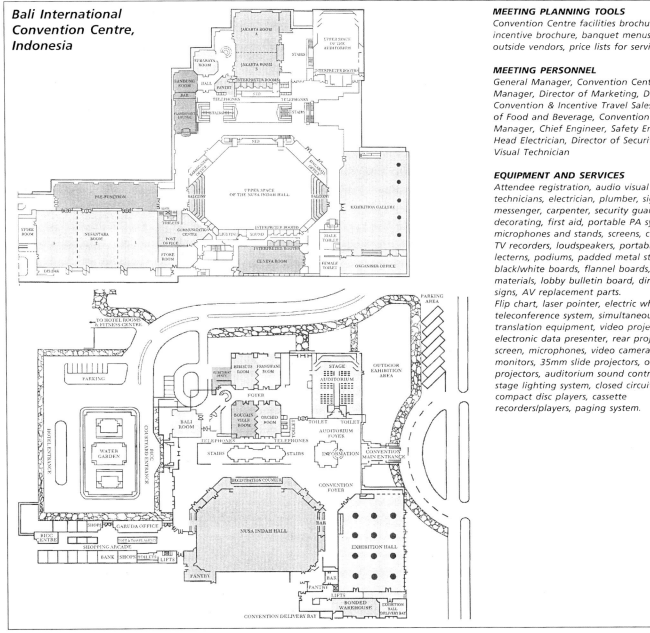

Bali International Convention Centre, Indonesia

MEETING PLANNING TOOLS
Convention Centre facilities brochure, incentive brochure, banquet menus, list of outside vendors, price lists for services.

MEETING PERSONNEL
General Manager, Convention Centre Manager, Director of Marketing, Director of Convention & Incentive Travel Sales, Director of Food and Beverage, Convention Services Manager, Chief Engineer, Safety Engineer, Head Electrician, Director of Security, Audio Visual Technician

EQUIPMENT AND SERVICES
Attendee registration, audio visual technicians, electrician, plumber, sign painter, messenger, carpenter, security guards, decorating, first aid, portable PA system, microphones and stands, screens, closed circuit TV recorders, loudspeakers, portable stages, lecterns, podiums, padded metal stack chairs, black/white boards, flannel boards, writing materials, lobby bulletin board, directional signs, AV replacement parts.
Flip chart, laser pointer, electric white board, teleconference system, simultaneous translation equipment, video projector, electronic data presenter, rear projection screen, microphones, video cameras, VCRs, TV monitors, 35mm slide projectors, overhead projectors, auditorium sound control room, stage lighting system, closed circuit television, compact disc players, cassette recorders/players, paging system.

particulars of the site and its immediate surroundings. Questions of accessibility to the airport and other commercial areas of the city and the need for an integrated system of public transport must be addressed, as well as the planning strategy for the area and the city as a whole.

As a rule, the preferred location for congress centres – particularly when other community uses are involved – is in the heart of the city or resort. The trend in new trade centres is towards more peripheral siting, allowing easier access to the airport and highway network (see 3.2).

2.2.2 Site investigation

Surveys of potential sites must take into account the wider issues, such as the marketing needs of the facilities and the

planning policy for the area (see 1.3). An environmental impact study of effects on the neighbourhood, including traffic generation, is usually involved.

Nature and volume of use:
- Main activities to be accommodated;
- Profiles of visitors, types of facilities and services to be provided;
- Multiple use – separation of groups and activities;
- Patterns of use and numbers of people – tidal flows, peak occupancies;
- Impacts on locality, city and region, consultations with local communities;
- Demands on the tourism and technical infrastructures;
- Provisions for sustainability.

Palacio de Congresos, Centro Kursaal, Donostia, San Sebastián, Spain

Opened in 1999, the Kursaal Congress Palace is located facing the sea on a new beach and consists of an extended base out of which rise two translucent glass 'cubes', each housing an auditorium. The larger has seating for 1850 and a 340 m² stage with rehearsal, dressing and VIP rooms and full technical facilities. This has direct access and can be operated independently when required. The smaller auditorium can hold 580, and has a 120 m² stage. Both have six booths for simultaneous interpretation as well as projection and control services. In the base is a 625 m², flexible, multi-use hall with an adjacent exhibition/foyer area, 10 smaller meeting rooms, a banquet hall for 650, restaurant and coffee bar. The main 1000 m² exhibition hall, with 6.2 m high ceilings, has the option of direct and independent access. Parking is accommodated in a basement. The profile of the 'tilting' cubes forms a symbol for the palace.

Information: San Sebastián Visitor and Convention Bureau
Architect: Rafael Moneo Valles

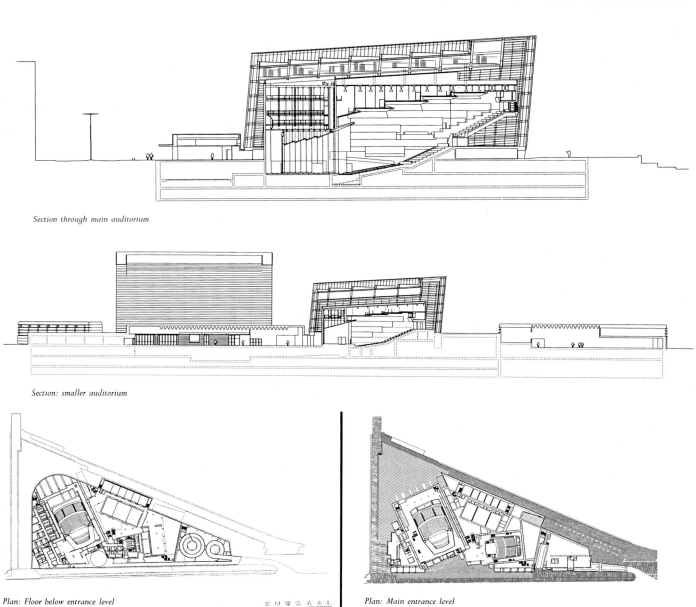

Section through main auditorium

Section: smaller auditorium

Plan: Floor below entrance level

Plan: Main entrance level

Traffic flow predictions:
- Existing traffic flows and intensity of road usage;
- Planned changes in road network (street closures, diversions, improvements);
- Estimates of traffic generation by:

Visitors and employees:
- transport options – modal splits (public/private, car/taxi/coach), multiple factors (persons/vehicle), vehicle movements, routes
- waiting, parking and disabled requirements, space allocations
- existing and planned parking provision in the area
- important visitors – specific provisions for reception and security;

Service vehicles (see 2.2.5):
- goods and services – types of vehicles, patterns of deliveries, requirements for access
- exhibition equipment, contractors – types of vehicles, peak numbers, provision of loading docks, goods lifts, waiting and parking arrangements, regulation of movements
- stage scenery/properties – vehicle details, waiting areas, access to workshops/backstage.

Emergency and occasional use:
- fire, ambulance, television/radio transmission – equipment and vehicle details
- building maintenance and plant replacements – particular requirements involved.

2.2.3 Site details

The site has a strong influence on the design and cost of the development. Particular aspects that must be examined include size and shape, environment, restrictions on development, and site conditions and work.

Size and shape

The area required for a new centre – or the extension or conversion of an existing premises – will depend on the range and capacities of the facilities to be provided, particularly the exhibition halls, main auditoriums, ballrooms and their foyers.

Site dimensions will dictate the way these are arranged – by vertical stacking or on the same levels – and the extent of basement construction.

As a broad guide, a medium-sized congress centre (8000 m²) in urban surroundings will generally require 1.2–1.5 ha (3.0–3.8 acres) and a larger development (14 000 m²) 2.4–2.7 ha (6.0–6.7 acres). In both cases this allows for external circulation and assembly areas, but practically no surface parking.

Projections of growth and trends that are likely to require future development and phasing must be taken into account.

Environment

The following must be considered:
- character of existing buildings and streetscape: integration of proposed building, relationships of scale and form, provision of public space and features of interest;
- prospects – views from and of the building, optimum locations for facilities;
- proximity to hotels, shops, restaurants: pedestrian routes;
- noise levels – road and rail traffic (including tunnel vibration), flight paths;
- potential noise generation by plant and activities (loading, equipment);
- orientation and climate – directions and intensities of sunlight, prevailing winds, rain and snow.

Restrictions on development

These may include:
- ownership and costs of land, (leasehold, freehold) legal procedures and time scales for acquisition; options for joint development, relocation of existing businesses, future enlargement; easements, covenants and other restrictions affecting the site;
- local planning and zoning provisions; land use designation and conditions;
- density, height, materials and other statutory requirements affecting the design.

Site conditions and works

Preliminary investigations of:
- levels and configuration, existing buildings and trees;
- geotechnical survey; trial bore holes, ground water levels, filled ground;
- other works; existing tunnels, mains services; requirements for road and mains diversions, shoring of buildings and site restrictions.

2.2.4 External relationships

See diagram on next page.

2.2.5 Visitor entrances

Separate access is required for visitors, staff, goods and service vehicles and emergency requirements. If the centre is also regularly used for theatrical or musical performances, it is usually necessary to provide an alternative entrance for the public (from the street or entrance concourse) which is independent from that used by conference visitors. This not only facilitates management and security, but also enables two or more congress events or exhibitions to be run independently in parallel.

FUNCTIONAL RELATIONSHIPS
PUBLIC/CONGRESS AUDITORIUM

CONGRESS/FUNCTION/EXHIBIT FACILITIES

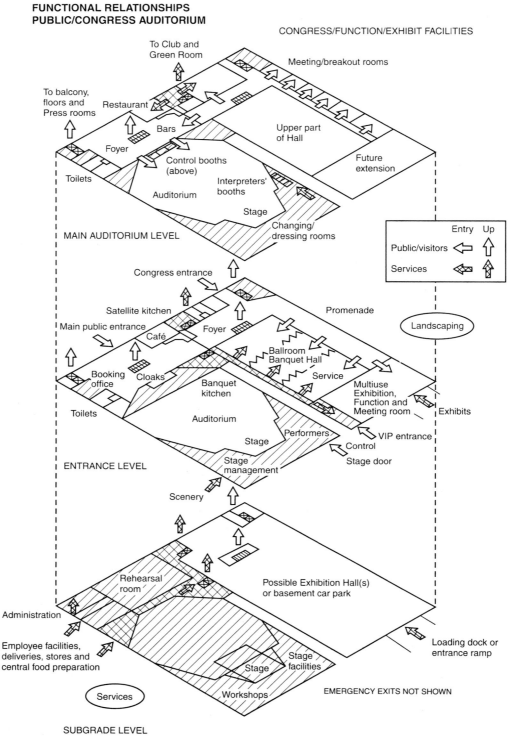

Notes

Diagrammatic representation. The actual layout will depend on the site area, ground levels and superimposed floor levels.

Key considerations:
- *separation of service areas (and deliveries) from public areas (and access);*
- *alternative direct access to banquet halls; separation of congress circulations from public areas when required for independent use but with the alternative of combined access for large events;*
- *separate access to exhibition halls when required independent of meetings;*
- *emergency escape routes and exits to safe assembly places;*
- *direct vehicle access for deliveries, stage scenery and exhibits (with vehicle waiting or parking bays);*
- *internal separation of service corridors to kitchens and stores from the public areas;*
- *supply of food to other function rooms, exhibition hall, Green room, etc.;*
- *restaurants, cafes, meeting rooms, break-out areas and lounges should overlook landscaped areas with terraces for extension of activities out of doors where possible;*
- *future extensions should be considered in the initial plan to minimize future disturbance, loss of business and structural difficulties.*

Pacifico Yokohama, Japan

The centre of a major urban redevelopment of the city and waterfront, the Pacifico Yokohama is one of the best convention complexes in Japan. Opened in 1991, it includes the National Hall, seating 5000, together with two other auditoria for 1000 and 390. There are also two multi-use halls (1366 m² and 792 m²), 16 meeting rooms and a huge exhibition/events hall of 10 206 m². The complex is linked to the soaring wings of the Yokohama Grand Inter-Continental Hotel.

Architect and Engineers: Nikken Sekkei

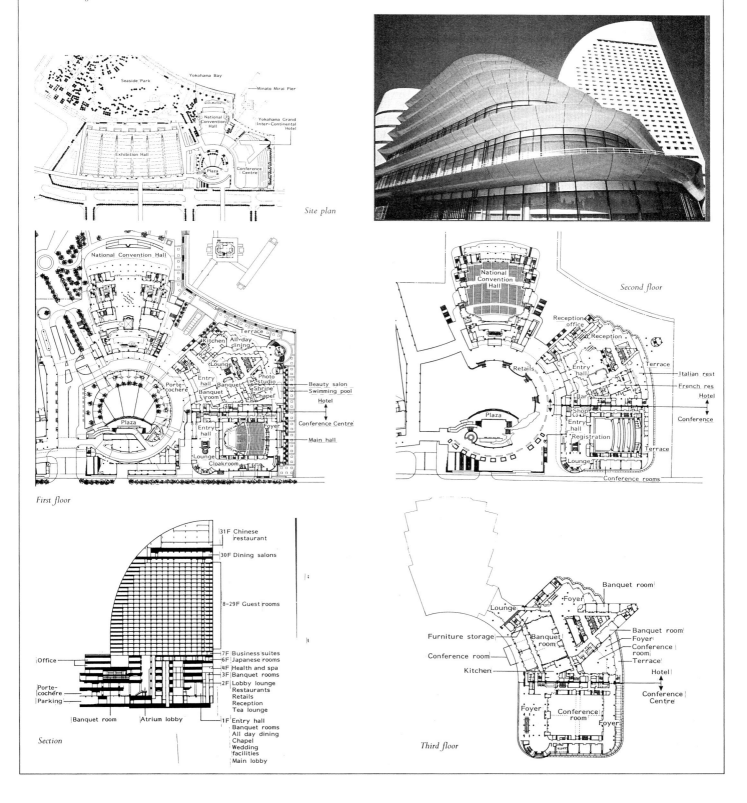

Site plan

First floor

Second floor

Section

Third floor

The public face of the building needs to generate interest, express its role and create a landmark whilst retaining harmony with the character of the setting. The frontage is best set back from the main street, with a pedestrian square or piazza providing a human scale of activity. In planning the main entrance, consideration must be given to:

- direct access from the public transport system (underground) or via a protected walkway from bus and rail stops and associated hotels (pedestrian routes to avoid crossing traffic lanes);
- vehicle access and parking – a one-way system with dual lanes to allow passengers from taxis, cars and coaches to alight without obstructing the entrance road, a lay-by with spaces for waiting taxis and coaches, and close proximity to parking (with sign directions);
- a canopy or portes cochere to provide protection over the entrances from inclement weather – canopies may extend over pedestrian routes to other doors;
- external lighting – flood and feature lighting of the building exterior and enhanced illumination of the entrance with the intensity progressively increasing through the lobby to the entrance hall; column lighting along the entrance roads and footpaths from outside car parking areas;
- signage and displays – an array of flagpoles and illuminated symbol and name; co-ordinated graphic design in all the signs and information throughout the building, with universal symbols adopted for exits, escape routes and other directions;
- entrance doors – automatic doors are essential for wheelchair users and several pairs of doors are required for peak departures (calculated); doors should be in two lines, at least 2 m apart, to form a draught lobby, and glass doors must have visible markings; fire escape requirements apply to all emergency exits (see 2.4.5);

Public areas	Operational services	Support services
Lobby, concourses	Information, displays	Public address system
	Shops, travel bureau	Rental space, deliveries
	Bank	Security, deliveries
	Cloakrooms, toilets	Attendants
	Box office	Front office, house manager
	First aid room	Access to waiting ambulance
	Restaurant/café, refreshments	Kitchen – food services[1], food and beverage, stores etc., deliveries
Entrance hall	Messages, paging	Public address system
	Public and house telephones	Telephone operator
	Information display	Press centre, business centre
	Welcome desks	Organizer's office
	Registration desks	Administration offices[1]
Foyer to banquet halls	Cloakroom, toilets	Attendants
	Information	Public address system
Banquet hall	Service lobby	Banquet kitchen – main kitchen[1], deliveries, beverage stores; linen, china, silver stores; furniture stores, displays, loading dock
Function rooms	Service corridor	Satellite kitchen – main kitchen[1], deliveries, beverage stores; linen, china, silver stores; furniture stores
Foyer to meeting rooms	Refreshments	Service lobby, kitchens[1], stores
	Information	Public address/CCTV systems
Meeting rooms	Interpretation booths	Access corridor, restrooms
	Operator's/control booths	Access routes, equipment stores[1]
	Furniture arrangements	Service lobby, stores, loading dock
	Equipment	
Foyers to auditorium	Refreshments	Service lobby, food service stores
	Drinks bar	Beverage and glass stores, deliveries
Information	Public address/CCTV systems	
Auditorium	Interpretation booths	Access corridor, restrooms
	Operator's/control booths	Access to equipment housings, stores[1]
	Stage	Back-stage equipment, stores, scenery dock, stage management, property stores, production workshops[1], assembly areas, performers' areas
	Dressing/changing rooms	Stage door keeper, stage door entrance
Green room	Food and beverage service	
	Practice room(s)	Instrument, etc. stores
Exhibition halls	Entrance lobby	Registration facilities, visitor access, cloakrooms, toilets, organizers' offices
	Exhibition area	Food and beverage services, service routes, technical services, plant[1], loading docks, vehicle access, security control

[1]With corridors leading to employee changing and rest areas, personnel offices, etc. and employee entrance. Food services may be rationalized (see 8.1.4).

International Congress Centre, Munich, Germany

Opened in October 1998 as part of the new Munich Trade Fair development, the ICCM has seating for around 7000, in rooms for 30–3000, and 3500 m² space for exhibitions accompanying conventions. The modern architecture is an example of 'form following function', and is designed for flexible use (for conferences, theatrical performances, concerts and exhibitions), with all areas easily reached from the foyer. Halls are spread over three levels, with a large divisible ballroom (3000 persons) and other conference rooms on the first floor over the main exhibition area (3500 m²). In the separate auditorium, fixed seating for 1500 converts to allow intermediate rows of tables in a classroom format for 750.

Operator: Messe München GmbH.

Architect: Planungsgemeinschaft Neue Messe München: Professor Kaub, Dr Scholz, Dipl-Ing Jesse (München)

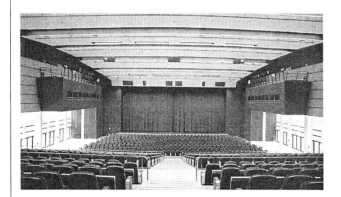

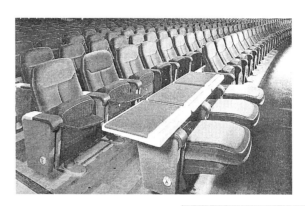

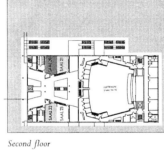

Second floor

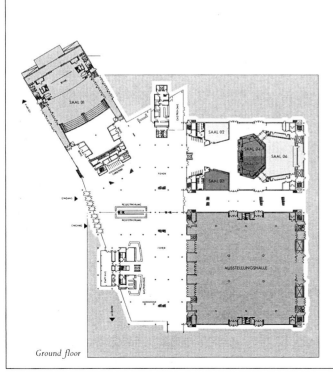

Ground floor

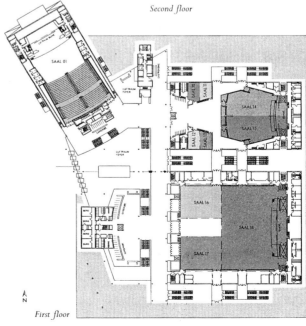

First floor

Valencia Congress Centre, Spain

The first meeting held in this landmark building, in July 1998, was appropriately titled Architecture and Cities of the Twenty-first Century. Shaped like a boat rising out of the fountains, with the roof a shimmering aluminium shield orientated for energy efficiency and soaring on slender columns above translucent and transparent facades, the interior layout of the Valencia Congress Centre is highly practical. A curved 100 m foyer runs the full length of one side, giving access to three auditoriums arranged side-by-side and nine conference rooms, as well as exhibition (1077 m²), retail and support areas. The auditoria can seat 1463, 468 (with tables) and 250 (divisible into two) respectively. All are lined with maple, have excellent acoustic quality and sight lines and a highly energy-efficient air cooling system installed in the seat bases. A digital network throughout the building interlinks communication and control systems.

The Centre is the focal point of a new area of urban development in Valencia, part of a complex that will include a hotel and 7500 m² of open parks and squares. Located 2 km from the city centre, it is easily accessible from the airport by road, underground rail or tram. Events are organized by the Turismo Valencia Convention Bureau.

Architect: Foster and Partners
Information: Turismo Valencia Convention Bureau
Photographs: Nigel Young

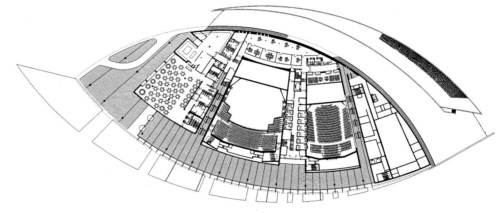

Level 2

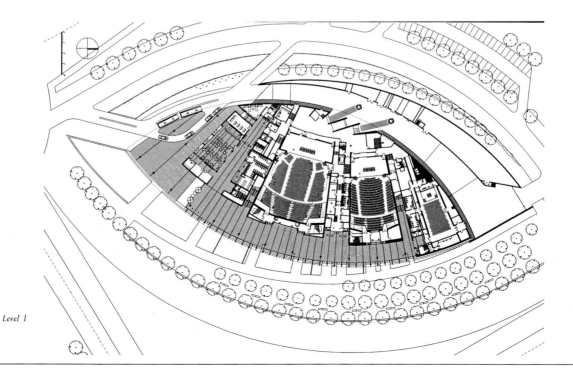

Level 1

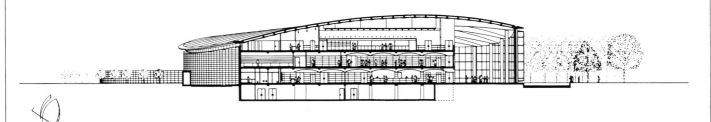

SECCION TRANSVERSAL A TRAVES DEL VESTIBULO

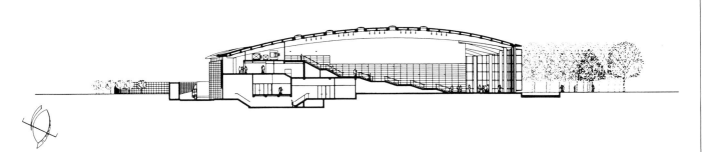

SECCION TRANSVERSAL ESCALERA PRINCIPAL NORTE

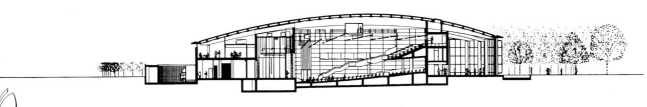

SECCION TRANSVERSAL AUDITORIO I

- access for the disabled – specific provisions include alloca-tion of parking spaces, identification of routes, provision of ramps, toilets and facilities designed for wheelchair and other disabled users in each main area.

2.2.6 Other entrances

Employee entrances should be separate from those used by the public and lead directly to a controlled area with time recording, changing rooms and other facilities. Personnel offices, interview/training rooms, wages/clerical records and security services are usually grouped in the same area. Corridors giving access to 'back of house' work stations must be separate from those used by visitors.

A stage door entrance for performers is required in centres for the performing arts. Entry is controlled by a small doorkeeper's office, and gives access to the backstage changing and dressing rooms, the 'green room', practice rooms and associated areas. Provision should be made for taxi and bus alighting points nearby.

Vehicular access is required for vehicles delivering food, beverages, supplies and equipment, for contract services and for removal of garbage. Facilities normally include a loading dock (with nearby vehicle waiting bay), checking office and direct transfer through level corridors to food, beverage and house-keeping stores and plant areas. If necessary, a good lift may be installed for transit to kitchens on higher or lower floor levels.

A separate area is required for storage of garbage, with containers for food waste (refrigerated), paper, glass and metals, together with compactors. The delivery area must be screened, located to minimize unsightliness and noise trans-mission, and designed for easy cleansing and control.

Exhibits: Delivery of exhibition stands and equipment and their removal is highly concentrated in time, and involves two or more loading docks for large vehicles. In planning the layout, exhibition halls should be at the access road level to allow vehicles to enter and reach the individual stand positions, thereby reducing the need for handling and transfer.

In smaller centres, direct access may be limited and, in some cases, transfer by goods lifts (at least two) to other floors may be unavoidable. Parking arrangements for transport vehicles must be regulated; off-site waiting/parking is normally required with a call system and other management controls.

Stage scenery and properties: access is required to the rear of the stage area for large pantechnicons, with a waiting bay to allow loading without obstructing other routes. The delivery bay leads directly to the workshop and back-stage platform.

2.2.7 Internal planning: relationships

Planning involves a progressive series of steps:

- identifying the activities that need to be accommodated and the extent to which they may use the same areas or need to be separated;

- knowing the sequences of use and the type of facilities and services required, together with the most efficient and unobtrusive means of providing the services;
- deciding the sizes and optimum shapes of the areas and where they are best located taking into account their requirements.

The first two may be represented by relationship diagrams (see 2.2.4) and more detailed examination of requirements.

2.2.8 Horizontal and vertical arrangements

Side-by-side arrangement of the main facilities enables each to be designed individually, simplifying structural requirements and reducing vertical transportation. The auditoria, main halls and groups of rooms need to be linked by a public concourse, which is often designed as a uniquely distinctive integrating feature with vast areas of glass, lighting effects, commissioned artwork and other spectacular attractions. Such arrangements are often adopted in large complexes (e.g. Tokyo Forum, Leipzig, Birmingham) and centres built in resorts or adjacent to parkland.

Vertical stacking of the auditoria and/or main halls is more economical in the use of land, and enables space below tiered floors to be more efficiently used. Unit costs of construction are higher, and vertical transportation of people and goods may present difficulties (space, costs, means of escape, organiza-tion). Exhibition halls at levels above or below ground may require extensive ramp and loading bay construction (e.g. Hong Kong, Singapore).

Different levels may also be used to separate the public facil-ities from support areas such as plant and equipment rooms, stores, the main food production kitchens and employee chang-ing and support services.

2.2.9 Circulation planning

Movements of visitors and members of the public need to be carefully designed to ensure clear directions, convenience and safety. Particular attention should be given to the peak flows of people, particularly on egress from each main area of assem-bly, and the local code requirements for means of escape in case of emergency. As a rule, the aim is to ensure evacuation of any room or level within 2.5 minutes.

Signs

Directional signs should be provided at all junctions, changes in direction, escalators and lifts, and at entrances to the rooms. For ease of reading, the optimum position is between 30° above and 10° below the horizontal from the viewing position. A uniform graphic style must be adopted throughout, with clear, legible lettering.

For zoning events, the directions to specific rooms may be changed electronically or colour coded. Standard symbols with illuminated signs are used to indicate emergency exits, toilets and other services.

Corridors and passages

Corridors must be designed to serve as means of escape in the event of fire and lead to safe exits from the building. Minimum widths, fire resistance standards (usually 1 hour), limits to combustibility and surface flame spread and emergency requirements apply (see 2.6.7). The walls and flooring must resist marking and damage, and ceilings should allow acoustic absorption and access to services.

Long corridors and large areas of impersonal space – other than for emergency use – should be avoided. Whilst continuity of passages must be maintained for directional purposes, some variation in space and finishes should be introduced, including 'pockets' of lounge seating for informal gatherings between events. Extensive glazing of promenades, lounges and restaurants provides a refreshing contrast to the artificial lighting of the internal areas.

Landscaping and predominantly restful colours (pale blue, green) are often used in the decor of the ancillary areas. Illumination in corridors should allow for transition from daylight to interior levels, and change from day- to night-time requirements.

Changes in level

Steps must be positioned in line with walls and openings, where they can be anticipated, clearly indicated (by lighting, contrasting edges) and provided with handrails. Most codes stipulate no less than two steps and no more than 16 in a flight, with consistent 275 mm treads and 180 mm risers. Handrails are usually 900 mm above the pitch line and 1200 mm above landings, with solid panels or balustrades having gaps no more than 100 mm.

Ramps for wheel chairs should not exceed a pitch of 1:12 nor lengths of 4.5 m, and may need to be separated from other routes.

Escalators

The floor area taken up by escalators is extensive, but is justified in a large complex where the main assembly halls or auditorium are on floors above ground level. The angle of elevation is usually 30° (maximum 35° in restricted space), with approach lengths of 1.8 m and 2.7 m at the top and bottom of the incline. Safety provisions are incorporated, including means of sealing open escalators in the event of fire with water curtains, and exhaust ventilation of smoke.

Typical installations:

Speed (m/s)	Width (mm)	Capacity (persons/minute)
0.45–0.60	810	80–90
	1000	110–120

Elevators

Passenger elevators should be positioned near the main stairs, with a lobby waiting area adjacent. For light traffic and wheelchair users, one may be adequate (16 persons, 1100 kg), but at least two (22 persons, 1600 kg) may need to be installed for transporting people over three or more floors, and dedicated good lifts may be required for food and other equipment. Traction-drive elevators are most common, but hydraulic elevators may be more easily installed in existing buildings or used for heavy goods transport. For short distances single or dual speed (0.5–1.25 m/s) is normally suitable, but precise levelling is critical.

Requirements include fire resistance of the doors and shaft, and entry through a fire protected lobby from underground car parks. Immobilization in the event of fire means that alternative stairs and other routes must be provided.

2.3 SPACE AND FACILITIES

2.3.1 Space requirements

Mandatory minimum requirements for close seating in an auditorium and other places of assembly are specified in codes and regulations concerned with fire safety, floor loading and environmental health requirements, but these are generally inadequate for planning purposes. It is more appropriate to use typical space standards in the initial allocations, although the final capacities will vary with the shape and actual dimensions of the rooms as well as the layout of furniture (see 2.4.4).

As a rule, smaller rooms are less space-efficient than the larger halls. Two sets of figures are indicated; minimum areas assuming close seating with limited space, and space allowing for the higher standards of comfort and greater flexibility for conference use. In each case these allow for internal circulation.

Typical space minima

Space per person	m²	Notes
Theatre seating density	0.8–1.0	Auditorium area excluding stage
Theatre-style linked seats	1.0–1.2	Large flat-floored hall or ballroom
Theatre-style seat layouts	1.2–1.6	For medium-sized to smaller rooms
Classroom seating	1.6–2.2	With individual tables in large halls
Classroom layouts	1.8–2.4	In medium-sized rooms
Boardroom seating	2.0–2.2	Groups of 10–25 around table
Banquet	1.0–1.2	Depending on table arrangements
Reception buffet	0.8	Standing, including serving counters
Foyers	0.3–0.6	Based on hall seating capacity
Circulations per 100	2.0	Added to the above spaces
Exhibition stands	9.0	Modular shells usually 3 × 3 m
Poster or counter stands	4.0	Allowing 2 × 2 m space occupied

Exhibition visitors	0.5–0.7	Over total exhibit area (40% circulation)
Restaurant (high standard)	2.0–2.2	Overall – but excluding kitchen
Coffee shop, café	1.6–1.8	Excluding satellite kitchen
Refreshment bar	1.5	Mainly standing
Lounge bar	1.8	Lounge seating area
Men's toilets (per person)	0.05	(Minimum area based on 500 plus)
Women's toilets (per person)	0.07	(Normally increased and in several areas)
Cloakrooms	0.1	For attended cloakrooms
Lobby, reception hall	0.5	Including registration desks but not shops
Service areas		
Restaurant kitchen	0.5–0.7	per seat cover
Banquet kitchen	0.2	per banquet seat
Satellite kitchen	0.3	per seat in café
Food storage	0.1	Based on total restaurant seats plus
Beverage storage	0.1	50% banquet
Linen, glass, china, silver stores	0.1	capacity
Furniture stores	0.15	per seat in halls (if changed regularly)

2.3.2 Types of rooms and flexibility

Facilities for meetings include auditoria with tiered, permanent seating and a stage, and flat-floored halls and rooms using loose furniture.

The sloping floor of an auditorium limits flexibility in layout, but changes are possible by:

- removal of rows of apron seats to extend the stage or create an arena type flat floor;
- conversion of alternate rows of seats into tables (incorporated in the seat design);
- use of removable writing tablets (built into arms of seats);
- physical division of the space by closing off segments, particular levels or balconies;
- elevation of the seating and floor into the ceiling, leaving a flat floor exposed;
- rotation of blocks of seats to form separate rooms;
- use of telescopic (bleacher) seating over part or the whole area.

Physical changes to the space affect the volume, acoustic characteristics, air-conditioning and other technical services, requiring balancing and duplication of control systems and equipment. In halls intended primarily for music, this may involve some compromise in shape and design. Division of the auditorium also requires separation of the foyers and support areas to cater for the different groups involved.

Flat-floored halls can be rearranged to suit each event, and are used for a variety of requirements; receptions, functions, banquets, meetings, participating group activities, exhibitions. The limitations on sight lines and acoustic clarity for large group sessions can be compensated for by the use of video projection and loudspeaker systems.

Difficulties can arise from the need to move and store furniture, which requires stacking systems, storage and limitations in the choice of chairs and tables (dining chairs may not be suitable for meetings). Most large halls and meeting rooms have some form of partitioning to allow division into smaller areas. As with auditoria, this incurs additional requirements for servicing each area, including divided foyers and separate service access (see 2.3.7).

Vancouver Convention Centre, Canada

A phased construction programme, starting in 2001, is planned to triple the meeting space. Comprehensive redevelopment of the waterfront is planned to provide:

Exhibition hall: 24 000 m² (250 000 sq ft)
Glass-fronted delegate concourse along water front
Meeting space: 7600 m² (82 000 sq ft)
Ballroom: 4600 m² (50 000 sq ft)
Lecture theatre: 1500 seats
Harbour view plaza
Cruise terminal extension
Waterbus terminal
Three new hotels of more than 2000 rooms

Information: Greater Vancouver Visitor & Convention Bureau

Edinburgh International Conference Centre, Scotland

The design concept of the EICC was influenced by the shape of the site, street level differences and the need to create a compact but flexible building. Completed in 1996, the innovative drum-shaped building is based on a circular plan in which two theatres can be revolved to increase the capacity of the main auditorium from 600 to 1200 for plenary meetings, or provide three separate auditoria of 600, 300 and 300 for parallel sessions, each with full projection, lighting, staging sound reinforcement and control systems. On the level below are eight perimeter meeting rooms for 30–100 delegates, and at entrance level there is a spacious foyer and a 600–seat conference suite sub-divisible into three segments. The lowest level, with direct access from a secure loading bay, provides a hall of 1200 m² with a 3.5 m clear height and underfloor services grid for exhibitions or banquets.

The elevations are buff/grey sandstone colour, traditional in Edinburgh, with contrasting stone and strong colour for impact, which is enhanced by night-time lighting. The four facades each have their own character and, overall, the shape and prominent roof edge feature give the building a unique image.

Architects: Terry Farrell & Partners
Structural and services engineers: Ove Arup & Partners
Acoustic and theatre consultants: Sandy Brown Associates
Main contractors: G. A. Management

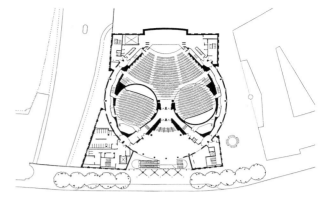

Main auditorium level

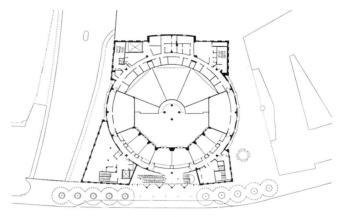

Level Two

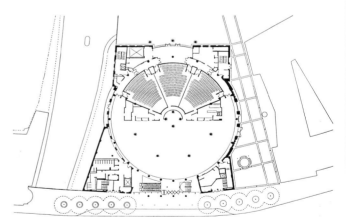

Entrance level

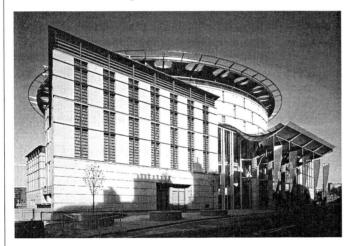

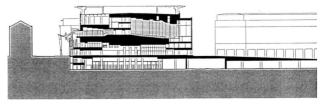

Section: Front to rear

Forum Grimaldi, Monaco

The latest addition to the congress and cultural facilities in Monaco, due to open in 2000, the impressive Forum Grimaldi is built on an extension to the seafront. It provides three auditoriums (1900, 800 and 400 seats), two interconnected exhibition halls (3940 and 4180 m^2) and 24 meeting rooms. Most of the building occupies lower floors than the tapering glass atrium which surrounds the entrance and sides of the Grand Hall at Esplanade level. Behind this, two upper floors accommodate three restaurants, bars, roof terraces and the larger exhibition hall, the central area of which is free from columns and has a ceiling height of 7 m, to allow for a variety of events.

Several new hotels are planned or under construction to support this development, including a 50 suite, luxury 5-star hotel and a 350 room, 4-star hotel being built next to the Forum.

Architects: Fabrice Notari & Frederick Genin

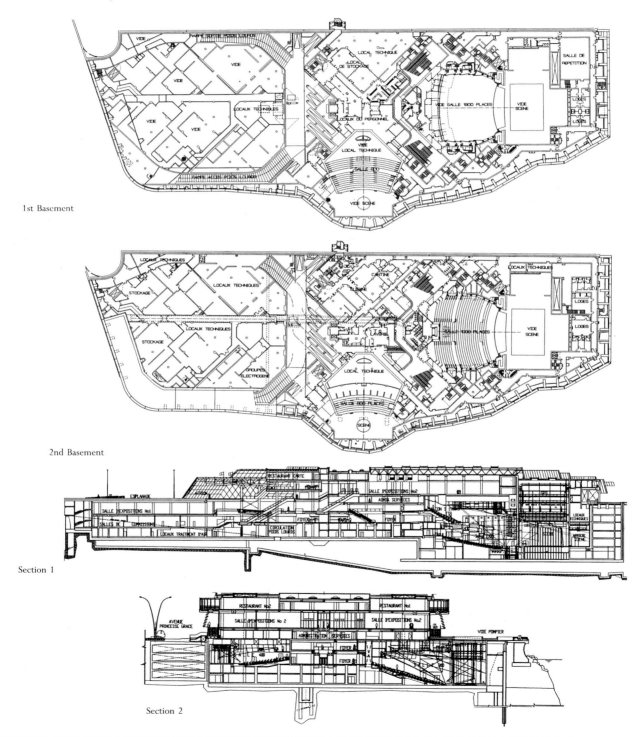

1st Basement

2nd Basement

Section 1

Section 2

1st Floor

2nd Floor

Ground Floor

Lower Ground Floor

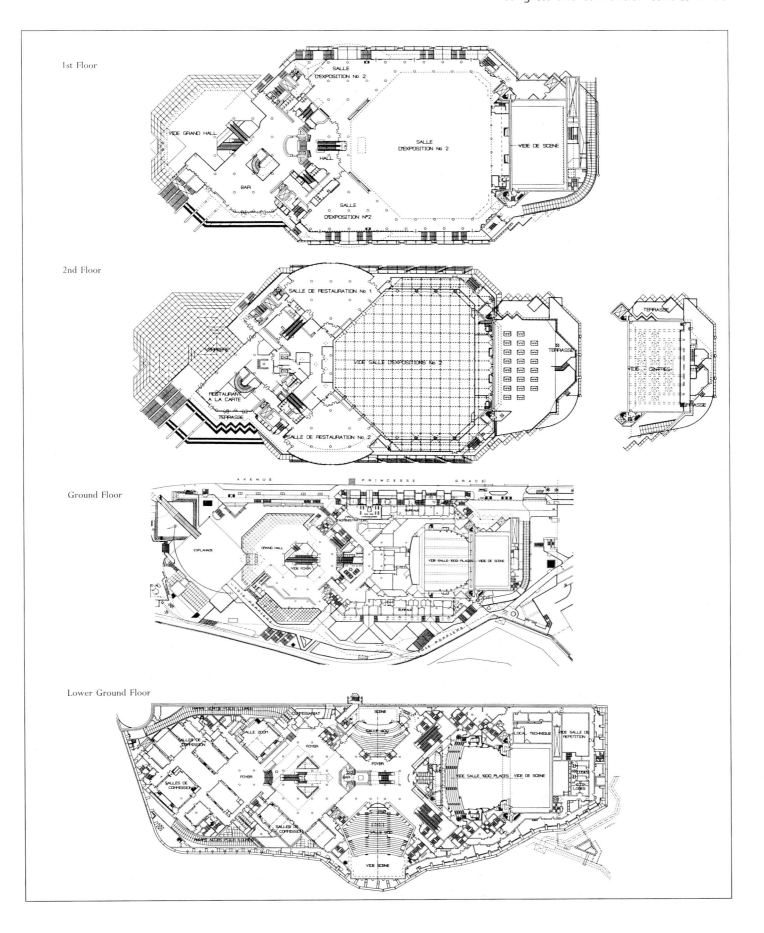

2.3.3 Ratios of space

Congress centres need to accommodate a wide range of activities and group sizes. Although very large congresses and conventions are important in terms of the publicity, demands on resources and economic impacts, the great majority of events are relatively small (see 1.4–1.5). Meetings and other organized events often overlap, requiring the provision of separate access, facilities and services.

Most congresses involve a range of activities, for example:

Plenary sessions	Large group meetings for the full attendance
Parallel sessions	Alternative choice of lectures/symposia
Break-out sessions	Group participation in workshops, seminars, etc.
Banquets, functions	Formal dining, usually with invited speakers
Receptions	Gatherings and introductions, social contacts
Exhibitions	Display of related products and information

Theoretically, for each seat in the main auditorium there should be an equal number of places for dining, for other meetings and for exhibit viewing. The capacity of the auditorium and main banquet hall (or ballroom) is important in marketing for large events, but the greatest demands are usually on the numbers of medium-sized and smaller meeting/function rooms. A total net area of 6.6 m² of public space per delegate is likely to be required to accommodate the various requirements of a large congress.

Ratios of public space (theoretical)	Minimum net areas m²	m² [1]
Reception/circulation		0.8 [2]
Auditorium	1.0 [3]	Foyer 0.4
Banquet hall/function rooms	1.2	Foyer 0.3
Meeting rooms	1.6	Foyer 0.3
Exhibition area	1.0 [4]	
Total area per delegate [5]	4.8	1.8

[1] Aggregated, including associated refreshment areas
[2] Including small lounge areas, business centre, corridors
[3] Excluding performing stage and back-stage areas
[4] Varies with markets: 0.7–2.1 m² includes exhibit stands
[5] To accommodate large congresses/conventions.

2.3.4 Rationalization: multiple use

A high ratio of utilization is necessary to justify the feasibility of this development. As previously indicated (see 1.2.5), the auditorium is often designed for the performing arts to increase community benefits. Banquet halls and function rooms also attract local markets for social events, and the exhibition areas may generate independent art, antique, business services and consumer shows. The demand for meeting/function rooms extends over association and corporate markets, and is mainly for groups of less than 300 persons.

To ensure flexibility to meet the particular needs of each event, areas are often designed for more than one use:

Area	Adaptations	Uses
Auditorium	Acoustic/lighting changes, stage/ back-stage facilities	Performing arts, public use, evening entertainment of visitors
Ballroom and Multi-use halls	Food, etc. services	Banquets, receptions, dinner parties, hospitality Exhibits, dances, discotheques
	Technical services Audio-visual support Space division	Meetings, product launches, presentations Separate groups, dual functions
Meeting rooms	Division of larger rooms Food services	Separate groups, interview rooms Social functions, business lunches
	Re-arrangement, technical services	Press rooms, training programmes Committee rooms
Ancillary services	Technical services Business centre Administration	Television monitoring, broadcasting Secretarial services, communications Promotion, public relations, marketing

2.3.5 Entrance halls

The entrance hall or lobby for congress visitors needs to be separated from that used by the public and is the main hub of circulation, serving as an assembly and meeting place and providing information, directions and other services. The registration and support services perform several functions:

- hospitality – introduction and personal welcome on arrival;
- defusing – point of contact to sort out problems and grievances;
- control – restrictions on entry, distribution of conference material;
- information – notices, general information, specific enquiries;
- registration – formalities, records and feedback for organizers;
- accounting – monitoring attendance and financial position.

The first impression is most important in establishing standards and attitudes. Signs must be clear and of professional quality, and sufficient space must be allowed for delegates to assemble in the lobby without congestion. Clearly defined circulation lanes to and from the registration desks and fast, efficient registration procedures are also vital. In many cases, delegates will have registered in advance and the registration formality is essentially a confirmation of attendance and briefing.

For registration and check-in purposes, two or three desks will usually be required, mounted in the lobby or foyer to one side of the main circulation area and permanently staffed throughout the period until the delegates leave. Specific provision must be made for access by disabled persons, including portable or permanent desks and rest areas.

Requirements within the area:

- public telephones and internal lines to the conference rooms;
- public address and paging system;
- lounge/waiting area with waiter service;
- exhibition and display space;
- good illumination, preferably with some daylight (300 lux – daytime; 200 lux – evening; increasing to 500 lux (shielded) over registration desks);
- air-conditioning with 3 l/s fresh air supply per square metre, based on floor area.

Space requirements: minimum, 0.5 m²/person; management offices, 0.1 m²/person (usually linked to the box office).

Direct access to a business centre associated with the administration and organizers' offices may be provided. In a large complex, other necessary facilities should be provided in the public concourse:

- tour, theatre and auto-rental agency
- banking and currency exchange
- news agency and other kiosks or shops.

2.3.6 Toilet and cloakroom facilities

High standards of sanitary facilities are necessary. These will be subject to a high coincidence of demand at the beginning and end of sessions, and will need to be discretely but conveniently located at a number of places – near the entrance lobby, at each auditorium foyer, the ballroom foyer, exhibition hall and groups of meeting rooms. Minimum legal standards, based on the total seating capacity in the area involved, are:

Large halls	Male	Female
Water closets	1 per 250 up to 500, +1 per 500 above	2 per 75, +1 per 50 above
Urinals	1 per 25	
Washbasins	1 per WC, + 1 per 5 urinals	1 per WC

As a rule, there should be at least two water closets in any group, and the approach to the male and female toilets should be discretely separate and clearly signed. The interior areas must be finished to a high standard, screened from external view and separated from any room by an intervening ventilated space. Separate provision, in the same area, must be made for a disabled persons' toilet with similar high standards of design.

Automatic control of lighting, flushing and hand drying should be installed, and corbel mounting of fittings with concealed pipework and cisterns is preferable. High levels of illumination (200–300 lux) and a separate system of mechanical extraction providing six to eight changes per hour are required. Noise reduction and maintenance are critical requirements.

Cloakrooms are required at each main visitor entrance, including the ballroom/banquet hall lobby, which may be used for external social events. For security, attendant operated services are preferred. The counter should be set back 1.2 m from the circulation route and, including this and the counter, the area is typically 0.1 m² per person.

2.3.7 Foyers

Separate foyers are required for each of the main halls and for groups of meeting rooms. The foyer provides circulation and assembly space leading to different parts of the hall, including each floor level, and any area that may be separated by division. It is also a place for personal contact and exchange between participants, and is often used for messages and information and service of refreshments during intervals. For social events the foyer contributes to the sense of occasion, and for conferences it provides a refreshing break between working sessions.

Key considerations:

- **Area** – 0.3–0.5 m² per person based on hall or auditorium capacity (minimum 0.3 m²);
- **Daylighting** – valuable for psychological contrast to internal areas, preferably with interesting views; transitional artificial lighting for both day- and night-time levels;
- **Décor** – for social uses (ballrooms, public auditoriums), the foyer should contribute to the sense of occasion; for conferences, a refreshing/relaxing neutral decor (green, blue) and informal atmosphere is preferable;
- **Vestibule** – entry to auditoriums must control sound and light penetration (insulation, sound absorption, screening); viewing panels or video monitors are required to show the interior during use (activities, performances);
- **Circulation** – routes must be recognizable and designed to allow easy, free flowing movement, without obstruction and cross flows; where there is more than one, all rooms and levels must be clearly signed;
- **Minimum widths** – to allow for peak egress conditions; door openings must be same width as corridors;
- **Fire safety** – to meet exit requirements (linings, fire separation); sprinkler systems normally installed and fire mode air flow controls;
- **Refreshment service** – access for food service trolleys; the location of counters must not obstruct circulations (queues, standing areas); supplementary lighting may be needed.

Facility provisions	Medium-sized congress centre	m² % of total	Large congress-arts centre	m² % of total	Notes
Main auditorium					
Seating	1200 @ 0.9 =	1010	2000 @ 0.9 =	1800	1
Stage area (10 m proscenium)		500		700	2
Projection/control/interpretation booths (gross)		150		220	3
Back-stage areas (gross)		400		480	4
Public foyers	1200 @ 0.5 =	600	2000 @ 0.3 =	600	5
Under stage and stores		140		200	
Total		2800 31.8%		4000 15.7%	
Auditorium 2					
Seating			800 @ 0.9 =	720	6
Stage area				330	7
Projection/control/interpretation booths (gross)				150	
Back stage areas (gross)				300	8
Public foyer			800 @ 0.5 =	400	
Total				1900 7.5%	
Auditorium 3/Studio theatre					
Seating	300 seats @1.0 =	300	400 @ 0.9 =	360	9
Stage		150		190	10
Projection/control booths (gross)		150		150	
Back stage areas (gross)		250		300	8
Public foyer	300 @ 0.5 =	150	400 @ 0.5 =	200	5
Total		1000 11.4%		1200 4.7%	
Meeting rooms					
Ballroom/banquet hall	500 @ 1.2 =	600	1000 @ 1.2 =	1200	11
Conference rooms	2 seating 100–150 @ 1.1 =	270	4 seating 100–150 @ 1.1 =	550	12
Meeting rooms	4 seating 40–60 @ 1.6 =	300	10 seating 40–60 @ 1.6 =	800	13
Break-out/committee rooms	8 for 10–12 @ 2.0 =	180	12 seating 10–12 @ 2.0 =	250	14
Assembly areas/foyers	500 @ 0.3 =	150	2000 @ 0.3 =	600	
Projection/equipment rooms		200		400	
Circulation and support areas		300		800	
Total		2000 22.7%		4600 18.0%	
Exhibition halls			4 halls @ 1000 m² gross =	4000	15
			Loading bays, storage areas	1000	16
			Entrance hall, public facilities	500	17
			Total	5500 21.6%	
Public areas					
Entrance lobby/booking hall		240	Concourse 3000 @ 0.3 =	900	18
Rentals: Post office, bank, shop				120	
Reception/registration hall	1200 @ 0.3 =	360	2000 @ 0.3 =	600	19
Organizers' suites of offices	Using meeting room, press office etc.			90	
Business centre		70		150	
Press room		50	80m² + 3 offices =	140	
Medical centre		30		50	
Circulation and support (cloakrooms, toilets)		150		250	
Total		900 10.2%		2300 9.0%	
Food and beverage areas					
À la carte restaurant	100 covers @ 2.0 =	200	200 covers @ 2.0 =	400	
Cafes/cafeteria	60 @ 1.7 =	100	200 @ 1.7 =	340	
Bars	Spilling into foyers		Lounges 150 @ 1.7 =	260	
Main/satellite kitchens and stores		300		700	
Gross area, including circulation, etc.		800 9.1%		2200 8.6%	
Administration and support areas					
Administration (gross areas)		230		650	
Plant, engineering and security areas		900		2600	20
Employee areas (changing, canteen, personnel)		170		550	
Total		1300 14.8%		3800 14.9%	
Total built floor areas		8800 100.0%		25 500 100.0%	

Notes:
[1] Area per seat allows for generous seating dimensions
[2] Stage area based on 10 m proscenium width, but will vary with types of productions required
[3] Includes booth areas, operator's equipment and circulation, but not plant rooms
[4] Average provisions for changing, dressing, green rooms and ancillary areas, but depends on use and status of hall
[5] Extends out into lounge areas with refreshment bars
[6] Alternate rows of seats convertible to tables
[7] Used primarily for congress meetings, product launches and repertory theatre; served by heavy goods lift
[8] Back-stage areas may be combined and rationalized, reducing these areas
[9] Seats may be telescopic type with alternative seating formats; used for rehearsals or meetings
[10] Stage is often portable to allow changes in seating plans
[11] Multi-purpose hall used for meetings, banquets, exhibitions, receptions; in medium-sized centres this area often extends into the foyer or other adjacent halls to accommodate larger banquet groups
[12] Rooms usually divisible into two or three sections for smaller meetings or meetings combined with functions; maximum capacity based on theatre-style seating and classroom seating will reduce these figures by 40 per cent
[13] Based on classroom-style seating; all rooms designed for flexible use
[14] Open square or boardroom seating
[15] Four halls linked together for separate or combined use; each hall will accommodate 50–60 stands (9 m²), combined capacity 220–230 stands
[16] Loading dock areas and goods lifts requirements depend on level of exhibition floor; normally this allows direct vehicle access
[17] Registration and entrance lobby (with cloakroom facilities) included to allow independent use of exhibition areas
[18] The arrangements for access and internal circulation to the halls depend on the design; in large centres this is often via a concourse extending through the complex
[19] To allow separate registration of congress groups; includes lounge areas, permanent and portable desks
[20] Widely variable depending on extent of roof mounted plant; includes all plant areas, control rooms, security offices, equipment stores, reserve storage and loading docks.

2.3.8 Analysis of areas

Requirements for individual congress centres vary widely depending on the brief and site characteristics. The following hypothetical examples (page 60) show preliminary estimates of the facilities and areas required for a multipurpose congress centre of medium size, and a larger complex with three auditoria and separate exhibition halls. In each case the auditoria are equipped with stage facilities for the performing arts. All areas are rounded for simplicity.

The arrangement of halls and rooms will depend on the site and access. Some rationalization and sharing of the foyer and prefunction areas is usually possible, but the need to provide for separate conference groups and other activities should also be considered.

2.4 AUDITORIUM REQUIREMENTS

2.4.1 Characteristics

An auditorium with tiered seats enables large numbers to be accommodated together in comfort with good acoustics, clear views and a close, individual relationship with the platform and presentations. This is particularly suited to plenary and information-giving sessions (lectures, seminars) with individual or panels of speakers and accompanying visual presentations (slides, films). In most cases this facility also serves for entertainment (for delegates and, at other times, for the public), requiring more elaborate stage and back-stage installations.

Location

Considerations:
- Public access separation from other conference activities;
- Stage/performers' access and back-stage provisions;
- Noise entry shielded by outer meeting rooms and double skin construction;
- Vibration – structural design, use of mountings;
- Daylight – in foyer and break-out areas.

Size and capacity

Large congress centres usually include two auditoria to cover the size ranges up to 2000 (exceptionally up to 3000) and up to 800. In medium-sized venues it is more common to provide one main auditorium seating 2000–2500 and designed for more flexible use (see 2.1.5, 2.1.7).

Space requirements depend on the seat geometry, seating density, number of floors and platform design. For well-spaced seating on one floor and including gangways, apron and booths, an auditorium area of 0.8–0.9 m² per seat (excluding the stage) may be used for preliminary planning.

In congress programmes, seats are occupied for long periods and must be comfortable, reasonably spacious and house the equipment needed (tables, communications, grilles). Excessive seating dimensions may lose audience social cohesion in addition to reducing the spatial efficiency. Seating densities should be more generous than the minima for theatres, and are usually in the range 0.55–0.65 m² per person for self-lifting (tip-up) seats.

2.4.2 Aural and visual considerations

Visual

Facial expressions can be discerned up to about 20 m (18 rows) away. For larger halls, cameras with video projection may need to be installed to show an enlarged view.

Screen viewing distances depend on image brightness (projection and screen characteristics) and legibility (character size and proportions), but is generally related to image width:

Viewing distance	Times image width
Maximum	6
Absolute minimum	1.4
Preferable minimum	2
Optimum seating	3–5

The viewing angle is the angle described at the centre of a flat screen by the viewer's sight line and the projection axis and is normally limited to 45°, but 30° is optimum. The vertical angle from horizontal eye level to the top of the screen (for front seats) should not exceed 35((see 6.5).

Screen viewing requirements

DIN recommendations for flat screen – white, matte, non-directional – assuming good standards of image brightness and legibility.

Plan showing optimum viewing areas for rectangular and fan-shaped rooms within 30° of centre line and a distance of 2 to 6 x screen width W. Fringe areas indicate the limit of 45° (40° barely tolerable) from the far edge of the screen and distance extremes of 1.4W and 7W.

The centre of row curvature is 1/8W behind the screen.

Sight lines

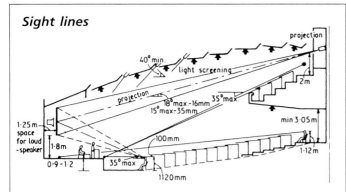

(a) Longitudinal section through a hall showing sight lines giving a minimum of 100 mm (4 in) clearance for each row producing a parabolic stepped floor. A clearance of 125 mm (5 in) is better. The steepness of the rake is also increased if the stage is lower or the speaker nearer the audience. For multi-purpose use the focus is taken to the back of the stage (and to the front for balcony viewing). Ceiling profiles are determined from sound ray diagrams.

Other considerations:

Unobstructed view of screen

Projection beam clearance

Maximum tilt of projection axis:

> *16 mm projection – 18°*   *(preferably less than 12°)*
> *35 mm projection – 15°*

Ceiling lights: minimum 40° cut-off angle for screening.

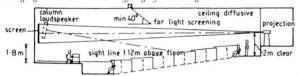

(b) Section through hall with 125 mm (5 in) clearance for alternate rows arranged with staggered seating. Maximum incline without steps is 10° (check local Codes)

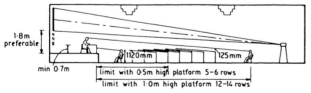

(c) Section through a hall having a flat floor allowing a minimum clearance of 125 mm each alternate row. Focus taken to table height (0.7 m).

Limiting distances:

with 0.5 m stage – 6.0 m from the speaker (5 to 6 rows)

with 1.0 m stage – 12.0 m from the speaker (12 to 13 rows)

If a portable screen is used this should also be 0.7 m minimum above the stage. A permanent screen should be fixed at least 1.8 m (6 ft) high to avoid the light dazzling the lecturer.

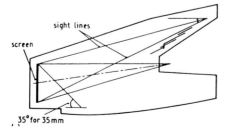

(d) Section showing alternative position of projection booth to facilitate separation of balcony.

Levels of illumination required in a congress hall are much higher than those for theatre or concert hall use, and this must be taken into account in designing lighting installations. Local individually controlled lamps (shielded) are often built into the backs of seats or tables – if used – to facilitate note taking. Lighting controls, including computer controlled stage lighting and dimming requirements, must be provided in an operator's booth sited centrally at the rear of the auditorium (see 2.9.3).

Aural

Acoustic clarity will depend on the size, shape and volume of the auditorium and the finishes and reverberation time, but for direct sound it is generally limited to 20 m from the speaker, reducing at the sides where the auditorium extends outside an arc of 140°. Natural sound can be reinforced by the placing of reflectors (ceiling panels, wall screens), but a sound amplification system with suitably placed loud speakers will be required to allow for wide variations in voice strength, panels of speakers and questions from the audience (see 6.3).

Speech perception mainly involves a frequency range of 200–6000 Hz, the frequencies between 700 and 5000 Hz accounting for some 80 per cent of speech intelligibility. In each frequency band there is a dynamic range (short time average) of about 25–35 dB from the loudest to faintest sounds. The voice power of individual speakers varies from about 40–150 μW, but is typically about 60 μW. Methods of measuring and assessing acoustic conditions for speech include subjective tests (percentage syllable articulation), frequency band analysis (articulation index) and reverberation measurement.

Optimum reverberation times (at 500 Hz) for speech range from 0.8–0.95, increasing with the size of the hall. In multipurpose halls this will need to be increased to 1.3–1.7; for symphony concert halls, 1.6–1.85; and for choral concerts, 1.7–2.1, requiring some adaptation for this change of use (see 6.1.8). Within the auditorium, the audience makes up 60–70 per cent of the absorption surface and the theoretical volume per seat required for speech is about half that for music.

Background noise becomes more evident as distance from the speaker increases. The masking effect is most marked in trying to distinguish consonants, and a signal-to-noise ratio of +7 dB or more is required to provide reasonable clarity. Distracting sounds, even at a lower level, cause switching of attention, particularly if they are recognizable (sirens, speech, music).

Design objectives for good acoustics

Pyschological conditions:
- Relationship between the speaker and audience – affected by size of the audience, circumstances, spaciousness, relative positions, elevation of the speaker;
- Arousal and appreciation levels – environmental and physical comfort, sound strength and clarity, masking, distortion and distraction.

Physical requirements:
- Good direct sound – determined by the shape and size of

the hall, distances to side and rear positions, row-to-row sight line clearances and design of balconies;

- Early reinforcement of direct sound – position and construction of reflecting panels and design of electronic amplification system;
- Freedom from discrete echoes and strong envelopmental sound – selective absorption and diffusion, adjustment of reverberation for differing conditions;
- Control of noise entry – limitation of masking/distracting noise by planning, zoning and separation of areas (sound locks), appropriate noise insulation standards and acoustic specifications for engineering services and equipment;
- Multipurpose use – acoustic regulation for music and other requirements includes adjustment of the shape, size and boundary conditions of the stage and auditorium and electronic modification of the growth and decay characteristics of sound (see 6.1.8).

Ambient noise control

Levels of noise in a building situation are measured over a spectrum of frequencies. These can be expressed in weighted sound pressures levels (dBA), speech interference bands (SIL), noise rating (NR) curves, noise criterion (NC) or the more stringent preferred noise criterion (PNC) curves.

Recommended standards	NR[1]	Conditions
Congress halls, concert halls, live theatres (<500 seats)	20	15 may be specified in concert halls
Live theatres (>500 seats)	25	
Lecture theatres, boardrooms		Quiet
Conference rooms (>50 people)		Conversation 3–10 m
Multipurpose halls, ballrooms	30	Raised voice 24 m
Banquet rooms, hotel guestrooms		
Small conference rooms	35	
Reception areas, corridors		
Quality restaurants and shops		Moderately noisy
Hotel lobbies, reception halls	40	Conversation 2–3 m
Large restaurants, bars, kitchens		Raised voice 3–10 m
Cafeteria, offices	45	Conversation 1–2 m
Raised voice 2–3 m		
Workshops, plant rooms	50–55	Noisy Normal voice 0.3–0.7 m

[1] PNC curves similar number. dBA levels for similar spectral shape = NR + 6. Source: Croome, D. J. (1970). Acoustic environment in buildings. *Journal IHVE*, May, 32–41.

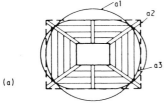

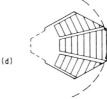

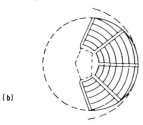

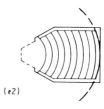

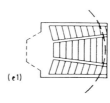

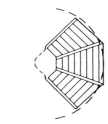

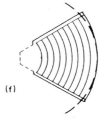

(a) 360° full encirclement for displays, spectator sports, shows. Directional and localized sound control essential. Used in arenas, coliseums and multi-purpose halls (using portable or bleacher seating). Various shapes.

(b) Wide arch: up to 135° for command. Lines of sight may limit use of side seats – particularly for screen viewing. Used with thrust stage. Typical in drum-shaped buildings without balcony seating. Provides large seating capacity.

(c) 90° arc: side and rear wall configurations vary and may approximate to an octagonal plan. Ensures good direct sound but the side seats may be obscured by a proscenium or for screen viewing. Usually includes balcony provision.

(d) 60° hexagon: a common arrangement in many multi-purpose theatres allowing flexibility in the stage and proscenium. Fixed seating may be kept to the perimeter and balcony leaving a flat central area for alternative uses. In the traditional theatre this may be modified to a 'horseshoe' shape.

(e) Rectangle: most multi-purpose halls are rectangular with an internal or extended (e1) stage. The side walls may be inclined towards the stage (e2) – this elongated 'shoebox' shape is traditionally favoured for concert halls. Side walls contribute to lateral reflections but require faceting or acoustic treatment.

(f) Fan shape: the angle of splay varies up to 60°. This shape is preferred for lecture theatres, giving best direct sound and screen viewing. The curved rear wall must be acoustically treated (e2 and f show typical 'continental' seating).

Scottish Exhibition and Conference Centre, Glasgow, Scotland

The SECC, located in an infilled dockland site in Glasgow, is the major exhibition venue in Scotland. In 1997 a new purpose-built Conference Centre was added to the exhibition complex, creating a distinctive profile on the skyline and a symbolic landmark building. With 3200 seats, the conference facility is one of only five in Europe with this capacity and is thus able to compete in attracting the larger conventions. The expansion also provided a new 5400 m² clear-span exhibition hall and conversion of an existing hall to provide break-out areas, including a flexible conference space seating up to 600.

Funded mainly by the City of Glasgow Council, with financial assistance from the EC, it is estimated that the new centre generates £26 million (US$41.3 million) per annum revenue and provided 1000 new jobs in Glasgow.

The Clyde Auditorium has three levels of tiered seating and rises to a height of 40 m. The roof is designed as a series of shells with metal cladding on a complex steel structure, the shape being generated entirely by 3D computer modelling techniques, and the foyer extends the full height at one end (810 m²) and is completely glass fronted.

Floor area, 13 000 m²; overall length, 120 m; width, 65 m; height 40 m
Area of roof: 10 500 m²
Project cost: £26 million (US$41.3 million)

Clients: Glasgow City Council SECC Ltd
Architect: Foster & Partners
Structural engineers: Ove Arup & Partners
M & E engineers: Ove Arup & Partners
Acoustic consultants: Sandy Brown Associates
Photographs: Richard Davies

Reference: The Arup Journal (1998), 33(2), 3–9.

SECC Construction sequence

Foundations

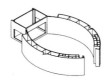

Buffer

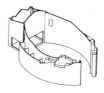

Auditorium

Seat Units

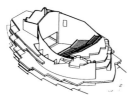

Floors

Superstructure

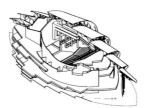

Cladding

Shells Completed

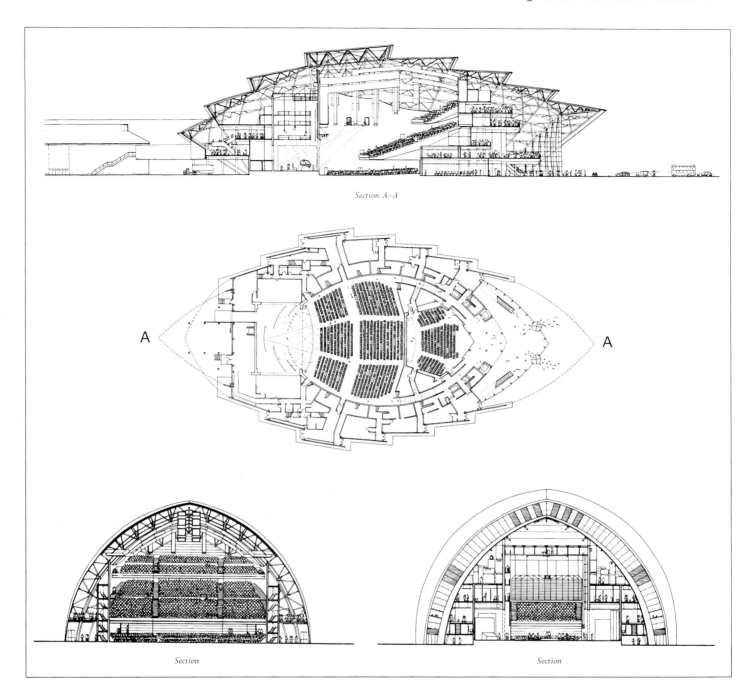

Section A—A

A   A

Section   *Section*

Sound absorption of a material depends not only on its intrinsic properties but also on its mass, thickness, method of fixing, air spaces, backing and surface treatment. To achieve the required reduction or adjustment over a spectrum of sound frequencies it is usually necessary to use a combination of techniques, including porous and membrane absorbers, dissipative surfaces and cavity resonators. Variations in occupancy levels and in uses can also have a significant effect on absorption and acoustic requirements (see 6.1).

Intrusion of noise from outside the auditorium, together with the risk of vibration from road and rail traffic (surface and underground), must be considered at the initial planning stage.

Preventive measures include the identification of potential sources and levels of noise, location of the auditorium with outer screening and insulation (double skin, mass), use of sound locks at points of entry, and specifications for equipment and services (see 6.2).

2.4.3 Plan shapes

The most common arrangements for seating facing a platform or stage are the traditional rectangular box, a modified box with the sides extended into a polygon or horseshoe shape, and the fan-shape auditorium (see page 69).

Rectangular plan

This is the most common plan for multipurpose halls with flat floors, being uncomplicated in construction, easily changeable in use and easily divisible by partitions.

A rectangular hall with height : width : length ratios of 3 : 4 : 8 or 2 : 3 : 5 is considered the optimum for concert music, giving a good balance between direct and indirect sound distribution and good orientation from lateral reflections. For speech acoustics, lateral sound reflections may produce standing wave resonance and echoes unless the side walls are made diffusive or absorbent. If the ceiling is high relative to width, the extended reverberation may call for the installation of suspended acoustic panels to shorten the reflection path characteristics.

Polygonal plan

The hexagon and its extended or modified forms is used extensively as the basic plan for multi-use theatre-congress-concert halls. It provides a compromise, giving good direct sound, controlled ceiling and lateral reflections, and scope for variations in seating arrangements and levels within the auditorium. For music, the sound may be electronically modified by assisted resonance to achieve satisfactory blending and quality.

For proscenium stage or side masking arrangements the sight lines from the extreme sides are liable to become too acute and obstructed, requiring sections to be closed off. This may also apply to screen viewing in the congress mode. To allow greater flexibility for a variety of uses, the central area of the main floor may be made flat using retractable seating with raised tiered seating round the perimeter.

Modifications of the building geometry to improve sight lines and intimacy include the horseshoe shape which, with balconies, is characteristic of the Georgian theatre and concert hall but is usually less suitable for congress use.

Fan-shaped plan

This plan enables the maximum number of seats to be concentrated within the arcs giving the best viewing and listening conditions. In speech the maximum strength of voice is directionally concentrated into an arc of 135°, but an apex angle of 90° is preferable for audience command. To avoid distortion, the viewing angle for screen projection should not exceed 45° and the relative width of the screen will also influence the seating plan.

To enable the side walls to add to sound reinforcement the angle of splay should be no more than 25°, and the wall angle may be acoustically reduced by the use of serrated or faceted walls or by introducing vertical panels inclined at a smaller angle. Panels of this kind can also be used to change the acoustic conditions of the hall for different uses.

A splayed area may also be combined with a rectangular or polygonal plan.

Rows of seats may be set in concentric curves (as in 'continental' seating) to provide each with a forward facing view of the platform. Alternatively, if dividing aisles are provided the side rows may be set at an angle to the longitudinal axis. In a wide hall these side sections may also be separated into areas and raised to higher levels to create variety in seating as well as more even lateral distribution of sound. The rear wall of the auditorium may be straight or concave, but will require acoustic treatment. Balconies are usually restricted to the rear.

Circular and oval plans

Encircling formats, as in arenas and coliseums, are also used for major convention and congress meetings, in addition to serving a wide range of community needs such as indoor sports, displays, rallies and pop concerts. The size of such enclosures and the distances over which sound and views of the proceedings have to be transmitted require the installation of complex loudspeaker and video viewing systems.

Each section of the audience is regarded as a sound-absorbing area at which sound signals of calculated amplitude are beamed from loudspeaker columns. This avoids the carry-over of sound, which could cause reverberation and echoes. Interval time delays are also introduced to synchronize the transmitted and direct sound. The acoustic design of the enclosure is not a significant factor, although sound reflectors may be located around the source. Similar approaches are used in the design of video systems (see 2.9).

Whilst the limitations for good acoustics are a drawback, the arena type of enclosure is able to accommodate extremely large numbers of people and generates the atmosphere of excitement and occasion. Most congresses and conventions only require plenary sessions at the beginning and end of the programme, the major part involving smaller, more specialized groups. Nonetheless, the ability of a venue to cater for all the delegates together is an essential selling point in attracting the large international and American conventions.

2.4.4 Seating arrangements

Layout

Seating geometry is mainly determined by the auditorium plan and the aural and auditory considerations. Rows of fixed seats may be straight, curved, partly splayed or in combinations, and fall into two main groups.

Traditional seating has the seats arranged in blocks separated by aisles or gangways. The maximum number of seats per row depends on local building codes/regulations, the seat clearway and access to gangways or aisles. The maximum number of seats with 405 mm gangways at both ends is 22, and with a gangway at one end is 11. The maximum travel distance along the gangway to an exit is 18 m (59 ft).

Multi-purpose auditoria seating

Comparisons showing (a) traditional seating and (b) continental seating in halls of similar size. Typical details of stage dimensions are also shown.

Normal proscenium widths are:

	m	ft
For drama	9–12	30–40
concerts	12–18	40–60
opera	18–24	60–80

Usual limiting distances are:

	m	ft
For drama	15–23	50–75
concerts and opera	30–38	100–125

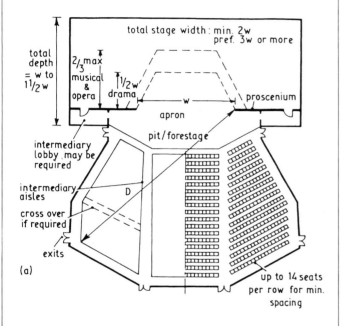

(a)

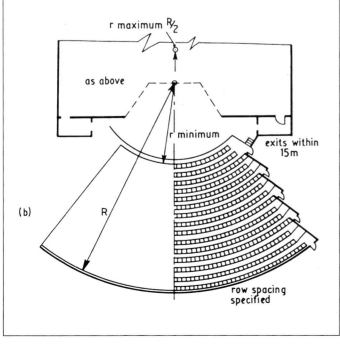

(b)

Fixed auditorium seating

Typical seat dimensions and spacing for traditional seating (a) and continental seating (b). Seat layouts are also shown in radial and straight lines

Typical dimensions, shown on the diagrams

		m	ft
a:	depth, seat down	650	25½
	tablet arm out	720	28½
b:	depth, seat up	380	15
	tablet arm down	510	20
c:	height of back	810	32
d:	to datum line	400	15½
e:	width	530–560	21–22
r:	row spacing (minimum*		
	traditional	815	32
	continental	965	38
s:	seatway (minimum*		
	traditional	305	12
	continental	460	18
t:	sightline	1120	44

Dimensions vary ± 25 mm (1 in)

*Subject to legal standards — see text

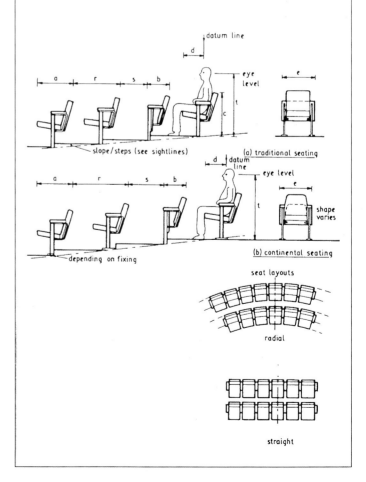

Continental seating has more than 22 seats per row, extending to gangways at each side and more exits. Requirements in the UK stipulate a clearway of 400–500 mm and maximum travel distances of 15 m from any seat to exits, with gangways at each end of the row leading away from the direction of the stage. In practice, the exits are usually provided for every three rows, each third row being blocked off so that equal risers of two steps can be provided.

The National Fire Protection Association (NFPA) recommends clearways of 18–22 inches (430–525 mm), increasing with the numbers of seats per row, a maximum of five rows between exit doors and limits to travel distances.

Seat design

Seats must provide a satisfactory standard of comfort over long periods of constrained movement, taking into account anthropometric and ergonomic principles and standards expected. The seats invariably have armrests and may incorporate equipment (cabling, microphones, voting systems, air ducts, concealed lighting, writing tablets) and tables for conversion of alternate rows. To reduce row spacing, tip-up seats are normally used, and the front rows may be removable to allow extension of a thrust stage.

Consideration must be given to the mechanism, durability, fabric covering and upholstery, fire risks, sound absorption balance, method of support and fixing, cleansing and life cycles for replacement.

Sight lines

When the audience is seated on one level, the sound is strongly absorbed at a low grazing angle above and around the heads of the audience. To some extent this can be improved by raising the speaker on a platform or stage and staggering seats in successive rows out of line.

In an auditorium the floor is also inclined in a series of steps to elevate successive rows of seats. To provide the profile, sight lines need to be calculated and drawn from representative seating positions in each row both across the longitudinal section of the hall and from other side angles.

Main criteria:

- Focal point on platform – stage heights vary from 800–1100 mm, and the focus is usually taken at 50 mm above the furthest point of the stage for acting (for multiple use); allowance must be made for any thrust stage;
- Eye level when seated – usually taken as 1120 mm along the central line;
- Vertical distance between the average viewer's eyes and top of the head – preferably 125 mm (minimum 100 mm);
- Maximum vertical angle – elevated view from nearest seats must not exceed 30° (discomfort); maximum angle down from balcony 35°, preferably 30° (vertigo);

- Recommended clearance is normally for successive rows; for widely spaced staggered seats it may be for alternate rows;
- Sight lines continue over cross aisles, balconies and other obstructions;
- The theoretical floor rake is a parabola; gangways may have a maximum slope of 1 : 10 (1 : 12 for wheelchair users) and at steeper inclines must have even, regular treads and risers extending the full width.

2.4.5 Means of escape in event of fire

An exit time of 2.5 minutes for evacuation of the audience from the auditorium is normally planned. Local fire requirements must be consulted, but the following are guidelines in the UK:

- Maximum travel distances – 18 m from gangway or 15 m from seat (Continental);
- Exits – at least two for up to 500 on each level, plus an additional exit per 250;
- Exit widths – based on 45 persons per minute per unit width of 520–530 mm.

Number of people on each level	Minimum exits	Minimum width
300	2	1200 mm
400	2	1350
500	2	1500
750	3	1500
1000	4	1500

(plus one additional exit per 250 people).

- Exits must be indicated with permanently illuminated signs; emergency lighting system must be installed (see 2.6.7);
- Exit route must lead directly to a place of safety with no reduction of width;
- Exit doors must open in the direction of egress with emergency release mechanism;
- Staircases must not have more than 16 steps in each flight nor fewer than two; treads/risers must be 275/180 mm and consistent;
- Ramps must not exceed 1 : 12 in lengths of 4.5 m; exit routes for wheel chairs may need to be separate;
- The fire escape routes must be enclosed by fire resisting construction, with limits on the combustibility and structural integrity of linings, and must be kept clear and maintained.

Fire control systems are outlined in section 6.8.5.

2.4.6 Ceiling requirements

Design requirements for the ceilings of halls are largely dictated by functional needs. In a large, purpose-designed congress hall, the ceiling construction would have to consider:

Congress Centre Messe, Frankfurt, Germany

Inaugurated in 1997, this centre is within a circular building shared with the Maritim Hotel and extends over four levels with a glass facade frontage. The foyer at the entrance level leads to small meeting rooms and offices on level 1, with the main hall on level 2 and other conference rooms and facilities above. The main hall (1890 m²), seating up to 2200, is designed for flexibility. Using retractable telescopic walls in the ceiling, the hall can be subdivided into five radial sections, three concentric rings and up to 15 rooms. Floors can be changed from level to a selected graduation, rising to over 3 m above the stage, using complex hydraulic technology. Extraction ventilation is also installed below the moveable floor. There are variable electronic signs around the rooms, infrared equipment with six interpreters' booths and video projection facilities. The hall is directly linked to the 10 000 m² Trade Fair complex and to an underground car park (466 spaces on two levels).

The Congress Centre was funded by awarding partial hereditary building rights for the hotel and an office building on the site over 99 years, the first 35 years free of ground rent.

Total hereditary building rights land: 12 500 m²
Building volume: 356 000 m³
Total floor area (Congress Centre, hotel and office building): 87 500 m²
Floor area of Congress Centre: 15 000 m²

Architects: Helmut W. Joos, J.S.K. Perkins & Will
Interior design: Andreas Ramseier Associates Ltd
Photographs: Congress Centre

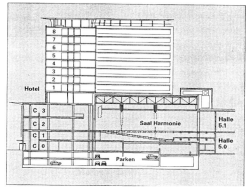

Teilungs- und Bestuhlungsvarianten im Saal Harmonie

Configuration and seating variations in function hall Harmonie

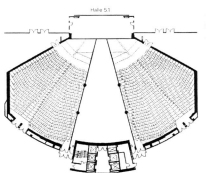

Teilung 3 mit Reihenbestuhlung für jeweils 727 Personen

Configuration 3 with theatre-style seating, each for 727 persons

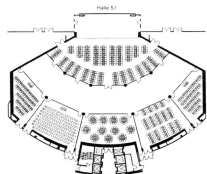

Teilung 2 und Teilung 5 mit gemischter Bestuhlung

Configuration 2 and configuration 5 with mixed seating

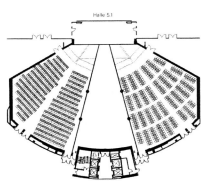

Teilung 3 mit Parlament- und Bankettbestuhlung

Configuration 3 with classroom- and banquet-style seating

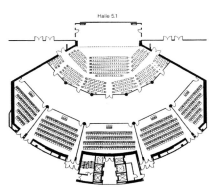

Teilung 2 und Teilung 5 mit Reihen- und Parlamentbestuhlung

Configuration 2 and configuration 5 with theatre- and classroom-style seating

Jyväsklä International Congress and Fair Centre, Finland

Completed in 1999 at a cost of US$12.5 million (excluding VAT), the new Congress Centre Pavilion is part of a programme for renovation of the Trade Fair buildings, which are adjacent to it. The pavilion is designed with two auditoria, each having 300 seats, which can be rotated to increase the 600 seating capacity of the main auditorium to 1200 or used independently. Each auditorium has its own stage and services and the pavilion is equipped to a high technical standard, allowing easy flexibility for meetings and entertainment with the minimum of staff required for operation.

Gross area, 6600 m²; Building volume, 53 000 m³

Architect: CJN Architects & Pekka Paavola
Structural engineers: Helander & Nirkkonnen
Mechanical engineers: Chydenius Ltd
Electrical engineers: YSP-Suunnittelu Ltd
Acoustics: Mauri Parjo

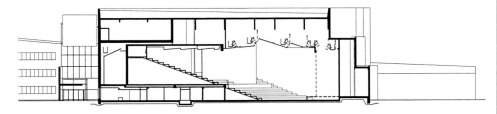

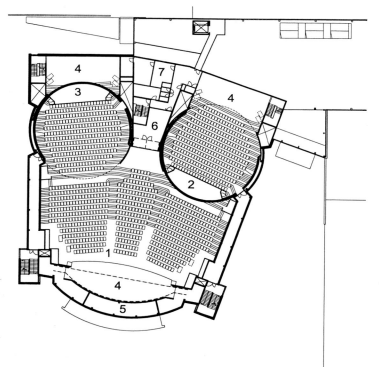

AUDITORIUM OF 1200 SEATS
CONSISTING OF:

1. AUDITORIUM, 600 SEATS
2. AUDITORIUM, 300 SEATS
3. AUDITORIUM, 300 SEATS
4. STAGE
5. BACK STAGE
6. INTERPRETERS BOOTHS
7. OFFICES

0   10 M   20 M

- Acoustics – profiled reflector panels and adjustable diffusers to ensure even distribution of sound over the whole seating area (see 2.4.2);
- Lighting – lighting bridges for access and supporting framework for stage and spot lighting in ceiling space over auditorium; lighting slots in ceiling construction providing screening; auditorium lighting equipment including emergency lighting; cable trunking (raceways) and connections;
- Air-conditioning – air ducts, diffusers and balancing dampers; energy sensors; noise attenuation and monitoring equipment, all with supporting hangers and means of access for servicing;
- Stage production – extended fly tower, gridiron and pulley suspension system for flying stage scenery; safety curtains etc. including access (see 2.5.2);
- Fire control – automatic water curtains, sprinklers and smoke vent releases; fire mode controls of air flows;
- Screen projection – clearance for cine, slide and television projection and video wall; load points and beams for screens and associated equipment;
- Changes to profile – mechanized lowering and rotating systems for volumetric changes, isolating balconies and separating spaces.

2.4.7 Changes in floor levels and areas

Changes in the level of floors to provide for multiple activities include:

- hydraulic ram or scissors-type stage lifts to raise or lower sections of a stage; these are often used to form an apron or thrust stage when fully extended, or to increase the seating area or form an orchestra pit;
- stages that may be retractable or made up from moveable platforms;
- stepped seating, which may be formed from wheeled or air floated rostrums, cut and fill rostrums, hinged units, retractable bleacher seating, hydraulically operated platforms or moveable floors (see page 68).

Vertical division may be practicable using:
- folded or telescopic extending partitions lowered from the ceiling or raised from the floor;
- lowered ceiling panels to cut off balconies;
- rotated whole areas of seating, including the enclosing construction, to create separate auditoria.

The positions for divisions must be carefully planned to take account of circulation, access, acoustic and environmental control conditions. Structural requirements, including loading implications, the means of housing the operating mechanism and safety considerations, must be examined. In most cases changes in the seating layout will also require modifications to, or the addition of, suitable stage or platform areas, projection and control booths and, where required, interpretation facilities.

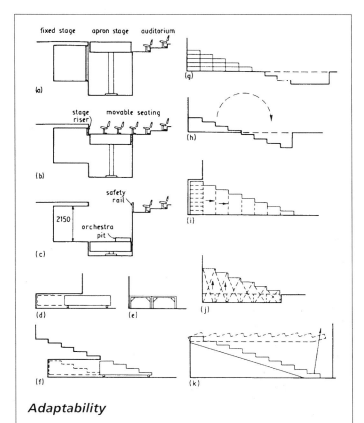

Adaptability

Changes in level of floors to provide for multiple activities include:

- *Hydraulic ram or scissor type stage lifts to raise or lower sections of a stage. These are often used to form an apron stage (a) when fully extended, or to increase the seating area (b), or to form an orchestra pit (c).*
- *Stages may also be retractable (d) or made up from moveable platforms (e).*
- *Stepped seating may be formed from wheeled rostra (f), cut and fill rostra (g), hinged units (h), retractable bleacher platforms (i), hydraulically operated platforms (j) or moveable floors (k).*

Adaptations in use of a conference auditorium to accommodate musical and other performances are outlined in section 2.5.3.

2.4.8 Projection, control and interpreters' rooms

Booths or rooms to accommodate interpretation services, projection equipment and control of lighting and sound are usually permanently installed in purpose-designed auditoria. Simultaneous interpretation booths are normally placed relatively near the speakers' platform and elevated to ensure a clear view of the participants, whilst projection booths and control rooms are located high at the rear of the auditorium central to the platform or stage. Back projection facilities are also required at the rear of the platform or stage. Details of booths are given in section 2.9.5, and systems are outlined in section 6.3.8.

Internationales Congress Centrum Berlin, Germany

Opened in 1979, the ICC Berlin ranks among the biggest, most advanced and successful convention centres in the world, as well as a landmark of post-war German architecture.

Every year the ICC Berlin hosts some 500 major conventions, attended by 250 000 delegates, and 70 shows attracting an audience of 200 000. A three-storey walkway links the ICC and Berlin fairgrounds (b) (160 000 m² hall space in 1999).

ICC Berlin can seat a total of 20 300 people in 80 halls and rooms. Hall 1 has 5000 tiered seats for major conventions, shows and concerts. Hall 2 has tiered seats for 1500, which can be raised to the ceiling to provide a flat floor for banquets, balls or shows. A 910 m² stage located centrally between these halls may be used from both sides (a), or combined for a total capacity of 7000. Hall 3 is an auditorium with 800 seats, and Hall 6 has seating in the round for 206 (c). There are six other main halls with flexible seating for 120–270 people and 17 smaller meeting rooms, as well as 8500 m² gross of exhibition space. A large press centre is located in the linking walkway, and there are two versatile seminar rooms in the fair grounds.

There is a multi-storey car park with 650 spaces.

Length, 320 m; width, 80 m; building height (stage section), 40 m; volume, 800 000 m³
Excavation: 350 000 m³

Client: Berlin Senate
Operator: Messe Berlin GmbH
Architects: Ralf Schuler & Ursulina Shuler-Witte
Engineers: Ingenieurburo Gerhard Bartels
General contractor: Neue Heimat Stadtebau

(a)

(b)

(c)

2.5 MULTI-USE HALLS: STAGE FACILITIES

2.5.1 Planning requirements

Large congress auditoria are often designed to allow alternative uses, with stage facilities for the performing arts. Significant extra costs are incurred both in stage construction and in the means of adapting space, acoustics and other requirements, but the feasibility may be justified by increased utilization and community benefits.

Multipurpose exhibition halls may be adapted for spectator sports and other types of performances, for product launches and large-scale events.

Ballrooms invariably use platforms for music, meetings, presentations and product displays.

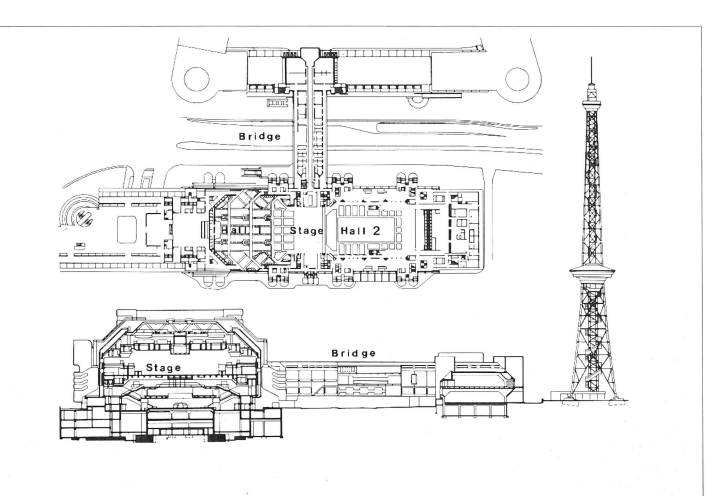

Bridge

Hall 1 Stage Hall 2

Stage

Bridge

Hall 1   Stage   Hall 2

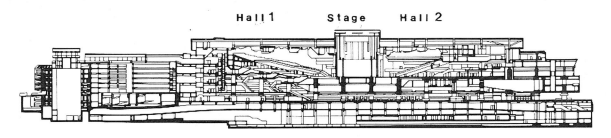

Planning considerations for multi-use facilities must take into account the need for access for stage scenery and other backstage requirements, for example:

- access for stage equipment, properties and displays – loading dock, goods lifts, direct routes, workshops, storage, control;
- entry and facilities for performers – control, changing/dressing rooms, green room;
- stage and event management – technical systems, administration, box office facilities.

2.5.2 Stage house

The installation of a fully equipped stage house with a flying system for scenery requiring a high fly tower for the suspension rigging will depend on the economics of the situation and practical constraints. In other cases, the grid system over the stage may be modified to become a simple structural framework supporting a variety of stage equipment. This will usually include pulleys and blocks for stage scenery, curtain track borders, a cyclorama track, stage lighting bars, a false ceiling and adjustable acoustic reflectors.

For conference use, or for orchestral and choral performances, the reflectors will usually need to be lowered between the lighting bars and rotated to direct the sound out to the auditorium. In other cases, individually controlled acoustic baffles may be located over the thrust stage and adjacent areas of the auditorium and/or pivoted side panels used to reinforce the direct sound (see 2.4.2).

Stage design is a specialized field, and this chapter only summarizes the types of stage equipment and basic requirements that should be considered in designing a multi-use centre.

2.5.3 Flexibility of use

Requirements for changing the mode of use are invariably more extensive than the installation of stage equipment. For musical performances it will be necessary to modify the acoustic characteristics of the auditorium, either physically (changes in volume, absorption/reflection) or electronically (extended reverberation, assisted resonance).

The front of a thrust stage (and even the stage itself) is frequently made convertible by means of a modular lift or elevator platforms or bridges, which can be raised or lowered over a variable of predetermined range of heights. It can be:

- raised to main stage level to form a thrust stage extension (for conventions, meetings, chamber music, large choral concerts);
- lowered to hall level, leaving a proscenium frontage to the stage and forming a flat apron area or increasing the seating capacity;

- lowered to below hall level to provide an orchestra pit;
- lowered to basement storage level to serve as a transporter for stage furniture (minimum clear storage height 2500 mm (8 ft 3 in).

In each case automatic safety barriers must be provided to close off any voids, and fire separation of the stage and auditorium must be maintained.

Changes in width and extension of the stage will usually affect adjacent seating areas. For example, reducing an open stage to the proscenium form will result in loss of satisfactory sight lines and screen angles from some of the side seats. In some cases, the central area of the auditorium is provided with a flat floor – with removable furniture – to provide greater flexibility of use.

Common types of modifications to facilitate congress or alternative uses may be summarized:

Changes	Provisions required
Acoustic response	Pivoted/adjustable ceiling and wall panels
Sound reinforcement	Loudspeaker system; induction loop (for deaf aids)
Sound modification	Changes in resonance and reverberation
Extension of stage	Modular lift, elevator platforms or bridges
Side masking of stage	Width adjustment of the proscenium opening
Stage removal	Folding or retraction into storage cavity
Seating capacity	Removal or addition of rows or blocks of seats
Screen projection	Suspension from flying system or self-contained structure with remote controls (see 2.5.2)

2.5.4 Relationship with audience

Both permanent stages and temporary platforms may be designed to be viewed from various degrees of encirclement.

270°–360° encirclement

This is used for maximum exposure to the audience, as in staged sports (boxing, gymnastics, snooker etc.), 'theatre in the round' performances and product launches (fashion shows, product displays). An arena stage or platform is open on at least three sides for audience viewing. Platforms are usually temporary, erected in the centre of a hall on a flat floor, which may necessitate the rearrangement of seating, turning on moveable platforms or bleachers to face inwards. Overhead scenery handling equipment with heavy load fixing points must be provided.

180°–220° encirclement

This is usually provided by a thrust stage extended out in front of the proscenium to provide a platform for meetings or accommodate large orchestral groups, massed bands, choirs, dance or pop groups. Long peninsular staging is often used for fashion displays. Installations include background lighting and supporting features. Acoustic reflectors may be required over the stage and its adjacent area.

60°–90° single- or multi-direction

Typical of the 'wide fan' and hexagon-shaped auditoria, stages of this type are fitted with side and proscenium masking when the widest angles of view need to be limited, such as for drama performances.

End stage

The stage or platform is located across one end of the room. This layout is common in multipurpose halls and ballrooms used for staging conventions. The platform is usually removable.

Proscenium stage

A proscenium wall creating a framed opening across the front of the stage approximately defines the acting area, provides side masking of the scenery and stage sets and enables the stage area to be separated from the audience by a safety curtain. The usual proscenium height for a theatre is about 6 m (20 ft), depending on sight lines, and the width varies from about 7–10 m (23–33 ft). The sets of many touring groups are designed for a 9 m (30 ft) proscenium. For other purposes (concert, opera and revues), the width may need to be increased to between 10 m and 14 m (33–46 ft) or more.

There are advantages in incorporating a moveable proscenium that can be adjusted in width, height and position relative to the stage, and this must be taken into account in structural design. The adjacent surfaces should also be adjustable in acoustic properties.

2.5.5 Stage dimensions

Overall stage dimensions are largely governed by the machinery provided for handling and changing scenery.

For theatrical productions the acting area is about 9 m wide and 4.5 m deep (30 × 15 ft). A space 2 m wide should be allowed around this for stage sets, with a further space 1.2 m wide outside for circulation. Thus the minimum dimensions overall for a small stage are about 15.4 m wide and 9.2 m deep (50 × 30 ft). Allowing for side storage of scenery flats and back stage equipment, the overall stage are will normally be 22–27 m wide by 9–12 m deep (72–88 ft × 30–40 ft), the latter being increased if a revolving stage is installed.

For orchestral concerts the stage is usually extended into the auditorium, adding to the envelopment and reverberation of sound and enabling instruments to be arranged to give a suitable balance of sound power between string, wind and percussion sections.

An orchestra of 120–140 players will require a stage area of about 160 m² (175 sq ft). This area would also accommodate a choir of some 220, with 60 musicians.

In multipurpose halls an orchestral enclosure within the stage house may be formed, using moveable ceiling elements (convex) and tilting side walls (with diffusing treatment) to project the sound towards the audience.

Stage construction

For easy adaptation and resilience, timber flooring is generally preferred. Fire requirements normally stipulate the thickness and construction, and the surface should be sealed (non-slip) and have a stage cloth or other covering when used for drama or meetings. Platform sections, including lift and elevator platforms, are usually formed in steel. If the understage is used for storage, fire separation requirements will apply.

2.5.6 Fire requirements

Many of the materials traditionally used in constructing stage scenery create a potential fire hazard, and legislation governing places of public assembly and entertainment normally requires the automatic separation of the stage from the auditorium should fire occur.

Conditional exceptions include small halls and constructions using approved materials that are non-combustible, inherently non-inflammable, made flame-resistant and durably flame-proof or self-extinguishing.

Separated stages must be fitted with a safety curtain capable of being closed within a set time (30 seconds) and able to resist passage of smoke, hot gases and flames from a severe fire, damage from falling scenery and displacement (by fire draught, air pressure) for a specified fire resistant period sufficient to allow complete evacuation of the building. With a fly tower the curtain is usually of a rigid-frame type, but with limited height a roller type may be installed. Water drenchers are fitted over the curtain. In other cases, a vertical water curtain alone may provide sufficient isolation.

Construction: The surrounding construction must have at least 2-hour, and any doors or openings at least half-hour, fire resistance. This also applies to all workshops and stores.

Ventilation: separate mechanical ventilation is required for the stage, including automatic exhaust outlets for smoke.

Exits: At least two exits remotely located must be provided, one of which must lead out through a protected lobby. Alternative means of escape are also required from fly galleries and gridirons.

Controls: Compulsory installation of smoke and fire detectors, together with automatic sprinkler systems, may be specified. A fire control station must be on or adjacent to the stage area, with indicators for emergency lighting and power circuits, sprinkler system, local alarm system, public address equipment and manual controls.

Evacuation from all parts of the auditorium to safe exits should be achieved within 2.5 minutes (see 2.4.5).

2.5.7 Stage operation

For theatre use, the speed of changing scenery is often critical both to meet stage production requirements and to enable the hall to be used between times for meetings and other purposes. Methods of changing scenery fall into three main categories depending on the equipment installed: flying; stage lifts, elevators or bridges; and horizontal movement.

Flying

Scenery suspended on counterweighted or winched steel ropes can be moved vertically up into a fly tower above the stage. The advantages of speed, minimum floor space and flexibility make this arrangement most suitable for theatres and opera houses. The pulley sheaves are fixed to a structural framework in the rigging loft of the tower or directly to the gridiron, which provides an access platform.

For a full flying system, the gridiron height must be at least 2.5 times the height of the proscenium opening. In theatres a grid height of 16–20 m is usual, increasing to 24 m or more for major opera houses. A further 2.5 m headroom is needed above the gridiron.

Counterweights must be guarded and, where possible, carried to the walls and cased in. Most are double-purchased to reduce the length of travel. The number of lines will depend on the size and requirements of the theatre: for a 500 seat theatre, about 40 counterweight sets together with fibre rope ('hemp') flying facilities for handled items is fairly typical.

To provide access to the flying sets and other equipment, there must be galleries at least two levels on each side of the tower. Additional loading and lighting galleries may also be required, the latter sometimes linking with lighting bridges over the auditorium.

Suspension fittings, either as part of the flying system or separately, must be provided for lighting bars, projection screens, curtain tracks, pelmets, maskings and borders.

Developments in power operated flying systems include the use of power operated winching incorporating sensitive transmission control, which may be programmed to co-ordinate several movements. Flying bars operated by hydraulic or electrical prime movers may be installed. Self-sustaining winching systems can also be used over open stages, being supported from a structural grid extending over the area.

Stage lifts, elevators or bridges

These are used to raise or lower modular platform sections making up the stage to the height of the rostrum, stage floor or basement level. If required, the stage may be stepped in level. Elevator or lift platforms are also used for thrust stages (see 2.5.3).

Mechanisms include screw jacks, hydraulic rams and pulley operated rope systems driven by electric motors. Travel distances generally range up to 10 m, and are set to predetermined levels. For safety, automatic barriers must be incorporated to screen off any voids.

Horizontal movement

In the simplest form, changes are made by moving scenery to one side or to the rear of the stage. Complete sets can be mounted on carrier wagons to be rolled or pivoted from either or both sides into the central acting area. Sets may also be built on revolves (single or double) for rotating into position. The revolves may be permanently installed or built for particular productions; in larger theatres they may be in semicircles made up in and elevated from the basement.

Stage dressings and sets

Apart from the design sets required for theatrical and other productions, a stage must be equipped with house and on-stage curtains, back-drops or cycloramas, projection screens and edge masking sets or curtains. For congress and convention use, stage design, including backgrounds, graphics and presentations of information, plays a significant role in creating the desired image and atmosphere for the event.

Scenery pieces may be constructed in workshops on the premises or transported to the theatre with a touring group. In either event there must be provision for loading and transferring scenery and properties, together with storage on and adjacent to the stage itself. Doors and corridors must have adequate clearance width and height. For a multipurpose exhibition area, this must include the facility to display and demonstrate heavy equipment, cars and other products.

2.5.8 Stage management

Within the general stage area there are requirements for stage control equipment, communication and public address systems, for prompting and direction (traditionally from the left), quick changing, and storage of properties and other frequently used equipment. The back stage must also be directly accessible (through sound and light locks) to workshops, stores, loading docks, changing and dressing rooms and the offices of managers and specialist staff directly involved in the operation of the stage area.

2.5.9 Dressing and changing rooms

Schedules of accommodation for performers will depend on the types of productions that are to be staged, their frequency and the length of the production run. As a rule it is not economical to provide for the largest possible cast. Touring companies are generally limited in scale, and the variety of use likely in a multi-use centre will demand considerable flexibility in room allocation. On occasions, a large choir or orchestral group may use hotel rooms or spare rooms within the centre as temporary changing rooms. A minimum provision for a multi-use centre in which concerts, recitals and plays are likely to be regularly performed is indicated below.

Requirements	Rooms	Places per room	Area of each room (m²)
Individual dressing rooms for principals, conductors, soloists	3–4	1[1]	15
Shared dressing rooms for minor principals	2	4	18
Communal changing/dressing rooms for musicians, choristers, supporting cast	3–4	8[2]	24

[1] Able to accommodate two performers if necessary
[2] for changing only (musicians), allow up to 16.

Provision must also be made for separate stage entry with a supervised office, and a green room for rest and refreshments with access from the food service areas. These areas will also be used for the speakers, reporters and other principals, for hospitality and other dual uses during congress and convention events.

2.6 MULTI-USE HALLS: ENVIRONMENTAL CONTROL SYSTEMS

2.6.1 Ventilation and air-conditioning systems

A wide range of air handling systems is used in conference centres, ranging from variable air volume (VAV) heat recovery systems in the main auditorium and large halls to fan coil air-conditioning in interpreters' booths and dedicated air-conditioning and cooling systems in the projection booths. Although thermal gains and losses are minimized by internal siting and the absence of windows, an auditorium presents particular problems in the design of air quality control systems due to:

- high ceiling heights and separated areas (balconies, stage areas) requiring zoned provisions;
- wide fluctuations in thermal loads with the occupancy increasing from 0 to 100 per cent at the beginning of sessions, then reducing to 0 during intervals;
- high installed heat loads from stage lighting and projection systems;
- a high radiant as well as convection component in the heat load from both the lighting and audience;
- requirements for very low noise emission levels from the air distribution system.

Systems used in large auditoria normally consist of two or more air handling units with variable speed controlled fans supplying 100 per cent fresh air at a rate typically based on 12 l/s per person, but may range from 10–15 l/s per person based on maximum seating capacities. This involves large supply and return ductwork, which must be integrated with the hall design and must be carefully balanced in dimensions to ensure even distribution. Airflow velocities are commonly 5.0 m/s (1000 fpm), reducing to 2.5 m/s or less in noise-sensitive situations. The ductwork is usually housed in ceiling voids, vertical service cores and roof top installations. In auditoria with fixed seating, either supply or return ducting is housed in hollow floor voids.

Acoustic treatment (including attenuation, directional flow streamlining, insulation, flexible connections and support) is necessary to reduce noise transmission. Recommended design criteria are usually NR 20 for large auditoria, but more stringent requirements for low frequency sounds may be stipulated, particularly where the hall is to be also used for music performances. NR 25 is usually acceptable for smaller halls seating fewer than 500 persons (see page 69).

2.6.2 Airflow distribution

Distribution of conditioned air through a large hall may be downward, upwards, across the space or in combinations, this being largely determined by the direction and momentum of the inlet air.

Upwards movement: Low level distribution of supply air under the fixed seats of an auditorium may be through grilles or mushroom outlets (in the floor or stepped risers) or through perforated plinths incorporated as part of the seat design. Low level discharge (or exhaust) velocities are usually reduced to about 1.5 m/s (300 fpm), and temperature differentials kept to 2–3°C to avoid discomfort. The upward movement tends to hold dust in suspension, but it generally ensures the most suitable conditions.

Downwards movement: This is created by the venturi/displacement action of supply air discharged through jets or diffusers in the ceiling or high level grilles in selected walls. The air is usually exhausted through floor or wall grilles. The air movement, particularly from side inlets, may be difficult to control, is liable to stratification and may not overcome the effects of natural convection. Jet action is normally circular, but may be linear.

A high velocity is usually acceptable if the ceiling is high: for diffusers a discharge velocity of 4.0 m/s (800 fpm) in auditoria and 2.5 m/s (500 fpm) in halls is common. Higher temperature differentials can also be allowed, reducing the quantity of air supplied. A difference of 4–8°C for cooling and slightly more for heating is often used in auditorium design. Downward distribution tends to hold smoke in suspension and create a higher fire risk (see below).

Cross flow: A variety of alternative arrangements are possible, as illustrated. In an auditorium, lateral movement tends to give rise to unequal distribution of conditioned air and this tends to become stratified. The possibility of draughts near points of discharge must also be considered.

Combinations: Both ceiling exhaust (from light fittings) and downward flows may be used. Special provision is also required for stage areas and under balcony seating (see 6.7.5).

Ballrooms, banqueting halls

In halls in which the floor must be kept clear to allow changes in furniture arrangements, supply air may be admitted through ceiling diffusers or perimeter grilles with exhaust air removed through wall grilles or by reverse flow through the ceiling. The inflow must be balanced with extraction from the service lobbies and kitchens. Airflow designs must also take into account the effect of room partitions, and enable independent control of each area as well as the whole.

Controls

Design proposals are normally tested by modelling and simulating the effects of varying conditions. New installations are normally controlled and regulated by building management systems, providing automatic adjustment of proportions of fresh air (with CO_2 sensors) and load conditions. Set programmes are provided to cover a range of operational requirements, including freshening during the intervals.

The air handling management systems are also interfaced with those for fire detection and control. In the event of fire, ventilation airflows will be automatically changed to the fire mode, ensuring that smoke is drawn away from the occupants and maintaining pressurized ventilation of escape routes (see 6.8.5).

Special areas

Dedicated supplies are required for projection booths (high heat emission, equipment cooling), interpreters booths (sound control, comfort) and stage areas (lighting loads, isolation and stage tower requirements).

2.6.3 Air handling plant

The plant should be located as near the supply zone as possible, but positioned and designed (mountings, isolation, enclosure) to avoid transmission of noise and vibration. Access is required for maintenance and eventual replacement.

Generally, roof mounting is most economic because of the shorter ducting involved and the close proximity of intake and chilling equipment, but the additional concentrated loading on large-span roof structures may introduce design complications. Plant is invariably supplied as packaged units, and two sets, each able to supply 60–70 per cent of the total, are often used to facilitate flexibility in operation and maintenance. In larger schemes several sets of units will usually be provided, each covering a main operation hall area of the complex.

2.6.4 Lighting systems in auditoria

Lighting systems in large auditoria can generally be divided into house lighting, stage lighting, emergency lighting and specialized requirements, such as for televising of events and visual aids. General details of lighting requirements are given in 6.4. The following details are more specific to auditoria and multiuse centres.

2.6.5 House lighting

Direct luminaires: Lighting installed in the auditorium ceiling is mainly direct, with a near vertical direction (slightly angled at 80° from behind the seating positions). To avoid glare, a cut-off angle of view for any light source must be above 40°, and direct luminaires are usually of the dark, recessed (fully or partly) type to provide screening.

Alternatively, the light fittings may be concealed in stepped recesses formed in the ceiling construction. Spot lights and other stage lighting equipment may also be housed in the ceiling voids, together with access provided by lighting bridges. For uniform illumination as well as a sense of order and orientation, a large number of luminaires must be used, arranged in regular patterns.

Indirect luminaires: This form is often used in perimeter lighting, either as washes or wedges of light over specific areas. Perimeter lighting reduces strong contrasts as well as providing a brighter and more relaxing environment, but it must not be so pronounced as to create visual distraction from the stage or speaker. The illumination must be positive, uniform and regular: it must not produce small patches, edge scalloping or 'haloes' from too close a proximity of luminaires. A visual cutoff angle of 45° is required.

2.6.6 Variations in lighting levels

Direct lighting from ceilings gives a high light utilization directed on to the seating areas. For a windowless room, an illumination of 400 lux on the horizontal plane at seat level should be provided, and this may need to be increased to 500 lux for a multipurpose hall.

All house lights (and stage luminaires) must have dimming facilities.

Conditions	Illuminance (lux)	Notes
Cine and slide viewing	5–10[1]	Minimum. Notes just perceptible with 30–50 lux provided at speaker's desk
Overhead projector	80	For easy note taking. May be increased to 80–100 lux for television viewing
Stage performances (house lights)	Down to minimum permitted	Safety lighting of aisles and exits maintained

[1] Depends on the type of projection. Minimum level.

Eye adjustment requires 5–10 s (optimum 6 s), but this delay can be irritating if repeated several times during a presentation and a delay of 3 s is generally adopted. At these reduced lighting levels, all luminaires must be screened.

2.6.7 Emergency lighting

Standards for emergency or maintained lighting are governed by legal requirements and should be related to the normal illuminance of the room. For auditoriums and halls that are normally lit to 500 lux, the minimum required level is usually 0.5 lux. The illumination need not be uniform and may be increased (up to a ratio of 4 : 1) over the escape routes (steps, aisles, stairs, exits).

Emergency luminaires need to be mounted as high as possible or screened to prevent glare or distraction. Emergency systems must be non-interruptible, and are usually battery supplied (constantly charged) with fault monitoring.

2.6.8 Stage and platform lighting

Stage lighting must be versatile to meet different requirements. Whilst the main cableways and controls are permanent, numerous alternative outlets and extension facilities must be provided in planning the circuitry, and most of the lighting equipment is moveable, allowing for rearrangement, adjustment and servicing.

In congress and convention use, stage lighting must provide for:

- balanced directional illumination of the speaker and other groups of people (chairperson, panels, etc.) on the stage or fore-stage;
- illumination of the stage area generally to avoid excessive contrasts;
- service levels of lighting, required for visual information and display boards (500 lux on vertical planar surfaces)
- separate controlled illumination of backcloths, emblems and other features;
- television and photography requirements (levels of lighting, contrasts, glare).

In a stage used for other purposes the overall illumination may need to be as high as 1000 lux, with full control allowing the level of lighting to be adjusted down to any level and varied in locational and directional emphasis for presentations and displays.

All these forms of lighting become more sophisticated when the stage is to be used for theatrical, musical and other staged productions, whether this is for entertainment or commercial promotions (such as product launches, fashion shows or televised broadcasts).

For multipurpose halls and theatres, a high-cost stage lighting installation can be justified on several grounds apart from

the difficulties of making subsequent alterations and the risks to safety that may be involved. A well-planned lighting system will extend the versatility of the hall or theatre, reducing the time required for setting up, allowing rapid changeover from one function or production (such as in a repertoire programme) to the next and ensuring a high utilization of the premises, including maximum rehearsal time.

In many cases a hall may need to double up as a congress hall during the workday and a concert hall or theatre in the evening, with the full conversion (and cleaning) taking place within 1–2 hours.

Lighting grids

In a large installation, the lamps are usually suspended from screened lighting bridges spanning over the auditorium above the ceiling. Side lights may also be housed in perches or wall slots, or suspended from hangers or vertical barrels. The lamps are usually fitted to the bridge or a grid system of bars, with short electrical connections from suspended trunking running above.

Numerous lamps are likely to be required, and the most powerful of these will extend well back over the auditorium to give the correct angle of light. The lamps must be well screened from the audience, and those over the auditorium are usually housed in stepped or screened ceiling recesses – these voids having black matt surfaces to reduce the emission of any light spillage. In addition to the installed lighting arrays, there is normally a requirement for manually operated spots from a high level at the back of the auditorium.

Access

Access to stage lighting is required for replacing, focusing and adjusting lamps, changing colour discs and maintenance. In a large auditorium, high level lamps require permanent access such as that provided by fixed lighting bridges across the ceiling void or cat ladders to individual platforms, or from higher floor levels outside the auditorium.

Access bridges and platforms need to allow a working width of 550 mm (21 in), increasing to 800 mm (31 in) for large lamps, and handrails and kicking (containing) plates must be fitted for safety. The platform surface should be quiet and electrically insulated. A headroom of 2000 mm (6 ft 6 in) should be allowed.

A 1000–seat theatre will usually have two to four lighting bridges in addition to the lighting bars fitted over the stage. In a small hall with a flat floor, servicing and adjustment is usually carried out from extendible towers of aluminium tubing.

Types of stage lighting

Most of the lamps used for stage and house lights are of the tungsten halogen type. Spotlights range from 500–2000 W, beam lights are generally 1000 W; individual floodlights

500–1000 W and compartment battens are made up of 150 W lamps. The projection of special effects (moving clouds, rain, smoke, dissolving colour and scenery backgrounds) is usually from large format slides requiring a more elaborate condenser-lens optical system and high wattage lamps.

Lanterns may have built-in colour filters, which must be of thin film, resistant to high temperatures, permanent in colour and non-inflammable. Colour changes may be obtained by remote-controlled colour change wheels fitted to the lamps.

A theatre or concert hall of 1000–1200 seats will usually require some 240–280 stage lighting circuits with 600–700 possible connections of lanterns, each (or each pair) with its associated dimmer. In a 300–500 seat theatre for plays and visiting companies 100 circuits are typical, providing some 180 connections for dimmers of which possibly 60 would be required for a production. An experimental theatre could have 60–80 dimmer circuits installed.

2.6.9 Lighting controls

Generally, lighting controls are concerned with two main areas – the lighting for the stage and auditorium lighting – although the two are interfaced.

In stage lighting, controls enable a smooth transition from one lighting sequence to the next. To set up a particular lighting array, the intensity of each group or channel of lights is adjusted by individual faders and the channels balanced. Changes in lighting patterns are made by cross-fading with master controls from one pre-set condition to the next.

In a large auditorium this regulation is operated automatically, the setting details being recorded in a memory control. Memory systems are made up from modular units with displays, keyboards, play-back controls, fade levers and wheels and core memories fitted into standard racks forming consoles. A typical memory system will have between 48 and 120 circuits connected.

Similar provision is made for controlling the house lights, allowing for programmed dimming and the various levels required for different uses, including cleaning. For congress purposes the general lighting may be supplemented by individually controlled lamps (screened) built into the backs of seats.

Lighting control rooms

In a congress hall or multi-use theatre this equipment is usually housed in a purpose-designed control room at the rear of the auditorium, enabling the operator to observe conditions directly. For congress requirements only, a minimum internal area of 2 m wide by 1.5 m deep is required; this increases to about 3 m by 2.5 m or more if the stage is to be used for theatrical or musical productions.

Lighting equipment should be located near to the projection booth and sound equipment room, allowing access from one to the other without spillage of light into the auditorium. These areas may be combined (as in lecture theatres and ballrooms).

Certain lighting controls will need to be interfaced or duplicated for projection services.

Access to control rooms should be from outside the auditorium and separate from the main public circulations. Separate air-conditioned ventilation must be supplied, meeting requirements for dust exclusion, fine temperature control (to avoid condensation) and minimum noise generation. The room itself must have high sound absorption and dark, non-reflective surfaces.

Heat- and noise-generating equipment, such as large thyrister dimmers, transformers, generators, batteries and mains controls, are housed in separate plant rooms that can be located in other parts of the building – taking into account economy of cable runs. Large storage rooms with suitably designed and labelled shelving, racks and benching will also be required for the numerous lamps, cables connections and spares that must be kept.

Requirements for sound control and projection rooms are examined in section 2.9.4.

For the varied needs of other areas, such as ballrooms, banquet halls and conference rooms, lighting controls may be mounted on trolleys, enabling the control unit to be located anywhere within the area where suitable terminal connections are installed. Controls of this type can be used to record and reproduce precise intensity levels for each sequence of use.

2.7 BALLROOMS, MEETING ROOMS, FUNCTION ROOMS

2.7.1 Types of rooms

A wide range of rooms is required to accommodate differences in the types of meetings, social events, hospitality and exhibition requirements, as well as in the numbers of participants. In many cases different groups also overlap, and the areas they use must be separated. Invariably the rooms provided for these purposes have flat floors to allow rearrangement of furniture, and the larger halls usually have moveable partitions to allow division into alternative sizes.

These rooms may be broadly grouped by size and function:

Type	Capacity	Other uses
Ballrooms/grand halls	500–2000+	Banquets, receptions, exhibitions
Meeting halls/large rooms	200–500	Banquets, functions, presentations
Seminar/conference rooms	25–100	Business lunches
Break-out/committee rooms	10–25	

2.7.2 Ballrooms and grand halls

Ballrooms are essentially dual-purpose, serving as the main banquet hall and the meeting room for very large groups such as in plenary sessions. In most cases, this room is also planned and equipped to accommodate exhibitions, product launches, dances, receptions and other social events. The maximum

Hawaii Convention Center, USA

Completed at the end of 1997, this spectacular centre has been designed to minimize the mass of the building, using separate yet interconnected structures and allowing the natural landscape and cooling trade winds to flow into open arcades, courtyards and terraces (only half the building requires air-conditioning). Visual lightness is created by a glass-fronted lobby rising the full height of the building, and soaring rooftop canopies resembling waves, sails and, at night, flower petals. Design representations of the cultural heritage of Hawaii extend throughout the interior.

None of the construction is below ground: building height is reduced by locating parking spaces for 802 cars within the structural frame depth above the exhibition hall. The exhibition hall at ground level is 9.14 m (30 ft) high and is divisible into three areas, each accessed from a total of 19 covered loading bays remote from the public entrances. On the third level there is 9940 m² of meeting space in 51 adaptable spaces, including two high technology audio-visual presentation theatres (seating 332 and 465), a teleconferencing centre and a press room.

On one side of the fourth floor, set back from the street facades, is the 3344 m² (36 000 sq ft) Grand Ballroom, entered through a prefunction area with dramatic views of the lobby, and on the other is a 1.0 ha (2.5 acre) roof garden used for special events and allowing for future extension of exhibit space.

Architects: Wimberly Allison Tong & Goo associated with Loschy Marquard & Nesholm
Design/builder: Nordic/PLC joint venture
Structural engineer: Skilling Ward Magnusson & Barkshire Inc.
M & E engineer: Syka & Hennessy
Convention centre operations: Leisure Management International

Fourth floor

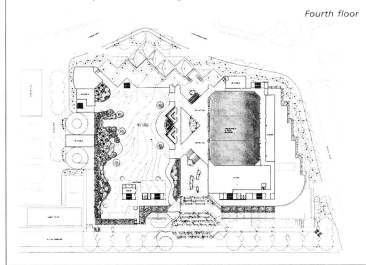

capacity will depend on the function and furniture set up, for example:

Arrangement	Theatre style	Classroom style	Reception/Banquet buffet	
Area/seat m² [1]	0.85	1.6	0.7	1.2
(sq ft)	(9.2)	(17.2)	(7.5)	(12.9)
Room size 500 m²	580–600	310–325	710–725	410–425
(5380 sq ft)[2]	capacity – number of occupants			

[1] Minimum net areas per person
[2] Range depends on room dimensions, furniture sizes and projection/platform requirements; numbers may need to be reduced for extended platform or difficult dimensions.

The design is influenced by the need to create an impression of grandeur for social events and formal occasions, but must also take account of divisions and service needs (see 2.7.3, 2.7.4). Windows are not necessary, and may present difficulties with noise entry and light distraction.

Seating plans

With a flat floor it is necessary to raise the speaker on a platform or dais to improve the sight lines and direct sound. Using a 0.5-m high platform, the maximum distance for clarity is 6.0 m (about five to six rows); a platform height of 1.0 m extends this distance to 12 m (12–13 rows).

For most situations a system of sound amplification will be required, and this must be designed to suit the proposed seating layouts. Similar considerations apply to the design of projection facilities and screens, including ceiling mounted video projectors.

In planning this area, provision must be made for:

- fire escape requirements – maximum travel distances to safe exits for each mode of use;
- service entrance to each area from banquet kitchen and furniture store;
- access for exhibits, with direct routes from a loading dock
- public access and foyer, including cloakroom and toilets, which may need a separate entrance independent of the internal circulation (depending on local market demand).

Ballrooms are normally planned to allow division into two or three smaller areas, and this may require some compromise in design.

Design considerations

Optimum plan dimensions	3:2 for large halls divisible into three areas
	2 : 1 for halls up to 250 m² divisible into two
Roof design	Large span structures: high partition suspension loads
Roof/ceiling construction:	High sound and heat insulation
Roof-mounted equipment	Plant: location, isolation mountings, access, dimensions, loads, weather-proofing
Ceiling heights	Proportionate to area: large halls typically 3.9–4.6 m, but may be increased to allow for exhibits
	Lines of division may be lower than in the central areas
	Ceiling voids sealed above partitions (fire, sound flanking)
Wall surfaces	Must resist damage (furniture movement, equipment)
	Very low rate of surface flame spread (class 1)
	Design features to break up large expanses of surface
Floors	Sprung floors: preferred for frequent ballroom use (with locking system and removable carpeting)
	For exhibits: designed for distributed load of 5 kN/m²
	Large items (vehicles): concentrated 3.6 kN on 300 mm square
Floor and ceiling services	Ducts in grids to suit room divisions and layout plans
	Individual control for each divided area as well as the whole
	Balanced air-conditioning for each zone of use

	Sensor and sprinkler systems, fire mode air flow control
Noise insulation	Sound transmission class (STC) ratings for walls and partitions separating:

Exterior; mechanical spaces, kitchens	45–50
Similar conference rooms, lobbies, corridors	40–45
Exterior; sheltered, quiet	35–40

Sound control	Acoustic adjustment for reverberation and side reflection
	Sound amplification system installed
	Noise insulation requirements (see 6.2)
Main doors	Central with separate doors for each divided area
	Attractive durable surfaces and furniture
	Silent, easy opening and controlled closure
	Fire resistance requirements (usually 30 minutes)
	Secondary escape doors to meet fire code standards
Service	Entrances to each divided area from service lobby
	Vestibule to limit noise and light entry
	Space for temporary serving counters (mobile)
	Access to banquet kitchen and furniture stores
	Large access doors for exhibits (2.8 m × 2.6 m)
Support	Types of projection systems, locations of booths and equipment
	Simultaneous interpretation provisions – usually portable

2.7.3 Room division

Division of a large room into separate areas involves several design complications:

- large, heavy partitions must be used;
- the spaces formed are often disproportionate in shape;
- problems may arise in access, the locations of projection rooms and other support services;
- high levels of sound insulation are difficult to achieve;
- complex technical systems are required to meet the changing volumetric conditions.

To provide STC 40–45, it is usually necessary to use twin panel leaf or double partitions. Flanking sound paths (through edges, suspension area, ceiling voids) must also be sealed, and transmission of impact noise and vibrations controlled.

The main types of moveable partitions are:

Type	Components	Noise insulation techniques
Sliding	Tracks	Edge sealed by expanding strips
Perpendicular folding	Sections	Insert and overlapping joints tightened together
Horizontal folding	Continuous	Flexible sheets or joined panels hollow filled.
Housed in wall recesses	Rigid panels	Resilient linings with heavy cores, edge sealing
Housed in ceiling or floor	Panels or continuous	Flexible or rigid as above, wall edges sealed
Relocated or demountable[1]	Panels	Pressed against or fixed to sealing strips or stiffened frame

[1] For small rooms; removed to store or reposition.

The operating mechanism must be simple, and panels should be capable of being assembled, moved and stacked by one person. Complex large wall systems invariably need to be mechanized, and the weight, ceiling loading and upward/outward thrust must be considered in structural design. Floor tracks may not be suitable (dance floors), and the panels must be both resistant to damage and consistent with the interior design.

2.7.4 Food and beverage service

Ballroom and banquet areas (including divided space) need to have individual service access from the kitchens and pantries supplying food and beverages. Close proximity is essential to ensure rapid service, and the banquet satellite kitchen or pantry is a specialized area equipped with large capacity refrigerators and regeneration ovens (often combined) based on the maximum numbers and menu choices to be provided.

Basic preparation of the food may be carried out in a central kitchen, requiring some form of dedicated system of food transportation between the kitchen areas. Consideration must also be given to the location of dishwashing facilities and the method of transporting soiled dishes (see 4.5.3). Service access is also required to the beverage stores, wine cellars, furniture and equipment stores, and for exhibits.

Table and seating plans within the banquet room must take account of the positions of both the public and service entrances. The latter must be located and designed to facilitate speedy, efficient, inobtrusive service, and minimize:

- risk of accidents, spillages, etc. (servery design, graduated lighting, non-slip flooring);
- distraction to activities, speeches, (vestibule limiting entry of bright light and noise);
- views of work areas (location, screening).

2.7.5 Furniture requirements

The range of furniture required to meet the different functions of the ballroom requires some rationalization, and flexibility is a key consideration. Other essential requirements include:

- ease of handling and storage – weight, stacking, damage in stack, trucks and dollies required for transportation, storage space and dimensions;
- strength and mechanism – frame and joint construction, method of folding, breakdown and assembly, simplicity of locking and fixing, strength and stability in use, risk of injury from protruding, sharp or serrated parts;
- appearance and durability – suitable for banquets and other uses, consistent with the room design and decor, durable in use, means of cleaning and renovation;
- interchangeability and multiple use – inter-changeability of components (table tops and bases), multiple uses (platforms) and varied shapes and layouts (buffets, banquets); method of linkage and extension.

2.7.6 Furniture layouts

Optimum room dimensions depend on the proposed furniture layouts, and alternative seating plans must be prepared for the capacities required for each mode of use. For a banquet, dinner or business lunch, the net area per place must include the table area and occupied seat area, plus an allowance for seat movements and space around for circulation and service. Similar allowances apply to classroom layouts, with space for a seat-way behind each row of occupied seats. Seat-ways are required in front of each row of occupied seats arranged theatre style.

Banquets, dinners

Two arrangements are commonly used:

- for social gatherings – separate circular tables seating 6, 8 or 10 (sometimes 12);
- for formal occasions, weddings and speeches – a top row of joined tables with other rows (sprigs) at right angles.

A minimum space of 1.2 m² per cover is normally required for either layout, depending on the dimensions of the room and platform. This is based on a 600 mm length per cover, which is also suitable for place settings. Rectangular tables are usually 750 mm across to allow flexibility. Circular tables are typically 1.20 m (seats 6–7), 1.50 m (8–9), 1.80 m (10) or 2.3 m (12) in diameter.

To give neat level abutment, tables must have screw-adjustable legs and simple connecting pieces (recessed to avoid knee injury or damage during stacking). Table legs must be designed to allow clearance for knees, and the cantilevered design is generally most convenient. Tops must be smooth, dimensionally stable, non-staining and suitably edged. A baize underlay is often used with the tablecloth.

Theatre-style seating

Close seating in rows gives the maximum capacity for meetings, which is often critical in marketing the venue. This is usually based on a seating density of 0.85 m² per person. In large halls, individual chairs will need to be joined or ganged together to prevent their displacement, and must be light, strong and stackable with upholstered coverings that meet fire codes (inflammability, emission of toxic fumes) and are resistant to marking, sagging or pilling.

The design must ensure suitable back and seat support for comfort and, as a rule, has to be appropriate (in appearance and dimensions) for both dining and conference use. Armchairs take up more space in the hall and may incur problems in storage, but are often preferable for conference use in the smaller halls.

Classroom-style seating

Interspacing of tables between rows requires a minimum space of about 1.6 m² per person. Worktables are usually 0.6 m deep and in 1.5 m lengths suitable for two people. Floor plans often allow for angling of the side tables to face the top platform. Tables may also be placed together in clusters for face-to-face group discussions, and other table formats (hollow or open square) are possible with lower numbers of participants.

2.7.7 Other requirements for large halls

Permanent or folded or assembled temporary platforms are used as staging for speakers, shows, contests, bandstands or performances. The platforms must be strong and rigid when assembled, and give an even, level surface. The construction will need to satisfy legal and insurance requirements. Requirements for direct access to the stage, and installed services (lighting, power, microphone points), will usually limit the number of locations suitable and the options for alternative floor plans.

Retractable or telescopic seat platforms are permanent installations that can be extended to provide stepped levels for successive rows of seats. When not required the platforms retract back into the rear enclosure.

Lecterns are required for speakers addressing meetings or commenting on events, and both table- and floor-mounted equipment should be provided. The lectern may have a built-in light and projection controls, a microphone, local light and connections to floor terminals.

Audio-visual aid facilities may be provided or hired for each event. In a large hall these include:

- auto-cue facilities with reading screen and separate scanner, monitor and controls mounted on a trolley;
- a video projector and screen or video wall together with camera set up on tripod and control equipment
- a cine and slide screen with adjacent projector room (for back or front projection)
- simultaneous interpretation booths and installed system with connection points (see 2.9.5).

Counters for beverage and refreshment services in the foyer, information desks and reception counters are often made up from portable units. The units must be of a convenient standing counter height (900 mm), and may have shelves fitted to improve rigidity. Counter tops should be finished with plastic laminate for easy cleaning and resistance to heat marking.

Decorative items include floral arrangements, banners, stage displays, menus, graphics and table appointments. The requirements vary for each major event, and may be provided through contractual arrangements with local suppliers or directly by the organizers. The weights of planters and stage sets can be considerable, and delicate handling is required. Access to a loading dock must be provided for electric powered forklift trucks and other transporters.

2.7.8 Furniture storage

Storage requirements tend to be underestimated, leading to congestion, extra handling costs, damage and restrictions in use. In setting up a room, time is usually critical. Often the banquet area will need to be laid out whilst another meeting is in progress, and high utilization depends on a rapid change round in room function. To achieve this involves the smooth, efficient, almost silent movement of furniture from one section to the next, including to and from storage when required.

Access demands transport on the level direct to store or to goods elevators provided for this purpose. Doors must be double swing, and fenders and buffers are required to reduce damage. The size of doorways must allow for the larger sets that may be needed for displays and exhibits.

The storage area will usually need bays for stored furniture, hanging rails for curtains and drapes, racks and shelves for equipment and fittings and a separate room for audio-visual aid equipment. Security control is essential, and the area must fitted with smoke and fire sensors and controls. A high degree of fire resistance (usually 1 hour), precautions against rodent and insect entry, dampness, dust and temperature extremes, and good lighting (150 lux) and ventilation (one air change/hour) are essential.

2.7.9 Other meeting rooms

In addition to the ballroom and large multi-use halls, a congress centre must provide a wide range of smaller meeting rooms. These will be used independently for corporate meetings, association committees, business lunches and other groups — which make up a large part of the market — as well as for the working sessions or break-out areas required by the large congresses. Depending on the alternative facilities available in nearby hotels, the total capacity of meeting rooms should be comparable to that of the main auditorium for plenary sessions.

Meeting rooms generally fall into four main groups:

- large meeting rooms or halls for groups of 200–500
- meeting rooms for medium and smaller groups of 25–150
- break-out rooms for groups of 10–20
- boardrooms and other specialized requirements.

Large meeting rooms or halls

These are comparable to the ballrooms in larger centres and have similar roles, being used for dining, business lunches, special functions, receptions, presentations, product launches and large group meetings. Design requirements are also similar, but on a smaller scale. The majority of congresses and conventions fall within this size range, and most centres provide two or more halls to accommodate separate groups of 200–300 and 350–500. For the larger group meeting requirements, it is often feasible to install retractable platform or bleacher seating.

Medium-sized rooms

Medium-sized rooms often have the highest utilization; they are in demand for corporate meetings, committees and local groups, as well for the working sessions of larger congresses. The largest areas (100 seats) may be divisible, but most are modular-sized permanent rooms designed to suit the alternative furniture set-ups and arranged together in blocks around a foyer or along a corridor.

Dimensions are critical, and must be related to the furniture sizes and proposed layouts to ensure efficient use of the areas. Alternative seating configurations include theatre style, class-room style, closed and open square, inverted, clustered, and boardroom.

Small meeting rooms

Design requirements:

- Natural lighting – windows fitted with adjustable louvres and mechanized blackout screens; in noisy environments, double or triple glazing is required; air-conditioning with individual room controls; uniform spatial lighting (300 lux) with dimming control;
- Good sound insulation between rooms and other areas (STC45–50 or better); acoustic balance of sound absorption within rooms;
- Neutral decor without strong contrasts; light colours with a balance of texture and a carpeted floor;
- Furniture – good quality chairs and tables which are inter-changeable; classroom tables are typically 1500 mm wide (suitable for two persons), with a depth of about 400 mm;
- Fittings – retractable projection screen, removable white board and tackable panels; portable easel and flip sheets;
- Equipment – cine and slide projectors, plasma screen and controller, video projector, all with appropriate stands and wall fixture points; suites of rooms may be linked with video systems and camera installations (removable) for management training programmes; separate projection rooms may be provided between the meeting rooms;
- Limited food and beverage services (using a local pantry and trolleys) may be provided to one or more specific rooms if there is a market for business lunches.

Furniture layouts

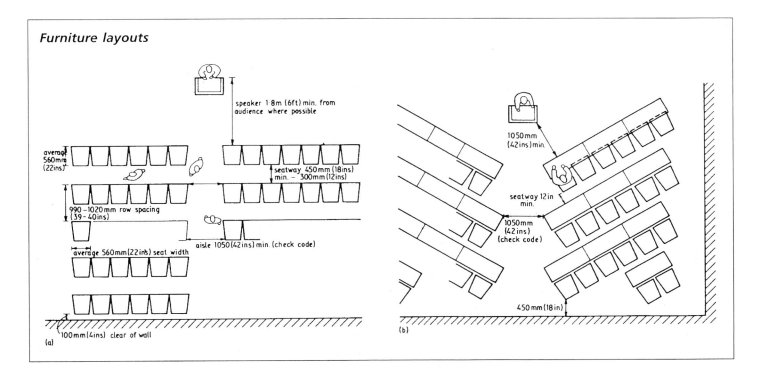

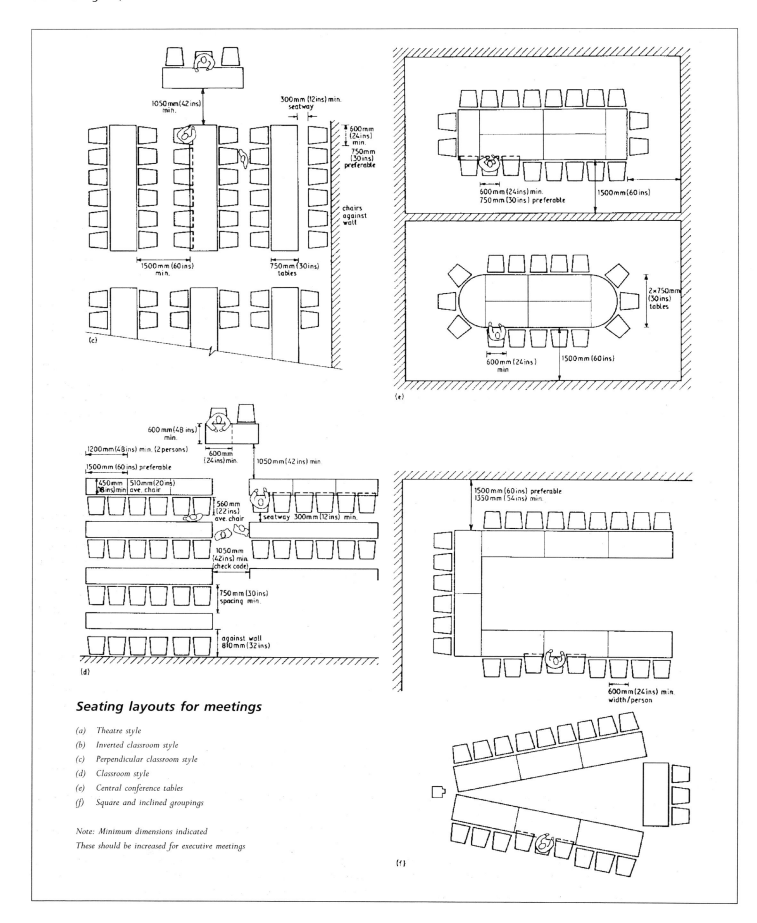

Seating layouts for meetings

(a)   *Theatre style*

(b)   *Inverted classroom style*

(c)   *Perpendicular classroom style*

(d)   *Classroom style*

(e)   *Central conference tables*

(f)   *Square and inclined groupings*

Note: Minimum dimensions indicated

These should be increased for executive meetings

Rooms suitable for 10–20 people are used for break-out groups, and also serve as additional offices (for organizers, administration, boardrooms, press and interviews). They must be well equipped for communications, with multiple ISDN lines and terminal points for computer hook-ups, telephones, facsimile transmission and television recording. Environmental standards are similar to other meeting rooms, but higher requirements for noise insulation, privacy and security may be specified for interview rooms and boardrooms.

2.8 EXHIBITION FACILITIES IN CONGRESS CENTRES

2.8.1 Benefits and feasibility

Exhibitions of products and services are often associated with large conventions and congresses. The benefits include:

- extension of interest for delegates (product intelligence, added practical dimension);
- enhanced value of attendance (time and cost incurred);
- a revenue source (sales of exhibition space and stand services, contribution to costs);
- facility availability for other events (consumer shows, regional trade fairs).

Compared with meetings, exhibitions are generally more profitable to the venue provider. The extended range of external services and employment generated also adds to the wider economic benefits. However, the market feasibility of this additional investment must also be considered, including a realistic evaluation of the utilization taking into account the availability of other trade fair facilities in the region, the practical problems of access and operation and the costs of city centre development.

Exhibition requirements can be broadly grouped into three main market segments; congresses and conventions, corporate meetings, and independent exhibitions.

Markets	Examples
Congresses and conventions	*Accompanying exhibits*
Medical, educational, scientific and technological interests	Equipment demonstrations, displays of products and services
Professional and service sectors	New systems and computer software
Associated with public seminars	Planning issues, employment and training opportunities
As part of social programmes	Fashion shows, leisure equipment, local culture
Corporate meetings	
Company sponsored events	Product launches and sample displays
Shareholders' meetings	Product range and company profile
Independent exhibitions	
Local consumer fairs	Art, handicrafts, antiques, hobbies, gifts, fashion
Regional trade fairs	Related to the main industries in the area

2.8.2 Range of facilities

Depending on location and scale of operation, the facilities in a congress or convention centre may provide:

- space in lobbies and entrance concourses for simple poster and information stands;
- multi-use halls that also serve for banquets and meetings;
- purpose-built halls designed specifically for this use;
- links to adjacent trade fair grounds.

Most specialist exhibits associated with meetings take up a net area of 500–1000 m², although some of the larger shows may require up to 1500 m²or more. About 50–60 per cent of the space in an exhibition area can be utilized for display, the balance of space being taken up by aisles, emergency fire escapes and support services for visitors. Hence, gross areas of purpose-built exhibition halls generally range from 1000–3000 m² in congress and convention centres. In comparison, banquet-exhibition halls in hotels are more typically less than 600 m².

Exceptions include the major convention centres in the United States and Canada, which are generally larger and combine trade shows with convention facilities. Many of the convention centres in Europe (notably in Germany) and Australia are linked to more extensive fair grounds.

2.8.3 Stand arrangements

Exhibitions in congress and convention centres are generally based on shell schemes, with divided booths or stands laid out in regular rows along gangways by the organizer. Display stands are modular, usually around 2.5–3.0 m wide and 2.5–3.0 m deep giving net areas of 7.5–9.0 m², and are varied to meet the different requirements of exhibitors. For larger exhibits an average stand area of 15 m² is more typical, and may extend over a number of shell modules or be purpose designed by the exhibitor (see 3.1.9).

An average trade show held in parallel with a convention could have about 60–65 shell stands covering a gross hall area of 1000 m² or up to 90–95 shell stands in a gross hall area of 1500 m², in each case allowing about 10 per cent larger stands. Major trade fairs require a higher proportion of large stands and a range of halls (see Chapter 3) for flexibility and better space utilization. Purpose-designed exhibition areas are often provided in two or more sections, which can be separated if required for smaller events or opened to provide visual continuity and free circulation from one section or hall to the next for the largest shows.

The stands are arranged on both sides of gangways or aisles that lead round from the entrance and give direct access to the emergency exits and any refreshment areas. Main aisles are often 3.0 m or more wide; side aisles usually are 2.0 m or 2.5 m wide depending on the types of exhibits.

2.8.4 Circulation requirements

Vehicular access for exhibits and contractors is essential and this should preferably be direct to the hall areas. This will require loading docks at street level or accessed via ramps. The build-up time taken for constructing and equipping stands prior to a show is critical, and dismantling (breakdown) times are even shorter. For a show that is open for 3 days during a convention, the build-up is usually no more than 3 days and breakdown often only 1 day, making a week's programme.

Direct access enables stands to be assembled quickly and exhibits to be taken to their positions with the minimum of handling. If the exhibition areas are within the interior of the building or on other floors, a system of goods lifts or elevators (a minimum of two) must be installed, capable of handling the largest sets, adding significantly to costs.

Visitor access is required directly from the congress or convention centre, with well signed routes. A separate entrance may also be provided for visitors attending independent exhibitions, and in this case there will need to be an entrance/registration hall with cloakroom facilities.

Safety requirements must comply with local regulations or codes. The aim is to enable an evacuation time of 2.5 minutes together with measures to delay the spread and scale of a fire.

- Maximum travel distances to exits (30 m measured along aisles) determine the positions and numbers of exits; at least two exits, remote from each other, must be provided.
- Exit widths for the various hall sizes are calculated on maximum capacity (1.5 m² per person. Minimum widths are typically 1.2 m (4 ft) for up to 300 persons, 1.4 m (4 ft 7 in) for 400, and 1.6 m (5 ft 3 in) for up to 500.
- The materials used in stand construction must not present a fire hazard within a hall — essentially, materials must be incombustible, inherently non-flammable or flame-proofed by impregnation or proofing. Plastics must be self-extinguishing in addition to having acceptable flame resistance.
- The construction must satisfy fire resistance and surface flame spread standards, taking into account alternative uses of the halls — as a rule, at least 1 hour fire resistance must be provided, increasing to 2 hours for separation of hazardous areas (garages, plant rooms, etc.) and for structural components[1].

([1] Examples based on the Greater London requirements: local codes may vary.)

Details of other fire prevention and control provisions are given in sections 6.8.5 and 6.8.6.

2.8.5 Construction requirements

Clear ceiling heights should be at least 4.3 m (14 ft) and, in the larger halls, should extend to at least 5.0 m (16 ft 6 in) to allow for tall exhibits and display features. Under any balcony or mezzanine floor, at least 3.6 m (11 ft 10 in) clearance is required for small stands.

In the case of a hall providing a clear height of 5 m or more, the view of the roof structure and associated engineering equipment is above 35° from the eye-line over most of the floor and visual intrusion will be minimal. If necessary, this can be further camouflaged by mounting lighting battens and other terminal equipment in the same horizontal plane providing masking illumination.

For halls of a lower height and for multi-use halls that also serve for banquets, a formed ceiling construction is desirable. The ceiling must incorporate luminaires, air diffusers, loudspeakers, smoke and heat detectors, sprinkler systems and other services (see 3.2.5) and provide structural hanging points for suspended equipment.

Walls of exhibition areas must be smooth and durable; the lower parts are liable to be damaged, particularly when stands are constructed or broken down and exhibits uncrated. Areas which are especially vulnerable (in corridors, entrances, exposed corners, goods elevators) should be protected by covers or fenders. In halls which are multi-purpose, a decorative, easily cleanable surface will be required, and this should incorporate sound diffusion and absorption to avoid echoes and air resonance from cross reflections

Floors have to withstand scraping and damage (dragged or dropped objects), spillages (paint, oil, water) and superimposed loading. For small exhibits the uniform floor loads rarely exceed 14–17 kN/m² (300–350 lbs/sq ft), but local concentrated loads will arise from wheeled vehicles and static units of equipment. Much higher loads are involved in large trade fair halls (see Chapter 3).

It is advantageous to support exhibition floors directly on the ground (access, technical services, alterations), and the form of construction is usually a screeded concrete slab (reinforced or otherwise) on a granular sub-base. During exhibition open days and other uses, the floor is covered with carpeting or carpet tiles.

2.8.6 Structural and utility servicing requirements

Modular dimensions for the structural, building and technical servicing components of the building must take account of the booth or stand dimensions and allow reasonable flexibility in show layout.

Structural grids are kept as large as practicable, depending on the construction above. Small halls associated with congress or convention centres are often based on a 10 m or 15 m structural grid, but light-weight roofs may span up to 30 m or more. The location of the columns has a considerable influence on the booth layout and, hence, on circulation planning and utility service grids.

Utility services to the stand locations generally include single- and three-phase electricity for lighting and power, ISDN telephone and computer links, closed-circuit and broadcast television lines, drinking water and drainage, compressed air and gas pipes. The latter three are often limited to particular areas.

Grid arrangements for the utilities in purpose-designed halls may be provided in:

- floor channels or trenches with access covers (usually at 3 m intervals);
- ceiling raceways or trunking (usually in 2.5 m or 3 m grids), with cable connections run down booms to the stands;
- wall trunking or enclosed raceways run round unobtrusively at skirting level (150 mm above the floor) or as a cornice near ceiling level.

Terminal boxes are also provided at fixed points around the hall and on the structural columns.

2.8.7 Environmental requirements

Apart from the utility services to individual exhibitors, provision must be made for air-conditioning, lighting, fire protection and other requirements of each hall. In multi-use halls these will need to designed for other uses, which may impose higher standards of provision. For exhibition use, the following guidelines are generally appropriate but may vary with individual circumstances.

Rates of air change: For limited exhibition use a rate of 6–10 changes/hour is usually adequate, but to allow for other requirements (such as banquets) 10–15 air changes/hour with control over the proportions of fresh : recycled air are necessary. The positions and design of diffusers must avoid airflow being concentrated over any particular exhibit area, and short-circuiting by the stand constructions.

Discharge velocities of the diffusers and the cross-sectional areas of airflow ducts will be determined by the ceiling or mounting height and noise emission – particularly for alternative banquet and other uses. In the latter case, velocities of 4 m/s (800 ft/min) reducing to 2 m/s (400 ft/min) may be the limit, depending on the degree of attenuation provided.

Air-handling units: Packaged units for air-conditioning are usually roof mounted or sited adjacent to each hall to provide independent zoned systems. Time and thermostatic controls, automatically regulated by external and internal conditions, are essential.

Airflow distribution must be balanced and be designed for automatic changeover to fire mode to control smoke and facilitate evacuation. Separate ventilation extraction is required from toilets, kitchens and plant rooms.

Natural lighting is not necessary although it can be useful during the setting up and breaking down stages. The positions and extent of any glazed areas must be limited (glare, heat gain/loss). During exhibitions windows diminish the impact of stand displays and introduce a security risk, and must be fitted with blackout blinds.

Hall lighting: The service value of illumination is usually 400 lux, with switching facilities to reduce this to half when supplemented by the lights from stand displays. Separate lighting circuits should be installed for each hall or section, and emergency lighting systems must be included.

2.8.8 Operational services

Security and communication systems are an important aspect of exhibition operations, particularly when valuable material is on display. Essential requirements include the following.

- **A public address system** with loud speakers zoned by area and adjusted for time delay and balance. A separate control room equipped with sound console, background music and announcement facilities, closed-circuit television monitors and fire indicator panels will be required for a large hall complex.
- **Closed-circuit television** to monitor the operation of the hall and maintain a security watch on goods entrances. The cameras should be motorized on swivel mountings to span an arc of coverage. Video monitors and plasma screens may be required to publicize the exhibition in other parts of the convention centre.
- **Fire alarms** with detectors for smoke and heat together with automatic sprinkler systems generally and CO_2 installations in electrical substations, as well as emergency lighting and generator systems, must be installed.
- **Associated facilities** include toilets and a first aid room, refreshment services for visitors and exhibitors, a press room, offices for the event organizer, and hospitality areas. The ancillary rooms are usually combined with other congress requirements.

Details of large exhibition venues are outlined in Chapter 3.

2.9 TECHNICAL FACILITIES IN AUDITORIA AND HALLS

2.9.1 Projection and control rooms

In large auditoria the booths or rooms for projection (slide, cine, video) and control of conditions (lighting, sound) are invariably permanent and installed at the rear of the room, elevated to ensure a commanding view of the stage and operations without being intrusive. Rear projection facilities are often also required behind the stage, and projectors need to be mounted in a suitable position (relative to the screen) with remote operation if required. Control and projection rooms are normally adjacent and have access from outside the auditorium and separated from the public areas.

Design requirements include good sound insulation, acoustic enclosure, screened lighting and measures to prevent light spillage into the auditorium, independent ventilation, communication with the stage, speaker and engineering control rooms, and adequate space and clearances to operate the master control panels, equipment and work benches.

2.9.2 Projection room

Either back-projection equipment, using a projection room behind the screen, or front projection, with a projection booth sited at the rear of the auditorium, may be used. To minimize distortion, the centre line of the screen should be symmetrical with the projector or, if there are two projectors, equidistant from each. The vertical rake of the projector is also critical (see 6.5.1, 6.5.3).

To allow access and operation there must be at least 750 mm (30 in) clear space around each projector, increasing to 1000 mm (39 in) around the larger video projectors. Typical internal dimensions for front projection booths, allowing for equipment, operation, rewinding benches and storage racks are:

	Minimum: two video projectors, two slide projectors and controls	Large auditorium including dual slide projectors and effects lantern[1]
Width	4.5 m (14 ft 9 in)	5.5–6.5 m (18–21 ft)
Depth	2.5 m (8 ft 2 in)	3.5–3.9 m (11 ft 6 in-13 ft)
Height	2.5 m (8 ft 2 in)	2.9 m (9 ft 6 in)

[1] Suitable for multi-use stage operations.

A port 0.5 m (20 in) high, designed to prevent light spillage, should extend across the front of the projection room – the sill height being determined by the projection equipment and angle of tilt – alternatively, individual ports for the projectors together with higher observation ports may be used.

The dimensions of back projection rooms are determined by focal length requirements of equipment and screen widths (see 6.5.2).

Sound insulation between the projection room and auditorium must be of a high standard, and the room must be lined with fire-proof, sound absorbent material.

Engineering services	General requirements
Power supplies	13 or 15 amp outlets for 16 mm portable equipment, 45 amp single-phase or higher rated three-phase supply for 35 mm equipment and high intensity lamps (rectifiers in separate room)
Lighting	Screened local lighting to avoid spillage through ports. For maintenance and editing, lighting levels of 750 lux (adjustable) are required
Water supply	Water cooling at 0.08–0.17 l/s may be required for high intensity lamps and large video projectors.
Ventilation	Conditioned supply (100 per cent fresh air) separate from auditorium and public areas. Direct ducted exhaust system may be required for large equipment. Suitable working temperature is 18°C (minimum 10°C)
Fire	Non-flammable film must be used (otherwise strict regulations apply). Services and exit routes must comply with local codes. A fire extinguisher must be provided. All doors open outwards
Cables	Accessible underfloor or cavity space must be provided for cable ducts. Auditorium lighting controls duplicated in separate room
Equipment	Separate plant rooms provided for lighting switchgear, rectifiers, emergency lighting batteries and other operating equipment

Details of screen viewing requirements and video projection are given in section 6.5.

2.9.3 Lighting control room

Sophisticated control of lighting is essential, and this is usually housed in a purpose-designed control booth adjacent to the projection booth at the rear of the auditorium, enabling the operator to observe conditions directly. Certain controls will be duplicated in the projection room, and direct access between these two areas is usually provided.

For smaller congress halls and exhibition requirements the minimum internal area is about 2 m wide by 1.5 m deep (6 ft 6 in × 5 ft), but for a large auditorium which is equipped with stage lighting for theatrical or musical productions, lighting control rooms increase to about 3 m × 2.5 m (10 ft × 8 ft). Access to the control rooms should be from outside the auditorium and separate from public circulation.

Lighting controls are mounted on panels or consoles made up from modular units and arrayed in front of the operator, with side benches for supplementary equipment. Individual air-conditioned ventilation must be provided, with dust exclusion, sensitive temperature and humidity control and minimum noise emission. The room must have high sound absorption and dark, non-reflective surfaces.

Separate plant rooms are required for heat- and noise-generating equipment such as the large thyrister dimmers, transformers, generators, batteries and mains controls.

2.9.4 Sound control and recording rooms

Control rooms for sound adjustment and recording are also usually located at the rear of the auditorium to provide a means of monitoring proceedings without distracting the audience. Siting is usually adjacent to the lighting control but remote from the projection area to minimize noise disturbance. The room has its own entrance direct from outside the auditorium, separate from public circulation.

The operator must be able to see and hear conditions in the hall if required, such as through a large sliding sash window. Otherwise, sound insulation from the auditorium and other areas must be high to exclude intrusion of equipment and fan noise.

Space requirements depend on the range of equipment, but an area 3 m wide by 2.5 m deep should be adequate to accommodate a sound mixer console with adjacent tape and disk equipment plus storage on both sides and some standby equipment.

Design requirements for booths

- Acoustics – high insulation construction with absorption linings;
- Services – extensive trunking and cable ways must be provided for future requirements;
- Working space – all equipment controls must be located within easy reach of an adjustable swivel chair; a shelf area must be fitted in addition to space for standby equipment, and storage must be easily filed and located;
- Access – all equipment must be easily dismantled for maintenance, and mobile trolley access must be provided;
- Lighting – high illuminance is required for servicing and editing work and should be adjustable up to 1000 lux; screened point sources (adjustable) are required for illumination of operating equipment during sessions, and internal surfaces should be painted matt black;
- Ventilation – the ventilation must be separate, filtered and maintained at 18–22°C and 45–65% RH, with the air speed not greater than 0.2 m/s (39 fpm) and minimum fan noise.

Sound control rooms are more elaborate in multipurpose theatres and concert halls, where they may need to include recording and broadcasting facilities.

2.9.5 Simultaneous interpretation booths

Interpretation systems are required for all major international meetings. In purpose-built congress halls the interpreters' booths are usually permanent constructions, whilst in ballrooms and other halls requiring flexible layouts, portable cabins are normally hired for each event. Installations may be based on cable or hard wired systems, induction loop systems or infrared systems of transmission, the last two allowing greater choice in seating layouts (see 6.3.8).

Standards for booths are laid down in ISO 2603 (built-in) and ISO 4043 (portable), prepared at the request of the International Association of Conference Interpreters (AIIC) and the Joint Service Interpretation – Conferences (JSIC) of the European Union.

Location

Booths must be elevated and built or sited at the back or side of the hall to allow an unobstructed clear view of the person speaking, the chairperson, black/white board and projection screen. They should be grouped together with a separate access passage (at least 1.5 m (5 ft) wide) entered from outside the hall through an area not normally used by delegates or members of staff, meeting safety and fire escape requirements. Similar requirements apply to the sound technicians' booth.

Minimum dimensions

Booths should accommodate the required number of interpreters comfortably seated side by side, and allow occupants to move in and out without disturbing each other.

No. of occupants	Minimum dimensions (m) (ft in)		
	Width	Depth	Height
No more than two	1.60 (5–3)	1.60 (5–3)[1]	2.00 (6–7)[1]
Two or three	2.40 (7–10)		
Three or four	3.20 (10–6)	2.40 (7–10)[2]	2.30 (7–6)[2]

[1] Standard depth and height for portable booths. With very exceptional space restrictions or internal transport problems where standard dimensions cannot be used, portable booths may be reduced to 1.50 × 1.50 × 1.90 m for no more than two interpreters.
[2] The larger dimensions are recommended for built-in booths.

Windows

Television may be installed for auxiliary viewing of close-ups and enlargements, but direct vision of the hall is essential. Front windows must span the full width of the booth, extending at least 0.8 m high above the working table surface with narrow vertical supports outside the central field of view. Side windows must extend back at least 0.6 m. The windows must satisfy sound insulation standards, be untinted and avoid acoustic reflection and mirror effects.

Sound insulation and acoustics

Insulation standards against noise from the hall and adjacent booths:

Location	Sound pressure level reduction (decibels) at frequencies of:				
	250 Hz	500 Hz	1000 Hz	2000 Hz	4000 Hz
Booth to hall	12	15	18	20	20
Booth to booth	18	21	24	26	26

Reverberation and sound reflection within a booth must be reduced with suitable antistatic sound absorbing materials (fireproof). When occupied, reverberation times should be between 0.3 s and 0.5 s in the octave bands 125–4000 Hz.

Environmental standards for booths

Requirements	Standards
Ventilation	Separate system from hall giving at least seven air changes per hour, adjustable at higher rates
Air speed	Not to exceed 0.2 m/s (39 fpm)
Air inlets	Positioned to avoid draughts and pollution
Noise emission	Kept below 40 dBA; vibration free
Temperature	Controlled between 18°C and 22°C
Lighting system	Independent from hall
Illumination	On working surface, at least 300 lux; adjustable between 100 and 500 lux
Glare	Lights shielded, matt finishes used
Colours	Non-distracting; dark or drab colours avoided

Working conditions

Each booth must have a strong, impact/sound deadened work top extending the full width, up to 0.5 m (20 in) deep, with a height of 0.73 m (29 in), allowing at least 0.45 m (18 in) unobstructed leg room. Each interpreter should have a comfortable chair with five legs on quiet castors, adjustable height and backrest, armrests and upholstery of heat-dissipating material.

A separate restroom and toilets should be provided.

Equipment

One set of controls (with language selector) and headphones must be provided for each interpreter. Microphones may be mounted on a moveable base or combined with the headset (to suit the operator). Outgoing channels should allow for tone control and selective communication with the speaker or chairperson.

When used with speech reinforcement systems, separate volume controls should be provided for individual adjustment to avoid echo and feedback from the loudspeakers.

All plugs must be distinctive to avoid wrong connection, and equipment in operation indicated by red or amber lights.

Details of interpretation systems are given in 6.3.8.

3 Trade fair and other exhibition centres

3.1 RANGE OF ACTIVITIES

3.1.1 Exhibition facilities

Exhibition facilities are provided to meet a wide range of community and commercial needs. They are used to enable visitors to see and obtain specific information about, for example:

- works of art, historical artefacts, scientific discoveries, technological achievements, environmental diversities and cultural heritages;
- products and services which are available to consumers generally or to identified groups of users.

Those serving the first group are purpose-built to house mainly permanent collections, such as in art galleries, museums and science centres, and are subjects requiring more detailed examination outside the scope of this text. However, the principles and techniques involved in such displays are often also employed in the design of stands and other types of commercial exhibitions (art, antique, fashion shows), and a few examples to illustrate the main features have been outlined in later sections.

The second group covers three main types of activities:
- permanent or long-term displays in show cases, visitor centres and design centres;
- temporary exhibitions in venues designed and operated for this purpose (trade fair centres, exhibition centres);
- temporary exhibitions set up in other places (in-store demonstrations, concourse stands, agricultural shows, village halls, leisure centres, stadia).

Visitor centres may be provided by large industrial organizations and utility companies to promote public awareness of their products and services. They are also used extensively in tourist locations to inform visitors about the area, its history or ecology and particular features of interest (see 3.3.5).

Temporary use of halls designed primarily for other purposes invariably imposes restrictions on the types of exhibits that can be displayed and the services that can be provided. Particular difficulties may arise from inadequate power supplies, terminal points, space and security for the exhibits, as well as limitations on stand design. Shows of this kind are normally to attract local visitors.

The following sections examine the requirements for large purpose-built trade fair and exhibition centres.

3.1.2 Characteristics of trade fairs and consumer exhibitions

Trade fair and exhibition centres are usually involved in both trade shows and consumer exhibitions, each of which tend to have different characteristics:

Features	Trade shows	Consumer exhibitions
Attendance	Invited potential buyers and trade representatives. May include 'public' days for other visitors	Open to public
Charges	Normally free to *bona fide* trade/business users	Visitor entrance charges are large part of revenue
Subjects	Specific to the sector. Large international fairs may have specialist sub-sections	Usually wide ranging domestic products and home furnishings; may be targeted on leisure, toys, gifts, fashion, antiques, art, computers, employment, boats, cars and hobbies
Size	Restricted visitors: the 'quality' in terms of their buying intentions is more important than numbers	Often large numbers of visitors
Hospitality	Separate lounges and rooms with food and beverage services	Not involved
Open period	Mostly 3–4 days; large international fairs may extend to 5 days	Large shows often 6–10 days; local events 2–3 days
Market catchment	National: often with 5–10% or more international visitors. Regional: secondary shows covering particular market areas	Mainly regional or local visitors
Seminars	Invariably held in parallel covering related topics	Not usually involved
Associated entertainment	Mainly restricted to individual promotional activities	Often featured as an additional attraction

San Diego Convention Center, California, USA

Since its opening in 1989, the San Diego Convention Center has been a cornerstone of the thriving tourist industry and a catalyst for economic and cultural growth. In the fiscal year 1997, the Center hosted 88 shows, 69 meetings and seminars and 17 community events. The total building occupancy rate reached 72.9 per cent; delegates directly contributed almost US$278 million to the San Diego economy, and convention and trade show visitors utilized some 500 000 room nights, spending an average US$1113 during their stay. The Center employed 219 full-time and 560 part-time employees.

The design of the present centre is characterized by 'waves' of curved glass walkways and a sail canopied roof. At ground level, exhibition space (8.32 m high) extends over 23 164 m² (249 340 sq ft) and can be divided into four halls accommodating a total of 1388 booths (3 m × 3 m; 10 × 10 ft). On the upper level there is a ballroom (divisible) seating up to 4000 and 14 flexible meeting rooms, together with a large special events area (9290 m²) under the sail roof. A second phase of expansion — over the adjacent car park — is planned for completion in 2002, and this will more than double the floor space and increase the available market by 13 per cent. The expansion, estimated to cost US$216 million, is financed by US$210 million in bonds to be repaid over 30 years through increases in city hotel room taxes.

Operator: San Diego Corporation
Architects for the existing center: Arthur Erickson Architects; Deems / Lewis & Partners; Loschky Marquardt & Nesholm
Architects for the expansion project: Tucker Sadler & Associates; HNTB Architects Engineers Planners
Main Engineers for the existing and expansion projects: John A Martin & Associates; Syska & Hennessy Engineers
Design and Build Manager for the Expansion project: Golden Turner Construction Company
Photographs: Hawkins Productions

San Diego Convention Center

EXISTING BUILDING FLOOR PLANS AND PRELIMINARY EXPANSION FLOOR PLANS
(Expansion Completion Scheduled for Fall 2001)

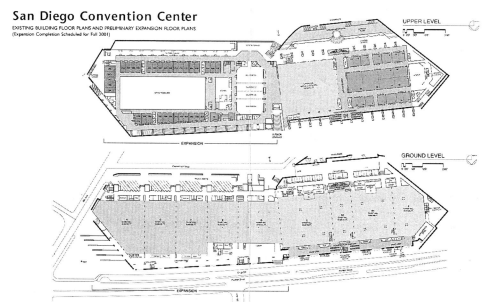

Combined events

Many trade show events which also have a wider public interest (tourism, leisure, motor shows) are extended to include days that are open to the public with charged admission.

Product launches

New products are often featured at both trade and public shows. Product launches may also be organized as separate events to attract individual publicity. These are often staged in prominent venues, including exhibition centres, and many centres provide suites of halls and rooms designed specifically for this purpose. Product launches often call for spectacular displays, extensive hospitality, and facilities to ensure wide press and television coverage (see 1.1.3).

3.1.3 Provision of facilities

Most of the large, purpose-designed exhibition centres or fairs are municipally owned, either exclusively or as a joint investment with the regional or state authority and other minority contributors (Chambers of Commerce, trade associations). The venue is normally operated by a semi-independent commercial company set up for this purpose, with a defined mission and policy objectives. Management of the centre may be direct or may be organized through management contracts.

Justification for public investment is usually on the grounds of:

- economic gains for the community, including direct and indirect employment, assisting tourism, generating a demand for many other support services and product suppliers (see 7.1.2);
- promoting the industry of the region, attracting visitors and buyers, and serving as a 'shop window' for trade and business;
- serving other community needs, such as a venue for consumer shows, entertainment and spectator sports and other events (see 3.1.6).

Most established exhibition centres operate profitably and are able to finance the capital investment debts and future phases of expansion. In some countries there is a trend towards 'privatization' of public facilities to attract private finance and more competitive commercial operation. Conversely, the expertise of many of the established companies is also widely offered as a consultancy or management service to new venues.

Some large venues are privately owned and operated, either as a result of the conversion and extension of other earlier properties or associated with other exhibit or sports facilities. The former are often located in urban surroundings, enabling easy public access, but are restricted in parking, loading and scope for extension. Sports grounds and arenas are able to provide extensive parking and public access, but often the technical services required for the efficient set up of large exhibitions are limited. In all cases, competitive companies need to have extensive programmes of continued investment and improvement.

3.1.4 Organization roles

The purpose of an exhibition, in this context, is the pursuit of trade and business; it is a forum in which buyers and sellers can meet, exchange information and see examples of products. These operations involve input from many organizations and groups of individuals, which may be broadly divided into:

- primary groups – exhibition visitors, exhibitors and exhibition organizers;
- secondary groups – exhibition venues, technical subcontractors, supporting agencies and local authority and utility services.

Exhibition visitors: Visitors or buyers attend exhibitions principally to meet companies involved in their particular fields of interest and assess their products. The number and buying intentions of the visitors is critical in attracting exhibitors and making the cost of exhibiting worthwhile. In consumer exhibitions, entrance charges are a substantial part of the overall revenue.

Exhibitors: The trading companies who rent space provide the main source of exhibition revenue. They also incur costs in stand construction, decoration and services, equipment, transportation and storage, insurance, promotion, hospitality, salaries, hotels and subsistence for stand personnel and support staff.

Specific reasons for exhibiting will vary with individual interests, but are mainly to:

- develop new sales leads, introduce and demonstrate new products and services;
- obtain sales and orders, meet existing clients, research markets and competition;
- recruit dealers, agents and distributors, and maintain company image and exposure.

Exhibition organizers create and manage shows, prefinancing many of the initial costs (hire of halls, exhibition promotion, management). The organizer will expect to recoup more than these costs through charges to exhibitors for space rental and other services, including advertising in the exhibition brochure. Other revenues may be provided by sponsorship, other advertisements, entrance fees (public) and negotiated commissions and free concessions. Exhibitions may be organized by the venues themselves or independently by professional companies or the associations involved in the subject. Many of the large organizer companies (such as Reed International) have wide interests in publishing and marketing. Most major exhibitions and trade shows are independently audited.

Exhibition venues provide the space and services required for exhibitions. Venue selection by organizers takes into account the location in relation to potential exhibitor and visitor markets, as well as the venue size, quality of service and availability at the preferred time. Contracts are drawn up stipulating access times, hall rentals, dates for staged payments, cancellation penalties, in-hall services and safeguards.

The venue receives revenues from hall rentals, catering, support services (parking, equipment hire, connection to technical services, administration and operating staff) and other facilities that may be required (seminar rooms, hospitality suites, press facilities).

Technical service contractors include the shell scheme contractors, stand designers and fitters, electricians, plumbers, graphic designers, freight operators, furnishers, florists, printers and others involved in putting shows together. These may be employed by the organizer or by the exhibitor directly. Ultimately, the costs are borne by the exhibitor.

Other agencies and services: Off-site services are provided by advertising agencies, trade journals and specialist publications (exhibition bulletin), transport and warehousing companies. All those involved in the exhibitions draw heavily on the services of hotels, restaurants, taxis and public transport in the area.

Local involvement includes the assistance of tourist and convention bureaux and trade organizations, as well as police, fire and customs services.

3.1.5 Development

Patterns

Once established, trade shows and exhibitions tend to use the same venue repeatedly as a regular calendar event. The repeat cycle is usually every 1 or 2 years, but may be 3 or 4 years for shows that rotate with other regions. This regular pattern is important in forward booking, negotiating contacts and reinforcing the status of the show.

Timing

Trade shows are generally seasonal, peak months being April, June, September and October, broadly coinciding with the patterns of business travel. The optimum depends on the business cycle for the industry concerned; the time when plans are made and orders placed for the coming year. This tends to result in competition for the best 'slots' in the calendar of events, and can lead to dilution when two or more similar shows are held about the same time. Apart from the peak vacation months, consumer events are more flexible but are also timed to suit cyclical family and individual interests.

Growth

Over time, successful shows grow in size, attracting more exhibitors and taking up more hall space, ultimately leading to a number of possible changes:

- phased expansion of the venue;
- relocation of the show to a larger venue;
- cloning of more specialist sub-sections.

Most large new venues need to have a policy of phased growth with space and infrastructure planned to allow future expansion, phased capital investment and high utilization of the initial hall capacity.

New shows are constantly being introduced; partly as a result of subject specialization in technology, partly through reorientation towards the service industries sector. In addition to major refurbishment, relocation and expansion of existing venues in Europe and North America, much of the investment in new centres has been in the developing regions of South East Asia and Australia.

3.1.6 Entertainment events

The large capacity halls required for exhibitions can also be utilized for big audience entertainment events (pop concerts, large-scale productions), spectator sports and other indoor activities. This increases the utilization of car parks, services and facilities between trade show programmes, and can be commercially viable where there is good public access from a major city or conurbation. Halls or arenas for this purpose need larger clear spans, flexible seating, provisions for stage construction and other adaptable facilities (see 3.2.3).

3.1.7 Exhibition operation

Typical programmes for trade shows and exhibitions are:

Programme	Small trade shows and specialist shows	International fairs and consumer shows
Build-up time for marking, setting up, constructing and decorating stands	2–3 days	7–10 days
Show open period	3–4 days	10 days
Break-down and clearing out of hall	1–2 days	4–7 days

There are wide variations in the arrangements for large international trade fairs and consumer exhibitions. Some may lease an exhibition centre for a month, taking 10–14 days for build-up.

Leasing charges to an exhibition organizer are generally costed on the overall time and floor areas involved. The organizer's rates for exhibitions are more often based on the net areas and open period of the show, with conditions stipulated about the time allowed for entry and removal of exhibits. Construction programmes usually involve:

Parties	Roles
Exhibition organizer	Allocation of space
Main contractor	Employed or nominated by the organizer to undertake the stand shell construction
Electrical and other sub-contractors	To connect distribution boxes and cable lines to stands; plumbing etc. connections
Exhibitor's own designer and sub-contractors	To set out stand display and special decorations. Sub-contractors may include window dressers, florists, graphics etc.
Exhibitor	Usually brings the items for exhibition to the hall. This may overlap with other decoration. (Long distance and imported items are usually sent in advance to storage/bonding warehouses)

3.1.8 Access and storage

Access

All exhibitions require good access for vehicles, construction equipment and exhibited items. The time allowed for setting up is short, and many vehicles will need to unload at the same time. Even if one main contractor is nominated for the shell construction, four or five pantechnicons may be required to build an average show covering 2000 m². Vehicles bringing in equipment, decorations and exhibits will arrive shortly afterwards. Peak traffic movements usually occur during the break-down period.

Essential requirements for handling exhibits to ensure a high turnover of hall use include:

- adequate parking for goods vehicles and trucks, with direct access to loading docks;
- vehicles able to drive to stand locations and drive out by an alternative route;
- supervision of vehicle entry to reduce congestion, combined with security control;
- off-site waiting and parking regulated by an installed call system;
- facilities for unloading and transporting exhibits and equipment direct to the hall, where possible at one level;
- doors, corridors and entrances that allow headroom and width clearance.

If transportation to another floor is involved, vehicular ramps and/or heavy duty lifts to each loading bay must be installed.

Storage requirements

Hall operations: storage for equipment, light fittings, signs, display items, audio-visual aid equipment, extra stands and decorations.

Exhibitors: crate and box storage whilst exhibits are on display – this may be off-site, with charges for handling and space. In other cases, removal of crates may be required.

Bonded secure storage (off site): for exhibits arriving in advance of the show or awaiting despatch.

3.1.9 Shell schemes and individual stands

Shell schemes are usually modular systems constructed by a contractor nominated by the organizer. Each is designed to a standard pattern, and often includes floor covering (carpet tiles), signs to identify exhibitors, standard lighting and basic furniture. Specific requirements, including an office or work area, display fittings and decorative items, may be added together, with variations in colours and features to provide individuality.

The cost is often less than half that of individually designed stands, and there are savings in setting up and exhibitor's time. Distribution of the many components to stand locations is facilitated by the use of pre-loaded trucks or racks.

Variations

North American booths are traditionally separated by drapes hung on a tubular framework, providing adjustable screening about 2.5 m (8 ft) high at the rear and reducing to 1.2 m (4 ft) on the sides approaching the gangways. Height restrictions may require the exhibits to be stepped down near the gangways.

Booths are generally provided with drapes, a duplex 110 V electrical outlet and standard signs, additional equipment being rented or brought in by the exhibitor. Unit sizes of booths are usually 3.3 m (10 ft) wide and 3.3 m or 2.6 m (10 ft or 8 ft) deep; aisles are normally 3.3 m or 3.9 m (10 ft or 12 ft) wide. This arrangement is often used in other countries outside Europe.

European shell schemes are more construction-orientated, using framed panels or modular systems of components for the back and sides, which allow attached fittings. Floor platforms may be needed to hide trailing cables. A standard shell scheme uses 2.75 m high wall panels which, together with framing and working space, requires the hall or balcony ceiling to have a clear height of at least 3.5 m. Stands are usually rectangular but may be octagonal or with rounded corners, depending on the system. Typical dimensions are 3 m deep by 3 m wide, but some 2.5 m modules may also be used in side aisles.

Individually designed stands are mainly used by the larger exhibitors to create a more distinctive identity and impact. They are usually constructed on a plinth, with framing and special panelling incorporating fittings, graphics and other features. Plasma screens are commonly used to convey images and information, and hospitality areas are provided on one or two levels. As a rule, exhibits over 4.0 m high need special permission.

The construction of all stands must comply with fire regulations, requiring the use of non-flammable materials and other conditions.

Arrangements

Stands may be individual or conglomerated in groups with associated interests under a single banner. The frontage may be

Messe Zurich, Switzerland

The new (1998) Trade Fair Centre in Zurich responds to the need in this region for medium-sized, well-sited and cost-optimized sites for fairs and exhibitions. Located 10 minutes from the airport with an integrated system of road, rail, tram and bus connections, the Centre provides 29 500 m² of exhibition space in a four storey building (including basement level) occupying a limited ground area of 15 900 m². A huge glass-walled entrance hall gives a view of all floors, which have seven halls planned for flexibility and high utilization. There are six restaurants and one café (total 650 seats) which, with sanitary facilities, are deliberately sited at the rear to draw visitors through the exhibits. The highest floor is multifunctional for smaller events, congresses, product presentations and banquets.

Two large ramps of 28.0 m diameter, 8.3 m travel width and 4.5 m clearance give trucks (40 and 28 tonnes) direct access to the three main exhibition levels for rapid construction and dismantling. There is parking for 26 trucks in the delivery area, plus 30 in the terminal. Car parking is provided in a new off-site garage (1500 spaces) and by a park and ride service (1000 spaces). Two sets of escalators (2 × 9000 persons/h) give access to all halls, as well as five large (21 person) elevators and two freight (10 t) elevators.

Underfloor cooling/heating ensures a maximum 26°C at 32°C outside temperature, and provision is made for 700 000 m³/h air circulation. Supply points at 45–50 m² intervals have electricity, telephone, ISDN, compressed air and water connections. A sprinkler system is installed for fire protection, and there are 2700 control points for security and building management systems.

Length/width/height: 137.2 m/115.8 m/33.4 m
Support grid: 19.2 × 9 m.
Halls: Seven: two on each of three levels, one on fourth level
Clear heights (floor levels): 7.4 m (1), 6.0 m (2 & 3), 5.0 m (4)
Floor loads (floor levels): 1500 kg/m² (1, 2 & 3); 1200 kg/m² (4)

Architect: Walter Waschle
Developer: City of Zurich
Manager: Hanspeter Meyer

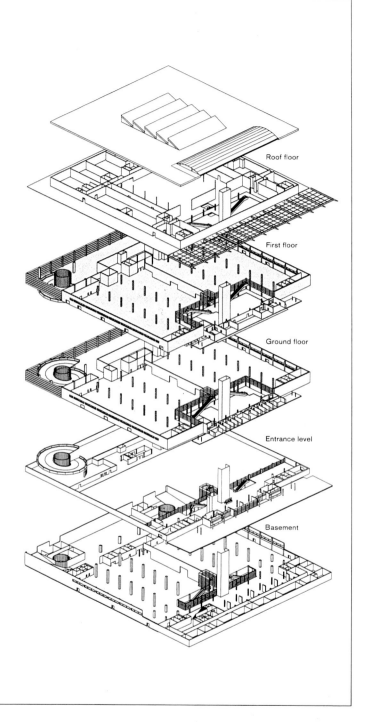

Roof floor

First floor

Ground floor

Entrance level

Basement

open on one, two or three sides, providing increasing exposure to visitors. Locations near the entrance, feature areas, refreshment points, escalators and main gangways are often at a premium, and routes should be arranged to draw interest to all parts of the hall by colour coding, location of catering outlets and other features.

Island sites are invariably individually designed and centrally located to provide landmarks and orientation. Small shell schemes may be arranged along the perimeter under and on mezzanine floors with escalator access, but the central area, over most of the hall, must be full height for visual and psychological impact.

Arrangements in halls must meet fire regulation standards for means of escape (see 2.8.4 and 6.8.5–6).

For economy of space as well as easy identification, the main aisles should be planned to run from fire exit to fire exit.

Depending on fire regulations and the type of exhibits, main aisles or gangways are usually 3 m wide for trade shows and 3.5–4 m wide for larger exhibitions; other aisles are generally a minimum of 2–2.5 m and 2.5–3 m wide respectively.

3.2 PLANNING AND DESIGN

3.2.1 Site requirements

Differences between purpose-designed exhibition centres and the exhibition facilities provided in most congress and convention centres are mainly in terms of scale and specialization. Exhibition or trade fair centres provide a range of large halls to serve any kind of show or exhibition required. To increase this flexibility, most of the halls are designed so that separating walls can be removed to open up the full area for major events.

Each hall is usually self-contained in that it can provide all the services required for exhibitors and visitors independent of the use of other areas, enabling events to overlap and run separately. Facilities are also provided for outside exhibitions or show extensions (large plant, buildings, structures), and sometimes for lake-based displays (boats, spectaculars).

Exhibition and trade fair grounds invariably include halls and rooms for seminars and meetings run in parallel with shows and in some cases are linked to purpose-designed congress/convention centres, extending the range of use to large meetings.

In most cases, one of the largest halls is designed for both exhibitions and multi-use spectator sports and entertainment. This dual use necessitates increased ceiling heights, the installation of telescopic arena type seating, and facilities for sophisticated lighting, air-conditioning, music and public announcement systems, video projection screens, reporters' booths and recording and broadcasting services. Multi-use halls usually have alternative entrances for independent operation, with reception and ticketing facilities together with public amenities (refreshments, cloakrooms, toilets).

Access

Good road access to a large market area is essential, together with parking and public transport facilities for the large numbers attending. The NEC, for example, provides over 15 000 car park spaces plus 300 spaces for delivery vehicles and coaches.

With very large numbers of arrivals during the first few hours of an exhibition opening, circulation planning must take account of:

- the capacity of feeder and access roads and intersections;
- the locations of car parks, coach and taxi stands and public transport stations;

- walking distances to the reception lobby and individual halls;
- signage and directions for the various traffic and pedestrian flows;
- transfers within the site from remote car parks and hotels.

Location

To facilitate vehicle access (for exhibits, contractors) and interconnection of space, halls are invariably single storey, large span structures. The extensive site area requirements together with the need for good access generally mean that new centres have to be located outside city centres. In some cases this can be an economic generator for redevelopment of redundant industrial areas or docklands; in others it may be part of a strategic master plan for the co-ordinated development of business and technology parks, retail centres, hotels and other services. Essential requirements for a major development include:

- a large site area allowing room for future phased expansion;
- direct access to the city by-pass and main highway network;
- convenient routes from the international airport, sea port and major urban populations;
- regular, fast public transport services, including a railway station linked to the site;
- a highly developed technical infrastructure, including adequate utility services.

Existing sites

Multi-storey hall construction may be required by the restrictions of the site in built-up areas and/or for further expansion of existing centres. The building costs of this option are significantly higher, involving large ramp construction for goods vehicle access to each floor, escalators and lifts for visitor circulations and, often, basement parking. This may be justified by the benefits of the location and established markets, but temporary accommodation for events may be required during the construction period. In other cases, relocation to alternative sites can release valuable land for commercial development, which can offset the costs.

3.2.2 Site planning

Locations for the main buildings and parking areas are often dictated by the access points (junctions, railways), surroundings and circulation routes. Floor plans need to separate the access for visitors and that from loading docks. Provision must also be made for future expansion and linkage between halls, and for landscaping to reduce exposure (wind, sun, drainage).

To shorten pedestrian circulation, visitor facilities may extend from a central reception area into a linear concourse

National Exhibition Centre, Birmingham, UK

With the 1998 addition of 30 000 m³ at a cost of £65 million (US$103 million), the NEC is one of the largest exhibition centres, providing a total of 190 000 m² of display space in 20 inter-connected halls plus 15 000 m² of outdoor exhibit areas. Located on a site of 220 ha (550 acres) with links to the Birmingham international airport, a main line rail station and major motorways, and two hotels on the site, the complex has more than doubled the original hall area since its opening in 1976.

Over 180 exhibitions are held annually, attracting over 40 000 exhibiting companies and three million visitors. The flexibility of layout enables exhibitions to be run alongside each other during the peak spring and autumn seasons. Examples of major events include the motor show, which takes up more than 75 000 m² of hall space and attracts 700 000 visitors with over 250 exhibitors from 30 countries taking part. During this period 2000 extra staff are employed on security, catering, traffic and cleaning. The IPEX (printing) show uses 125 000 m², with 2000 exhibiting companies and 90 000 buyers.

Source: NEC Group reports

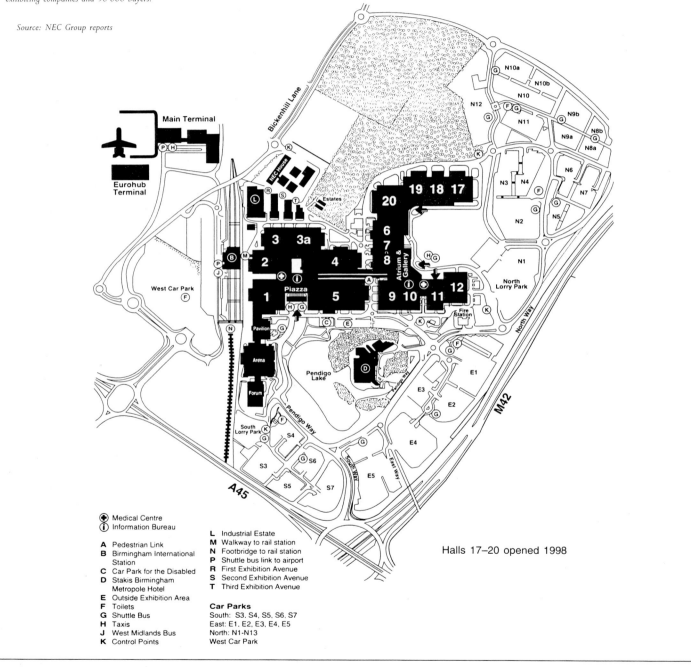

Halls 17–20 opened 1998

⊕ Medical Centre
ⓘ Information Bureau

A Pedestrian Link
B Birmingham International Station
C Car Park for the Disabled
D Stakis Birmingham Metropole Hotel
E Outside Exhibition Area
F Toilets
G Shuttle Bus
H Taxis
J West Midlands Bus
K Control Points

L Industrial Estate
M Walkway to rail station
N Footbridge to rail station
P Shuttle bus link to airport
R First Exhibition Avenue
S Second Exhibition Avenue
T Third Exhibition Avenue

Car Parks
South: S3, S4, S5, S6, S7
East: E1, E2, E3, E4, E5
North: N1-N13
West Car Park

along one side or between groups of halls. Alternatively a radial linkage may be used, allowing greater scope for separation of hall usage. Halls that are designed for public entertainment usually need separate, direct access.

The link buildings are usually extensively glazed to provide relief from the artificially created environment required for the displays, and may be on two or more levels to accommodate visitor services, circulation and assembly/waiting areas.

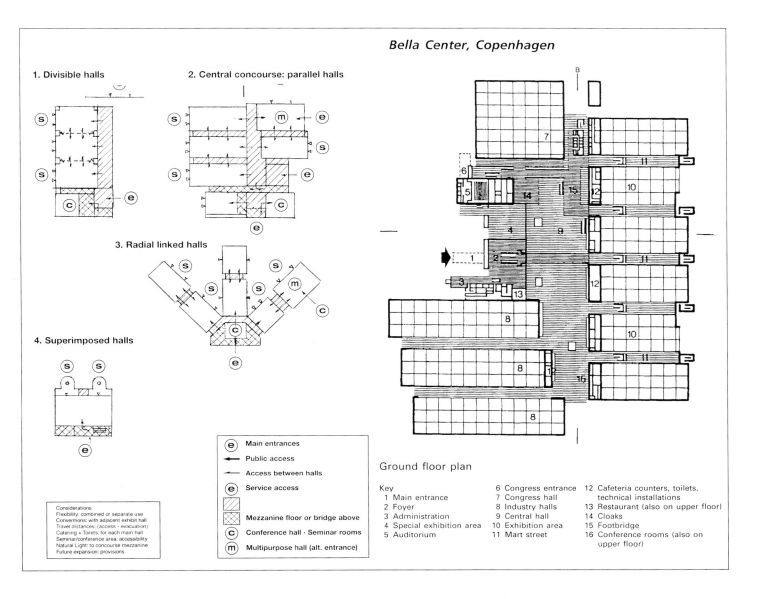

Bella Center, Copenhagen

1. Divisible halls
2. Central concourse: parallel halls
3. Radial linked halls
4. Superimposed halls

Ground floor plan

e	Main entrances
←	Public access
→	Access between halls
e	Service access
	Mezzanine floor or bridge above
c	Conference hall · Seminar rooms
m	Multipurpose hall (alt. entrance)

Considerations
Flexibility: combined or separate use
Conventions: with adjacent exhibit hall
Travel distances: (access · evacuation)
Catering + Toilets: for each main hall
Seminar/conference area: accessibility
Natural Light: to concourse mezzanine
Future expansion: provisions

Key
1 Main entrance
2 Foyer
3 Administration
4 Special exhibition area
5 Auditorium
6 Congress entrance
7 Congress hall
8 Industry halls
9 Central hall
10 Exhibition area
11 Mart street
12 Cafeteria counters, toilets, technical installations
13 Restaurant (also on upper floor)
14 Cloaks
15 Footbridge
16 Conference rooms (also on upper floor)

3.2.3 Hall design

Single storey halls are usually modular in design, using standard structural systems to facilitate prefabrication and rapid construction. Requirements vary with the type of shows and exhibitions targeted and the scale of operation, and the smaller halls are generally similar to those in convention centres, particularly when intended for multipurpose use such as for banqueting and large meetings (see 2.8).

For larger exhibition halls typical provisions are as follows.

Structures

Clear ceiling heights with lightweight roofs are usually 7.6–8.6 m (25–28 ft), but halls that are also to be used for entertainment may require clear heights of 16.0 m (52 ft) or more. Structural grids are kept as wide as possible, and may completely span the hall. In other cases, column spacings of 30 m across the hall with perimeter wall columns at 15 m intervals are common. The trusses spanning the bays are usually N- or V-braced box sections, serving as walkways to give access to overhead services. Other structural designs include two-layer space frames and cable stayed designs.

The roof structure has to be designed to take heavy suspension equipment, including division partitions.

Roof construction

The prominence and expanse of the roof may be designed to form a unique profile, particularly in an urban setting such as Brisbane, Hong Kong, San Diego and Vancouver.

In other cases, a distinctive image may be created by the design of tall features on the site (water towers, communication towers, special features). Surface water drainage from the roof may be used for landscaped lakes, cooling systems and irrigation.

The roof construction must meet specified standards for:

Leipziger Messe, Germany

The exhibition halls of the Leipzig Trade Fair provide a total of 102 500 m² of space with ceilings 8–16 m high and floors designed for loadings of up to 30 kN/m².. Standard beam spans are 37.5 m, but in the 16 m high hall this is increased to 75 m. There are over 500 hanging points for 50 kg and 100 kg loads, and utility services are provided in trenches at 5 m intervals (for water, sewage, power, compressed air, sprinklers, telephone, ISDN, data and image transfer and wide band communications) (a).

At the centre of the complex is the new spectacular vaulted Glass Hall, which is directly connected to each hall to allow independent use, and accommodates shops, a post office, bank, restaurants and childcare facilities (b). The new Congress Centre, accessed from the Glass Hall, also has extensive glass facades and extends over three levels arranged around an atrium (c). Above the entrance and registration level there is a multipurpose exhibition and banquet hall floor. At the higher Conference Level there are a large conference hall seating 1000, two halls each for 384 persons and a range of smaller meeting rooms.

Architects: gmp: von Gerkan, Marg & Partner; Ian Ritchie (Glass Hall structure); OBERMEYER Planen und Beraten

Structural Engineers: IPP: Ingenieurburo für Bauwesen

IHG: Ingenieurgellschaft Helmut Haringer

Building Services Engineers:

HLT: HL-Technik Aktiengesellschaft Beratende Ingenieure

EBI: Ebert - Ingenieure GdbR mbH

Project Management:

IRW: Ingenieurgemeinschaft Bernd Rauch und Peter Weise

(c)

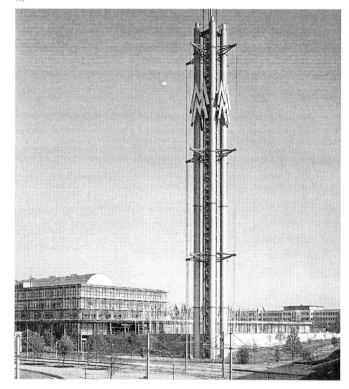

(b)

(a)

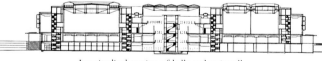

Longitudinal section of halls and stairwell

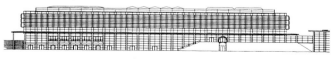

External view of congress centre

Congress Centre and Glass Hall: West elevation

Plate 1
Burj Al Arab by night, Dubai,
United Arab Emirates.

Plate 2
Burj Al Arab by day, Dubai,
United Arab Emirates.

Plate 3
The Jumeriah Beach
Hotel, Dubai, United
Arab Emirates.

Plate 4
National Convention Hall
of Yokohama

Plate 5
The Estel Hotel, Convention and
Events Center, Berlin, Germany

Plate 6
Bali International Conferen
Centre, Indonesia.

Plate 7
Hong Kong Convention and
Exhibition Centre – Interior

Plate 8
Scottish Exhibition and
Conference Centre, Glasgow,
Scotland (front view).

Plate 9
Scottish Exhibition
and Conference
Centre, Glasgow,
Scotland (side view).

Plate 10
Le Grand Motte,
Palais des Congrès, France

Plate 11
Brisbane Convention and
Exhibition Centre, Queensland,
Australia.

Plate 12
Hawaii Congress Center
by night

Plate 13
Cairns Convention Centre
Queensland, Australia.

Plate 14
International Convention
Centre, Birmingham, UK.

Plate 15
Dover Heritage Centre,
The White Cliffs Experience, UK.

Plate 16
International Convention Centre,
Birmingham. UK

Plate 17
Valencia Congress Centre,
Spain.

Plate 18
Hong Kong Convention and
Exhibition Centre.

Plate 19
De Vere Grand
Harbour Hotel,
Southampton, UK.

Plate 20
 Diego Convention Center,
lifornia, USA.

Plate 21
Sydney Convention and Exhibition
Centre, Darling Harbour, Australia.

Plate 22
International Congress Center,
Munich

Plate 23
International Convention Centre,
Durban, South Africa.

Plate 24
International Convention Centre,
Durban, South Africa.

Plate 25
International Convention Centre,
Durban, South Africa.

Brisbane Convention and Exhibition Centre, Queensland, Australia

Arising from a winning design and construction tender in 1993, the Brisbane CEC opened in June 1995 on time and within budget at a cost of A$170 million (US$ 107.5 million). With a total floor area of more than 110 000 m², the complex is huge and consists of a line of five halls, each 72 m × 72 m with 14 m clear ceiling heights, augmented by a 2200 m² ballroom, a series of meeting rooms from 30–1000 m², associated support facilities and basement parking for 1600 cars.

Four of the halls are for exhibitions; the fifth – the Grand Hall, adjoining the foyer – is highly flexible, providing staging with tiered seating for up to 4000, part of which can be elevated to provide a flat floor for banquets and exhibits. Both the Grand Hall and the adjacent exhibition hall can be subdivided by operable walls to halves and quadrants. A canopied concourse for pedestrian access to the halls extends along one side, and a continuous loading dock along the other.

To create a striking profile, each of the roofs is designed with doubly-curved hyperbolic paraboloid shells cut and folded about one diagonal and supported by a deep, 100 m long bowstring truss, which is triangular in section, together with edge and bracing members. This unique structure enables the roof loading to be mainly supported by shafts at the corners of the diagonal, and these have been adapted to house the services and extended as a feature of the roofscape. Although roof construction weighs only 45 kg/m², it is able to support heavy suspended loads and withstand near cyclonic winds.

The limited size of the site required the ballrooms and plaza to be built by bridging over an adjacent railway, and this also provides access to riverside gardens and other cultural build-ings. Construction had to cope with congestion, poor ground conditions and time limits, and involved fast-tracking, division of the work into manageable packages and extensive prefabri-cation. In addition to providing a dynamic landmark image for the city and winning many awards, the BCEC is projected to generate A$800 million (US$506 million) into the economy of Queensland during its first 10 years of operation.

Client: Q Build Project Services as agent for the Queensland Government
Architect: Philip Cox Richardson Rayner & Partners
Associate architects: Peddle Thorpe Architects
Consulting structural, civil, geotechnical and transportation engineers: Ove Arup & Partners Australia
Building Services engineers: Norman Disney & Young
Contractor, project manager: Leighton Contractors Pty Ltd
Hall steelwork sub-contractor: Evans Deakin Industries

Source: Ainsworth, I., Cardrae, R. and Short, B. (1996). Brisbane Convention and Exhibition Centre. The Arup Journal, 2.

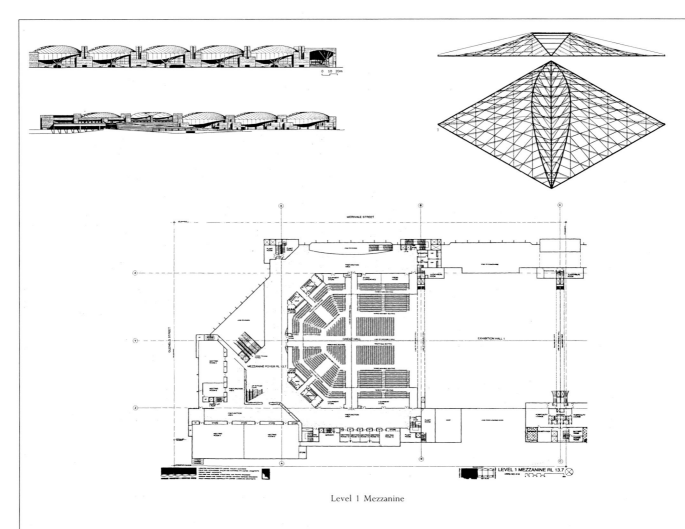

Level 1 Mezzanine

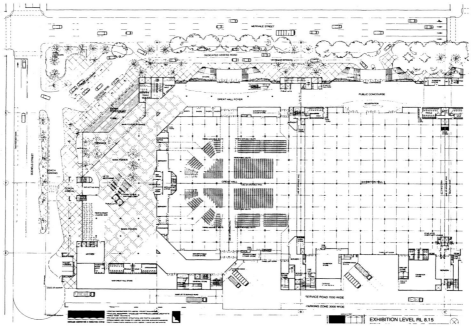

Exhibition level

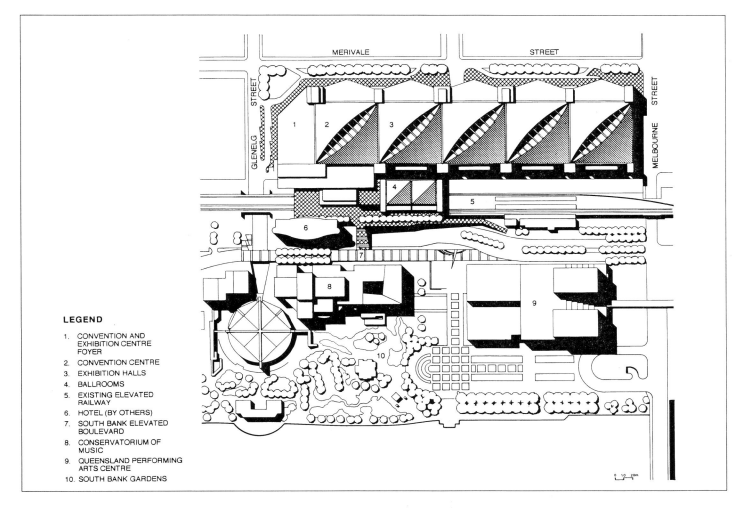

LEGEND

1. CONVENTION AND EXHIBITION CENTRE FOYER
2. CONVENTION CENTRE
3. EXHIBITION HALLS
4. BALLROOMS
5. EXISTING ELEVATED RAILWAY
6. HOTEL (BY OTHERS)
7. SOUTH BANK ELEVATED BOULEVARD
8. CONSERVATORIUM OF MUSIC
9. QUEENSLAND PERFORMING ARTS CENTRE
10. SOUTH BANK GARDENS

sound insulation (environmental noise climates, impact noise from plant, rain etc);
• thermal insulation and solar reduction (energy conservation, plant requirements);
• loading (climatic cycles, roof mounted plant, roof access, suspension loads);
• fire safety (surface flame spread, structural integrity, fire resistance);
• engineering equipment, ducting, cabling, pipe work, fittings (space, access, support);
• maintenance (access, protection, differential movement, condensation control).

As a rule, the ceiling voids are left open to allow access to ceiling mounted equipment. The view of ceiling structures is more than 35° above eye level over most of the area, and visual intrusion, with a high lower plane of lighting, is not significant.

Walls

The lower levels of walls (to a height of at least 2 m) are liable to be damaged by scraping and impact, and are usually constructed of smooth concrete or rendered brickwork or blockwork which can be painted as required. The upper areas may use systems of panelling or sheeting which meet fire safety standards and provide a degree of sound absorption. Doors giving access from loading docks must have large, high openings for vehicles, and are usually mechanized for easy movement. Separate exit routes are usually required.

Floors

Heavy floor loads may be involved, and design specifications are often based on a uniform loading of 200 kN/m² (2 tons/sq ft), with up to 50 kN (5 tons) on a 300 mm square plate for point loads. Floor construction is usually screeded concrete with composition finishes to prevent dusting and allow repairs. Grid trench systems are normally provided for service connections to stands (see below).

3.2.4 Stand layouts and circulation

Stands

Both shell and individual stands are normally used in major exhibitions. Although there are wide variations depending on the type of products displayed (from motor cars and boats to jewellery and fashion), shell stands are mainly planned on the basis of 9–15 m² (97–160 sq ft) units although free-form displays can be much larger. The options for stand and aisle layouts are affected by the positions of columns and exit points, dimensions of the hall and grid lines for engineering utilities.

Occupancies

Maximum occupancies for exhibition halls are based on 1.5 m² per person, including stand personnel, and this is used in calculating emergency exit widths. Although flow patterns vary widely research suggests that, over the period of a show, there are about two to three visitors for each square metre of rented stand area in specialized trade fairs, rising to 10–20 or more visitors/m² in consumer exhibitions.

Circulation routes

Visitor circulation in the hall should be planned on a simple grid arrangement, with stand frontages on each side of the aisles. Free-standing displays are mainly sited in the centre of the hall, to create animation and variety. Access to emergency exits within the required travel distances must be maintained. Main aisles extending through the hall are usually 3m wide, increasing to 4 m for larger exhibitions, whilst side aisles are at least 2 m and usually 2.5–3 m wide. As a rule, the maximum ratio of net stand space to circulation and support areas is about 55 : 45.

Uniform and repeated signposting, together with the use of identifying symbols, numbers and colour codes, is essential for orientation and direction to particular areas, and this is even more important where the exhibits may be spread over several halls.

3.2.5 Engineering services

Engineering requirements within each hall fall into two main groups; those services needed to maintain the functions of the building, and the utility supplies required by the individual stands.

Utility services to stands

Engineering services to stands are invariably run in underfloor channel or trench systems with 3 m or 6 m spacing and removable covers to suit stand layouts. Access to services is provided by underfloor galleries and basement plant rooms. The utilities include single- and three-phase electricity, ISDN telephone and computer lines, compressed air, drinking water, drainage and gas supplies. Vacuum points may also be installed for stand and hall cleaning. Regulations governing the positions of pipelines and cables, colour coding, screening, metering and provisions for isolating valves and switches, overload protection and other safety requirements must be observed.

Building engineering services

Environmental services are mainly housed in the ceiling voids, and include air ducts, electric cabling or busbars in trunking or raceways, fire detection and sprinkler systems, and speaker, closed-circuit television and computer systems connected to information panels and screens.

Air-conditioning

Air changes: For large exhibition halls a rate of 6–10 air changes per hour is usually adequate, but for multiple uses higher rates may be specified (see 2.7.7). It may be necessary

---

Lille Grand Palais, Belgium

At the crossroads of five autoroutes and the fast TGV train network to five European capitals, the 50 000 m² Lille Grand Palais is made up from three main elements – the Zenith, Congres and Expo – arranged side-by-side under a single oval roof line. With a 5000 seat capacity (7000 standing), the Zenith is a convention centre/rock concert hall. The 20 000 m² Congres, in the middle, has three equipped auditoria of 1500, 500 and 320 seats, with the option of writing tablets or alternate rows of tables, together with 12 meeting rooms, a banquet suite for 1200 and flexible exhibition areas of 4200 m². The Expo is a serviced 20 000 m² exhibition area, sub-divisible into three halls. In the basement there is parking for 1250 cars.

This huge building was constructed in just 19 months on site and opened in June 1994.

Operator: *Lille Grand Palais*
Architects: *Rem Koolhaas/Office for Metropolitan Architecture, FM Delhay-Caille*
Engineers (structure and concept services): *Ove Arup & Partners*
Services and co-ordination: *Sodeg Ingenierie*
Photograph: *OMA*

to supplement heating to ensure quick recovery of temperature after a show has been set up, and air curtains may be provided over loading doors to reduce wide fluctuations in temperature.

Distribution: The positioning and design of diffusers must avoid air being blown into any particular exhibit area and also the obstructive effect of the stands. Discharge velocities of diffusers and the distribution and cross-sectional areas of air-handling ducts are determined by the mounting height and noise emission. In large halls with heights of 10.5–15.5 m and the risk of air lamination and temperature gradients, discharge velocities of 6–10 m/s (1000–2000 fpm) are usually necessary to provide effective distribution. The return air ducts must be designed to ensure a balanced airflow distribution.

Plant: Packaged air-handling units are mounted on the roof or in an energy centre adjacent to linked halls to provide independent zoned systems. The associated equipment will include an air intake, a mixing chamber for variable proportions of fresh and recycled air, an automatic filter, a cooling coil with refrigeration equipment, a heater (usually gas fired) and supply and return air fans. Access and servicing requirements must be considered.

Controls: Individual areas have time and thermostatic controls, with automatic monitoring and regulation to optimize conditions and energy usage. Energy recovery systems are usually installed. In the event of fire, automatic changeover to fire mode with smoke outlets is necessary.

Ancillary areas: Separate ventilation extract is required for areas such as toilets (six changes per hour) and kitchens. Supplementary heating will be required in entrance lobbies and cloakrooms, whilst offices and suites are generally provided with fan-coil units. Separate air conditioning zones are used for restaurants, lounges and other public areas.

Lighting

Natural lighting is often a disadvantage in display halls (see 2.7.7), but must be provided in concourses, entrance lobbies, restaurants and other ancillary areas. Luminaire design depends on the height and character of the hall and, during open days, will be supplemented by the higher levels of lighting provided by the stands.

Service levels of illumination are normally 400 lux, with switching to reduce this to 200 lux. In large halls with high level fixtures, colour-corrected 1000 W high-pressure mercury discharge lights are common. For lower ceiling areas, balanced fluorescent lighting in battens or ceiling systems may be more appropriate.

Security and communication systems

Extensive provision must be made for safety, security and communications (see 6.8). In large halls the requirements may extend to entertainment displays and spectator events, involving large video walls or screens, projection equipment, camera monitoring, editing and relay facilities (including outside broadcasts) and sophisticated sound amplification systems.

More generally, computerized systems are required for automatic recording of visitor enquiries, reservation/visitor profiling and auditing, accounting, personnel, maintenance and other management controls (engineering, security, circulation, safety, energy).

3.2.6 Reception and registration facilities

The central reception hall is the main focus of circulation. Its location is determined by the need for convenient pedestrian access:

- from public transport terminals (rail station, bus and tram stops links to airports);
- from car and coach parks (or transfer terminals);
- to the various halls and other facilities.

Often the reception hall forms an extended public concourse linking the halls and accommodating public facilities (as in the arched glass hall of the Leipzig Centre and central hall of the Bella Center, Copenhagen).

Registration facilities

Facilities for reception and registration of visitors should be provided centrally for major shows and separately for events running in parallel. The area required for the registration hall, counters, attendant desks and turnstiles must be calculated for the peak rates of arrivals, and the objective is to process visitors through with minimum delay and congestion.

Separate provisions are normally made for stand representatives, pre-registered visitors and general visitors, and registration details are usually programmed into data systems with badge reading bar codes for exhibitor information.

Conference and seminar facilities

Most exhibition centres include facilities for conferences and seminars, which may be offered independently as well as in parallel with trade and consumer shows. The conference halls may be sited off the public concourse or grouped together with other meeting and hospitality rooms, banquet facilities and support services.

Seminar rooms usually incorporate extensive audio-visual aid services (video projection, multiscreen presentations) for product information, and may include equipped areas for demonstrations of craft skills or product launches.

Studio facilities

One or more specialized halls may be offered for product launches, displays and demonstrations. These are designed as flexible studios with arrays of lighting, sophisticated sound and lighting controls, neutral surroundings and adaptable telescopic

G-Mex, Manchester, UK

The G-Mex (Greater Manchester Exhibition and Event Centre) in the heart of Manchester is an exhibition centre converted from a Victorian railway station. Under an arched roof 26 m high, it has 10 350 m² of column-free space, which can be divided when required into two halls. A new linked seminar suite accommocates five suites with a total seating capacity of 1100 plus a restaurant.

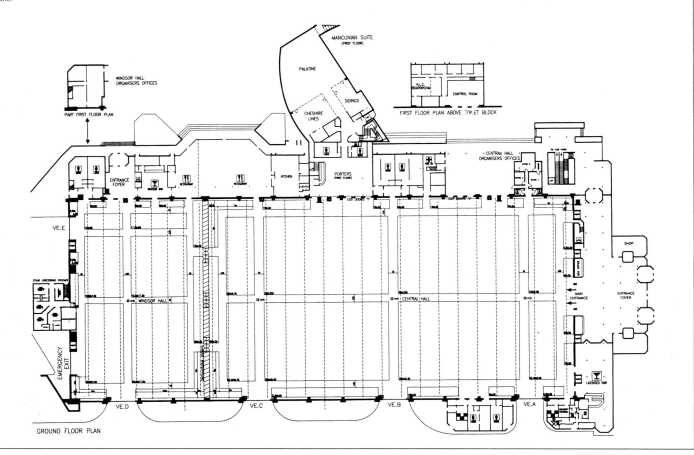

seating. Access must be provided for large display products, such as vehicles and sets, together with facilities for outside broadcasts as well as film and television recording.

Studios are an extension of exhibition work for wider dissemination of product information, advertising and promotional activities. They may be used in conjunction with other exhibits, or hired independently for sales meetings or production of advertising material.

3.2.7 Other accommodation requirements

A comprehensive range of services must be offered to both visitors and exhibitors. As a rule, this will include a choice of food and beverage service, cloakrooms, toilets, first aid facilities, offices, hospitality rooms, travel and hotel reservations, public telephones, paging and announcements, a press centre and some shopping facilities.

Sanitary facilities

At varying times these will be required for contractors and other pre-opening workers, catering, cleaning and maintenance staff, exhibitors and visitors. For employees, the facilities must also include washrooms and changing rooms (with lockers) which are separate for the sexes. Employee facilities are generally grouped together with personnel offices, time monitoring and security controls (see 6.8.1–3).

Depending on the scale of operations, sanitary facilities for contracting and delivery staff may be provided near the loading dock area. Separate facilities may also be allocated for exhibitors, including changing and locker room areas, and these can be grouped with food service cafeteria and restrooms provided for exhibitors' use.

Visitor facilities must include cloakrooms, which are usually attendant operated to minimize queuing and congestion. Toilets are typically located near the entrance, but in a large hall complex, additional toilets should be provided near café and restaurant services. In each case, a toilet area for the disabled must be included. Toilet requirements are:

For maximum occupancy (visitors plus exhibitors)	per 500 m² area of the hall
Men	
Water closets	2
Urinals	5
Washbasins	5
Women	
Water closets	7
Washbasins	7

Other requirements

First aid centre: In larger exhibition complexes, more than one first aid centre should be provided. A centre usually consists of a reception area, a treatment room fitted with a clinic sink and waste disposer, and a small staff office. Often a disabled person's toilet is included in the centre.

Exhibition organizer: An office will be required by the resident organizer over the whole period of the show, together with a secretarial office. In a larger fair this will be extended to a suite of rooms.

Press room: This usually includes exhibition literature, offices and facilities for interviews and photography.

Travel bureau and other shops: For overseas visitors and exhibitors requiring travel information and other assistance, a travel bureau is required in all international fairs. This is usually provided as a permanent unit in the public concourse, together with a bank/currency exchange and one or two retail outlets.

Shipping and forwarding office: This facility is required to arrange the ordering, customs clearance and despatch of exhibited products. One or more offices will be required for an international fair.

Hospitality rooms and suites: These may be needed for the use of exhibitors if their stands are not large enough to entertain important guests. Rooms and suites may be reserved in an associated hotel, and in other cases meeting rooms can be temporarily converted to this use.

3.2.8 Food and beverage services

Service modules

For operational reasons, food service areas, bars and kitchens are usually grouped together to form service modules which can be largely standardized in design. Separate modules must be provided in each hall or main divided section to allow each area to be used independently. It is an advantage to limit the size of each restaurant or cafeteria in order to offer a wider choice, individual service and flexibility.

Requirements

The number of places required will depend on many factors, such as the location, alternative facilities available, nature and length of the exhibition and the numbers attending each day. As a rule, the main use of restaurants arises from specialist trade shows whilst public exhibitions generate a greater need for snacks and self-service facilities.

Food service areas need to be open for most of the time an exhibition is in progress, with a high seat turnover at peak demand times (12.00–14.30 hrs). In most cases, each 40–50 m² (430–540 sq ft) of exhibition space will require one cafeteria or restaurant place (1.5–1.8m²) plus about 1 m² of bar and lounge space. In addition, snack and refreshment services should be provided, using either permanent bars or portable counters. Arrangements may also be made for distributing refreshments to stands and for a cafeteria to be reserved for exhibitors.

Organization

Food services may be operated by catering contractors using outside sources, or be mainly supplied from a central production kitchen. The latter is grouped with bulk stores for food and beverages, laundry and other supplies, and will include facilities for preparation and initial cooking of food together with snack and sandwich-making sections.

Distribution arrangements for prepared food and collection of waste must be planned to avoid visitor circulation routes. Final preparation and dishwashing are normally decentralized, using satellite kitchens adjacent to the food service areas (see 4.5.1–4).

3.3 PERMANENT AND SEMI-PERMANENT EXHIBITIONS

3.3.1 Range of facilities

Exhibits that are displayed in a permanent/semi-permanent arrangement or for relatively long periods of time are usually housed in purpose-built premises such as museums or art galleries. In some cases, such as travelling exhibitions or commercial displays, space may be leased for this purpose in similar buildings or in a more commercial setting. Exhibitions of this kind can be broadly grouped into three main categories, depending mainly on their roles.

Roles	Types of centres	Types of exhibits
Cultural	Visitor centres	National collections
	Museums	Regional collections
	Art galleries	Local collections
	Science centres	Private collections
Commercial–cultural	Visitor centres	Company sponsored
		Privately operated
	Private collections	Designed exhibitions
Commercial	Design centres	Company displays
		Leased space
	Trade centres	Featured exhibitions
	Display cases	

Telecom World, Hong Kong

Designed as a voyage of discovery, the Telecom visitor centre is designed as a series of seven galleries each dedicated to a different aspect of telecommunications with special effects and hands-on interactive and virtual-reality exhibits. A visitor 'smartcard' is used to personalize the choice of language, exhibits and games as well as to access extra information. The centre covers 3160 m² (34 000 sq ft) on the fifth and sixth floors. Business visitor facilities are provided on the fourth floor.

Clients: Hong Kong Telecom
Centre design: MET Studio Ltd

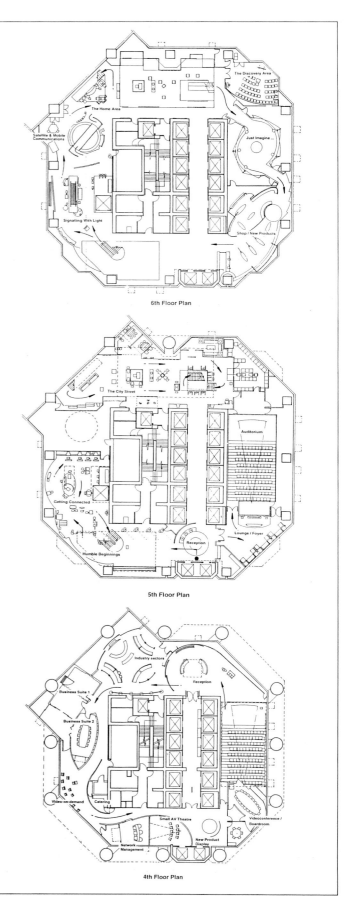

6th Floor Plan

5th Floor Plan

4th Floor Plan

3.3.2 Museums, art galleries and visitor centres

The roles required of museums, art galleries and many visitor centres are often much broader than the mounting of the exhibitions. In particular, where national and regional collections or important works of art are involved the facilities must provide for a wide range of operational needs as well as careful planning of the visitor movements around the exhibition halls and provision of a wide range of visitor services.

This complexity of planning for museums and art galleries calls for extensive consultation and specialist input. For a more detailed examination of requirements, reference may be made to G. Matthews' *Museums and Art Galleries: A Design and Development Guide* (1991) and M. Sixsmith's *Touring Exhibitions: The Touring Exhibition Group's Manual of Good Practice* (1995).

The following general summary (3.3.3–3.3.9) can be applied to most centres and, to a large extent, is relevant in planning similar kinds of commercial exhibitions.

Operational requirements for the larger centres include facilities for a number of associated activities and services, as well as space for temporary display of travelling exhibits. In addition to the exhibition area, the associated operational functions usually include:

- research, conservation, workshops;
- open and closed storage of items not on display;
- technical support, recording, photography;
- labelling and graphics, exhibit design;
- receipt and dispatch of material for travelling exhibits and new acquisitions;
- administration, security and control of access.

The individual requirements of each exhibition centre vary widely, and will need to be considered at the inception stage of planning as part of the briefing process.

3.3.3 Planning exhibition areas

Exhibition requirements need to take into consideration the objectives in providing displays (education, information, research), and the types of markets targeted. The trend in museums is towards more responsive involvement of visitors, particularly in science and history subjects, by means of animation and interactive exhibits – adapting techniques employed in theme parks. In other cases, the priority is usually to safeguard treasures and works of art whilst allowing opportunities for close viewing in surroundings which provide a contextual setting. In each case, it is necessary to pursue a step-by-step planning procedure to identify:

- the roles of the centre and aims in displaying exhibits;
- the characteristics and interests of the target markets;
- visitor groupings, patterns of movements and peak numbers;
- circulation, routes, control points, disabled access;
- access for exhibits, dimensions, weights, handling requirements;

- orientation, introduction to subject(s), features, directions;
- zoning of exhibits, relationships, densities of displays, flexibility;
- types of displays – passive, communicative, animated, interactive;
- viewing and activity requirements, spaces, heights, rest areas;
- building design, vertical/horizontal layouts, clear ceiling heights;
- orientation, fenestration, solar screening, external noise climates;
- the design of displays, mountings, floor loads, viewing positions;
- environmental conditions – illumination, air-conditioning, humidity, noise;
- engineering services, light fittings, air distribution, power, communications;
- risk assessment (fire, damage, security), monitoring and control systems.

3.3.4 Exterior areas

Exterior exhibits such as excavated ruins, archaeological features and commissioned works of art should be integrated with landscaping and the arrangement of buildings. Particular considerations relating to the site include:

Aspect	Checklist
Public access	Modes of transport, waiting areas, parking facilities
Climatic conditions	Shelter, drainage, paths, hard standings, landscaping
Sensitive areas	Protection against vandalism and damage (railings, moats). Incorporation in layout (courtyards, glass conservatories)
Security generally	Control of access points, surveillance systems
Flood lighting	Illumination of building and outdoor exhibits (lighting systems, locations). Lighting of entrance and approach
Maintenance	Grounds maintenance, building fabric, window cleaning
Emergency access and egress	Location of exits and assembly points. Vehicular access, water hydrants, emergency lighting
Technical plant	Plant room requirements, location, limitation of noise, vibration; effluvia, storage and safety requirements
Exhibits and other deliveries	Loading dock requirements, dimensional clearances, handling equipment, security controls, weather protection

3.3.5 Visitor facilities

Requirements for visitors depend on the importance and location of the centre. A national collection in a capital city will usually offer extensive research and educational programmes as

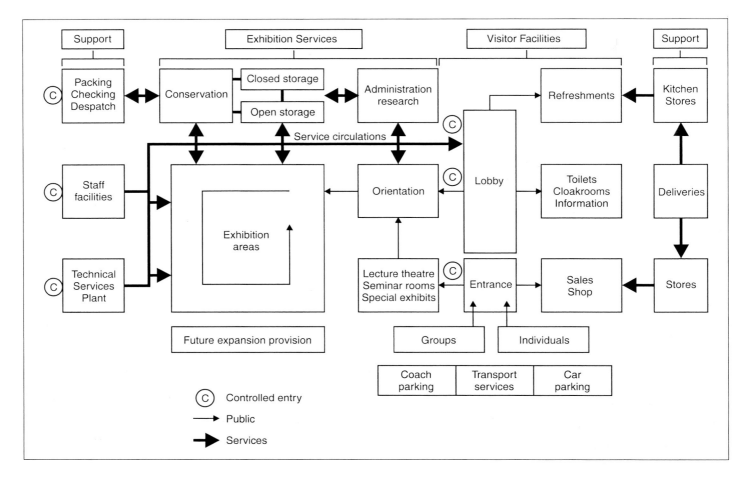

well as serving as a major tourist attraction. Visitor centres in important historical sites also include extensive orientation and amenity facilities (cinema, meeting rooms, museum, souvenir shops, restaurants), and these are often associated with the car parking areas to maintain traffic free zones around the monuments and archaeological exhibits.

In other cases, where suitable alternative commercial facilities are available nearby, a simpler arrangement may be adequate, such as using the reception area for other sales to save duplication of staff.

Circulations

In planning major centres, consideration should be given to the way visitors are to circulate around the building and relationships between the various areas:

- location of main entrance (surroundings, modes of transport);
- secondary group entrance leading to assembly points (coach bays)
- access routes to lobby, facilities for the disabled, controls;
- direct access to assembly points, shop, cloakrooms, toilets, restaurant;
- controlled access to exhibitions, library, meeting rooms;
- lecture theatre/cinema, meeting rooms, activity areas;
- orientation area introducing the exhibits and directions.

3.3.6 Interior areas: entrance hall

The entrance hall serves a number of functions; it is an easily identified place of entry to the building (distinctive), an assembly point (waiting space), access route to public areas (directions) and information and control point (reception desk, barriers). As the main thoroughfare it will be subject to intensive traffic and wear and tear, and is difficult to close down for long periods of repairs.

Aspect	Checklist
Entrance doors	Shelter from weather, design and furniture, opening mechanism, draught lobby, floor mat, monitoring system, security, means of escape
Disabled access	Specific routes indicated giving access to all main areas. Trolley parks may be required
Hall circulation area	Based on 0.3 m² (3 sq ft) per person at the peak times. Queuing and waiting areas planned to avoid cross-circulations. Some seating provided
Finishes	Durable and attractive, easy to clean and maintain. Floors non-slip. Fire regulations apply. Notice boards and signs
Reception desk	Information counter, ticket issue and control (duplicated in large centre). Monitoring system. Separate brochure stands.

Cloakroom	Attended, about 0.1 m²/user; locker hangers, 0.18–0.16 m²/user depending on type		seating up to 70; 50 m² (540 sq ft) for meeting room for up to 25)
Shop	Important revenue generator and tourist facility. Adjacent to entrance hall, within view of reception desk. Allow about 0.8–1.2 m²/customer (8–12 sq ft) at peak times, depending on layout. Storage area, about 10 per cent of shop area. Near vehicle access.	Offices and general stores	The duty manager's office and a stationery store should be adjacent to the entrance hall. Other administration may be elsewhere. Ancillary storage and cleaners' rooms located on main floor levels.
Meeting/lecture rooms	Adaptable areas for information, films, meetings, audio-visual presentations (typical areas: 70 m² (750 sq ft) for auditorium	Lighting	Entrance hall, corridors and stairs: 150 lux with transitional zones. Counters and displays: concentrated lighting, 500 lux (see 6.4). Daylight is preferable in offices, refreshment areas, meeting rooms

Techniquest Science Discovery Centre, Cardiff, Wales

Techniquest is an educational charity with one of the leading 'hands-on' science and technology exhibitions in the UK. The Discovery Centre in Cardiff, completed in 1995, has been converted out of a disused heavy engineering workshop and is one of the principal visitor attractions in the Inner Harbour of Cardiff Bay. The site has been planned to provide public access to the harbour front, and one of the old cranes has been retained as a feature of the past.

Using the exposed cast and wrought iron structure of the mid-nineteenth century building, the new facades are largely of glass supported by lightweight tubular steel space frames, creating a light spacious environment. On the dock side the wall is shaded by external sun screens in transparent black fabric, whilst a series of stepped curved walls in engineering brickwork shelter the building from the north.

Exhibits occupy most of the interior, and include a small library and reference area with adjacent workshop. There is also a small semicircular lecture theatre, a mini-planetarium and a shop as well as offices and ancillary rooms. Internal finishes are in muted colours (grey, white, silver), providing a background to the primary colours of the Techniquest exhibits.

Financed by the Welsh Office and the European Regional Development Fund, this project has won several prestigious awards.

Operators: Techniquest
Architects: Ahrends Burton & Koralek
Structural and services engineers: Buro Happold
General contractor: Shepherd Construction Ltd

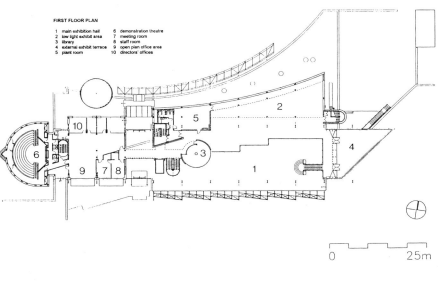

FIRST FLOOR PLAN

1 main exhibition hall
2 low light exhibit area
3 library
4 external exhibit terrace
5 plant room
6 demonstration theatre
7 meeting room
8 staff room
9 open plan office area
10 directors' offices

0   25m

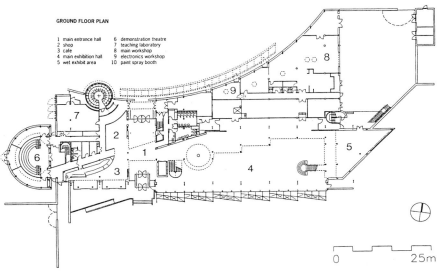

GROUND FLOOR PLAN

1 main entrance hall
2 shop
3 cafe
4 main exhibition hall
5 wet exhibit area
6 demonstration theatre
7 teaching laboratory
8 main workshop
9 electronics workshop
10 paint spray booth

0   25m

Dover Heritage Centre: The White Cliffs Experience, UK

Curving round the archaeological remains of two historic sites, this 5000 m² complex in Dover, England, provides exhibition spaces, a theatre, museum and craft shops. A pedestrian route extends through the site, linking two major streets. The building consists of two and three storey elements in grey brick with bands of light cream brick emphasizing cornice levels and surrounds. As a contrast, delicate glazed crescent structures with steeply sloping roofs look out over historical sites on each side. Archaeological remains are also exposed in the building as part of the environmental experience. Completed in 1991, the building won a Civic Trust Award in 1992.

Client: Dover District Council
Architect: Ahrends Burton & Koralek
Structural engineer: YRM Anthony Hunt Associates
Services engineer: Michael Jones & Associates
Management contractor: Bovis Construction Ltd
Project Manager: Richard Ellis

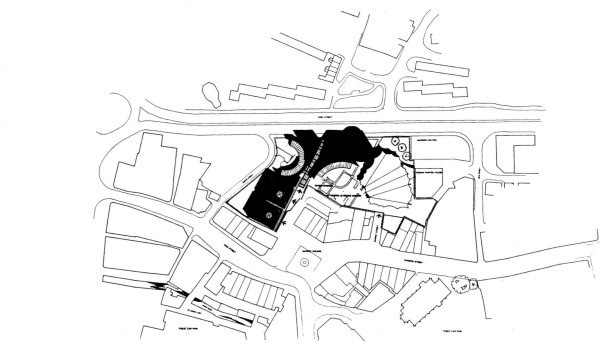

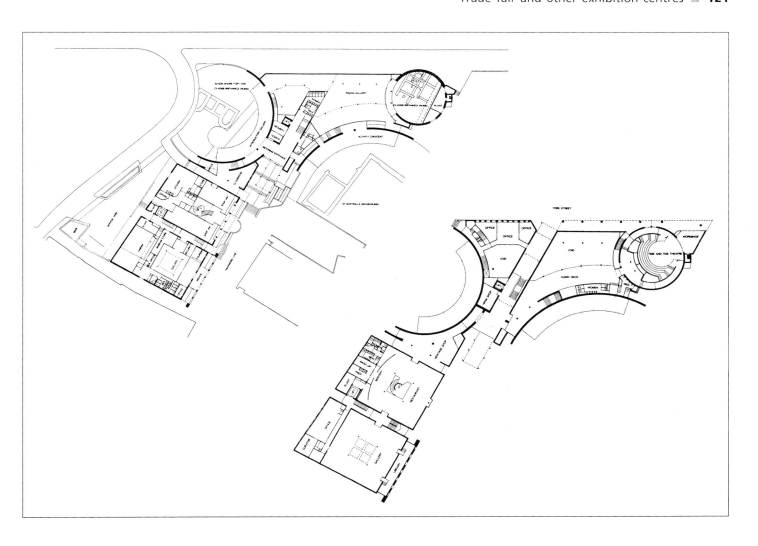

Air-conditioning	Zoned system with automatic control of fresh/recycled air. The proportion of fresh air increases from the lobby (in-leakage) to corridors and exhibition areas	
Toilets:	Locals requirements apply: typical standards:	

	Men	*Women*
Waterclosets	2 up to 500 1 per 500 above	2 up to 75 1 per 50 above
Urinals	2 up to 100 1 per 100 above	
Washbasins	1 per WC plus 1 per 5 urinals	1 per WC

Refreshments:	Depends on the facility and its location. Normally a snack bar or cafeteria will suffice. Provision may be made for business and social functions. Typical areas per cover:

	Dining area m^2/*seat (sq ft)*	*Kitchen/stores* m^2/*seat (sq ft)*
Snack bar/café	1.2–1.4 (13–15)	0.4–0.6 (4–6.5)
Cafeteria	1.4–1.6 (13–17)	0.5–0.6 (5–6.5)

3.3.7 Management requirements

Separate entrances that lead directly to control and personnel areas, together with toilet and changing facilities, should be provided for employees. If required, interview, training and wages clerk offices can be grouped in this area. The focus of front management control is normally the reception desk, and this should have access from associated offices (direct or by rear corridor) without crossing the visitor circulations. Similarly, major exhibit areas should have unobtrusive, rear access routes to allow for changing of displays, maintenance and technical services.

Management of a large centre will include archive and library services, responding to various enquiries and facilitating research studies. For administration purposes, management systems generally cover:

- reception desk: ticketing, accounting, recording, visitor profiling;
- exhibits – origin, provenance, photographs, details, valuation, insurance;

- personnel – accounting, work scheduling, employee records;
- engineering – monitoring conditions, energy, security, maintenance;
- management – daily, weekly, seasonal and annual data, financial analyses
- library: card identification, filing systems, records, loan details.

3.3.8 Exhibition requirements

Design requirements vary both in the different areas of a centre and in the provision of suitable environments for different kinds of displays. The concept in the exhibition halls may be to create a dramatic theatrical setting, recreating the illusion of contextual historical or environmental conditions in which the exhibits can be better appreciated. In an art gallery, the approach is more commonly to provide a neutral background, avoiding distraction and possible reflected coloration, veiling or damage to the works of art.

The following summary outlines some of the key matters that should be taken into account in the planning stage.

Viewing and spatial requirements

The viewing arc for acute (foveal) vision without moving the head is up to about 54° wide, 27° upwards and 10° down from the horizontal, and this is the basis on which displays, exhibitions and notices are normally planned and positioned.

Eye levels depend on age, sex and racial characteristics, but for European populations the following norms are usually taken for viewing notices and displays:

Standing eye level heights (mm)	50%[1]
Adult men aged 18–40 years	1737
Adult women aged 18–40 years	1546
Boys aged 12 years	1458
Girls aged 12	1468

[1] 50th percentile. Half the population is below this height, half above. (Source: Tutt, P. and Alder, D. (1979). *New Metric Handbook*. Architectural Press.)

Large displays and paintings need to be viewed from a distance of about 1.5 times the maximum width of the object.

Exhibits may be mounted in display cases which can be the full standing height, viewed from one, three or all sides, or lower, showing the view (tilted or level) from the top. Many exhibits are best assembled into tableaux showing the items in the context of their natural environments or settings. All exhibits and works of art must be clearly labelled, preferably in a position where the label can be read from the same viewing position as the display.

Viewing gangways between two display cases must be at least 1.4 m wide. If the gangway is also used for circulation or

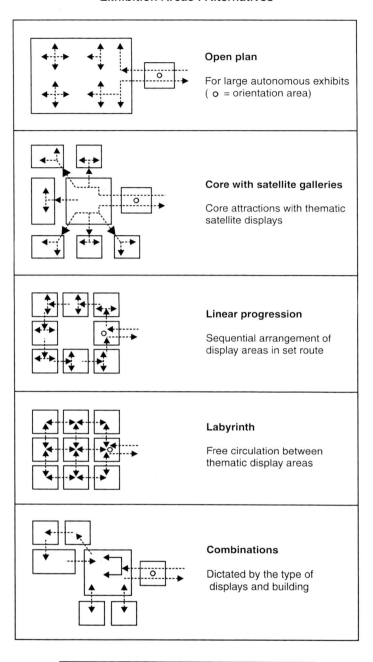

Exhibition Areas : Alternatives

Open plan

For large autonomous exhibits (o = orientation area)

Core with satellite galleries

Core attractions with thematic satellite displays

Linear progression

Sequential arrangement of display areas in set route

Labyrinth

Free circulation between thematic display areas

Combinations

Dictated by the type of displays and building

Planning considerations
• Types of exhibits, visitors and activities
• Primary attractions and main circulations
• Flow patterns, time required for each activity
• Peak numbers, room capacities, queue formations
• Information, directions, signage, assistance
• Exhibit servicing, cleaning, maintenance
• Security, protection, fire safety

is between large exhibits, the width should be increased to 2.8 m. Extra space may be required for exhibit access, and barriers may be required to protect displays and set the minimum viewing distance.

Floor loadings are normally a minimum of $4.0 \, kN/m^2$ for temporary exhibits, increasing to $5.0 \, kN/m^2$ for general display areas. Storage areas may have to be designed for two or even three times this loading for rolling racks, book stacks and equipment.

3.3.9 Environmental conditions

Illumination of works of art

In art galleries soft diffused natural lighting is often preferred, to provide a balanced spectrum and accurate colour definition. The risk of glare, pronounced surface irregularity or reflection from the angle of light and damage from ultraviolet rays must be considered. With artificial lighting, the spectral qualities of the light source(s) and their locations are critical. For more precise specifications of display illuminance and colour, the following standards are representative:

Objects	Maximum illuminance recommended (lux) and colour classification
Metal, stone, glass, ceramics, stained glass, jewellery, enamel	Not restricted but rarely necessary to exceed 300. Subject to radiant heat and display considerations Colour temperature: 4000–6500 K
Oil and tempera painting, natural leather, horn, bone, ivory, wood and lacquer	150–180 in service Colour temperature: approximately 4000 K
Textiles, costumes, water colours, tapestries, prints and drawings, stamps, manuscripts, miniatures, paintings in distemper media, wallpapers, gouaches and dyed leather	50 (less if possible) Colour temperature: approximately 2900 K

Source: Dempster, M. J. F. (1977). Art and lighting. In *International Lighting Review*, Vol. 2. Eindhoven.

To reduce the destructive effects of light on organic material, paintings and other works of art, illumination levels should be kept down to 150 lux and reduced to 50 lux for more delicate articles. The relative damage factor, based on the deleterious effect of ultraviolet and visible radiation per unit of illuminance, can be used when comparing different light sources. Lamps with a low factor should be used in such displays.

Display and exhibition lighting

In general display work, the lighting must be used to create visual variety and stimulation. Whilst direct lighting is gener- ally more emphasized, giving higher illuminances, extreme contrasts of brightness must be balanced by some diffused and background light to avoid discomfort glare. Techniques employed in lighting schemes and lighting equipment are outlined in section 6.4.

Air-conditioning

Standards for air quality must be considered from two aspects; the risk of damage to sensitive exhibits, and conditions of comfort for the visitors.

For delicate exhibits, the main concerns are changes in temperature and relative humidity, air pollutants and uneven distribution of airflows. In a sophisticated arrangement, a relative humidity of 50 ± 5 per cent is maintained by sensing the absolute humidity of return air lines, outside conditions and treatment plant. For particular works of art and delicate materials, conditions may need to be even more closely controlled. For example, the specification may require:

Temperature	$21°C \pm 1°C$
Relative humidity	$55\% \pm 5\%$ RH
Air cleansing	Maximum content and size of particles
General lighting	Colour-corrected fluorescent lamps behind diffusing panels
Screening	Ultraviolet filters
Spot lighting	Specified distance to track line fitting

Conditions for comfort require:
- stipulated quantities of outdoor air supply based on the numbers of occupants;
- temperature and humidity adjustment taking into account heat gains and losses;
- air cleansing to remove fumes, dust and impurities;
- even air distribution giving suitable velocities, particularly at head level, for freshness;
- screening of near radiant heat emission or absorption surfaces.

Details of air-conditioning and other technical requirements are given in section 6.7.

Noise control

The large volume linked spaces and hard floor and other surfaces often required in halls tend to generate impact and reverberation noise. Some absorbent materials may need to be introduced, such as carpet strips and acoustic panels, to reduce excessive noise levels. Other provisions include zoning of noise generating activities and attenuation of plant noise, particularly persistent high-pitched sounds. Further details are given in section 6.2.

4 Hotels

4.1 MARKETING OPPORTUNITIES FOR HOTELS

4.1.1 Roles of hotels

Hotels are invariably the main beneficiaries of meeting, incentive travel, convention and exhibition business. In most destinations, some 60–65 per cent of total delegate expenditure is on accommodation and meals in hotels even where the main venue for meetings is elsewhere. Investment in municipal facilities generally leads to upgrading and expansion of the hotel stock in the area to supply the higher standards expected by conference delegates.

The role of hotels varies; depending on where the main meetings are to be held, they may supply:

- accommodation and some meals only;
- accommodation, meals and seminar rooms for supplementary sessions;
- facilities for associated receptions, banquets and supportive events;
- inclusive residential conferences and meetings.

Many of the large congress centres and exhibition complexes have hotels built on or directly linked to the site, and some hotel companies, such as the Maritim Hotel chain (Germany), have made extensive investments in this segment of business. The hotels provide both accommodation and additional meeting and banquet facilities, with mutual benefits from the association. Over-dependence on a congress-convention or exhibition centre as the primary focus of business can, however, present difficulties for hotel operation, leading to pronounced peaking and wide fluctuations in demand. Most hotels in this situation try to develop other balancing demands.

In resorts, the benefits gained by hotels are particularly important. Conventions and exhibitions are predominantly held outside the peak holiday seasons, extending the demand for services, increasing annual occupancies and financing improvements. The provision of a multi-use centre is often a valuable addition to the holiday attractions as well as a venue for marketing larger events that could not be staged in the hotels.

For the largest conventions it may be necessary to extend the range and capacity of accommodation available to convention visitors to include self-catering or serviced resort properties, condominiums and university campuses. Agreements releasing empty properties for this purpose may be drawn up at the initial planning stage.

4.1.2 Meetings in hotels

Hotel investment in multipurpose meeting rooms can be justified on several grounds:

- meetings are an important source of revenue, not only in creating a demand for food, beverages and other services as part of the event, but also from the resultant room sales;
- many small meetings and combined business lunches tend to be held on a regular basis, representing repeat business;
- the rooms used for meetings can be used for other functions such as banquets, private parties, receptions and dances at other times, particularly at weekends;
- being divisible and adaptable, a room can often serve both as a meeting place and as a reception, banquet and/or exhibition area.

Economic appraisal of such investment is based on both the higher room occupancies that can be achieved and the revenue flows generated. The average expenditure of resident conference guests is invariably higher than that for other hotel markets. Although there are wide individual variations, studies of several hotels in Europe (Lawson, 1982) showed the average spend by a conference resident compared to that of other guests was: 2.38 : 1 for a rack rate guest; 1.92 : 1 for a corporate booking; 1.98 : 1 for a travel agent booking; and 3.07 : 1 for a tour group contract. Similar or better results have been reported from convention hotels in the United States.

The economic benefits must also take into account other revenue streams that may be generated, such as from the use of this space for entertainment, local banquets, weddings and functions (see 4.1.5).

Expansion of meeting and conference business may be subject to operational limitations, not just as a result of the location and unsuitability of the hotel. Large groups of delegates tend to have a disruptive effect on the hotel services (bar, lounges, restaurants, pool and sport facilities) for other guests. The fact that the hotel is full may mean it loses valuable regular bookings. Often, when a hotel already has a high Monday to Thursday business occupancy, it is necessary to limit the proportion of rooms allocated to convention use.

The optimum ratio of convention business to other users will depend on management policy as well as on the pattern of business, but for most chain hotels 15–20 per cent is generally regarded as a suitable balance. Weekend and out-of-season demand, on the other hand, is often geared to encourage convention use, often with two-thirds or more of the rooms available for this purpose. Tailored convention packages with special rates and combinations of meetings with sport and other team building events are often offered and backed by extensive sales campaigns.

4.1.3 Profile of business: Europe

Most of the meetings in hotels in Europe are held by companies; the corporate : association market mix is difficult to discern, but some national surveys suggest this is 3 : 1 or more. Practically all local meetings and over one-third of all those arranged by large national companies do not extend beyond 1 day. Only about 25 per cent of the meetings held by the large national groups last longer than 2 days (see 1.5.4, 1.5.5).

Corporate meetings in hotels tend to be small. Excluding sales force meetings, which often involve 100–200 participants at national level, and product launches, which can be almost any scale of promotion but tend to be in the range 50–200, the vast majority of management and training meetings are for less than 50 people. Most of these are for groups of 12–25.

Association meetings in hotels, although fewer, are often much larger – many having 100 or more delegates – and generally extend to 2, 3 or 4 days. Compared with corporate events, associations are usually more location- and cost-conscious in choosing accommodation and invariably make tentative reservations well in advance.

Company choice of hotel is often made first on the basis of its location in relation to the company's business interests, and on its availability. Other factors, rated in order of importance, are:

- the standards of the meeting facilities;
- an efficient/attentive service;
- the quality of food and beverage services (including a choice of menus);
- clear terms and conditions;
- competitive rates;
- good standard sleeping accommodation;
- car parking on site.

Specific requirements may apply in particular cases, such as the availability of exhibition space and business services, and in some instances exclusive occupation of the venue may be an essential condition. In most cases three alternative venues are considered before making a decision and, when satisfied, over half of the companies concerned return to the same venue or use it for other events (MIA, 1997).

For convenience of access for delegates from a wide travel area, proximity to an airport or inter-city rail station are important considerations. Many of the hotels located near major international airports have extensive meeting facilities, and in some cases this is the major segment of their business.

4.1.4 Hotel meetings in North America

About 85 per cent of corporate meetings and over 80 per cent of association meetings in the United States are held in hotels. Although two-thirds of corporate meetings and about 45 per cent of association meetings are for small groups, hotels also attract the larger corporation events as well as state and national conventions.

Average attendance figures for regular off-premises corporate meetings in the United States are also somewhat higher than those in Europe, but generally range from less than 50 for management and board meetings to 100–200 for most others. Most meetings last between 2 and 3 days, but major company conventions and incentive trips usually extend over 5 days.

Regular association committee and board meetings are also for less than 50 participants, increasing to 100–200 for professional association workshops and seminars. However, some 9–10 per cent of major association conventions attract over 1000 delegates, and those which have accompanying exhibits range over much larger sizes.

These attendance figures are important in drawing comparisons between the regional design requirements for convention hotels. Many American convention hotels feature huge ballrooms (divisible into several sections), which are needed for the plenary meetings and banquet functions of the association markets, as well as large numbers of guestrooms to accommodate such gatherings. This pattern is also the trend in Japan, Hong Kong, Singapore, Canada and South America. Apart from those associated with municipal congress centres, relatively few hotels in Europe can accommodate meetings for more than 1000 people.

4.1.5 Other uses

Receptions, dinner dances, banquets, wedding parties and other local functions tend to be seasonal in emphasis and mainly occur at times between the peaks of meeting demands, such as at the weekends and in the festive/vacation periods. The types of facilities required for these events are generally equally suitable for meetings and business users, but may be elaborated by decorations and addition of other features. These types of activities tend to generate large food and beverage expenditures with relatively high margins of profit.

Other potential dual uses for these areas include:

- exhibitions of art, antiques, fashion goods and gifts, including product launches, fashion shows and promotional events;
- special interest group meetings, lectures, films, demonstrations and festivals as part of packaged holiday and short break arrangements;
- conversion of weekday syndicate rooms for business meetings to family rooms at the weekend.

Cairns International Hotel, Queensland, Australia

Designed by the architects to capture a 'sense of place' reflecting the essence of the tropical colonial past in a style of casual elegance, this 321 room hotel in the heart of Cairns with commanding views of the harbour and surrounding hills has basement parking for 193 cars, three restaurants, four bars, a health club, three pools, a landscaped roof deck and a shopping village with 54 speciality boutique shops.

The flexible convention facilities, approached by a grand staircase and lifts with the pre-function area open to the lobby below, provide up to 11 meeting rooms for 50–590 theatre style, the large ballroom seating 530 for a banquet.

Site area: 0.8 ha (2 acres)

Floor areas: Basement parking, 7104 m²; hotel building 27 810 m² (enclosed) and 6758 m² (balconies/decks); retail shops: 1170 m² (enclosed) and 636 m² (balconies)

Matson Hotels Resorts
Developer: Solander Industries Pty Ltd
Planners and architects: Wimberly, Allison, Tong and Goo
Interiors: Chhada, Siemieda & Associates (Australia) Pty Ltd
Photographs: Willem Rethmeirier

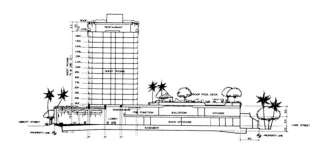

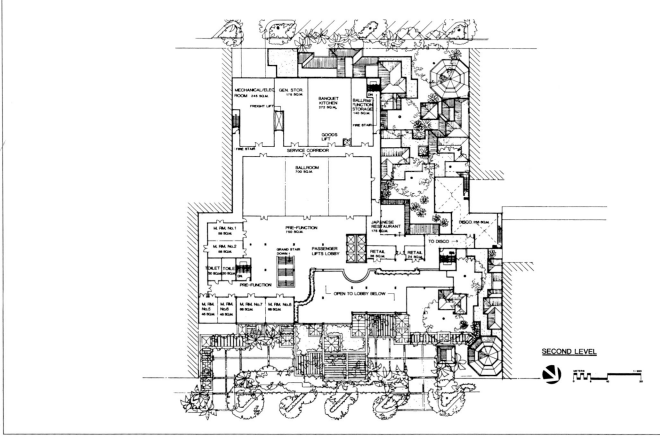

SECOND LEVEL

Cairns International Hotel, Queensland, Australia

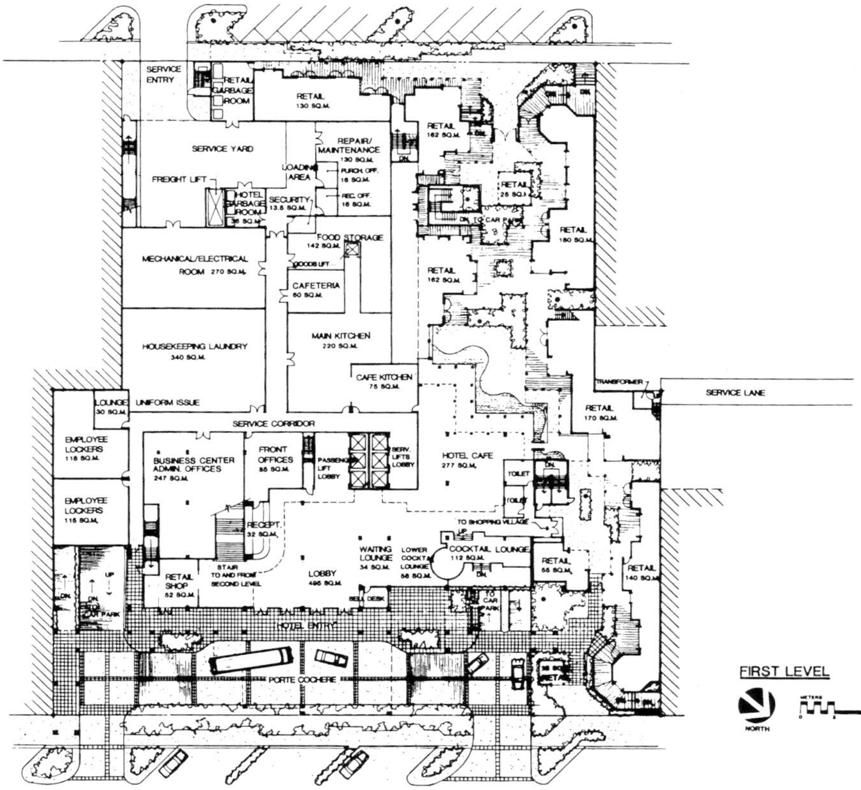

SERVICE ENTRY
RETAIL GARBAGE ROOM
RETAIL 130 SQ.M.
SERVICE YARD
FREIGHT LIFT
HOTEL GARBAGE ROOM 36 SQ.M.
SECURITY 13.5 SQ.M.
LOADING AREA
REPAIR/ MAINTENANCE 130 SQ.M.
PURCH. OFF. 16 SQ.M.
REC. OFF. 16 SQ.M.
RETAIL 162 SQ.M.
RETAIL 25 SQ.M.
TO CAR PARK
RETAIL 180 SQ.M.
FOOD STORAGE 142 SQ.M.
GOODS LIFT
MECHANICAL/ELECTRICAL ROOM 270 SQ.M.
CAFETERIA 60 SQ.M.
RETAIL 162 SQ.M.
HOUSEKEEPING LAUNDRY 340 SQ.M.
MAIN KITCHEN 220 SQ.M.
CAFE KITCHEN 75 SQ.M.
TRANSFORMER
SERVICE LANE
LOUNGE 30 SQ.M.
UNIFORM ISSUE
SERVICE CORRIDOR
RETAIL 170 SQ.M.
EMPLOYEE LOCKERS 115 SQ.M.
BUSINESS CENTER ADMIN. OFFICES 247 SQ.M.
FRONT OFFICES 85 SQ.M.
PASSENGER LIFT LOBBY
SERV. LIFTS LOBBY
HOTEL CAFE 277 SQ.M.
TOILET
EMPLOYEE LOCKERS 115 SQ.M.
RECEPT. 32 SQ.M.
TO SHOPPING VILLAGE
WAITING LOUNGE 34 SQ.M.
LOWER COCKTAIL LOUNGE 58 SQ.M.
COCKTAIL LOUNGE 112 SQ.M.
RETAIL 55 SQ.M.
RETAIL 140 SQ.M.
RETAIL SHOP 52 SQ.M.
STAIR TO AND FROM SECOND LEVEL
LOBBY 495 SQ.M.
BELL DESK
TO CAR PARK
HOTEL ENTRY
PORTE COCHERE
RETAIL

FIRST LEVEL

NORTH

METERS 0 5 10 20 1:300

TENNIS
POOL
JACUZZI
BAR
RETAIL MALL
GUEST ELEV.
STAIR
SERV. ELEV.
MAID
HEALTH CLUB
STAIR
CORRIDOR
STAIR
GUEST ROOMS
GUEST ROOMS

3RD. LEVEL

NORTH

METERS 0 5 10 20 1:300

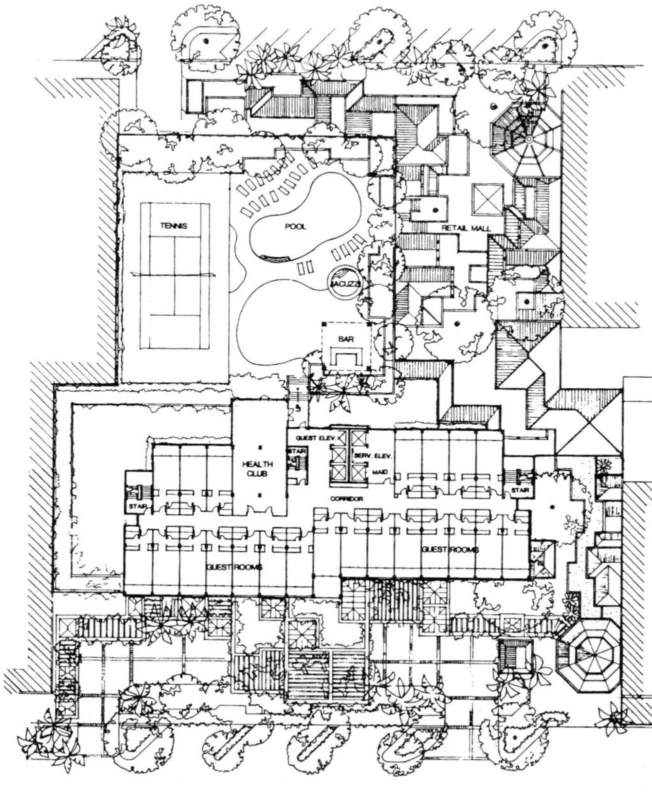

Four Seasons Hotel Chinzan-so, Tokyo

Oriented around an historic 6.8 ha (17 acre) garden, laid out in 1877 by Prince Arimoto Yamagata, this 286 bedroom luxury hotel is an oasis of calm in the centre of Tokyo. The angularity and colours (polished rust-coloured granite and with amber-tinted window details) of the 13 storey building provide a subtle background to the gardens. Only a few of the guestrooms are in traditional Japanese-style (a), but all are spacious (minimum size 45.5 m²) and equipped for business travellers. The 600 hotel staff are bilingual.

Whilst hotels in North America and Europe depend largely on bedroom business, in Japan food and beverage services and functions – particularly weddings – are a major source of revenue. The opulent public rooms, with marble-clad walls and exquisite collections of Asian art, occupy the four floors of the podium and provide over 2400 m² of meeting and banquet space, including a ballroom (630 m²), eight banquet halls, four meeting rooms, two boardrooms and a high-tech amphitheatre with permanent tiered seating for 100, equipped with front and rear projection, and audio-visual projection booth and simultaneous interpretation.

There are four restaurants – Chinese, Japanese and Western styles – all providing room

(a)

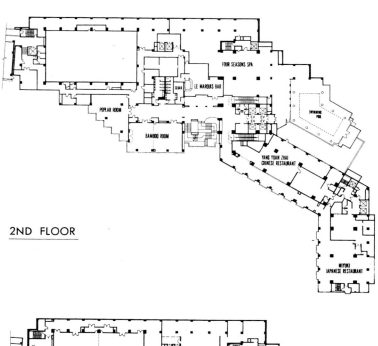

2ND FLOOR

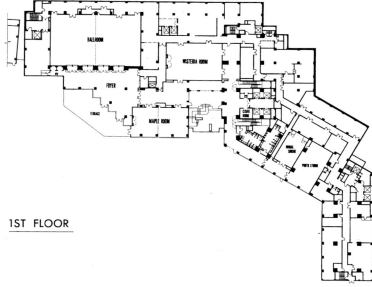

1ST FLOOR

service; extensive provisions for weddings (including a wedding chapel and Shinto wedding hall); shops and gallery; a business centre; and a spa, pool (b) and Japanese bathhouse using natural spring water.

Number of floors: 13 above ground, two below
Building area: 5754 m²
Floor space: 42 693 m²
Guestrooms and suites: 286 (45 m² to 283 m²)

Developer: Fujita Tourist Enterprises Co. Ltd
Operator: Four Seasons Hotels and Resorts
Design Architects: Wimberly, Allison, Tong & Goo
Architect of record: Kanko Kikaku Sekkeisha (KKS)
Interior design: Frank Nicholson
Photographs: Robert Miller

(b)

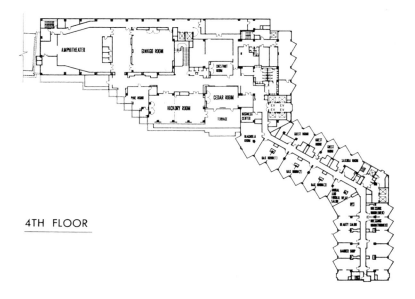

4TH FLOOR

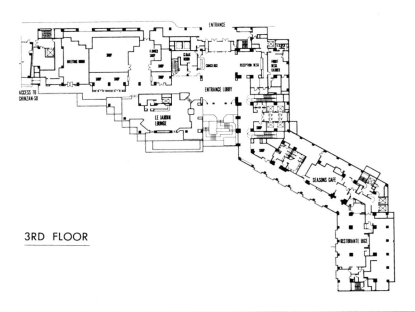

3RD FLOOR

4.2 TYPES OF HOTELS AND RESORTS

4.2.1 Locations and range of properties

As a broad comparison, the main types of hotels involved in providing meeting facilities can be grouped into five categories:

Types of hotels and locations	Main types of meetings accommodated	Locational requirements	Distinctive features
Large city centre business hotels, 250–600 guestrooms	International meetings[1], medium-large conventions[2], association meetings[3], regular corporate events[4], product launches[5]	Central location, commercial/business districts nearby, good access/public transport, car parking	High standard business services, large ballroom, spacious lobby, room service, leisure/fitness centre
Medium-sized suburban/motor hotels, 100–250 guestrooms	Corporate meetings, associations meetings[3]	Near major junctions, access to highway routes and downtown	Meeting rooms for 25–100, work stations in guestrooms, easy acess and car parking, small gymnasium
Large resort hotels and integrated resorts, 300–1200 guestrooms	Major conventions[2], corporate training and events, incentive travel	Near resort centre and/or attractions, spacious grounds	Large ballroom(s), extensive meeting and function rooms, pools and recreation facilities, golf course[6]
Airport hotel, 250–400 guestrooms	International meetings, regular corporate events, association meetings	Linked or near to terminal, easy access to city and regional transport and highways, signposted	May have purpose-designed lecture theatre. Usually a range of medium-sized and small meeting/function rooms, health and fitness suite, extensive glazing and soundproofing
Country hotels, boutique resorts, 80–120 guestrooms	Exclusive corporate meetings	Remote locations, spacious grounds	Small meeting rooms and suites, high quality services, health and fitness suite, golf course

[1] International congresses and other meetings
[2] Full membership association meetings
[3] Committee, professional development and similar association sponsored meetings
[4] Management, sales, stock holders' and other corporate meetings
[5] Mainly for the services sector and fashion goods
[6] Golf course on site or nearby.

4.2.2. Standards of hotel

To meet the requirements of convention and conference organizers, the grading classification of the hotel is often critical. Space standards for convention hotels, on the whole, are much larger than those in other hotels of the same grade. A high proportion of this space is taken up by the meeting and function areas themselves, but more spacious lobbies, reception, circulation and services areas are also needed to cope with the greater concentrations of simultaneous use.

As a rule it is not practicable for a hotel reception desk to cope with 150–200 or more delegates all arriving at about the same time, and arrangements must be made for pre-registration or a separate registration area to be set up for this purpose. This can often provide information and other specific services for the delegates. For larger conventions, and also for marketing large facilities for independent banquets, it is usually necessary to provide a separate entrance, lobby and foyer exclusively for this use.

Similar difficulties may arise in other areas – for example, inadequate car parking, restaurant service, cloakrooms and toilets – unless specific provision is made in planning these facilities. A common complaint of inefficient and slow food service often stems from unsuitable cooking and counter equipment as much as from staffing arrangements.

As a rule, most city centre and resort convention hotels are the equivalent of 4 star grade, and smaller hotels which market facilities for business meetings are usually 3 star grade or better. Although there are notable exceptions, such as exclusive country hotels and remote boutique resorts, the majority of convention hotels are large in terms of the numbers of guestrooms (200–600 or more) and range of amenities provided.

4.2.3 Guestroom requirements

Most corporate meetings and association meetings with a work-related purpose, particularly those of short duration, require a high percentage (often over 90 per cent) of single occupancy rooms. In suburban hotels with a high conference and business traveller demand it is often an advantage to provide one double (or king-size) bed rather than twin beds in the majority of rooms. The space thus freed can be used to set up a workstation with a writing desk, television screen with terminals for use with a desktop computer and an ISDN line telephone with facsimile and computer hook-up facilities. However, in most cases it is necessary to take into account marketing requirements at other times, particularly at weekends and during the vacation periods.

As a contrast, major conventions, international meetings and incentive travel arrangements generate a high multiple occupancy factor, particularly for hotels in resorts and interesting or exotic destinations. One of the major considerations in selecting venues for such events is whether the image of the destination and attractions will generate a high attendance response from potential delegates.

Preliminary space requirements for convention hotels (high, first class or 4 star grade) are typically as follows:

	European (m²)	American (sq ft)
Guestroom area (net)	30.0 (+5%)	350 (+5%)[1]
Gross area (gross factor 40%)	44.0	515
Public and support areas	18.0	200
Total area per room	62.0 (667 sq ft)	715 (66.4 m²)
Ratio of residential : total area	70.1%	72.0%

Notes: European model is based on high site costs. American model allows for larger rooms and more extensive convention areas.
[1]Net internal area of ensuite room. +5% of total rooms are suites occupying two bays (see detailed analysis in 4.5.9).

4.2.4 Access requirements

In planning convention hotels accommodating large groups of people, particular attention must be given to:

- easy access with clear visibility, signposting and advanced warning of entrances;
- peak arrival and departure rates, which are concentrated into 15–30 minute periods before and after events such as banquets and receptions;
- coincidental flows from other guest arrivals and departures and the effect on traffic and car parking
- Well-illuminated car parks with marked out bays and paths, preferably divided by landscaped borders, with clear signs and lighting over paved routes to the entrance;
- Regulation and control of car parking areas for security and efficient use;
- Alighting and waiting bays for coaches;
- Space in the forecourt and entrance area for cars and taxis to set down and pick up guests – preferably under cover of a canopy or *portes cochere* – without impeding other circulation

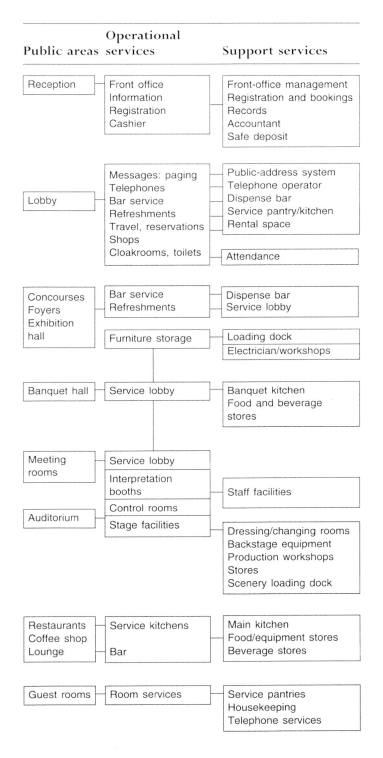

- provisions for access for the disabled, together with dedicated parking bays, ramps and suitable door mechanisms;
- distinctly separate access for goods and service vehicles leading to screened loading dock area, and direct access to the ballroom for exhibits.

Harrahs Sky City, Auckland, New Zealand

Situated in the heart of Auckland amongst the bustling shops, restaurants, theatres and night clubs, Harrahs Sky City occupies a prime site overlooking the harbour. A vast development, the complex includes a 344 room hotel, casino and VIP gaming room, 700–seat theatre (with auditorium, stage and changing rooms), conference centre and landmark 328 m high telecommunications tower – the Sky Tower – with three observation decks, revolving bar and restaurant. A swimming pool and fitness centre are located on the roof, and there are six other restaurants and bars, a shop, and underground parking for 2700 cars.

The conference centre occupies Level 3, with its own exclusive foyer, and is adjacent to the theatre and hotel lobby. It provides a ballroom (570 m²) seating up to 700, which can be divided into three, and six flexible meeting rooms (60–160 m²) separated by removable walls. Sky City is designed to be a New Zealand experience. The choice of building materials and use of strong primary colours reflect this indigenous theme, and commissioned works of art representing different aspects of New Zealand's heritage are exhibited throughout the interior.

Operators: Harrahs Sky City Ltd

Architect and interior design: Craig Craig Moller

Structural, mechanical and services engineers: Beca Carter Hollings & Ferner

Project managers: Terra Firma Group

Main contractors: Fletcher Construction

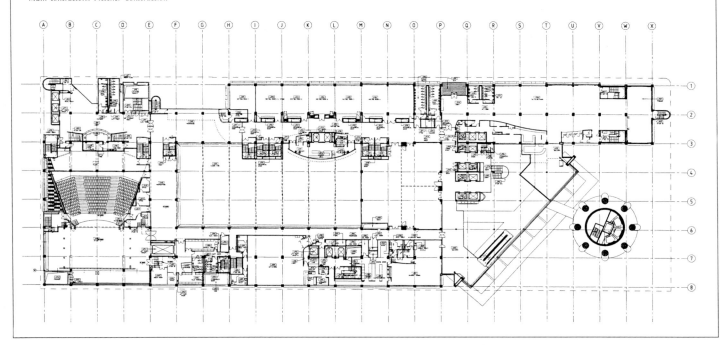

4.2.5 Car parking requirements

To estimate car parking and coach spaces, it is necessary to analyse the maximum levels of demand for all activities over a 24–hour period; modes of transport, load factors and the arrival and departure times. The provision of car parks will depend to a large extent on the hotel location, conditions for using alternative facilities (municipal car parks), availability of good public transport systems and arrangements for group transfers from the airports. Typical provisions for city or resort centre hotels are:

User	Per car park space	Notes
Banquet places	10	Evening demand
Convention hall places	10	Day demand
Hotel guestrooms	2–3	3 in city centres
Motor hotel guestrooms	1	Total 1.2 per room
Staff numbers	5–10	Depends on transport

Car parking is expensive in space, and multi-storey or basement parking is usually feasible in city sites. In each case, lifts must be provided together with stairs for emergency use, within fire-proof enclosures, entered through smoke control lobbies and leading directly to the reception lobby. Overall areas for surface parking, with parking : circulation ratios of 55 : 45, are about 24 m²/space (European) and 300 sq ft/space (American).

In many new resorts, car parking (after unloading) is situated off-site to ensure traffic-free environments. In boutique hotels, valet car parking arrangements or the provision of limousine collection is common.

4.2.6 Service access

Separate entrances, roads, waiting bays and loading docks are required to deliver goods and provide services to the hotel operational areas. These will include regular deliveries of food,

Harrahs Sky City, Auckland, New Zealand

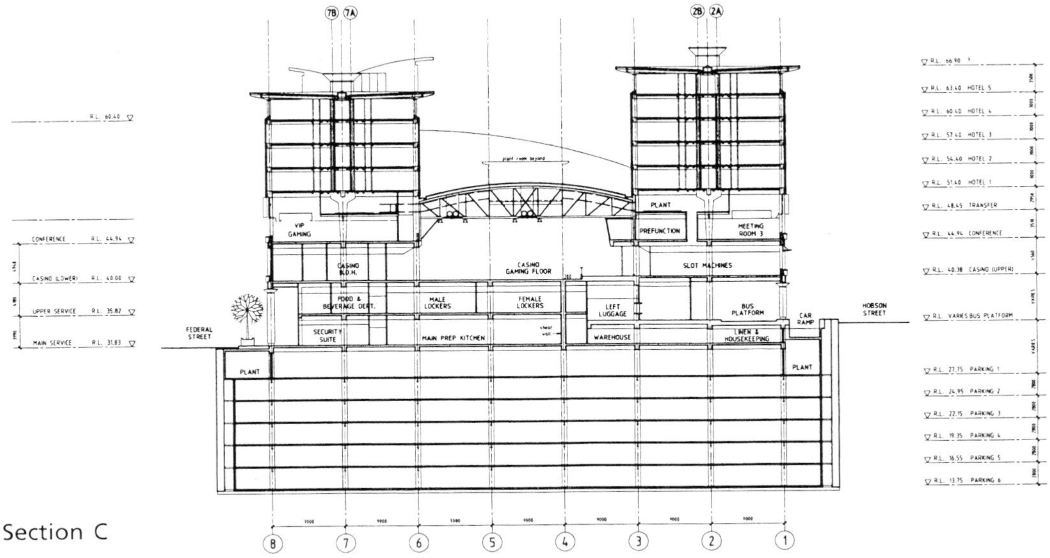

Section C

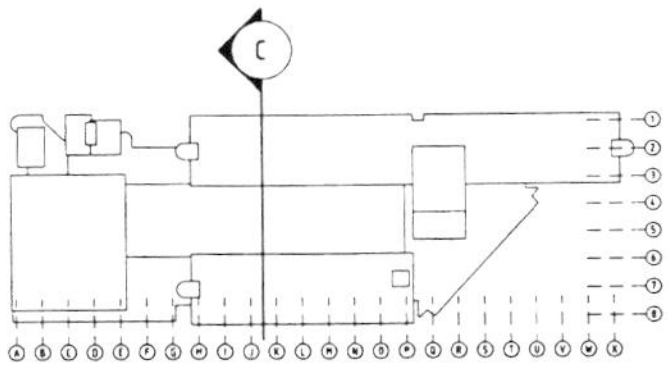

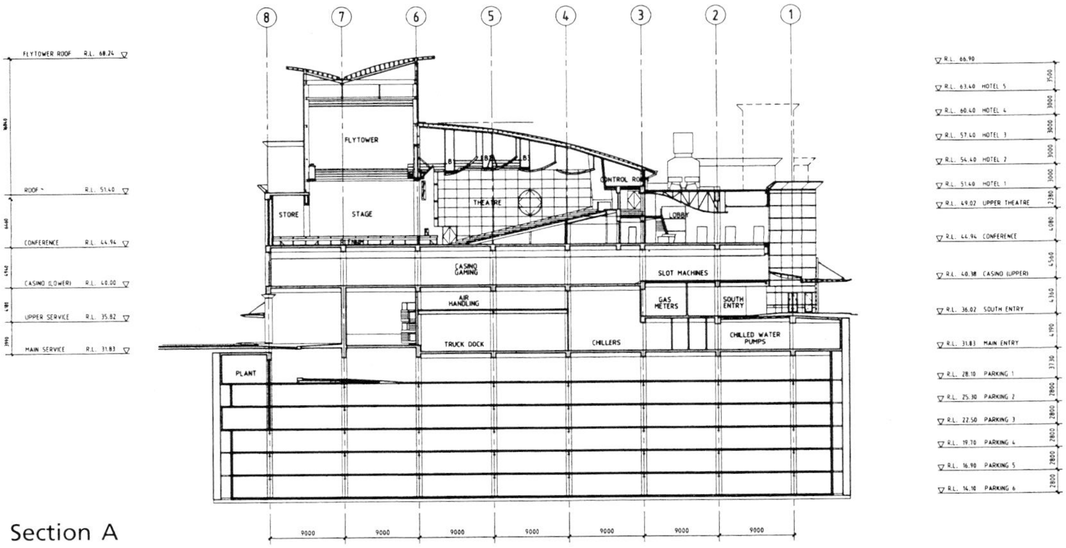

Labels (left elevation levels):
- R.L. 60.40
- CONFERENCE R.L. 44.94
- CASINO (LOWER) R.L. 40.00
- UPPER SERVICE R.L. 35.82
- MAIN SERVICE R.L. 31.83

Grid references top: 7B 7A — 2B 2A

Interior labels:
- VIP GAMING
- CASINO B.O.H.
- FOOD & BEVERAGE DEPT.
- MALE LOCKERS
- FEMALE LOCKERS
- SECURITY SUITE
- MAIN PREP KITCHEN
- CASINO GAMING FLOOR
- LEFT LUGGAGE
- WAREHOUSE
- PREFUNCTION
- PLANT
- MEETING ROOM 3
- SLOT MACHINES
- BUS PLATFORM
- CAR RAMP
- LINEN & HOUSEKEEPING
- FEDERAL STREET
- HOBSON STREET
- PLANT
- plant room beyond

Right side levels:
- R.L. 66.90
- R.L. 63.40 HOTEL 5
- R.L. 60.40 HOTEL 4
- R.L. 57.40 HOTEL 3
- R.L. 54.40 HOTEL 2
- R.L. 51.40 HOTEL 1
- R.L. 48.45 TRANSFER
- R.L. 44.94 CONFERENCE
- R.L. 40.38 CASINO (UPPER)
- R.L. VARIES BUS PLATFORM
- R.L. 27.75 PARKING 1
- R.L. 24.95 PARKING 2
- R.L. 22.15 PARKING 3
- R.L. 19.35 PARKING 4
- R.L. 16.55 PARKING 5
- R.L. 13.75 PARKING 6

Grid numbers bottom: 8 7 6 5 4 3 2 1 (9000 spacings)

Key diagram marker: C

Section A

Grid numbers top: 8 7 6 5 4 3 2 1

Left elevation levels:
- FLYTOWER ROOF R.L. 68.24
- ROOF R.L. 51.40
- CONFERENCE R.L. 44.94
- CASINO (LOWER) R.L. 40.00
- UPPER SERVICE R.L. 35.82
- MAIN SERVICE R.L. 31.83

Interior labels:
- FLYTOWER
- STORE
- STAGE
- THEATRE
- CONTROL ROOM
- LOBBY
- CASINO GAMING
- SLOT MACHINES
- AIR HANDLING
- GAS METERS
- SOUTH ENTRY
- TRUCK DOCK
- CHILLERS
- CHILLED WATER PUMPS
- PLANT

Right side levels:
- R.L. 66.90
- R.L. 63.40 HOTEL 5
- R.L. 60.40 HOTEL 4
- R.L. 57.40 HOTEL 3
- R.L. 54.40 HOTEL 2
- R.L. 51.40 HOTEL 1
- R.L. 49.02 UPPER THEATRE
- R.L. 44.94 CONFERENCE
- R.L. 40.38 CASINO (UPPER)
- R.L. 36.02 SOUTH ENTRY
- R.L. 31.83 MAIN ENTRY
- R.L. 28.70 PARKING 1
- R.L. 25.90 PARKING 2
- R.L. 22.50 PARKING 3
- R.L. 19.70 PARKING 4
- R.L. 16.90 PARKING 5
- R.L. 14.10 PARKING 6

Grid spacings bottom: 9000 9000 9000 9000 9000 9000 9000

Key diagram marker: A

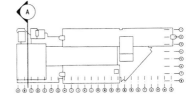

De Vere Grand Harbour Hotel, Southampton, UK

A 5 star luxury hotel, the De Vere Grand Harbour is designed in a Y shape to provide as many as possible of the 172 bedrooms with views of the Solent waterfront. The main confer-ence/banquet suite seating up to 450 (theatre style) has its own entrance foyer and separate external access for exhibits. Divisible into three, the suite has a 4.5 high ceiling with a concealed hanging system that supports 75 kg/m, as well as full technical services. At mezza-nine level there are four conference rooms (40–50 seats) and six boardrooms (26–35 seats). The hotel facilities include a main restaurant for 200 covers, an à la carte restaurant for 45, a cocktail/lounge bar, lounge and well-equipped leisure club.

Hotel operators: De Vere Hotels
Architect: Igal Yawetz & Associates

GROUND FLOOR PLAN

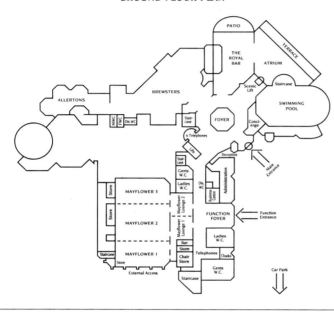

MEZZANINE FLOOR PLAN

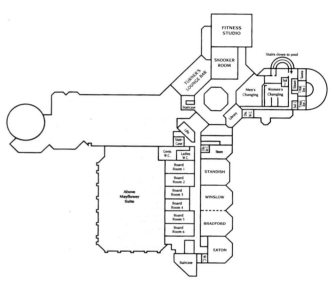

Disneyland, Paris, France

The Disneyland resort has seven themed hotels (5700 rooms) with two convention centres offer-ing 10 500 m² (113 000 sq ft) of modular meeting space with the latest technology, plus recreation, group activities and golf. In 1998, there were 1400 corporate meetings and incen-tives for 10–3000 delegates, producing 165 000 room nights

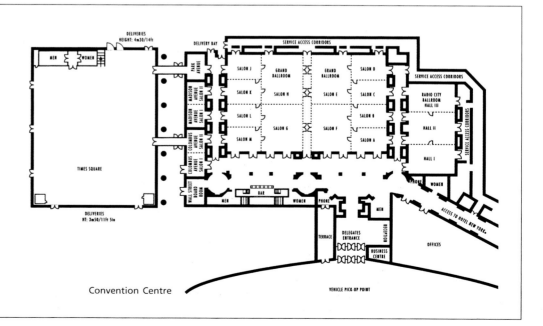

Convention Centre

beverages, laundry, furnishings and equipment, maintenance and contract services, and the removal of soiled laundry, waste and garbage.

Additional provisions must be made for transport and handling of exhibits, large plant replacements and emergency access for fire appliances, ambulances and security vehicles. Service routes and loading docks must be screened from other areas to reduce noise and unsightliness, and must have security controlled access. Space must be allowed for queuing and manoeuvring.

The loading docks are invariably covered (partially or fully), illuminated and have platforms at a suitable height with impervious surfaces to facilitate cleansing, leading directly to storage and plant areas. For exhibits, there must be direct access to the back stage/display area with adequate clearances and load-bearing floors.

4.2.7 Structural considerations

The need for large, tall, column-free ballroom or hall spaces has a strong influence on the structural design of convention hotels. Superimposition of modular guestroom units on top of large-span areas introduces a number of difficulties from the additional loading, access and servicing requirements. Three alternative arrangements are commonly adopted:

- A bridging structure over the hall area, providing a building platform for the guestroom construction and a service floor to intercept and divert the vertical services;
- A podium extension to the main building for large halls on one or two floors at ground level;
- A separate building housing the ballroom and ancillary facilities, with covered linkways to the main hotel reception lobby and between the service areas.

The last arrangement is also the norm for integrated resort developments.

4.2.8 Entrances

Many hotels with extensive banqueting and convention markets provide a separate entrance leading directly to the ballroom foyer with its own cloakroom and reception facilities. In bypassing the hotel lobby, this has mutual benefits for the visitors (exclusive attention) as well as for hotel guests and operation (reduced congestion, security).

This first contact is most important in establishing standards and attitudes. The entrance must be prominent and wide yet inviting, offering shelter, easy access and assistance if required. In most cases a draught lobby is required together with air-conditioned interiors, but some resort hotels may take advantage of cooling air currents with open views of the beach activities and sea. To demonstrate the international status of the hotel and as a courtesy to foreign visitors, a row or grouping of flagpoles should be provided in all major centres.

Sufficient space must be allowed for delegates to assemble in the reception lobby without congestion. Clearly defined circulation lanes to and from the registration desks and fast, efficient registration procedures are essential. Often supplementary reception tables are set up in the lobby or foyer (to one side of the circulation areas) to welcome groups, provide personal assistance and distribute papers, badges and other material. These should be manned over the duration of the convention.

Key considerations:

- arrangements for identifying, handling and transferring luggage to rooms; luggage storage and security;
- pre-registration systems and procedures for checking room, dietary, disabled and other requirements;
- design of doors – widths and numbers of openings, operating mechanism, weather protection, location in relation to front desk (observation), security controls, fire exit requirements, furniture, visibility of glass, durability and maintenance requirements;
- luggage entrance – location, coach waiting bay, pavement area, labelling system, access to storage room, trolley design, porter (bell captain) desk in lobby; luggage lifts to guestroom floors;
- draught lobby (at least 3 m deep), transitional illumination, cooling/warming system, floor mats.

4.2.9 Hotel reception lobbies

The reception lobby of a hotel is the main hub of circulation, serving as an assembly and meeting place and providing information, directions and other services. For management control and security, the circulations for non-resident resident visitors (to restaurants, shops, meeting rooms and function areas) are planned to be distinct from those leading to the guestrooms. Circulation routes may be indicated by signing, carpet strips (secured) on a hard flooring (marble, terrazzo) and visible barriers (planters, balustrades). The minimum width must allow for two people passing with luggage (2.125 m).

Design: To meet its marketing and public role, the design of the lobby is usually spacious, impressive and distinctive. Individually designed, the aim is normally to create a 'sense of place', with artefacts and representations giving a flavour of the location. At the same time, business hotels (particularly those with chain affiliations) have to maintain company procedures and brand identity to give an assurance of standards. Design policies of different companies vary from minimal guidance to a high degree of standardization.

Space: Generally the overall space is based on 1.0 m² per room for resorts ranging to 1.2 m² per room for city centre hotels, both including a lounge area and front desk facilities. One or two small shopping kiosks may be located in the lobby.

Jumeirah Beach Hotel and Conference Centre, Dubai, United Arab Emirates

Self-contained within its own private grounds, the Jumeirah Beach Hotel and resort offers two spectacular hotels, a marina and sports club together with a purpose-built conference centre and wide range of attractions. Designed in the shape of an Arab dhow at sea, the conference centre includes a fully equipped 416–seat theatre, a video conferencing facility and 12 meeting rooms, with a ballroom and banqueting area on the ground floor for up to 1600 people (1326 m²) and capable of division into four exhibition areas. It is served by an underground car park for over 300 vehicles. Opened in September 1997, the centre caters for corporate, incentive, social and commercial events and celebrations.

Operators: The Jumeirah Beach Hotel
Architects, engineers, project and construction managers: W. S. Atkins
Interior designer: Leo A. Daly

Jumeirah Beach Hotel: Seaview elevation

Jumeirah Beach Hotel: Section

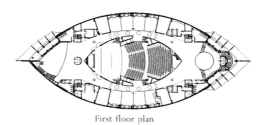

First floor plan

Conference Centre

North side elevation

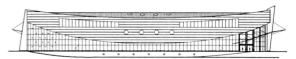

South side elevation

Longitudinal section

Ground floor plan

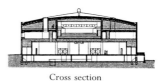

Cross section

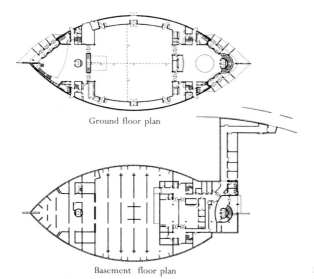

Basement floor plan

Site plan:
1 Burj Al Arab
2 Jumeirah Beach Hotel
3 Conference Centre
4 Sports centre
5 Aquapark
6 Beach chalets
7 Marine restaurant

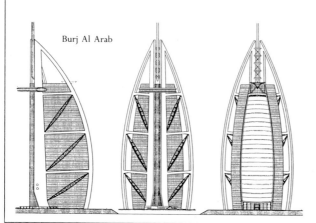

Burj Al Arab

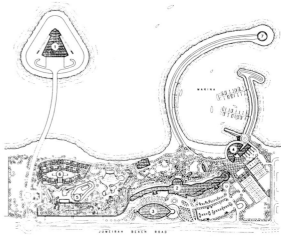

In most large resort developments and some city hotels a separate mall or parade of shops is provided, extending to the street frontage.

Front desk: This must be located to one side of the main circulation routes, set back 2.5 m or more to allow for queuing, and visible from the entrance. Typical areas are:

Guestrooms	Desk length, m (ft)	Stations	Area, m² (sq ft)
100–150	4.5 (15)	2–3	14.0 (150)
200–250	7.5 (25)	3–4	23.2 (250)
300–400	10.5 (35)	4–5	32.5 (350)

The reception desk must have direct access to a front office, providing back-up, and broadly covers the following services:

- cashier – safe deposit/vault, currency exchange, credit card verification, daily balances, point of sale accounting and billing systems; comptroller;
- registration – mail sorting, registration files, database, room allocations, guest requirements; reservations office, front office manager;
- mail, keys – messages, paging, communication, brochures, information, information directions; fire control monitors; security installations; telephone operator's room; business services centre.

Lobby lounge: For guests, waiting arrivals and meeting places, the lobby lounge usually occupies about 10 per cent of the lobby area. A refreshment service is usually offered.

Lift lobby: Lifts are essential for hotels of three or more storeys, and are usually provided in all cases to assist elderly, disabled or other guests. The lift lobby must be located in view of the reception desk, remote from public areas to provide a measure of control. Security monitoring systems should be installed. The numbers of lifts are determined by the numbers of guests to be transported, the height of the top guestroom floor and the standards of speed and sophistication required (round trip time) to achieve an acceptable waiting delay.

Special lift systems are required for rooftop restaurants and bars, for basement car park service, for staff movements and for goods and luggage.

4.3 PLANNING HOTEL FACILITIES

4.3.1 Unit areas

Unit space requirements for conventions and meeting requirements generally are summarized in section 2.3.1. For hotels, actual capacities will depend on room dimensions, seat arrangements, locations of aisles, the areas required for platforms, sight lines and screen viewing limitations, and other particular needs of each event. As a broad guide, two sets of figures should be considered:

Event	Large ballrooms		Small meeting rooms[1]
	Minimum m² (sq ft)	Optimum m² (sq ft)	Minimum m² (sq ft)
Conferences			
Theatre style	0.80 (8.6)	1.00 (10.8)	1.60 (17.2)
Classroom layout[2]	1.60 (17.2)	1.80 (19.4)	1.80 (19.4)
Open U-shape			2.50 (26.9)
Closed rectangle			2.00 (21.5)
Boardroom			2.40 (25.8)
Receptions	0.75 (8.1)	1.00 (10.8)	
Banquets	1.00 (10.8)	1.20 (12.9)	

[1] Room dimensions are often critical: actual capacities vary widely.
[2] Parliamentary-style layout may give higher density of 1.50 m² (16.1 sq ft).

Since the maximum capacity is often critical in marketing hotel facilities to convention groups, this is often based on the minimum space per person. In practice, more generous areas are usually required to allow for easier circulation and variations in the arrangement of furniture to provide more working space, which is preferable for small group executive meetings in high quality hotels.

As an initial guide, other spatial requirements are summarized below. These areas are typical for most convention hotels, but may need to be modified for very large group facilities.

Examples of space analysis in hotels

Minimum areas/user	m²	Notes
Foyers for assembly	0.3	One-third of the hall areas
Exhibitions	1.5	Maximum numbers of visitors + exhibitors
Interpreters' booth	6.0	Temporary: including access (see 2.9.5)
Hotel registration desk:		
200 guestrooms	18.0	Counter length 7.5 m
400 guestrooms	30.0	Counter length 10.5 m
Congress registration desk:		
Each group	9.0	Separate desk
Larger groups	14.0	Temporary counter set up
Services:		
Tour agency	14.0	Also most small shops
Other shops	23.0	
Main restaurant	1.8–2.2	Per seat (cover)
Café/coffee shop	1.4–1.6	
Speciality restaurant	2.0–2.4	High quality
Main kitchen	0.7–1.0	Per restaurant cover served
Satellite kitchen	0.3	Per cover in café/outlet served
Banquet kitchen	0.25–0.3	Per seat in banquet hall
Furniture stores	0.15	Per seat – for frequent changes
At the front desk:		
Hotel reservations	28.0	Typical office requirements for large convention hotel
Cashier/deputy manager	11.0	
Front office manager	11.0	

Telephone switchboard   23.0
Administration offices (main central offices only) (1):
General manager   19.0
Secretary   11.0
Marketing/sales director   14.0
Sales office   19.0
Food and beverage manager   14.0
Accounting comptroller   14.0
Accounting office   19.0
Secretarial office   23.0
Secretary offices: each   11.0   For the departmental heads

[1] Other offices are required near: housekeeping areas, employee areas (personnel, paymaster, security), food and beverages areas (chef, purchasing manager), technical areas (engineers, plan room). These are not included in this list.

4.3.2 Main types of meeting rooms

Requirements for meeting areas will depend on the market analysis, but generally fall into two main categories:

- **One or more large halls** that are column-free and capable of division into two, three or more sections, each section having its own entry for delegates and separate access for the operational services. The halls must have individual sectional control over engineering services for lighting, air-conditioning and audio-visual aid equipment.
- **A larger number of smaller meeting or syndicate rooms** that can accommodate groups of 20, 50 and up to 100 people with theatre-style or classroom arrangements. One or two of the small rooms may be set out as boardrooms. The rooms are usually arranged in suites around a common foyer.

Main halls

The design and size of the main halls may be dictated by other needs – for example, the marketing opportunities for large banquets and dinner dances. Account must also be taken of potential exhibition requirements in terms of both the space and engineering connections to stands. In most cases, the over-riding consideration is the need for flexibility in space, layout and equipment to enable the hall to be changed over quickly from one function to the next with the minimum of noise, disturbance, labour and cost.

This need for flexibility and multiple use limits the choice to a rectangular room with a flat floor. Very few hotels offer an auditorium with raked seats. Those that do so are in locations that generate a frequent demand for permanent meeting facilities with sophisticated communications, interpretation services and electronic displays, such as those near airports.

Small meeting rooms

These are usually of two kinds:

- those that are regularly used as meeting rooms or boardrooms and are kept more or less fully furnished and equipped for this purpose, although extra items of furniture may be brought into the room and rearrangements made to suit particular group needs;
- those that can be adapted from guestrooms or suites; the design of guestrooms for dual use generally calls for inter-connecting doors, more space (including space for storage of the furniture which is not in use) and higher standards of air-conditioning and services.

Meeting rooms must be zoned or concentrated on one or two of the lower floors to minimize overlap with other hotel users and maintain security and management control. Directions to the meeting areas must be clearly indicated, and in a large hotel an escalator is essential if the meetings floor is not at ground level.

The larger meeting rooms also serve for private social parties and club functions in addition to providing dining facilities for the delegates. The locations of these rooms in relation to the kitchens, bar stores, service lifts and furniture stores must be considered at an early stage of planning

4.3.3 Ballroom design

Hotel ballrooms need to be large, impressive areas, providing an appropriate ambience for both formal and social activities on a grand scale. Traditionally places of ornate grandeur with elaborate plasterwork, chandeliers and mirrors, modern designs tend more to express an air of quiet elegance and sophistication, the atmosphere of each event being created by the furnishings, decorations and stage sets brought in for the occasion.

Entrances

Each ballroom area requires its own foyer, which serves as an assembly, information and control point as well as a break-out area for refreshments and relaxation between sessions. This is typically 0.3–0.4 times the ballroom area.

Direct access is essential for food and beverage service, furniture/equipment changes and exhibits, with sound locks and service pantries.

A separate entrance (to the back stage area) may also be provided for entertainers, speakers and technical services (television, projection). Booths and equipment may brought in or permanently installed for interpretation, projection and environmental control (sound, lighting, audio-visual aid systems).

Dimensions

Minimum areas are usually determined by the maximum capacity required for banquets, based on 1.1–1.2 m² per cover.

Minimum dimensions take account of structural restraints (column spacing), modular group sizes and alternative layouts (see above).

Heights of large ballrooms are usually 3.6–4.3 m (11–13 ft) clear, but may be increased to 4.6 m (14 ft) to allow for exhibits. The central areas are often higher to allow for featured lighting, air grilles and other systems. Smaller halls (500 m^2) should be 3.28 m (10 ft) clear. At least part of the ceiling must be sound absorbent.

Entrance doors must be in proportion to the space and allow for concentrated traffic and equipment. Typically they are 2.0–2.30 m (6–7 ft) wide, depending on the numbers of entrances. Graduated lighting, sound attenuation and viewing panels should be fitted.

Floors

Floor loadings – floors are usually designed for 5.0 kN/m^2 (100 lb/sq ft) distributed loads with provision for concentrated wheel loads if required.

Floors are almost always carpeted, but provision will need to be made for dancing (carpet removal/storage or dance squares). Purpose-designed dance floors must be sprung and have securing bolts. The use will affect locations of floor socket outlets and partitions.

Décor

Whilst allowing for partitioning and other function needs, a banquet hall should create a sense of occasion and excitement. Wall mirrors and panelling together with featured lighting are often used to extend the impression of spaciousness, but the effects on projection and filming needs must be considered.

Analogous colour schemes are commonly adopted to avoid excessive contrasts and conflicts with other uses, allowing colour to be introduced by decorative highlights, floral displays, table appointments and stage sets.

Technical services requirements

Extensive cabling installed within a network of ducts or conduits to a range of terminal points and controls. Key requirements are flexibility in room layout and use; frequent changes in connections and equipment; easy access and space for additions.

User systems: microphone, sound amplification, interpretation, data and telephone communication, projection controls, co-ordinated lighting controls, prompting systems.

Building systems: air-conditioning, balancing and regulation; energy management, fire sensing and defence; fire mode ventilation/smoke control; lighting sub-circuits and controls, power ring mains and terminals.

Audio-visual systems: sound amplification systems and speaker arrays, closed-circuit television networks, camera/ recorder points and remote controlled projectors, video, cine and slide projectors with mechanized screens, language interpretation systems and operators' booths. Interpreters' booths are usually portable to allow changes in use.

Details of technical equipment and systems are covered in section 4.4 and Chapter 6.

4.3.4 Division of areas

Adaptability of meeting space is usually a critical factor in marketing and achieving high utilization. On the other hand, partitioning of rooms adds significantly to the duplication of services and to costs, and is not normally practical for rooms of less than 80 m^2. In planning room division, consideration must be given to the following:

- resulting room dimensions (in relation to furniture layouts, height) – optimum ratios of length : width are 3 : 2 for division into two (each 1.5 : 2) and 2 : 1 for division into three (each 0.67 : 1);
- division into three is preferable in larger halls since it allows for three separate rooms or two rooms with two-thirds and one-third areas;
- each of the separated areas must have its own direct access from the foyer (which may be common or itself divided), and access to the service lobby (from the kitchens and stores);
- both the main hall and each divided area must have individually controlled technical services (for air-conditioning, lighting, communications and audio-visual aid equipment); airflows, scalar illumination and electricity networks must be balanced for both the full volume and the spaces when divided;
- high noise insulation standards must be specified, including the sealing of flanking paths through the ceiling and other areas and the reduction of impact noise (from kitchens, furniture changes, vibrations);
- a balance of sound-absorbing surfaces is required to prevent standing wave reverberation (and microphone howl-back), particularly with disproportionately high ceilings in the divided areas;
- fixed positions for equipment such as stages and projection booths may limit flexibility, and this should be considered at the initial stage of planning.

Dividing walls and partitions are invariably positioned in line with the structural beams and columns. The ceiling height around the perimeter and over the lines of dividing partitions is often lower than that in the centres of the halls, to house the suspension gear, air ducts and other technical services whilst allowing spacious central voids for more sophisticated lighting fittings.

Partitions must be simple to fit into position and fold easily (motorized or balanced) and neatly (into designed recesses) when not required. The structural loading on ceiling hangers must be considered in suspended systems, as well as the upward thrust in expanding sealed panels. The main types of partition systems are summarized in section 2.7.3.

4.3.5 Flexibility

Optimum ratios to provide maximum flexibility for meetings, based on 100 per cent guestroom occupancy by delegates, are illustrated for a 200 guestroom hotel. In practice the conference delegate occupancy of the hotel would rarely reach this level, and other marketing factors would have an influence on the function room sizes required.

Meeting rooms	Alternative arrangement: seat numbers		
	Theatre style	Banquet	Classroom
Main hall[1]	240	200	130
divided into three sections	3 × 80	3 × 60	3 × 40
Subsidiary hall	200	170	110
divided into two sections	2 × 100	2 × 80	2 × 50
Small rooms (flexible; used for meetings or associated purposes)	2 × 50	2 × 40	2 × 25

[1] The main hall can be divided into two-third and one-third areas or three one-third areas. Actual capacities will depend on room dimensions when divided.

This representative example involves the provision of some 500 m² of net hall space (2.5 m²/room) and a gross area of about 800 m² (4.0 m²/room), including foyer, satellite kitchen, stores and added circulation, together increasing the overall built area of the hotel by 6–7 per cent. Feasibility analyses of this kind are often used in evaluating market and economic opportunities.

In practice, most hotels of mid-grade (3 star) or better offer meeting facilities of some kind and, in many cases, a significantly larger proportion of space is provided for convention and banqueting use. In the UK, the average conference hotel of 81 rooms offers some 4.4 m²/guestroom of meeting space, although 74 per cent of all the halls are for groups of less than 200.

Analysis of a wide spectrum of international convention hotels also indicates that net meeting capacities are about 2.7m²/guestroom.

Division of a hall not only allows for a range of group sizes to be accommodated but also for different activities to go on at the same time. For example, part of the hall can be set up for a function whilst another is in use for a meeting. In other cases, the divided areas can provide more rooms for small syndicate groups following a large plenary session in the same hall. The relative sizes of subsidiary halls is also important in adding to this range of use, particularly for the smaller corporate meetings which dominate hotel operations.

4.3.6 Banquet hall requirements

As indicated above, the need for flexibility has a major influence on the design of ballrooms and must be considered in detail at the initial planning stage. Often some compromise is required to accommodate different needs.

Provision for meals must be made for the vast majority of hotel meetings, including day events. Delegates will wish to dine together, whether at a business lunch or formal evening meal, in order to exchange views, comments and experiences. Often these are occasions to which guests are invited and at which after-dinner speeches or announcements are made, demanding high quality sound systems and elimination of all extraneous noise (from kitchens, adjacent areas and outside).

Expectations: Banquets provide special occasions for visitors and their partners to share with other guests, and are often sponsored as the highlights of a programme. The memorable experience of a banquet depends on many factors, but it is easily spoilt by inappropriate design and provision.

Banquet layouts are often specific to suit the occasion. The space is often estimated on 1.1 m²/seat, but at least 1.2 m²/seat is usually required to allow for different set-ups. For formal occasions, tables may be arranged in rows (or sprigs) at right angles to the head or top table, Social events and conventions usually require clustering into separate groups, often using round tables seating 8, 10 or 12. Ten is normally the optimum to give the highest seating density.

Circulation planning is necessary to ensure a fast, efficient service. Wide (1.2 m or more) service routes must be allowed from the service entry with separate in-out routes. Mobile serving trolleys and side tables must be positioned at a number of points to reduce travel time and congestion.

Service areas must be designed to facilitate hygiene, with washable surfaces, adequate lighting and good extraction systems, hand-washing facilities and suitably designed serving trolleys and equipment. A sound attenuation lobby must be installed at each entrance to reduce noise entry and balance ventilation. To avoid distraction, the lighting will need to be graduated from the brighter service areas to the level of illumination in the ballroom, particularly for dinner dances.

Dinner dances: Broadly similar layouts are used for dinner dances and entertainment events. An area of carpet may be removed or covered by a dance square and the tables arranged radially around to maximize the view, often with minimal space between seats. Performers usually require changing/rest rooms, a separate stage entrance, microphone and power points and featured lighting (lighting rigs or permanent fittings).

Furniture: Furniture dimensions must be based on anthropometric data for the main market populations served. Framed chairs of traditional design are most common, the frame forming an edging to the back to minimize marking, with a seat angle of 0–2° and a back rest angle of 98–102°. Where chairs are against a wall or barrier, additional space must be allowed for the back slope and seatway access.

The seat height must be related to that of the table. High backs tend to obscure views, and arms to the chairs may add to access and stacking difficulties. Table legs and frames must be cantilevered to allow knee clearance and adjustable for levelling. The underside of the table must be free from protrusions, and rectangular tops must allow joining. A choice of tabletops is required.

All chairs and tops must be light and easily stackable (without marking or damage) on trucks or dollies for removal to storage. Storage areas for furniture and equipment can add up to 5–10 per cent of the hall area, and should preferably be on the same level.

4.3.7 Meetings and conventions

The ballroom provides the venue for plenary sessions and large group meetings arranged theatre-style to achieve the highest seating density. Traditional banquet seats, although elegant, are often not ergonomically suited to this purpose. The layout of the seating must be related to the viewing requirements for screens as well as providing adequate sight lines for the audience to view and hear the speaker. Particular considerations include the following.

Chair layouts

Fire regulations may require chairs to be secured together in lengths of four seats and the end seats to be fixed or secured to the rows in front and behind by floor bars to maintain the integrity of the rows.

Depending on the shape of the room and the positions of aisles, rows of seats may be in parallel lines or have the side rows set at an angle (up to 45°) to face the platform.

Row spacing is determined by the seatway clearance between the edge of the seat and the back of the one in front. With the minimum seatway (305 mm) there is just about room for the knees to clear the backs of the seats in front (assuming average body dimensions), but this should be increased for comfort and to allow others to pass along the row. The seatway determines the number of seats allowed per row. If there are differences in floor level, the minimum seatway is increased and rows may be limited to 12 seats (New York Code).

Seatway mm (in)	Number of seats per row Aisles at both ends	Aisle at one end
305 (12)	14	7
330 (13)	16	8
355 (14)	18	9
380 (15)	20	10
405 (16)	22	11

Based on GLC Regulations; local codes may vary.

Typical row spacing for loose chairs fixed in gangs is 990–1020 mm (39–40 in).

Gangways or aisles

Gangways must lead to protected exits, providing a means of escape in the event of fire. At least two separate, independent means of egress, with the exits sufficiently remote from each other to allow alternative directions of escape, must be provided for up to 500 occupants. An additional exit is required for every 250 occupants (or part) above this capacity.

Widths of aisles and passages are based on the unit width of a person, nominally 560 mm (22 in). A minimum width of two units, 1100 mm or 1200 mm (43 or 44 in) is stipulated in most codes. The widths between rows as a rule must be uniform, and the ends of the chairs must be fixed in line (see 6.8.6).

Travel distances

To ensure safe evacuation within a limited time (within 2.5–3.0 minutes), the longest distances of travel to a safe exit are stipulated:

Type of use	m (ft)[2]	Measured from:
Traditional seating	18 (60)	Any aisle or gangway
Parts not used for close seating (including banquets)[1]	30 (100)	Direct distance; actual route distance not more than 45 m
Large exhibition halls (exits not more than 60 m (200 ft) apart)	30 (100)	Exits must be remote each other (more than 45° from any other exit in the hall)

Based on GLC Regulations. Comparable US distances are shown in ft.
[1]Other codes limit travel distances to primary exits in banquet halls to 85 ft.
[2]Representative of US requirements.

National Fire Protection Association recommendations allow travel distances to be increased from 33 m to 49 m (100 ft to 150 ft) if automatic sprinkler systems are installed.

4.3.8 Operational requirements

Sound clarity

When the audience is seated at one level, sound is strongly absorbed at a low grazing level above and around the heads of the audience, as well as the view being obstructed. To some extent this can be improved by placing the person speaking on a higher level, such as on a stage or platform.

Sight lines: Direct sound and visibility can be assessed by drawing sight lines from eye level (1120 mm) positions of the seated audience to a focal point on the platform (often table height) giving an unobstructed view of the speaker. The limiting distances for clear sight lines are:

Stage height	Distance to speaker (seats in line)	Rows distant
0.5 m	6.0 m	5–6
1.0 m	12.0 m	12–13

This may be improved by varying end seat widths in alternate rows so that the seats are in line with those two rows in front. However, with untrained voice clarity, direct sound is unlikely to be adequate beyond 14–16 rows.

Limiting angles of elevation: To avoid physical discomfort, the maximum viewing angles of elevation from the nearest seats is 30°. This determines how far the front row will need to be set back from an elevated platform or screen.

Platform design

The design of the platform will depend on the intended uses of the ballroom and may range from a fully rigged stage suitable for entertainment events and product launches to a simple platform. The platform height should not be less than 0.3 m (1 ft) to avoid loss of command over the audience, nor more than 1.2 m (4 ft) to avoid screening the stage from front rows of the audience.

For congress and convention meetings the minimum depth is 2–3 m (6–9 ft) and the minimum width 4–5 m (12–15 ft), allowing a range of activities such as discussion panels and supporting displays. The platform must be fully serviced for a mobile lectern, prompt facilities and floor sockets (electricity, communications, control, microphones) to allow plugging in from any position.

Sound amplification, simultaneous interpretation

A system of sound amplification must be built into all large halls, with facilities for changeover and sound balancing of each divided area if required. With large volume halls and high ceilings, line source speakers in vertical columns are usually necessary (see 6.3.7).

Simultaneous interpretation may use hard-wired (with cable lines), induction loop or infrared systems. In most cases the booths are purposely designed and equipped cubicles hired for the event, but suitable locations must be planned and terminal connections and access provided (see 6.3.8).

Slide, cine and video projection.

Projection equipment may be permanently housed in a booth, back-stage area or adjacent projection room, or be temporarily set up within the hall when required. The location and size of the screen in relation to the seating layout is critical. As a guide, optimum viewing conditions for a flat screen are within 30° of the centre line and within a distance equal to two to six times the maximum screen width. The bottom of the screen must be at least 1.8 m above the platform, and higher if simultaneous camera views of the speaker are shown. Facilities may be required for outside television and radio broadcasting services (see 6.6.8).

4.3.9 Exhibitions

Apart from the largest convention hotels, exhibits are mainly concerned with:

- equipment and demonstrations accompanying conventions;
- independent art, fashion, antique and gift fairs;
- franchise, finance and service industry products and services;
- product launches (cosmetic, fashion and fancy goods shows);
- career opportunities and company presentations.

This range of products is suited to a carpeted floor and ballroom environment, although additional rooms will usually be required for meetings, interviews, sample presentations, poster sessions and hospitality. Special requirements will apply where vehicles and large stand displays are involved. Stand layouts must take into account travel distances and fire escape needs (see 4.3.7).

Exhibits require extensive power connections for stand lighting and equipment, as well as communications and other services. The loading on building systems, including air-conditioning, must be taken into account in planning networks. Safety considerations also affect the types of products and stand constructions accepted, and automatic sprinkler systems are invariable required (see 2.3.2–4 and 6.8.5–6).

4.4 TECHNICAL SYSTEMS

4.4.1 Range of technical installations

Technical systems in convention hotels are increasingly sophisticated. They cover the operating requirements of equipment such as lighting and air-conditioning, and include automatic sensing and adjustment to ensure optimum conditions as well as the identification of faults. Mostly these are integrated with building management systems which incorporate a range of other services, for example security and safety monitoring and response measures (alarms, location indicators, changes to fire mode), maintenance planning, records and budgeting.

The range of business services available to guests and conference users is also extending. Current developments not only cover communication services (voice mail, facsimile and data transmission, video conferencing) but also include support facilities in business centres and help in the organization of conventions and other events (set design, equipment hire etc.).

New developments in audio-visual aid equipment available to conference groups include computerized white boards and plasma screens as well as rapid advances in video filming, projection and transmission. In hotels it is normal for the more complex equipment to be hired to meet the particular requirements of each event, but it is necessary to anticipate the space and service connections likely to be required.

Hotel management systems also cover a wide range of operating services (reservations, accounting, personnel), and have extended into areas like direct marketing (internet, e-commerce) and forecasting.

General information on technical equipment and services is given in Chapter 6, and particular aspects relating to hotel facilities are summarized below.

4.4.2 Lighting requirements in ballrooms and large halls

Environmental services in ballrooms and other hotel function rooms, including lighting systems, are complicated by the need for these areas to be divisible. Each area must have individual circuits and controls and be suitably balanced as a whole. To allow for flexibility, lighting installations will usually provide:

- at least three separate lighting circuits for general space lighting (including a combination of downlights and diffusing lights);
- separate circuit(s) for perimeter lighting (wall lighting, pelmets and drapes);
- a separate circuit to spotlights (minimum three) for illumination of the speaker, displays and exhibits;
- separate control of main feature lights (chandeliers, etc.);
- an emergency lighting circuit giving at least 0.5 lux illumination;
- balanced dimming controls to give lower levels of illumination (usually pre-set) for projection, dancing and other needs, with co-ordinated control circuits to motorized blinds.

In smaller meeting rooms, four, six or eight lighting circuits with dimmer switches are usually installed, with main controls on the wall behind the speaker also operated from the lectern and a hand-held controller.

4.4.3 Air-conditioning

Air-conditioning requirements in hotels range from mono-zone systems using centrally controlled, variable air volume (VAV) plant to supply individual ballrooms and large halls, to multi-zone systems in other areas in which occupancy conditions and activities may vary, requiring local adjustment.

Ballrooms and large halls

Requirements are usually based on a 100 per cent fresh air supply to meet peak conditions, with ratios of recycled air adjusted as appropriate. Large plenum and exhaust ductwork is involved, which must be incorporated in the hall design, and the plant is normally located in the close vicinity (roof mounted or in plant room) with provisions for access and control of noise transmission.

Supply air is usually discharged through ceiling diffusers, with exhaust grilles arranged to avoid stratification or short-circuiting (cross or reverse airflow movement). In a hall which may be divided into separate areas, air supply and exhaust branches to each division must be suitably balanced with pre-set dampers for isolation when necessary.

A slight positive pressure should be maintained to ensure directional flow towards service lobbies and kitchens. Acoustic treatment is required to achieve the specified design criteria NR25, and the risk of sound carry-over from one section to another via ductwork must be considered.

Small meeting rooms

Air-conditioning in smaller rooms is usually with fresh conditioned air (from central plant) supplied to terminals such as fan coil or induction units, enabling air to be finally adjusted and part recycled within the room.

4.4.4 Electrical services

Extensive ducting must be installed for equipment and control connections, with separated conduits or raceways for standard and low voltage cables. Alternative positions for speakers' platforms and audio-visual aid equipment should be planned, and terminals (socket outlets, jack points) arranged in appropriate positions – both in floor boxes and wall outlets.

4.4.5 Control rooms

Permanent projection, lighting and sound control rooms may be installed in a large ballroom, positioned at the rear of the room (based on the full seating plan) and elevated to give a clear view of the platform or stage and also projection clearance. Requirements are similar to those for auditoria, but are usually less elaborate. For other situations requiring stage lighting (product launches, displays, entertainment), lighting consoles may be trolley mounted.

In smaller halls, lighting controls are usually housed in wall panels with numbered and coded switches, the panels preferably being mounted in the service lobbies adjacent to the room. Local switches, controlling some of the lights, must also be provided within each room at the point of entry.

Purpose-designed conference facilities may provide permanent projector rooms between pairs of meeting rooms, allowing either front or back projection to be used, as well as independent access, lighting and sound control, equipment storage and working areas.

Provision must be made for installing simultaneous interpretation booths if international congresses are likely to be involved. Booths are invariably hired for this purpose, but the seating plans must allow for the location and design standards specified (see 2.9.5).

4.4.6 Audio-visual aid equipment

Although basic equipment such as slide and video projectors, screens (retractable and portable), easels, white boards and flip charts are usually provided by each hotel, more complex equipment is often supplied by the organizer or hired (with an operator). The economics of specialist in-house equipment must take account of the costs of trained staff, maintenance and life-cycle replacement (typically 3–5 years), but may be justified by marketing advantages. Details of audio-visual aid equipment are given in section 6.5.

4.4.7 Other business facilities

Suitably located hotels with a regular demand for local business meetings may offer more specific facilities to develop this aspect of their business. The options include:

- a floor or group of **syndicate rooms** which, at weekends and vacations, convert to family rooms or suites;
- dedicated **executive floor(s)** of guestrooms with an exclusive lounge and other facilities;
- a fully equipped **business centre** for guests and local business users (membership fees);
- an **executive conference centre** with a suite of conference rooms with built-in facilities (teaching walls, projection booths, technical support, media room) and an allocated block or wing of guestrooms for delegates;
- **video conferencing facilities** with purpose-designed studios for extended conference programmes or independent rental.

4.5 HOTEL SERVICES AND FACILITIES

4.5.1 Food and beverage services

Food services in hotels cover a wide range of requirements. The outlets include:

- restaurants, cafés and coffee shops open to residents and the public;
- function room and banquet services to pre-arranged groups and events;
- individual service to guestrooms and hospitality rooms;
- employee meals;
- serviced apartments, shops and off-site outlets.

Each type of production and distribution arrangement has different characteristics but, to a large extent, several of the preliminary stages (bulk storage, preparation and initial cooking) can be rationalized and combined in a central production facility. In high standard hotels, the need to maintain quality through control of food and beverage services means that the central production is invariably operated by the hotel company itself.

4.5.2 Systems of food production

Meal service generally falls into four types:

Service requirements	Examples of outlets
Meals prepared to individual order	Main restaurant, gourmet service
Menu rationalized, limited choice	Coffee shop, café, speciality service
Fixed menu, pre-ordered	Banquets, functions
Self-selection, set range of choice	Buffet, cafeteria

Individual call orders require large kitchens, extensive equipment and a high ratio of staff to customers. Greater efficiency and quality control can often be achieved by limiting menu choice to a popular range, scheduling production, and preparing food in advance and using chilling or freezing systems of preservation and storage.

Chilling and storage at 0 to 3°C is preferable since it is quicker and avoids any loss in texture and flavour of the food. Chilled food has a short storage life (1–3 days) and is most suitable for pre-ordered meals, such as for banquets and buffets.

Deep freezing and storage at −20°C involves more time in regeneration of the food (25–30 minute cycles) and higher energy costs. The shelf-life of frozen food is extensive (1–3 months), and applications include remote outlets, *à la carte* menus and speciality dishes (see below).

Both processes involve three main stages:

- Preparation/initial cooking, using conventional batch cooking equipment in the central kitchen; large catering units may use continuous cooking/assembly equipment;
- Chilling or freezing – food containers are transferred to blast chillers/freezers and then stored in large chilled/freezer cabinets;
- Regeneration/end cooking in special combination ovens/radiant heaters; heated food is plated and served directly from satellite units adjacent to each outlet.

4.5.3 Planning requirements

Location	Central kitchen, relationship to food and beverage outlets and other activities
	Noise and disturbance, discharge of fumes, engineering plant, staff facilities
Deliveries	Access needs, shelter from weather, screening/part enclosure
	Vehicle dimensions, manoeuvring space, waiting bays, service vans
	Loading docks, checking/control office, passages to stores, handling equipment; security
Garbage	Storage of food waste; chilling and compaction machines; glass etc. recycling; returnable containers; washing, waste containers and vehicle areas

Stores	Frozen, chilled, fresh and dry foods, wine cellar, liquor, other beverages
	China, silver, glass/china, linen, reserves and other stores
	Delivery/consumption schedules; storage volumes, layouts, controls.
Production	Location of kitchens, production requirements (meals/outputs), equipment
	Layouts; areas; engineering plans, building plans/sections, finishes.
Distribution	Location of outlets, meal requirements; means of distribution and control
	Integration with other services, design of service routes, lift systems
Satellites	Menu requirements, meal preparation and service, dishwashing, stores
Staff	Job specifications, work schedules, staff numbers, employee facilities
	Management roles, offices, personnel services, security/control

Kitchens require high rates of air extraction (40 air changes/hour over equipment zones), using hoods or ventilating ceiling tiles, and this must be balanced by conditioned (or tempered) air distribution allowing controlled inflows from the restaurant or banquet service area. Provisions for fire safety include high fire resistance separation (1–2 hours), fire dampers over equipment exhausts and extinguishing equipment.

The walls must have glazed tiles up to at least 2 m (6.5 ft), and impervious, non-slip drained floors. In large installations, steam cleansing may be stipulated. Provision must be made for noise containment, particularly in noise producing areas such as dishwashing, as well as some sound absorption (with vapour sealing) in the ceiling/upper walls.

Equipment is normally gas or electric heated, and may be island or wall sited – the latter being more common in smaller units. Modern cooking and reheating equipment is invariably in stainless steel and designed to facilitate speed, automatic control and cleansing. Hand washing and first aid facilities must be provided in every food handling and equipment area.

Kitchen areas are based on the numbers of meals served over the peak period, with savings achieved through economies of scale. Although these will depend on the systems and menus operated, typical figures are:

Central kitchen (including stores)

Output (meals/day)	Area m²	(sq ft)
500	300	(3300)
1000	500	(5400)

Satellite kitchen (plus local stores and dishwashing)

Covers (seats) served		
100	60	(650)
200	100	(1100)

Banquet pantry (equipment plus serving trolleys)

Covers (seats) maximum		
500	200	(2150)
1000	300	(3200)

4.5.4 Restaurant, lounge and bar design

The public areas of a hotel or congress centre have to serve a range of marketing, merchandizing and functional roles: they are constantly used by most if not all the residents; they need to compete with other facilities in the area and attract other visitors; and they must maintain the standards and reputation of the hotel or centre.

As a rule this involves offering a choice of places, menus and experiences to suit different needs at varying times, ranging from, for example, a quick convenient breakfast to a business lunch and a celebration evening meal. Some restaurants may be designed for easy conversion to allow dual use (breakfast buffet-coffee shop); others may be designed around a particular style of food service (theme restaurants) or menu (speciality restaurants).

Design must be guided by the requirements of the guests, taking into account market profiles, circumstances and expectations. The emphasis may be classical, traditional, modern or *avant garde*, and may be based to a greater or lesser extent on a theme or association. In all cases, however, certain principles apply:

- consistency – in decor, table appointments, menu and service style;
- order – deliberation and tidiness in arrangement, whether formal or contrived informality;
- appropriate seating plans – each area offering specific benefits (views, intimacy, social grouping);
- atmosphere – ambience, lighting and features to create the desired responses.

The same principles apply in lounges and bars. Bars are often designed to encourage clustering and crowding in order to create a lively atmosphere. The bar itself is the focus of attention, with sparkling lights, mirrors and standing patrons providing animation.

Type of outlet	Typical space per cover, m² (sq ft)
Coffee shop, cafe, speciality restaurant	
Compact seating	1.3–1.5 (14–16)
More varied seats	1.5–1.7 (16–18)
Quality restaurant	1.8–2.0 (19–22)
Dinner dances	1.9–2.2 (20–24)
Bars – popular	0.6–0.9 (6–10)

For further information, see Lawson (1994).

4.5.5 Housekeeping and laundry services

Hotel housekeeping services cover two main areas:

- guestrooms – cleaning, bed making, linen replacement, renewal of consumable items (toiletries, stationery, drinks, etc.), removal of waste;

- public areas – cleaning, removal of waste, renewal of consumable items.

In all cases, housekeeping has also a vital role in checking the quality and performance of these areas and reporting deficiencies and defects.

Detailed systems and procedures for reporting and recording action are a mandatory function of management and apply equally to congress centres and other public buildings.

Laundry requirements depend to some extent on the location and size of the hotel. The space, costs and energy consumption of an in-house laundry are large, and economies of scale apply, often warranting centralization of the main laundry services. The benefits of self-provision include better control, turn-around and savings in linen stocks. Even when laundry is mainly contracted out, hotels usually retain services such as guest laundry, staff uniforms and specialist needs.

Laundry equipment generates noise, steam and fumes, and this area is liable to become a fire hazard (lint). The operation must be carefully planned around the sequence of receiving/sorting, washing, drying, roller pressing, ironing, airing and clean storage areas. Siting must be near plant rooms (services), housekeeping lifts/chutes, linen stores and loading areas.

4.5.6 Staff facilities

Large numbers of staff are employed in hotels and congress centres. Employment tends to be hierarchical, with management, supervisory, skilled and semi-skilled categories. Although employee turnover in hotels (particularly semi-skilled groups) is often high, and may be seasonal in demand, hotels generally offer opportunities for long-term careers. In most congress and exhibition centres, a higher ratio of the lower grade jobs are casual or periodic, and contract services tend to be used to a greater extent.

Staff facilities include entry and leaving recording equipment, changing and locker rooms, toilets and shower facilities, and restrooms/canteens for meals and personnel services. Provisions must also be made for interviews, first aid and training areas. Many requirements are laid down in employment legislation, and must be based on the maximum numbers involved (peak conditions).

The ratio of employees in good (4 star) convention hotels is normally from 0.8 per room in developed countries to 1.2 per room or more in developing regions.

Minimum toilet facilities (for up to 100)

	Males	Females
Water closets	4	5 (preferably 6)
Urinals	4	
Washbasins	5	5 (preferably 6)

Plus 1 WC and washbasin per 25 or part over 100. In the case of males, one in four of the additional WCs may be substituted by a urinal.

Typical net areas per 100 male or 100 female employees

Facility	m² (sq ft)
Sanitary facilities	25 (270)
Changing, lockers and showers	35 (380)
Staff meal areas (0.9 m²/seat) for up to 30% at any time	30–40 (320–430)
Security, time keeping and personnel	50 (540)

4.5.7 Administration and business services

Administration offices need to be located in several areas:

- front office – adjacent to the front desk;
- personnel – largely near employee facilities;
- engineering – near plant areas (also security monitoring);
- food and beverage sales – near banquet halls/function areas;
- general – flexible, but with access to front office.

The front office services usually include telephone operators, paging and communication services. In most convention hotels these are extended to provide a business services facility to guests, and this type of service is usually also available in congress and exhibition centres.

The range of business services may be extensive, covering:

- typing, copying/scanning needs, communications, marketing data, local information;
- photographic, television and editing work, preparation of slides and display material;
- private meeting and hospitality rooms, hired offices, secretarial assistance;
- deposit vaults and secure storage for documents and valuable items.

Hotel guestrooms also offer an increasing range of work-related and information facilities, including two or more ISDN lines for telephone, computer and facsimile transmissions, and interactive television screen systems (local information, booking/reservation services, personal account payment).

4.5.8 Leisure facilities

Leisure attractions are important in marketing hotels to both business and tourist groups. In city centre locations facilities are normally enclosed, as health, fitness or lifestyle suites, to ensure all-year round availability. Exceptions may apply, as in tropical climates, where an outdoor landscaped pool may also provide an attractive vista for surrounding bedrooms and restaurants.

Resort areas are aimed at the tourist demand and hotels provide extensive outdoor recreation, from poolside activities to tennis, golf, sailing and other sports. Indoor facilities may also be offered for out-of-season conventions and winter skiing seasons.

Leisure facilities represent a relatively high investment and may generate significant revenue from:

- local club membership subscriptions and sales;
- professional coaching and sports retail services;
- competition tournaments and promotional events;

- associated real estate sales (fairway houses, condomiums, marinas).

4.5.9 Indicative space standards

The examples illustrate typical areas and percentages of space for: (a) large convention hotels of high (4★) standard in city centres and (b) suburban/airport hotels of mid-standard (3★)

Facilities	City centre	area (m2) %	suburban	area (m2) %	Notes
Residential areas					
Number of guestrooms	400		200		
Number of storeys	12 + 2 basement		4 + 1		
Guestroom areas	400 × 8.0 × 3.75	= 12 000	400 × 7.4 × 3.65	= 5400	
5% suites (extra bays)	20 @ 30	= 600			
Circulation	+40%	= 5000	+35%	= 1890	1
Gross residential area (% of total)		17 600 71.0%		7290 75.9%	
Public areas					
Lobby	1.2 m² per room	= 480	0.8 m² per room	= 160	
Shops	2 @ 30 m²	= 60			
Main restaurant	100 @ 2.0m²	= 200	120 @ 1.6 m²	= 190	2
Coffee shop/café	250 @ 1.6 m²	= 400			
Speciality restaurant	60 @ 2.0 m²	= 120	80 @ 1.8 m²	= 140	2
Hotel bars	150 @ 1.5 m²	= 220	80 @ 1.4 m²	= 110	
Cocktail lounge	50 @ 1.6 m²	= 80			
Circulation: excluding lobby	+20%	= 310	+20%	= 120	
Gross public area (% of total)		1870 7.5%		720 7.5%	
Conference areas					
Ballroom	600 @ 1.0 m²	= 600	100 @ 1.0 m²	= 100	2
Foyer	600 @ 0.3 m²	= 180	100 @ 0.3 m²	= 30	
Conference rooms	300 @ 1.6 m²	= 480	80 @ 1.6 m²	= 130	2
Circulation, storage, business centre	140 + 60 + 70 m²	= 270	30 + 10 + 60 m²	= 80	
Gross conference areas (% of total)		1530 6.2%		340 3.5%	
Leisure Health Club	with indoor pool	= 450	no indoor pool	= 80	3
Circulation and storage	20%	= 90		= 20	
Gross leisure area (% of total)		540 2.2%		100 1.1%	
Administration					
Total including circulation (%)	400 @ 1.6 m²/room	= 640 2.6%	200 @ 1.2 m²/room	= 240 2.5%	
Back of house					
Main + satellite kitchens	400 @ 1.0 m²/cover	= 400	200 @ 0.7 m²/cover	= 140	
Banquet kitchen	600 @ 0.2 m²	= 120	100 @ 0.2 m²	= 20	
Circulation and storage	20% + 15%	= 180	20% + 10%	= 50	
Total food and beverage service (% of total)		700 2.8%		210 2.2%	
Receiving area and general stores	0.6 m²/room	= 240	0.4 m²/room	= 80	
Housekeeping	0.5 m²/room	= 200	0.4 m²/room	= 80	
Laundry	0.8 m²/room	= 320	0.7 m²/room	= 140	4
Engineers workshops & plant	1.8 m²/room	= 720	1.1 m²/room	= 220	4
Employee and personnel facilities	1.1 m²/room	= 440	0.9 m²/room	= 180	
Total back of house: gross (% of total)		1920 7.7%		700 7.3%	
Hotel total		24 800 100%		9600 100%	
Built area per room	62.0 m² (667 sq ft)		48.0 m² (517 sq ft)		

Notes
[1] Gross factors increase with restrictive sites and single loaded corridors
[2] Higher capacity depends on local market and competitive advantage
[3] Indoor pool may be warranted by club membership and feasibility
[4] Depends on extent of services contracted outside hotel.

4.6 ACCOMMODATION FOR DELEGATES

4.6.1 Hotel classification

There are advantages in housing all congress or convention activities, inclusive of accommodation and food services, in one establishment. This leads to better cohesion between delegates and control over their location, as well as savings in time and costs.

Where delegates and accompanying persons have to be accommodated elsewhere, a range of choice and price variation should be offered. It is also important to ensure there is close liaison between the hotels and main congress venue in relation to meal arrangements, leisure activities for accompanying persons and suitable means of transportation for transfers and tours.

Categories of hotels and other accommodation, together with prices, must be clearly defined and their locations shown on a street map of the area accompanied by general information. Hotel classifications generally fall into five grades, although there are many variations.

Rating	General characteristics
5 star	Deluxe hotels offering the highest international standards of facilities and furnishings together with impeccable services. Rooms are generously sized and appointed, and include a high ratio of suites
4 star	High class business and convention hotels furnished to a very high standard of comfort and having extensive facilities and services. All rooms have en-suite bathrooms. Most international chain hotels fall into this category
3 star	Similar, well appointed but less sophisticated hotels offering a wide range of amenities at a medium price. Large resort hotels of this grade often cater for packaged tourism
2 star	Simpler, comfortable accommodation, often in older hotels or budget-orientated accommodation. Services and amenities may be limited
1 star	Economy grade accommodation with good basic facilities. Food services are usually limited or separate, and bathrooms may need to be shared

Most tourism authorities operate some form of grading or classification system, and international hotel companies specify their own standards for branding and marketing purposes.

4.6.2 Room descriptions

Standard terms used to categorize rooms are:

- single – occupied by one person;
- double – one large bed for two persons;
- twin – two single beds;
- twin double – two double beds;

- studio or executive – room with convertible beds for use as a parlour or bedroom;
- suite – parlour with one or more bedrooms;
- junior suite – room partitioned into sleeping and parlour areas;
- duplex – two storey suite with internal stairway;
- lanai – room with balcony overlooking water or garden;
- hospitality – function room or parlour for entertaining.

4.7 INCENTIVE TRAVEL REQUIREMENTS

4.7.1 Roles of incentive travel

Incentive travel is aimed at identified groups within a company or organization whose individual efforts can directly affect the way the company is able to achieve its set goals.

The target groups may be employees, sales representatives, agents, dealers or retail outlets.

The objectives of a programme may be to reward performance, engender loyalty, achieve higher sales or profits, promote the introduction of new lines or products and/or create corporate bonding and exchange of ideas.

In devising programmes and organizing events, companies may use the services of professional incentive travel managers meeting standards laid down by the Society of Incentive Travel Executives (SITE) and other representative bodies. A comprehensive programme will need to:

- define company goals, the participating groups, time scales and means of assessment;
- decide appropriate types of incentives and how these are organized and implemented;
- evaluate results, short- and long-term benefits and future strategies for the company.

4.7.2 Incentive travel products

Incentive travel borders on corporate hospitality and team building activities, and may include similar events. Depending on location, the numbers of award winners taking part in any travel programme is usually in the order of 15–50 and, in every case, they are encouraged to bring wives or partners. For large groups, cruise ships may be hired; others may use scheduled or charter aircraft to fly to the destination. All arrangements from start to finish must be highly organized and aimed at providing a rewarding, memorable experience.

Selection of products	Requirements in general
Destination	Exotic, unusual, exciting or sophisticated. The image is important – it should not be that of a routine place for holidays
Venue	High quality hotels offering an appropriate social atmosphere, services and facilities
Recreation	Wide range of organized activities (golf, tennis, shooting, sailing etc.) plus opportunities for relaxation (pool, bars, entertainment)
Visits	Courier-accompanied programme of work-related[1], general interest and social/hospitality visits to selected places and events
Facilities	Large meeting room for group welcome, receptions, address by the chairman and award ceremony. Suites of seminar rooms for exchange of ideas and proposals are also likely to be required
Gifts	Mementoes of the places, prizes for competitors, gifts for the partners, floral bouquets and decorations, complimentary fruit, drinks and gifts in rooms
Transport	From home (limousine) to and from airport, courier assistance, organized luggage, lounge and flight arrangements, ground transport and courier services throughout at the destination

[1] The extent of work-related visits depends on the interests of the client group. They may include invitations to company sites or research and development centres, or opportunities to see and try new products in action. Alternative visits should be arranged for partners.

5 Other types of conference and training centres

5.1 EXECUTIVE CONFERENCE CENTRES

5.1.1 Concept

The executive conference centre is a relatively new development, stimulated by demands for higher standard meeting facilities for small groups in a pleasant, distraction-free environment that is dedicated to this use.

In Europe, conference centres fall broadly into two main types; those that have been converted from existing buildings such as mansions and hotels, and properties that have been built specifically for this purpose. The latter stem from the introduction of the original Scanticon centre in Aarhus, Denmark, in 1969, and this concept has been widely developed in the United States, Denmark, Sweden and other countries.

The main features of executive conference centres are:

- conference facilities specifically planned around the needs of small meetings;
- high technology services and equipment with professionally trained support staff;
- inclusive food and beverage services and comfortable residential accommodation;
- opportunities for recreation and group activities outside work sessions;
- location in a catchment area of major market users, with convenient access;
- a quiet, landscaped setting.

5.1.2 Marketing considerations

Although most involve groups are of only 20–50 participants, small meetings represent the largest segment of the total meetings market (see 1.5.) They include a high percentage of the corporate meetings, particularly those which have a pattern of repeat requirements, such as management meetings and training sessions. The need for small meetings is constantly increasing with changes in law, finance, technology and management structures, making it necessary for both companies and professionals to keep abreast of new developments.

Market sectors	Examples of activities
Corporate	
Management	Executive meetings, management development programmes
Sales	Regional sales force meetings, product information presentations
Training	Company induction programmes, management training courses
Association	
Professions	Professional development programmes, pre-qualification courses
Others	Educational courses, special interest groups, society meetings

Major markets for executive conference centres are the large companies involved in insurance, banking, accounting and financial services, telecommunications, pharmacy and medical supplies and franchising services.

Executive meetings are a specialized market, and the location of conference centres is critical. Although some may be remote retreats for highly confidential and sensitive meetings at a political or senior management level, most centres need to be conveniently accessible to a well-developed business catchment area. Locations such as the periphery of business and research parks, university grounds and quiet country sites relatively near airports and cities are often preferred.

The feasibility of investment may warrant provision for dual markets, which will affect planning and operation:

Main conference users	Other complementary markets
Monday to Friday cycles	Weekend leisure breaks, social and special interest groups
Outside vacation periods	Tourist accommodation, educational programmes
Gaps in programmes	Organized business activities, sports, team building
Country hotels and resorts	Separate wings or blocks dedicated to conference use

Educational and special interest groups include associations and societies whose members have cultivated interests in the arts (such as courses in art, languages, literature, music) or more specialized fields.

Scanticon Borupgård Helsinger, Denmark

Comwell first introduced the executive conference concept with the Scanticon Centre in Aarhus in 1969. By 1999, Comwell Scanticon operated 10 units in Scandinavia, both in self-owned and managed properties, specifically aimed at the small meetings market. All the meeting rooms are adaptable to meet customer requirements, and each area can operate independently from the others.

Opened in 1989, Scanticon Borupgård Helsingor is the centre most frequently used for international meetings in Denmark. It was created from a restored ancient manor farmhouse and extended by 12 000 m³ of new buildings arranged in the original courtyard plan (a). The facilities extend around a central entrance lobby, providing: a block of 149 double rooms including four suites (b); five lecture rooms for 350–76 people plus 16 smaller conference and syndicate rooms, all with high technology equipment (c); an à la carte restaurant; comprehensive banquet functions; and extensive recreation facilities (pool, fitness rooms, tennis, volley ball, games rooms).

Operators: Comwell Scanticon
Architects: Friis & Moltke MAA
Contractor: H Hoffman & Son,
Photographs: Helge Kassgaard Oleson

(a)

(b)

(c)

Scanticon Borupgård Helsinger, Denmark

Keys:

Site plan
1 Conference wing
2 Guest room wing
3 Landscaped court
4 Administration
5 Restaurant wing
6 Kitchen entrance
7 Mechanical equipment
8 Conference/syndicate rooms
9 Conference/dining/lounge area
10 Pond
11 Tennis court

First and ground floor plans
1 Foyer
2 Administration
3 Guest rooms
4 A la carte restaurant
5 Bar
6 Conference restaurant
7 Café
8 Kitchen
9 Hall
10 Reception hall
11 Lounge
12 Meeting room
13 Auditorium
14 AV-studio
15 Banquet room
16 Personnel canteen

First floor

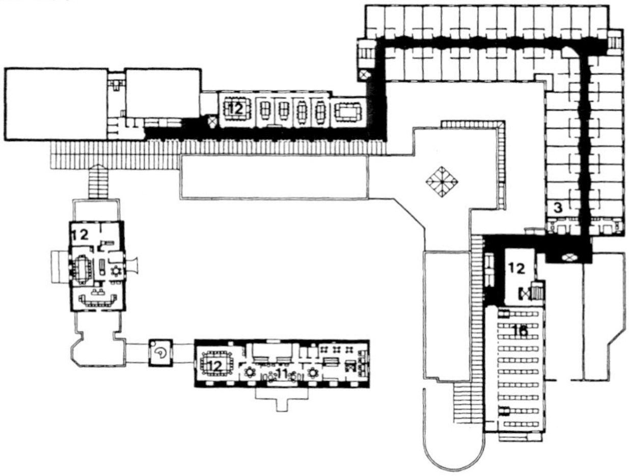

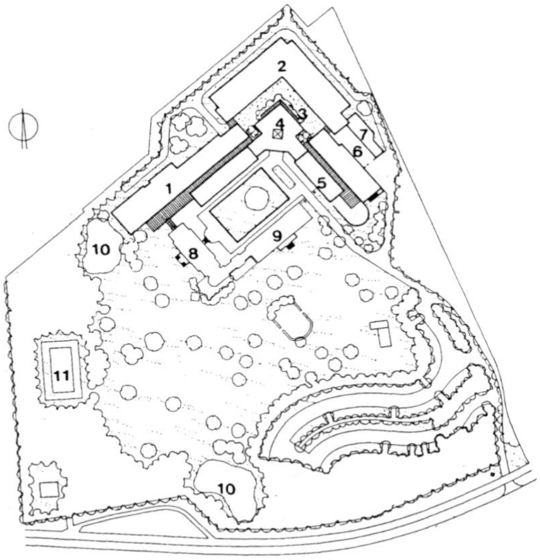

Site plan

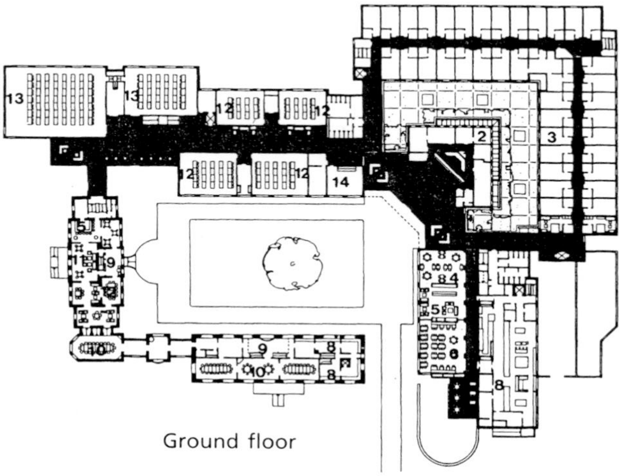

Ground floor

5.1.3 Variations

Executive conference centres are normally operated on a purely commercial basis and are available for use generally, with quoted and negotiated prices.

Corporate centres may be provided by large companies to accommodate their own requirements for in-house management training and development, either on an exclusive basis or partly available for general hire. The premises may be company owned or leased, and operated either directly or under management contract. Many corporate centres are non-residential, although arrangements may be made to use nearby hotel accommodation. The range includes employee training centres and conference centres for middle and senior management meetings.

Country hotel and resort conference centres are also operated as commercial enterprises. They are invariably set in extensive grounds, with championship standard golf, tennis, and/or other sports of appeal to a business clientele. As a rule these facilities are marketed to both conference users and, at other times, to other high spend tourists. Both guestrooms and public areas are usually larger to accommodate this market variation.

University conference centres offer en suite guestrooms of a higher standard than student accommodation and a dedicated conference facility to attract year-round professional and business markets. Often these are associated with postgraduate business schools and other MBA and management/professional development programmes as a profit-generating extension to university academic courses. Conference centres may be purpose-built or converted from other properties and they may be owned and operated by the university or leased to and operated by commercial companies under contract.

Robinson College, Cambridge, UK

Located in a 140 ha (350 acre) riverside site with a business and leisure village, this Executive Conference and Training Centre opened in 1999 and offers two conference rooms (240 seats combined), seven training and 16 syndicate rooms. There are 80 double en suite bedrooms in a linked building, and more on site. Extensive facilities include an 11.5 m swimming pool, spa, health suite, studio, fitness testing and therapy.

Robinson College (Cambridge) Management Training Ltd

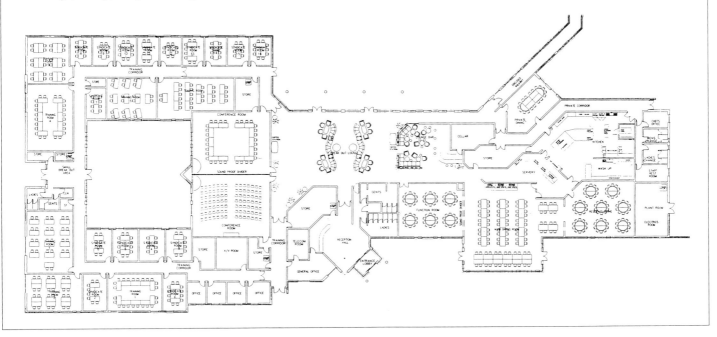

Centres in the United States are generally larger than those in Europe and typically provide 220–340 guestrooms – about twice the size of most European developments. Guestroom areas, particularly in resort-based conference centres, also tend to be more generous. Many of the American conference and training centres are operated by companies for their own in-house management development and training programmes, and have specific design requirements. Although this chapter provides data that are largely common to all regions as a basis for planning, reference may also be made to American examples in Penner (1991).

5.1.4 Planning executive conference centres

Market feasibility studies: Market surveys take into account the nature and scale of commercial activities in the region, economic indicators of growth, socio-economic and demographic characteristics and specific market generators (headquarters of large companies and institutions, universities, hospitals, government offices, airports). They indicate the size and value of potential demand, projected revenues and operating costs, and the likely return on investment.

Location: Accessibility to the main markets is critical, but sites must be in a quiet, distraction-free environment (rural, suburban). Most centres are low-rise buildings (one to three storeys) in landscaped grounds, ensuring a degree of privacy and seclusion. The buildings may be arranged around courtyards or extended into wings to facilitate separation of the activities.

Zoning: Residential, public amenity, conference and back of house areas must be zoned to facilitate operation and management as well as to minimize disturbance. As a rule, the entrance lobby is not only the point of reception and information, but also serves as the hub leading directly to the conference rooms, public areas and residential buildings or floors.

Parking: The approach to the entrance is usually via a circular drive. After unloading, cars are often parked in a separate area away from the buildings. A ratio of 1.2 total parking spaces per guestroom is normally required, but it may need to be based on the capacity of the largest hall for day meetings.

Size: To provide the individual attention required, executive conference centres are relatively small. In Europe they tend to fall within the range of 100–160 guestrooms, whilst in the United States centres more typically extend from 220–340 guestrooms.

Space: Depending on the location and market structure (particularly the ratio of day meetings), the residential areas usually take up about half the total built area:

Edinburgh Conference Centre at the Heriot-Watt University, Scotland

This purpose-built conference centre set in the parkland university campus opened in 1990 and was extended in 1999 to provide a 620–seat conference venue, 700 m² of exhibition space and up to eight seminar rooms. Seventy en suite bedrooms are available all year round, plus 1224 bedrooms during the vacations. Near Edinburgh airport and the motorway network, the centre is within 1 hour's drive of 60 per cent of Scotland's business community.

Architect: Merrylees and Robertson
Client: Heriot Watt University Estate Office

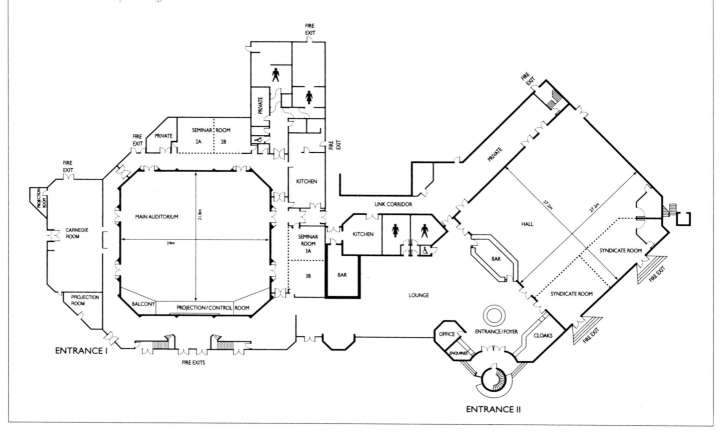

Allocation	Range (% of built area)
Residential areas	48–52
Public areas	8–10
Conference areas	17–21
Recreation areas	3–5
Back of house	11–15
Total built area	100

A more detailed analysis is in section 5.1.9.

Comparisons: Executive conference centres allow more generous spaces for meetings, lounges and dining areas than convention hotels. Most also include an indoor pool and health suite. With relatively few guestrooms to support this infrastructure, the total built area per room is often 80–95 m² (860–1022 sq ft), some 30–50% larger than that of convention hotels.

5.1.5 Guestrooms and public areas

Guestrooms are usually designed to accommodate both conference users and other weekend/vacation markets. As in business hotels, most rooms are based on a double (1.5 m × 2 m) or king-sized bed, allowing a separate area near the window for a workstation.

To allow market flexibility, a convertible sofa bed is often included and a proportion of rooms may offer 1.0 m × 2 m twin beds. All rooms must have en suite bathrooms, and one or more must be suitable for disabled visitors. The décor is generally light and stylish, suitable for either male or female visitors.

Extensive power points, two ISDN telephone lines, television screen connections for personal computers and high levels of illumination over the work areas are essential.

The lobby is the centre of circulation, reception and information. In addition to hotel functions, the front desk specifically provides information and assistance for organizers and participants when conferences are being held. The lobby area usually extends into two or more small lounge areas as places for waiting-assembly and individual discussions.

Restaurants: Food and beverage outlets are generally

Scanticon Denver, Colorado, USA

Located in a landscaped business park with architecture reflecting the character of the Colorado High Plains, the Scanticon Executive Conference Centre, Denver, has a built area of 35 500 m²
(350 000 sq ft) extending over five floors. On the upper floors are hotel rooms and suites, whilst on the lower floors are restaurants, lounges, a health club, boutiques, banquet hall lobby and
conference areas. The conference rooms and restaurants extend into two parallel wings linked to the main building by glass-roofed promenades. There are 33 sound-proofed meetings rooms equipped
with high technology services.

Architects: Friss & Moltke A/S
Operator: Scanticon Corporation Princetown
Engineers: KKBNA Inc. Jaros, Baum & Bolles
Photograph: Timothy Horsley

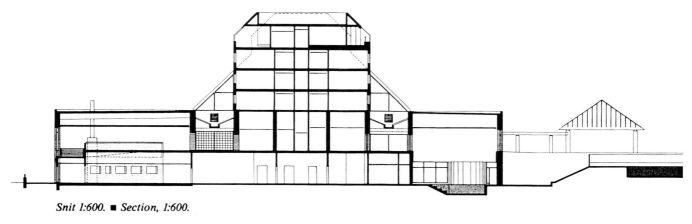

Snit 1:600. ▪ *Section, 1:600.*

rationalized to one main dining zone adjacent to the kitchens, but with separate conference dining room, *à la carte* restaurant and café areas to accommodate the needs of different conference parties and other visitors. Seating arrangements must be flexible to provide for changing conference groupings and social clusters.

A large banquet hall is normally required to accommodate the largest groups (typically seating up to 350 at a banquet), as well as receptions and other events.

The main bar-lounge is usually adjacent to the dining areas for practical reasons, but also to generate social atmosphere. One or more coffee-bar-lounge areas are also required

near groups of meeting rooms. Lounges are usually planned to provide distinctive areas of seating with which conference groups can identify.

Circulation areas are designed to provide a contrast to the indoor work sessions. Often the corridors and foyers are extensively glazed, and feature indoor landscaping and works of art. Foyers often have adjacent patios to allow breaks to spill outside.

Recreation and healthy lifestyle feature strongly in residential conference centres. In Europe some centres include an indoor pool and sauna as well as a fitness/lifestyle suite, and a few offer spa services. The grounds usually include tennis courts and pitches for group competitions.

Scanticon Denver, Colorado, USA

Key:
 1 Main entrance
 2 Reception
 3 Lobby
 4 Street
 5 Conference room
 6 Conference service
 7 Meeting room
 8 Control room
 9 TV production studio
10 Graphic art studio
11 Offices
12 Toilets
13 Private dining room
14 Gourmet restaurant
15 Kitchen
16 Specialty restaurant
17 Conference restaurant
18 Banquet room
19 Bar/pub
20 Fire side lounge
21 Auditorium
22 Board room
23 Storage
24 Technical equipment
25 Service facilities
26 Exercise room
27 Indoor swimming pool
28 Locker rooms
29 Golfclub facilities
30 Employee facilities
31 Outdoor terrace

5.1.6 Conference areas

The unit space per person allowed in conference rooms is more generous than that in hotels, and the required seating plans dictate dimensions for the rooms Practically all rooms – even those described as auditoria – use flat floors to allow frequent changes in seating layouts. Stepped floors with fixed seating in a lecture theatres or with fitted tables in amphitheatre arrangements are not normally required for executive conferences, but may be provided in more specialized company-operated training centres (see 5.2.2).

Depending on the market structure, conference areas generally provide three sizes of conference rooms and a large number of small meeting or breakout rooms. The latter are used for face-to-face groups of 10–20 persons, and together account for some 40 per cent of the conference area.

Space per seat

The space required per seat in a conference room varies with the set-up required (theatre style, classroom, boardroom etc.), the standards of comfort to be provided and the room dimensions. In conference centres, seating plans are based on high executive standards, using comfortable chairs and 0.6 or 0.75 m wide (24–30 in) tables. For classroom and similar arrangements, 1.5 m long (5 ft) tables are normally used with two seats.

Larger centres usually include a ballroom to accommodate the maximum market group size, which may be indicated by local as well as residential demands. A centre with 250 guestrooms is likely to require a ballroom (seating up to 350), one large conference room, three or four medium-sized rooms, four or five small conference rooms and 20 or more small break-out rooms with similar sizes to those indicated above.

The main conference rooms are usually grouped together and entered through a spacious foyer. Break-out rooms are more commonly clustered into suites of rooms to facilitate organization. Room divisions may be provided to increase the flexibility of space, but the partitions must provide high noise insulation standards. All conference and break-out rooms allow natural lighting, but solar screens and blackout blinds must be fitted.

5.1.7 Technical support

One of the marketing advantages of executive conference centres is the extent of technical equipment and support services provided. The main conference rooms are equipped with projection rooms, often with two rooms served by a central back-projection area. Support facilities usually include:

- conference service manager's desk and office; trained staff;
- audio-visual aids – front and rear screen projection rooms with separate staff entrances;
- a central equipment distribution centre, stores and workshops; a separate room for clients' equipment;
- a graphics centre – for signs, badges, printing, copying, artwork and photography (darkroom);
- trainers' offices – two or three offices and a common room;
- coffee and refreshments pantries adjacent to break-out areas;
- Furniture and materials stores.

5.1.8 Typical facilities in conference rooms

All meeting rooms are well equipped with audio-visual aid equipment, and the larger rooms have permanent booths for slide and video projection. Seating and facility arrangements are often flexible to meet specific client requirements. A typical arrangement would provide:

Typical facilities

150 guestrooms	Area m^2	Theatre seats	Classroom seats	Hollow square seats	Boardroom seats	Open square seats[1]
Large conference room[2]	300	200	120			
Large conference room	150	100	60			
Medium conference rooms × 2	100	60	40			
Small conference rooms × 3	75	40	24			
Meeting rooms × 6[3]	50–60			20–22		12–14
Meeting rooms × 10[4]	30–40				12–18	

[1] All seating capacities allow for average comfort and spacing, but depend on room dimensions.

[2] May also be used as a banquet hall seating up to 250, but this may present zoning problems. Banquets are more commonly accommodated in a separate hall or ballroom.

[3] Used for small group meetings and break-out sessions. Chairs are often grouped round tables boardroom style. Alternatively, chairs may be fitted with writing tablets and arranged informally to suit discussion groups.

[4] Small rooms are usually more space efficient for face-to-face groups.

- a permanent teaching wall with hinged panels or hanging rail system having one or more white boards, a pin board (tackable), flip chart and one or two screens;
- slide and video projectors (in projection room) and an overhead projector;
- comfortable chairs and writing tables; armchairs with writing tablets may also be provided;
- lighting switches with separate circuits for general lighting, accent lighting on teaching surfaces and wall washers; controlled dimming with operation of mechanized blinds.

Larger rooms usually have two screens for dual presentations, and a permanent or removable stage. The video projector is usually permanently fitted. More sophisticated equipment may be available for video-conferencing and/or data presentation (see 6.5).

5.1.9 Calculation of space requirements

Centre with 150 guestrooms	m^2	% of total area	Notes
Guestrooms, 150 @ 28.0 m²	4200		1
Suites, 4 @ 28.0 m	112		
Common lounge areas, 4 @ 12	48		
Circulation, service areas, 45%	1960		2
Total residential areas (gross)	6320	52.0	
Public areas:			
Lobby, 1.5 m per room	225		
Conference dining room, 80 @ 1.5 m²	120		
À la carte dining room, 40 @ 1.7 m²	68		
Café, 30 @ 1.6 m²	48		
Private dining rooms, 50 @ 2.5 m²	125		
Main lounge, 70 @ 1.8 m²	126		
Individual lounges, 80 @ 1.5 m²	120		
Circulation, cloakrooms, 25%	208		
Total public areas (gross)	1040	8.6	
Additional areas:			3
Banquet hall, 300 @ 1.2 m²	360		4
Foyer and support areas, 150 m²>+ 20%	260		
Conference areas:			
Large conference room, 120 @ 2.5 m²	300		5
Large conference room, 60 @ 2.5 m²	150		6
Medium conference rooms, 2 × 40 @ 2.5 m	200		6
Small conference rooms, 2 × 24 @ 3.0 m	144		6
Meeting/break-out rooms, 16 total, 240 @ 2.2 m	528		7
Total conference rooms (net)	1322		8
Projection and equipment rooms	120		9
AVA and graphics room	50		
Assembly and circulation space, 40%	598		
Total conference and support areas	2090	17.2	10
Recreation:			
Enclosed swimming pool	250		11
Exercise room/gymnasium	75		

Centre with 150 guestrooms (cont.)	m^2	% of total area	Notes
Changing, lockers, toilets	75		
Circulation, plant and storage, 25%	100		
Total recreation built area	500	4.1	
Administration:			
Front office, reception and conference desk	220		
Executive, accounting and sales offices	150		
Circulation and storage	130		
Total administration: gross built area	500	4.1	
Back of house:			
Main kitchen and stores	350		
Satellite kitchens	100		
Housekeeping and laundry (mainly off-site)	200		
Engineering and maintenance	450		
Employee facilities	320		12
Loading dock and circulation, 20%	280		
Total back of house (gross areas)	1700	14.0	
Total built area for centre	12 150	100	
Built area per room	81.0 m² (872 sq ft)/room		

Notes:
[1] Guestrooms in resort conference centres are generally larger at 30 m². In American executive conference centres, guestrooms range from 300–325 sq ft (28.0–30.2 m²).
[2] Gross factors are relatively high (40–45%).
[3] Larger conference centres (250 rooms) include a large ballroom/banquet hall. In other cases, this additional facility will depend on the local demand. The addition of a ballroom increases the total built area/guestroom to 85.1 m² (916 sq ft)/room.
[4] Including banquet service and storage areas.
[5] 120 in classroom style, 150–200 in theatre-style seating.
[6] Classroom style
[7] Face-to-face meetings in closed square or boardroom arrangements. Rooms in various sizes to seat 24, 22, 18, 16, 14, 12 and 10. Density depends on dimensions, and varies from 2.0 to 2.5 m² per seat. Open square groups require 3.0–3.5 m² per seat.
[8] Includes some dual use private dining rooms.
[9] Projection rooms sited between conference rooms
[10] Minimum; conference areas range between 17 and 20 per cent of the total.
[11] Based on 20 × 8 m or smaller swimming pool. Minimum deck area with jet pool in surround.
[12] Excludes employee sleeping accommodation.

5.2 OTHER TYPES OF CONFERENCE CENTRES

5.2.1 Conference resort and country hotel centres

Residential conference centres and country hotels that offer high quality recreation facilities, such as championship golf courses, invariably cater for tourists as well as conference groups. To ensure compatibility, marketing must be aimed at the top socio-economic segments and high standards of accommodation, facilities and service are demanded.

The conference requirements are similar to those of executive centres, but with larger guestrooms of 30 m² (325 sq ft) or more, and more extensive public facilities will be required to accommodate non-conference guests, if necessary with separate restaurant and lounge areas. Conference zoning is particularly critical, and the conference areas may be linked to wings of guestrooms dedicated to conference users.

In vacation resorts an alternative approach is to provide a convention/conference centre which can contribute to the marketing of all the hotels in the resort. Such centres are non-residential, often publicly funded through the municipal authority, and aimed at a wide market coverage. Details of convention centres are given in Chapter 2.

5.2.2 Corporate conference and training centres

Many large corporations have requirements for:

- management development centres – for middle and senior management conferences, meetings and seminars;
- human resource training centres – for lower management/supervisor courses, company orientation programmes and employee career development.

Management development

The types of accommodation and facilities required for management conferences and meetings are similar to those for executive centres. Depending on the structure and size of the company, the options may be to use other commercial facilities (conference centres, hotels), lease these services or provide a company-operated conference centre, which may be non-residential or residential (fully or in part). Design requirements are generally similar to those for executive centres, but may be dictated by particular company requirements (size of groups, inclusion of amphitheatres, technical systems).

Human resource training centres are generally purpose-designed around company operations, and have many similarities to educational institutions. Accommodation is invariably in single study-bedrooms, and the conference facilities include tiered lecture theatres or/and amphitheatres with sophisticated AVA facilities and special requirements such as computer rooms and resource learning centres.

Corporate centres are usually located near to the headquarters of the company or its regional office.

5.2.3 University conference centres

Almost all universities market their facilities for conferences and exhibitions. In the main these are concentrated in the long vacation periods, when the university teaching facilities and student accommodation are not required for the main academic programmes. Conferences may be initiated by the univer-

sity as part of organized programmes and courses, or as individual seminars or congresses stemming from academic interests. Space and services may be also be hired by independent organizers of educational programmes, language courses, meetings and exhibitions.

Universities and colleges offer many marketing advantages over other venues: they are often located in attractive grounds with good sports facilities; the teaching facilities are usually extensive, modern and well equipped; accommodation, food and other services are relatively inexpensive; and the association with the university may lend prestige to the event.

In general, the main limitations of universities as venues for business conferences arise from:

- the limited period available, vacations being out of phase with the main seasons of conference demand;
- the quality of student accommodation, which is set by other economic criteria and is often inadequate for more mature business visitors;
- the design of classrooms and lecture theatres, which is mainly dictated by larger group teaching needs and may not be able to meet the standards and flexibility required for conference organization.

Universities market their facilities both directly and collectively through university accommodation consortia. New forms of accommodation are often planned to offer higher standards with en suite bedrooms and combination suites, and dedicated conference centres may be provided as part of management faculties or business schools.

Planned university conference centres invariably have a dual role: they accommodate teaching programmes for intermittent short courses and they are available at other times for professional and management conferences. They may use other university accommodation set aside for this purpose, or include residential units as part of the centre. In some cases, a historic university building has been converted as a distinctive conference venue (for example, Warwick University); in others the centre has been purpose-built as a self-contained facility within the campus grounds (for example, Princeton University).

Space requirements for university conference facilities are broadly similar to those for executive centres (see 5.1), but recreational facilities are invariably those provided for the university as a whole, and many of the back of house services are also centralized.

5.3 OTHER VENUES FOR MEETINGS

5.3.1 Non-residential conference centres

Non-residential facilities targeting the markets for conference facilities in cities range from banqueting halls to purpose-designed conference centres. The latter may be operated commercially as an independent venue serving the local business district, or be part of a serviced office complex, business centre or World Trade Centre marketed to other users as well as a service to the office tenancies.

The facilities are usually offered on a half-day or full-day basis, inclusive of refreshments, business lunches or/and evening functions.

5.3.2 Institutions and charitable organizations

A wide range of residential and non-residential centres are provide by institutions and other organizations in pursuit of their educational or training objectives. Many of these are operated on a non-profit making basis and are limited, for example, to participating members, trades unions or religious orders. Rooms at college centres may be available for commercial leasing or hire on a daily or residential basis.

5.3.3 Unusual venues

Many sporting complexes have space designed for multiple use, which is available both for hospitality events associated with games or races and at other time for business meetings. Invariably these are non-residential, but large new sports venues often include a hotel as part of the complex, and others have arrangements to use hotels in the vicinity. The facilities may be limited to a conference suite of rooms or extend to the use of the whole sports arena for large conventions or exhibits.

5.3.4 Cruise ships

Cruise ships, ferries and other pleasure vessels can often be hired for meetings and incentive travel packages. The public rooms can usually be easily adapted for conventions, banquets and entertainment, and the larger suites may be suitable for break-out sessions. Travel itineraries vary widely, and may include outbound and/or return flights to facilitate exchange visits between two centres or enable delegates from more than one country to participate.

Cruise ships and out-of-season ferries may also be used for promotional visits to potential or growing market destinations. The larger public rooms are laid out with selected exhibits, and other areas are used to provide facilities for hospitality and private meetings.

6 Technical requirements

6.1 ACOUSTIC DESIGN OF MEETING ROOMS AND AUDITORIA

6.1.1 Importance of acoustics

Acoustic considerations influence many aspects of design for meeting rooms (such as the layout, volume, floor raking interior linings and ceiling construction) as well as equipment requirements (sound amplification, interpretation systems). Moreover, in many cases congress auditoria have to enable changes to be made in acoustics for various theatrical and musical performances. Approaches to acoustic design are also changing, with a shift away from dependence on physical characteristics and towards the use of electronics to achieve the desired acoustic effects.

6.1.2 Variations in sound levels

The subjective loudness of sound may be expressed by a logarithmic relationship between the stimulus strength and perceived hearing response. These comparative levels of sound power, pressure and intensity are usually scaled in decibels (dB), the measurement being compared with the average auditory threshold as the reference level.

The loudness scale of human hearing from the auditory threshold (0.002 Pa) to the threshold of pain (200 Pa) is 140 dB. Sound levels change rapidly, and the dynamic range (ratio of maximum to minimum short time average) of live and recorded speech is about 36 dB, with peaks of up to +12 dB. Recorded music is similar, but live music such as a symphony concert has a larger dynamic range of around 70 dB with peaks of +15 dB.

Subjective impressions of loudness also depend on the frequency of sounds, the human ear having maximum sensitivity in the region of 3–4 kHz. This non-linear relationship between sound pressure levels and frequency can be represented **by equal loudness contours**.

Measuring instruments are designed to respond in a similar way to the human ear, having electronic A, B or C weighting networks. For acoustic measurements, the A-curve is generally used.

6.1.3 Characteristics of speech

Speech is a complex flow of sounds initiating from oscillations of the vocal folds forming **harmonic partials**, which are then amplified by resonance in the cavities of the vocal tract and articulated by movements of the lips, tongue, teeth and palate interrupting or constricting the breath stream.

Speech sounds, called **phonemes**, differ from each other in the characteristic way they build up and decay, their duration, harmonic composition, total intensity and distribution of intensity over the frequency range.

The English language includes about 16 different vowel sounds and some 22 consonant sounds. Other European languages have similar basic characteristics.

Vowel sounds are mainly carried by the harmonics of the resonant or formant frequencies of the voice. They predominate both in intensity and duration, giving the voice its individual identity.

Consonant sounds are nearly all of a transient nature. They are short, rapidly changing, often expressed without definite tone and extend over the higher frequencies of the speech range. The energy content of the unvoiced consonant is less than 1/1000th of that of the average vowel. Consonants are easily masked by other noise and, because of their high frequency content, they tend to become distorted by absorption and transmission loss.

The ear is less sensitive to high frequencies, especially in older age groups. Yet it is the consonants that convey most of the information needed for comprehension, and these play a major role in speech communication. Congress halls should ensure the articulation loss (A_{is}) is less than 10 per cent consonants.

Rapidly changing in amplitude and frequency, the elemental sounds, lasting about 30 ms (0.03 s), are combined to form a sequence of syllables, words and phrases. In English each syllable lasts about 100–125 ms, and the interval between syllables is about 100 ms.

The speed of speech varies both with the situation and the individual, from a formal address of some 120–160 words per minute to a typical conversation with 160–200 words per minute, the latter corresponding to about four syllables per second.

Speech perception

Good perception of speech involves a frequency range of 200–6000 Hz. Frequencies between 700–5000 Hz account for some 80 per cent of speech intelligibility, and the frequencies between 1000 and 2500 Hz for 50 per cent.

Relative weightings of octave bands affecting speech intelligibility

Octave band	63	125	250	500	1000	2000	4000	8000
Weighting factor	0	0	4	13	20	31	26	6

The contribution of sounds over this frequency range is used to measure the articulation index (AI).

In each frequency band there is a dynamic range of about 25–35 dB from the loudest to the faintest sounds. Changing the level of loudness by raising or lowering the voice affects the whole frequency range to about the same extent.

The voice power of individual speakers varies considerably from about 40 up to 150 microwatts (μW). Without amplification, the weaker voice is unlikely to be heard beyond the fourth row of a large auditorium.

6.1.4 Acoustic design for speech

Two key considerations are involved in setting out design objectives for good acoustics in a hall or auditorium:

Psychological conditions

- The relationship between the speaker and audience: this is affected by the size of audience, circumstances, spaciousness of surroundings, relative positions and the elevation of the speaker.
- Arousal and appreciation levels: these refer to environmenal and physical comfort, sound strength and clarity, masking, distortion and distraction.

Graphical analysis of sound

(a) Human auditory sensation area showing typical spectrums for the male voice and for music.
(b) Contribution to intelligibility from frequency bands, each dot representing 0.01 contribution to the articulation index. Frequencies between 1000 and 2500 Hz account for 50 per cent of speech intelligibility. Each band has about 30 dB range of amplitude
(c) Effect of distance on sound. The graph represents an open-air condition (absorption unity) with sound pressure levels relative to the sound power level reducing by 6 dB for each doubling of distance from the source. In a room or hall average reductions, each time the distance is doubled, range from about 5 dB (highly absorbent linings and large volumes) to 4 dB (medium conditions) to 3 dB (with sound reinforcement by surface reflection and reverberation), to 2 dB

or less (small rooms with low surface absorption). Attenuation is increased by the occupants and furnishings
(d) Effect of masking by background noise showing PNC 25 and 30 superimposed on the reduced sound spectrum. The articulation index is represented by the number of dots above the appropriate PNC curve. In the example there are 29 dots above PNC 25 (appropriate for a large auditorium or lecture theatre) representing an AI of 0.29.
Source:
(1) Turner, N. (1974). Acoustic performance standards for offices. Building Services Engineering, 41, 223–30.
(2) Bains, A. (1973). Information sheet, Environment 1, Acoustic factors. AJ handbook of Office Building. Architects' Journal, 28, November, 1329–35.

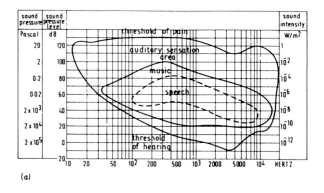

(a)

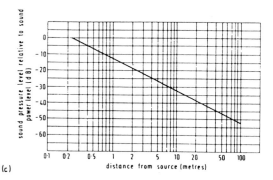

(c)

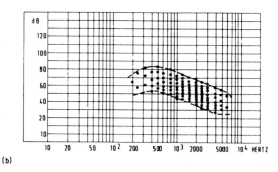

(b)

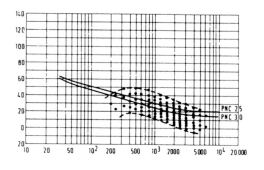

(d)

Physical requirements

- Good direct sound: direct sound is determined by shape and size of the hall, the distance to rear and side seating positions, row-to-row sight line clearances and the design of balconies.
- Early reinforcement of direct sound: this is achieved by the position and construction of reflecting panels and the provision of electronic amplification.
- Freedom from discrete echoes and strong envelopmental sound: this is provided by selective absorption and diffusion and the adjustment of reverberation for differing conditions.
- Control of noise entry: control of masking/distracting noise is effected by the planning, zoning and separation of areas, appropriate noise insulation standards and acoustic specifications for engineering services and equipment.
- Multipurpose use: acoustic regulation of speech/music includes the adjustment of the shape, size and boundary conditions of stage and auditorium, and the electronic modification of the growth and decay characteristics of sound.

6.1.5 Direct sound

Plans and sections of an auditorium are largely determined by the need to ensure the maximum solid angle of sound from the speaker is directed at the audience. This, together with a clear view of the person speaking and any visual aid presentations, may be provided by raising successive rows of the audience on stepped tiers (see 2.4) and/or raising the relative height of the person speaking on a stage or dais. To avoid eye and neck muscle strain, the angle of elevation from the nearest seats should not exceed 30°.

The voice produces largely directional sounds, with a significant reduction in sound power in the higher frequencies (on which intelligibility largely depends) outside an arc of 140°. As far as possible, the auditorium or hall seating should fall within this angle. To some extent, this can be compensated by the use of angled reflecting panels set above and behind the speaker's position.

Binaural listening helps to localize voice signals and to separate meaningful information from other background noise. Directional effects are also important when designing for the reinforcement of sound (whether speech or music) by reflection or electronic amplification.

Reductions in direct sound can result from:

- obstructions causing strong sound shadows (and variations in frequency diffraction);
- the distance from the speaker – discounting the effects of the enclosure, an attenuation of 6 dB results each time this distance is doubled, producing a typical reduction in AI of between 0.15 and 0.20;
- air absorption of the sound – this occurs particularly at high frequencies (altering tone colour) and low humidities (RH 15–30 per cent);

- absorption at the boundaries, around the audience and contents of the room and through grilles and other openings.

Background noise tends to mask the sound, particularly in trying to distinguish consonants. Even with a signal-to-noise intensity ratio of +3 dB, speech is barely perceptible. A ratio of +7 dB is required to produce reasonable clarity, and up to 18 dB to ensure clear distinction between consonants (see 6.2.2).

6.1.6 Audible distance

Apart from variations in the voice power and clear articulation of the speaker, the distances over which speech can be heard will depend on the design of the hall or auditorium and the extent to which sounds are reinforced by reflection and masked by other noises.

As a general rule, a hall or meeting room with a flat floor will usually provide adequate clarity for groups up to 80 without sound reinforcement. A purpose-designed lecture theatre or auditorium will be suitable for groups of 100–500 without amplification by electronic means, but this should be installed to allow for weaknesses in speech, for questions and for panels of speakers. Electronic systems of speech reinforcement are essential for larger audiences, rooms having low ceilings or high surface absorption, or rooms that are large in relation to the size of the audience.

Typical limits of speeches, lectures, group addresses	m (ft)	Note
In a hall or room with flat floor (without sound reinforcement)	12 (40)	Volume of hearing distance – 400 m³ (allowing average absorption)
In a purpose-designed lecture theatre or auditorium with stepped or tiered seats	20 (65)	Volume – 2000 m³, with facial expressions visible up to 25 m (80 ft)
With an auditorium extending round sides of stage, outside an arc of 140°	13 (43)	

6.1.7 Reinforcement of direct sound by early reflections

Provided the interval between impulses of direct and reflected speech signals is not delayed more than 25–35 ms (0.2–0.35 s), the impulses blend together and intensify the sound. To achieve this, the difference in lengths of direct and reflected sound paths must not exceed 12 m (40 ft).

However, the minimum time delay required to produce this effect will depend on the relative power of the voice and the tempo of the speech. It will also vary for other sounds; for instance, the optimum for most music is between 150 and 250 ms.

Other acoustic effects influenced by sound reflections include:

- **fullness of tone**, which depends on a good balance between direct, reflected and reverberant sound fields, the energy ratio also affecting the 'warmth' of tone;
- **clarity** – for clarity, the amplitude of the direct sound and first reflections (within 20–35 ms) must be much greater than the reverberant sound which follows;
- **spatial responsiveness** – this is the subjective impression of the directions and sequences in which reflections reach a listener; spacing of reflections in the first 60 ms is particularly significant.

Means of sound reinforcement

Reinforcement may be provided by the use of reflections from the ceiling or from fixed or moveable reflectors suspended over the auditorium, and by early reflections from the walls.

In auditoria and lecture theatres where speech is the primary source of sound, the ceiling may be deliberately profiled to assist even distribution. Adjustable convex ceiling reflectors are also used to allow acoustic changes for music.

Side walls adjacent to the source may also be angled to reflect sound towards the audience. Side walls can contribute to a sense of envelopment (particularly for music), but for clarity and directional orientation the reflections must immediately follow the direct sound (within 8 ms). Elsewhere, faceted or absorptive surfaces may be required to prevent cross-reflection, echoes and standing wave formation. For music, concentration of reflected sound may affect fullness of tone unless accompanied by long reverberation, and selected surfaces may need to be made dispersive.

Some local reflection in the stage area is desirable to enable individual orchestral players to distinguish their own and other instruments. Similarly, for speeches and lectures some acoustic feedback (including moderate reverberation) is important in reducing the effort and strain on the speaker, particularly in a large auditorium or hall.

Reflecting surfaces must be smooth and non-porous with a high density – at least 5 kg/m^2 for speech and 25 kg/m^2 for music – to minimize low frequency absorption.

6.1.8 Adjustments in hall and auditorium acoustics

Delay and prolongation of sound wave patterns may detrimentally affect the acoustics of a hall, causing **echoes** when the direct and reflected sound paths differ in length by more than 20 m (66 ft) – a delay of 60 ms – and **near echoes** with loss of intelligibility when the delay is above 40 ms.

Flutter echoes and **standing waves** can result from repeated reflections between parallel surfaces such as walls of

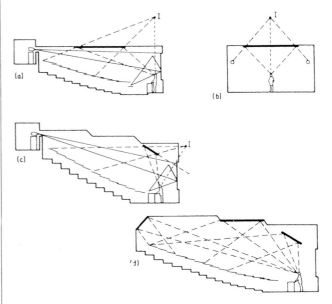

Direct and reinforcing sound

(a) Construction of sight lines giving equal clearance from row to row producing a parabolic floor rake. Reinforcement of sound by means of ceiling reflection showing the method of determining the reflective image I and the area required

(b) Cross-section of (a)

(c) Moving the speaker nearer the audience or to a lower relative level increases the rake of seating. With a high ceiling sound may be reinforced by angled reflectors suspended above (or to the sides) of the speaker

(d) Progressive development of ceiling reflection in a larger hall. Reflective surfaces may be plain, convex or parabolic in section or faceted to give equal distribution. Extensive areas of plain surface are liable to give rise to resonance, harmonic distortion and amplification of background noise. The difference between direct and reflected rays should not exceed 12 m.

a rectangular hall or between a reflective ceiling and hard floor. In each case, elimination involves the selective use of absorbent or dispersive surfaces.

Reverberation adjustment

Reverberation is the time (in seconds) for sound to decay by 60 dB. A long reverberation time gives fullness to tone and sonority, but without definition and clarity. The short reverberation appropriate for speech tends to be too dry and harsh for music.

It is the first 160 ms or the time taken in the first 15 dB of decay which provides the main subjective impression of reverberation, later reflections being largely masked by new sounds. The slopes of the decay curve will also differ with different sources of sound, different surface absorptions (including the size of the audience) and their relative positions, and the volume and shape of the enclosure.

Reverberant sound in an auditorium used for speech can increase fullness of tone and contribute to the sense of occasion and spatial responsiveness. However, if reverberation is excessive in relation to direct sound, and prolonged, it may mask the transients of speech and thus affect clarity. Reverberation will also increase the level of distracting noise from within or outside the hall.

Optimum reverberation times

Use	Volume (in m³)	Reverberation time at 500 Hz seconds
Syndicate rooms and adaptable suites		0.4–0.5
Small conference rooms/lecture theatres[1]		0.6–0.8
Large auditoria for speech[4]	to 1000 m³	0.8
	2000 m³	0.85
	5000 m³	0.93
	10 000 m³	0.97
Television studios[5]	1000 m³	0.3–0.4
	5000 m³	0.7
	10 000 m³	0.75
Concert halls for symphony and choral concerts[2]	to 5000 m³	1.5
	10 000 m³	1.6–1.85
	20 000 m³	1.7–2.10
Multipurpose halls		1.3–1.7
Restaurants, banquet halls		0.5–0.6
Display areas, reception areas[3]		0.3–0.6

[1] Varies with occupancy: usually based on 1 s – when empty, 0.8 s – two thirds full, 0.6–0.8 s – full.
[2] Optimum depends on power of instruments, grouping (solo, ensemble or orchestra), rhythm and speed of music, and need of purity for reproduction.
[3] Lower reverberation times indicate degree of privacy for personal communications.
[4] Source: Knudsen, V. O. and Harris, C. M. (1962). *Designing in Architecture*. Wiley.
[5] Source: Parkin, P. H. and Humphreys, H. R. (1969). *Acoustics, Noise and Buildings*, 3edn. Faber & Faber.

6.1.9 Sound absorption

Within an auditorium, the audience make up the most significant absorption surface – typically 60–70 per cent (at 500 Hz) for theatre-style seating. Changes in audience numbers and seating arrangements and closing off sections, such as a balcony, may affect acoustics. As a rule, empty seating (with carpeting) should be designed to have similar absorption characteristics to those occupied.

Absorption should be balanced across the full frequency range, although prolongation of the bass frequencies tends to give quality and warmth to music tone whilst high frequencies may need reinforcement for speech.

Sound absorption methods in a hall include the use of dissipative surfaces, as in porous linings and furnishings which mainly absorb the higher frequencies, membranes such as panels for low frequencies, and cavity resonators, which can be designed to give selective absorption of sound in the middle frequency range.

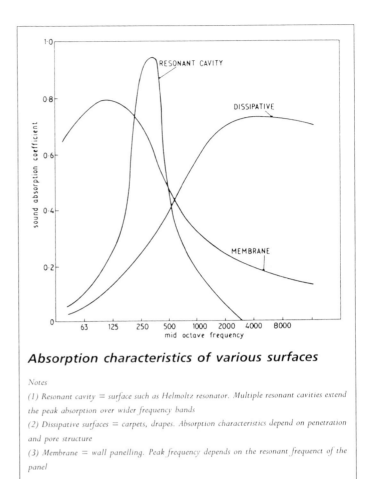

Absorption characteristics of various surfaces

Notes
(1) Resonant cavity = surface such as Helmoltz resonator. Multiple resonant cavities extend the peak absorption over wider frequency bands
(2) Dissipative surfaces = carpets, drapes. Absorption characteristics depend on penetration and pore structure
(3) Membrane = wall panelling. Peak frequency depends on the resonant frequency of the panel

Suitability of linings and materials

Many other factors have to be considered in selecting acoustic linings and methods of application:

- fire hazards – combustibility, surface flame spread, fire resistance or separation, fire stopping of cavities and behaviour of material in fire conditions;
- decoration – its suitability for a particular room, the method and cost of decoration renewal and its life-cycle;
- durability – resistance to damage (e.g. moving furniture or occupants), its repair limitations and maintenance costs;
- permanency – the effectiveness of jointing and sealing under conditions of use;
- function – access requirements and the need for movement.

6.2 MULTIPURPOSE USE AND NOISE CONTROL

6.2.1 Acoustic requirements for music

Compared with design for conference use alone, acoustic requirements for music are much more demanding. Audiences are usually acutely sensitive to even slight variations in precision, clarity and quality, and the optimum volume and acoustical requirements will change from one instrumental grouping and arrangement to the next. Furthermore, it is usually difficult to correct basic faults in shape and size by subsequent adaptation.

As a rule, some degree of compromise has to be accepted in single multipurpose halls. In larger complexes, separate halls may be provided for concerts, theatre and conference use. The basic requirements which apply to concert hall design are as follows:

Acoustic design	Objectives
Steeply raked seats, especially in large halls	Good direct sound and vision For definition and clarity, particularly in fast-moving music (presto and allegro movements). Also for binaural hearing and localization of sounds
Early reflections within first 50 ms, especially from side walls and reaching all seating positions	
Balance of later reflections (after 50 ms)	Fullness of tone, resonance, blending of notes
Evenness of decay through first 30–40 dB	For subjective effects of reverberation
Uniform diffuse distribution of sounds at all frequency levels throughout the hall and orchestral area	For performers to achieve synchronism and balance amongst the various sections Also to blend and unify composite sounds in the hall
Positioning and contouring of instrumental groups in order of acoustical strength	For instrumental balance and indentification (particularly strings and woodwind)
Adjustable angled reflectors over and around the stage.	To reduce excessive loudness in the playing area and front of the hall
Extension of orchestral area into main body of hall	
Control of reverberation by selected absorption and compensation	To balance frequencies and harmonization. For depth of tone, reverberation of bass sounds (125 Hz) may need to be extended by a factor of 1.25–1.50
Supplementation by electro-acoustical means	For deficiencies in frequency adjustment and amplification

6.2.2 Multipurpose halls: adjustable acoustics

To allow for changes in acoustic requirements four main alternatives are possible:

Accepting a compromise between reverberation times and other characteristic parameters:

- relative frequencies of use must be considered and weightings of importance attached to the criteria; certain incompatible uses may need to be excluded.

Installing changeable elements:

- controlling the decay rate of reverberation time by the use of retractable or reversible absorption surfaces in the rear and main body of the hall;
- intercepting projection of sound energy (often first 50–100 ms) with adjustable absorption areas near point of generation;
- increasing directional projector of energy (first 50–100 ms) to particular areas be means of adjustable tilting reflectors;
- shortening delay time (first 50 ms) of initial reflection by lowering canopies;
- changing perimeter and depth of stage enclosure to allow greater projection or concentration of sound;
- extending forestage to bring source of sound (orchestra etc.) into the main body of the hall;
- extension or removal of seating, including use of extendible bleachers or rising platforms to improve sight lines.

Providing moveable structures:

- using moveable walls to acoustically separate certain parts of the room volume from the main space (altering temporal and directional distribution of sound, reverberation and absorption as well as the seating capacity);
- using retractable screens to separate off sections above or below balconies;
- raising or lowering ceiling sections to separate off balconies.

Electro-acoustic modification of sound:

Methods depend on the main purpose of the hall
For speech in halls designed for music

- directional amplification – installation of loudspeakers having strong directional characteristics for speech; the

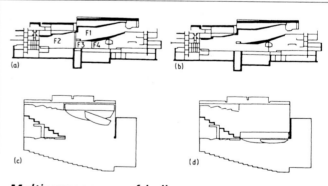

Multipurpose use of halls

Congress Centre, Geneva, Switzerland (top): Sections showing the convertible rooms provided within the modular design. Sound-proof partition walls can be moved automatically.

(a) Four separated rooms with 120 to 800 seats each
(b) All partitions removed giving 2500 seats
(Courtesy: CIC, Geneva)

Civic Theatre, Nancy, France (bottom): The ceiling of the large theatre (c) can be lowered to form two smaller theatres (d)
(Courtesy: EMI Pathe: Sores)

sound should be directed into specific sections of the audience;

For music in halls designed for speech
- ambiophonic systems – generating artificial reverberant sound effects by the use of feedback loops which transmit sound back into the diffused sound field of the hall with a delay (typically 40 ms);
- assisted resonance – using electro-acoustic assisted resonance to replace loss of energy from selected modal frequencies;
- multi-channel reverberation systems – adding reverberation back into the hall for music from a separate reverberation chamber through many speakers arranged to reinforce the natural pattern of reflections and sound diffusion;
- sound equalization techniques – to produce an even frequency response over the complete audio-frequency range by cancelling out excessive peaks or dips caused by the room acoustics, using feedback response through active filters.

6.2.3 Amplification of sound: acoustic conditions

Where electro-acoustic systems are to be used, the acoustic design of a hall is simplified in that there is less need to provide for natural reinforcement of direct sound. This has considerable advantages in, say, banqueting halls, where the use and seating arrangements will change from one occasion to the nest. Reverberation may also be simulated, enabling a hall of limited volume to serve for a variety of purposes (concerts, music recitals and speech). Acoustic conditions in a room with sound amplifications may be summarized as follows:

- Higher room absorption is usually necessary as amplification (by 10–15 dB) tends to increase the ambient level of noise.
- Shorter natural reverberation times should be provided as reverberation may be amplified and distorted unless corrected.
- The distribution and time sequencing of amplified signals is critical. For speech to sound natural and appear to emanate from the person speaking, amplified sound must reach each section of the audience within 20–35 ms of the direct sound. Signals are normally sequences to provide an electronic delay to 10–15 ms plus the difference in time-distance involved.
- Room shapes should be designed to avoid long reflected paths (from either direct sound or amplified sound) liable to produce echoes.
- Loudspeakers must be integrated into the design at an early stage, including steps to avoid 'feedback' to microphone positions. Adequate space must be provided and loudspeakers must be correctly positioned and orientated.
- Loudspeaker systems may be centrally grouped (this is

typical for congress halls, lecture theatres and banquet halls) or distributed over the area (as in exhibition halls and multi-purpose recreation halls) (see 6.3.7).

6.2.4 Masking of sound

Masking of sound by background and intruding noise is greatest when the sounds are of similar frequency to those used in speech, especially in the range 600–4800 Hz. The most critical locations are:

- where hearing conditions are most difficult, such as the back of the room;
- where emission noise may be picked up by microphones (around the stage).

Measurement of the likely effects of such intrusive noise may be expressed as sound pressure levels (dBA), noise rating (NR) curves or preferred noise criterion (PNC) curves, the last two covering a range of frequencies.

Recommended standards

Situation	NR[1]
Congress halls, concert halls, opera houses Live theatres (< 500 seats) Studios for sound reproduction	20
Live theatres (> 500 seats) Large auditoria, lecture theatres Television studios Conference rooms (> 50 seats)	25
Board rooms, conference and lecture rooms (20–50 people) Multipurpose halls, libraries, banqueting rooms, cinemas	30
Hotel guestrooms Public rooms in hotels, ballrooms	30
Small conference and seminar rooms Small restaurants, cocktail bars Quality shops, banking halls	35
Reception areas, corridors Hotel lobbies Large restaurants, bars, nightclubs	40
Toilets and washrooms Gymnasia Kitchens, laundry rooms Computer rooms, accounting machine-rooms, offices Cafeteria Swimming pools Covered garages	45
Workshops, plant rooms	50–55

Note
[1] PNC curves similar number; dBA levels for noise sources of similar spectral shape are approximately equal to NR +6.
After: Croome, D. J. (1977). Noise, Buildings and People. Pergamon Press, Oxford 1977.

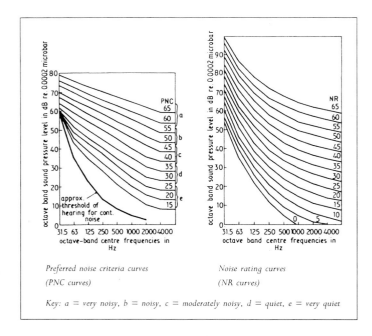

Preferred noise criteria curves
(PNC curves)

Noise rating curves
(NR curves)

Key: a = very noisy, b = noisy, c = moderately noisy, d = quiet, e = very quiet

6.2.5 Reduction of noise

The main sources of disturbing noise in congress rooms and auditoria are:

- outdoor noise (traffic, aircraft, plant);
- noise from adjoining rooms, particularly service areas (kitchens, bars, toilets, plant rooms and offices);
- corridor noise (entering through doorways);
- ventilation and other engineering equipment;
- self-generated noise (people talking, footsteps, chair and table movement, door slamming, projection and sound equipment).

Noises which are of a pulsating nature or of a constant pure tone tend to be more annoying to a conference audience than random noises. A weighting of 5–10 dB should be added to the recorded level of such noise.

Noise reduction methods – control of noise entry

A high standard of insulation against noise intruding from external sources is essential. As a rule, the areas which are particularly sensitive to noise (auditoria, meeting rooms and banquet halls) should be isolated by:

- planning – the interposition of foyers, galleries and circulation areas etc., to provide an intermediate zone of rooms, with high internal absorbency where appropriate;
- separation – by the use of double doors and lobbies;

Use of area	Standards of insulation separating walls or partitions		
	Adjoining area	STC	Hearing conditions
Multipurpose hall	Exterior		Intruding noise practically inaudible
	Mechanical equipment spaces, kitchens, toilets	55–60	
	Other halls	50–55	Very loud noise heard only faintly
	Restaurants, shops		
	Exhibition spaces		
	Corridors and public areas	45–50	Loud speech can be heard but only faintly
	Entrance foyers		Normal speech inaudible
	Administrative lobbies		
	Conference rooms		
Conference rooms	Kitchens, restaurants	45–50	
Seminar rooms	Toilets		
Meeting areas	Mechanical equipment space		
	Hotel bedrooms		
	Other similar areas	40–45	Loud speech can be heard but not clearly; normal speech heard faintly, if at all
	Offices, corridors and lobbies		
	Exterior: sheltered quiet	35–40	Normal speech can be heard but not clearly
Exhibition areas	Exterior		
	Conference rooms	45–50	
	Restaurants		
	Offices		
	Toilets		
	Kitchens		
	Plant rooms		
	Corridors and lobbies	40–45	
	Other similar areas		

Source: ANSI Standard Z24 19.1957. *Laboratory Measurement of Airborne Sound Transmission Loss of Building Floors and Walls*, American National Standards Institute.

- construction – the use of double construction for external walls and ceilings, with sufficient mass to provide a high transmission loss over the frequency band ranges from 20.75 up to 4800–9600 Hz;
- flanking – the stopping of sound flanking paths, including noise entry through grilles and ventilators;
- vibration – isolation from ground vibration due to plant or traffic noise in the range 10–50 Hz by means of floating floors, anti-vibration mountings for nearby equipment and structure-borne sound insulation mountings.

Windows present a particular difficulty, since as well as an environmental benefit they may also reduce sound (and heat) insulation and necessitate the use of curtains or blinds. On balance it is better if auditoria do not have windows, but natural lighting should be provided in the associated restaurants, promenades and galleries used by delegates for relaxation between sessions. Syndicate rooms should also have natural lighting.

Multipurpose function rooms in hotels generally must have windows to cater for wedding receptions and day-use requirements. Usually the windows overlook courtyards, sheltered gardens and patios with glazed doors to allow outdoor extensions of the internal activities. The external amenity area may include a swimming pool which, if used by other guests, could become a source of noise annoyance to conference users of the room.

Where necessary windows must be double-glazed against noise entry, with sound absorbent linings to the intervening space. A gap of at least 100 mm (4 in) and perferably 250 mm (10 in) is necessary for insulation against traffic noise.

6.2.6 Standards for noise insulation

Reduction in sound passing through a solid barrier (wall, floor, etc.) may be represented by the mass law curve, with a decline of approximately 6 dB for each doubling of mass. A barrier separated into two unconnected leaves at least 500 mm apart is more effective than mass alone, and doubling of the air space reduces sound transmission by a further 5 dB and more if this space is lined with visco-elastic materials to damp the vibration.

Insulation standards of a construction can be evaluated by measuring its performance against standard curves covering a range of frequency bands representing Standard Transmission Classes (STC).

6.2.7 Flanking paths

The effectiveness of insulation may be greatly reduced if there are doors or openings (for services) in the separating wall, or if there are significant flanking paths for noise passing round ceiling or wall cavities or gaps in edge sealing.

Flanking transmission is particularly liable to occur in light-weight structures, partitions without firm anchorage, light suspended ceilings, poor fitting doors and windows and moveable partitions which have inadequate edge seals.

6.2.8 Impact noise ratings

In a conference, impact noise can be generated by footsteps, mechanical equipment, door opening, tip-up seats, creaking chairs and transmitted vibrations. Impact noise within the room can be reduced by the use of resilient coverings such as carpets, and the specification of performance standards for air-conditioning and other equipment.

6.2.9 Noise from adjacent areas

Noise control can be improved by zoning and separating areas which are noise generating from those which are highly sensitive to noise disturbance. Noise generating areas include kitchens (in which noise climates of 66 dBA and peaks of 85 dB are common), toilets (noise from flushing and door closure can rise to 78 dBA and above), unloading docks, plant rooms, and machinery such as lifts.

Separation can be provided by intermediary areas, designed to absorb sound and fitted with quiet, self-closing doors.

6.3 SOUND SYSTEMS AND EQUIPMENT

6.3.1 Types of systems and equipment

Systems of equipment for reproduction, transmission and amplification of sound have many applications in congress centres and hotels. The choice of equipment and quality of performance specified will depend very much on marketing and economic considerations:

- the standards of facilities offered, extent of specialization conference business and marketing and promotion considerations;
- the scale of operation; size of the hall, frequency of use, and relative costs of installation, operation and maintenance;
- alternatives available, such as hire facilities, comparative charges and services.

6.3.2 Permanency of installation

Changes in audio–video equipment occur continuously as existing items become defective or obsolete and new developments

System	Areas of application
Public address To relay announcements, paging and emergency instructions etc.; background music from a radio receiver; broadcast relay or wired services or by reproduction from disc or tape	Public areas of hotel or centre – lobby, bar, restaurants, coffee lounge and foyer etc.
Extensions to guest rooms may be provided with a local selector panel for tuning to radio programmes or hotel music. It also may include television controls, message indication and emergency instructions (over-riding other controls). *Integrated room systems* may also provide for room status indication, security monitoring and energy regulation	Guest rooms, staff restrooms
Sound relay For transmission of conference proceedings (direct or from recordings) to other rooms by audio or video relays. It may also be used for playing back concerts, recitals and other events	To seminar rooms and ancillary areas used by delegates and by operational staff
Speech reinforcement This comprises microphones located at strategic points, mixing and controlling equipment and loud-speakers designed to suit the room acoustics	Conference rooms, congress halls, multipurpose halls, banquet halls, theatres
Simultaneous interpretation This facility enables speech to be relayed to and from the delegates via the interpreters' booth and a master set controlled by the chairman. Communication networks many be hard-wired with individual cables, or use infrared radiation (radio frequency induction loops less suitable)	Multi-lingual conference facilities
Electronic voting This consists of displayed (and recorded) voting by means of electronic relays, with various protection devices	Purpose-designed assembly and congress halls; multipurpose halls and arenas used for sports and competitive events
Acoustic modification of sound Systems provide for changes in the character and reverberation of sound by means of assisted resonance, extended reverberation and other electronic techniques	Multipurpose rooms used for congresses as well as for concerts, functions and entertainment
High-fidelity This system is essential for music reproduction and amplification and is usually combined with lighting effects	Halls used for concerts, discotheques, theatres, ballrooms
Sound reproduction from cine film tracks	Cinemas, conference rooms and other halls used for film projection
Closed-circuit and ultra-high-frequency television distribution This system is either combined with sound relay or exists as an independent system	Intended for conference rooms, large auditoria and suites of seminar rooms for operational control and security
Intercommunication system Communications can use either ring or radial networks or operate on the basis of radio telephones	To and from control room for instructions to operators; in theatres for backstage announcements; for communication between offices; for contact with security, maintenance and housekeeping staff
Exhibition and demonstration sound systems These include tape–slide presentations, back-projection and video recording–playback equipment	For background sound, paging and announcements, local units
Recording and broadcasting This is required for television and sound radio	For interviews, recordings of proceedings and events, studio work

become available at competitive cost. Maintenance charges are high and the trend is towards planned life-cycle replacement of equipment or components. At the same time, regular servicing and cleaning is essential to maintain good standards of performance.

To facilitate repair, replacement and extension, all equipment must be readily accessible. Standard modular design is essential, using interchangeable components. In the case of control panels and consoles, the modules should be mounted in racks, allowing any to be removed and replaced without major rewiring.

Equipment for which the positions are fixed, such as loudspeakers and motorized controls, must be incorporated into the design of the room, whilst allowing for access and eventual replacement. Other equipment may be portable and set up in a variety of positions when required. In all cases, provision must be made for cables and wiring to be installed and extended to suitable terminal points to which equipment can be connected without long trailing leads.

For purpose-built lecture theatres and auditoria with fixed seats, the cable runs and connections are more or less defined, extending from the lectern or stage to control booths and rooms housing the equipment and to other predetermined points. In multipurpose halls such as banquet halls, in which the function and seating layout will change from one occasion to the next, it is less easy to plan cable layouts with precision. For both, however, the cable-ways must be accessible to allow future addition, extension and replacement of the wiring, and separated for different voltages and screening requirements.

The cable-ways may be in floor ducts (with access covers at junctions), trunking or enclosed raceways allowing continuous access (in skirtings, carpeted floors, hollow partitions, accessible ceilings), or conduit leading to specific connections.

6.3.3 Comprehensive audio systems

Audio systems are made up from complementary sets of equipment which receive inputs of sound patterns (or broadcast frequency waves) and change them into electronic signals, pre-amplified as necessary. The signals are then corrected, balanced and further amplified (such as in a sound mixer) and transmitted to loudspeakers or headsets from which sound waves can be emitted at the required level of loudness, with or without modifications in quality.

Inputs	Control and mixing	Outputs
Microphones, radio receivers, external wired services, reproduction (from tape, disk, sound or film), artificial signals (process control, prewarning, emergency, etc.)	Switching, simultaneous fading in and out of signals power amplification of signals, volume or gain control, tone control, signal modification (frequency selection, filtering, delaying, extending, etc.)	Loudspeakers individual headphones and earphones

Usually audio-equipment is supplied as an integrated package, designed to meet specified requirements either on a sub-contracting basis or as a turn-key project.

Standards

Specifications laying down overall standards of performance for sound systems must take account of the purpose of the equipment and also the quality of sound likely to be expected by the audience. The latter will depend on the particular listening conditions. British Standard Code of Practice 327 recommends three main categories of quality (see next column):

In each category, standards are stipulated for maximum variation over frequency ranges, limits to distortion and electrical hum and noise, balance of stereophonic systems and electrical stability.

Reference should also be made to the recommendations of the International Electrotechnical Commission, IEC.

Type	Quality	Listening conditions	Examples
1	Highest quality of reproduction for speech and music	Critical listening under good acoustic conditions	Auditoria: for reinforcement of speech and music reproduction for concerts and theatrical use
2	Intelligible and natural sounding; good reproduction of music quality	Listening conditions suitable or capable of being made suitable by minor interior changes	Small halls and function rooms. For speech amplifications generally
3	Intelligible but not so natural in sound; acceptable music quality	For secondary interest, e.g. background music. Where acoustic conditions poor, e.g. high background noise or prolonged reverberation	Background music in lobbies, bars, restaurants

6.3.4 Control rooms and audio equipment

Audio equipment is easily damaged by mishandling, by dust and by moisture. There is also a security risk involved. Operational access for regulation and servicing must be provided, and in a more complex installation an operator may need to be continuously in attendance whilst the equipment is in use (for recordings, announcements and adjustments etc.). Control facilities generally fall into four main groups:

- **Public address and background music in hotels.** Components are mounted in racks and housed in metal cabinets, which can be located in a general operational room with other equipment (usually near the reception area). The enclosed equipment must be adequately ventilated and fitted with indicator lamps to show when it is working.
- **Sound amplification and recording; reproduction from tape, film, disk, in lecture theatres and congress halls.** Sound equipment should preferably be housed in a separate control room in which the operator can see and hear conditions in the theatre or auditorium. Preferably sited separate from, but adjacent to, the lighting control room, although these facilities are usually grouped together for small lecture theatres.
- **Simultaneous interpretation of speech.** Separate booths are required for interpreters. The central control and monitoring equipment may be grouped in the main sound control room or separately.
- **Mobile equipment for sound reproduction and control.** May be provided in hotel banquet halls, exhibition halls and other areas to provide local adjustment, amplification, background music and announcements. More exotic facilities are installed in discotheques and ballrooms.

Sound control rooms

Space requirements depend on the range of equipment, but an area 3 m wide × 2.4 m deep (10 × 8 ft) should be adequate to accommodate a sound-mixer console with adjacent tape and disk equipment, plus storage on both sides and some standby equipment.

All equipment must be easily dismantled for maintenance. A doorway and ramp should be designed for mobile trolley requirements.

Environment

High illuminance is required for servicing and editing work, and should be adjustable up to 100 lux. Screened point sources (adjustable) should be provided for the illumination of operating equipment during sessions, and internal surfaces painted matt black. Ventilation should be controlled with an air speed not greater than 0.2 m/s, and with minimum for noise. Incoming air must be filtered and maintained at a temperature between 18–22°C and 45–65 per cent Relative Humidity.

Sound control rooms are more elaborate in multipurpose theatres and concert halls, where they may provide recording and broadcasting facilities.

6.3.5 Microphones

Microphones are used to receive and transmit sound for speech reinforcement in auditoria and halls, for broadcasting announcements through public address systems and for intercommunication. The performance of the equipment will depend on its technical specification and acoustic (directional response) characteristics, the latter being chosen for the particular use and location.

Microphones must be supported free from vibration, and adjustable to an optimum distance of 0.5–0.7 m from the mouth. If greater distances occur, excessive reverberation is picked up, although highly directional microphones can be used for long-distance stage work. Where several microphones are used together as inputs to a sound system, they must be connected in correct phase relationship. When being used from alternative positions, such as in receiving questions from delegates, only one should be left on at a time to avoid adding to reverberant noise. The location relative to loudspeakers may be critical to avoid regenerative feedback.

Technical characteristics

The main types of electro-acoustical transducers used in microphones are electrostatic (condenser and electret types) and electrodynamic (moving coil type). Considerations influencing choice include cost, simplicity, power requirements, minaturization, technical specifications and directional characteristics.

The sensitivity to sound arriving from different directions is represented by polar diagrams, and may be omnidirectional (all-round sensitivity), cardioid and hypercardioid (increasingly directional in sensitivity) or bidirectional (sensitive from front and rear). Directional properties are used to discriminate against reverberant and background sounds, and reduce the risk of regenerative feedback whilst allowing the distance from the speaker to the microphone to be increased.

Congress facilities

In a hall that is to serve for a variety of purposes, a combination of several types of microphones with different directional sensitivities should be used to enable the best effects to be obtained by simply switching from one set to another. Such arrangements are essential for stage acting, shows and concerts. Congress or convention requirements for a large hall normally specify the following microphone facilities as a minimum:

Location	Microphones
Chairman's table	One or several table microphones on flexible shaft mountings or adjustable stands (vibration-free) with individual on–off controls.
Speaker's lectern	A fixed microphone, adjustable in height and angle, with anti-vibration mounting. A miniature lavalliere microphone (worn around the neck) to allow the speaker to comment on slides.
Delegates' questions	At least two microphones on adjustable stands temporarily erected in the aisle *or* two hand-set ('roving') microphones with leads long enough to reach all delegates *or* permanent microphones built into armrests or recessed backpanels of seats with a minimum of one microphone per three seats in same row, one microphone per four seats in two rows.

6.3.6 Sound amplification

Reinforcement of speech is usually required in purpose-designed auditoria – even where the seating is raked – when the audience capacity is more than about 400. For multipurpose halls and rooms in which the seating is at one level, sound amplification is often found necessary for an audience upwards of 100 and desirable for 80, particularly where the ceiling is low and the surroundings highly absorbent.

Sound reinforcement in an auditorium may also be required for orchestral and instrumental music, for reproduced sound (music or speech) from disk, tape or film, or sound transmitted from other areas.

In designing sound reinforcement systems, a number of acoustic and technical criteria must be satisfied. The design must:

- ensure reinforcing sounds arrive at every part occupied by the audience within 20 to 35 ms of the direct sound, in order to coalesce the initial and reinforcing signals:
- create the impression that the reinforcing sound originates

from the person speaking, by delaying the reproduced signal so that it follows the original with an optimum delay (of about 10–15 ms); it should also be capable of adjusting the amplitude appropriate to this delay (up to a maximum increase of 10 dB);

• provide an output power sufficient to meet the peak requirements with an adequate margin; this should also be capable of adjustment to suit both the sound input (speech, music, etc.) and changes in room conditions (audience numbers, reverberation times, etc.);

• avoid distortion of frequencies over the full range, but with the means of adjustment to improve the naturalness of the sound (e.g. by restricting the bass response in speech to reduce boominess);

• provide all flexibility in the layout and use of room whilst reducing the risk of feedback or regenerative howling from loudspeaker to microphone, vibration noise and other effects.

6.3.7 Loudspeakers

Loudspeaker systems in large halls and auditoria can be broadly classified into two systems; central (or high level) and distributed (or low level).

Central or high level

This system uses a few loudspeakers located near the source, usually placed above and to one or both sides of the speaker and tilted forward 5–10° so that the beam is mainly projected over the rear two-thirds of the audience.

Distributed or low level

In this arrangement a larger number of loudspeakers are located (usually in the ceiling) over sections of the audience where there is a need for sound reinforcement, usually starting 6–8 m from the source. The reinforcing signal must have a time delay (see 6.2.3 and 6.3.6).

Loss of clarity may occur if a listener can hear sound from a number of speakers, and the volume and beam characteristics should be adjusted to ensure even distribution. To avoid feedback when roving microphones are used, each speaker should be capable of being switched off.

Low level distribution systems are also used for background music and public address systems in other areas of hotels and congress centres, each loudspeaker covering a specific section of the area with a peripheral overlap.

Types of loudspeakers

Direct radiator (cone) loudspeaker:

In this system a comparatively large diaphragm, usually cone-shaped, is vibrated by a moving coil. The frequency range of

Typical power ranges

Type	Application	Power range (W)
Cabinet speakers with or without volume control	Background music and announcements in hotels, foyers, shops	2–8
Column speakers	For music or speech in multipurpose halls and function rooms	12–20–32
Column speakers	For high-fidelity output in theatres, etc.	60–75
Column speakers	For speech reproduction with minimum feedback for bad acoustic conditions in halls	6–8

Source: Rank Audio Visual Ltd.

each diaphragm is generally limited, and at higher frequencies (above 1000 Hz) directional beaming and side distortion become pronounced. This effect reduces with diameter, and to extend the frequency range multiple speakers of different sizes are assembled together in cabinets, flat baffles or directional baffles. Acoustical efficiencies are in the order of 1–5 per cent. Cone loudspeakers, e.g. 200–250 mm, are often mounted in the ceilings of foyers, lounges and restaurants for background music and announcements. Mountings must be vibration-free and accessible for adjustment and servicing. The coverage spreads at about 45° around the centre line, and spacing is determined from 2 × (height – 1.5 m). For ceilings higher than 6 m, line source loudspeakers are more appropriate. Cabinet assemblies are widely used in portable equipment.

Horn loudspeakers:

The use of a horn coupled to a small diaphragm with a moving coil enables sound to be radiated in a fairly narrow beam, and gives efficiencies of about 10 per cent or more. For lower frequencies horns must be large and, in this size, are folded to take up less space. Multi-cell units are generally used, with two or more exponential horns in one flare forming splays up to 90°. Horn assemblies in cabinets are often used in cinemas. Horns in exhibition halls are mounted to beam sound over a specific section of the occupants, to give high local absorption and thus limit reflection.

Line source loudspeakers:

When several loudspeakers (usually radiator type) are connected in phase with signal loudness tapered, and mounted in vertical columns, the radiation pattern forms a flat-shaped beam concentrated vertically. The horizontal angle is about 110°. The concentration increases with length, which should be at least 1.2 m (4 ft) and may be up to 3.3 m (11 ft) for very reverberant conditions. Compared with other single sources the intensity is increased, and this does not fall off so quickly with distance. The front may be curved to reduce side wave formation. The beam

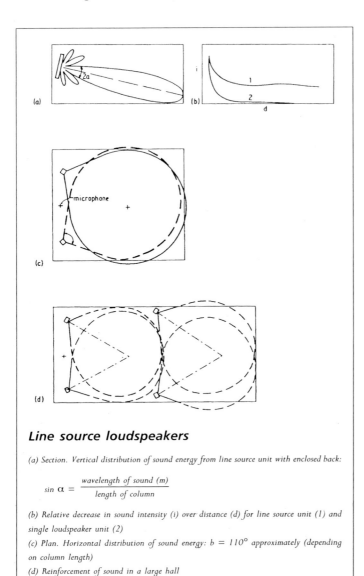

Line source loudspeakers

(a) Section. Vertical distribution of sound energy from line source unit with enclosed back:

$$\sin \alpha = \frac{wavelength\ of\ sound\ (m)}{length\ of\ column}$$

(b) Relative decrease in sound intensity (i) over distance (d) for line source unit (1) and single loudspeaker unit (2)

(c) Plan. Horizontal distribution of sound energy: b = 110° approximately (depending on column length)

(d) Reinforcement of sound in a large hall

characteristics are particularly suitable for speech when fitted with tone control filters (bypassed for music). Typical sound outputs are 6 W for speech and up to 60 W for music.

Electrostatic loudspeakers:
Generally of very high quality, but more expensive, electrostatic loudspeakers are also more slender and suitable for medium-size rooms.

Headphones

Individual headphones or earphones are used for simultaneous interpretation systems. The most common are the 'stethoscope' type, which have a single miniature receiver acoustically coupled to twin earpieces. Most headphones operate on the moving coil or electro-magnetic principle. The ear pieces should be removable for cleaning and disinfection.

A minimum 1.7 m (5 ft) length of flexible cord should be provided, with strain cords or cord grips at both ends. Connections to the permanent installation may be made through terminals in the arms of individual seats or in the hollow backs of the seats in front.

6.3.8 Simultaneous interpretation systems

Three types of simultaneous interpretation systems are available; cable or hard-wired, induction loop and infrared.

Cable or hard-wired system

This is a permanent installation of the required number of language selector cables with built-in terminals located conveniently to hand for each conference participant. The cabling is usually run through the bases of seats in ducts extending from row to row and across aisles in ring mains. Wired systems usually provide facilities for delegates to participate in the discussions, including request indicator lamps, microphones and holding switches.

Equipment controls may be built into the hollow arms of chairs, or into panels provided in the backs of the preceding seats.

Portable microphone units may also be provided for conferences. There are normally placed on the desks in front of delegates and used together with individual headphones or small loudspeakers. The units are connected in series to a central control desk and then to the interpreter's sets for translation and relay.

Induction loop system

The induction system uses transmission by a magnetic field generated by a looped wire around the auditorium. The field, which is subject to broadcasting regulations, generally allows up to six carrier frequency bands which can be picked up by a small portable monitor provided for each participant.

Limitations in the induction loop system arise from the restricted frequency range (generally 50–100 kHz), which only allows a narrow waveband width for each of the carrier channels, thus limiting the audio frequency bandwidth to about 3.6 kHz – a quality comparable to the sound of a telephone.

The induction system is fairly flexible in seating layout and allows participants to move about. There is, however, some loss of security from transmission outside the room and a risk of distracting crosstalk between channels or transmission interference from adjacent rooms.

Infrared system

Modulated infrared radiation from a number of sources in the room is used to transmit signals at different channel frequencies

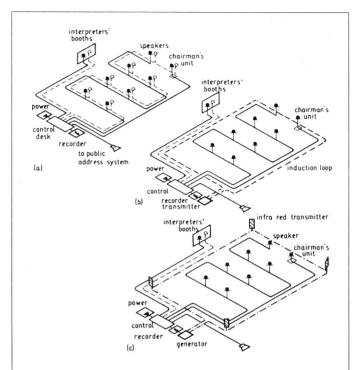

Simultaneous interpretation systems

Key

──┴── *conference cable with individual microphones*

─ ╷ ─ *programme cable directly wired to each position (a)*

─ ─ ─ ─ *induction loop aerial used with portable receivers (b)*

─·─▨─·─ *infrared transmitter used with portable receivers (c)*

Note: The conference cable may be limited to set speaking positions
The Technical and Health Committee of the AIIC and Groupe Technique of the European Union recommend that the induction loop system should be banned because of the poor sound quality, interferences from outside systems and potential hazard from floor cables. Whilst booths need to be elevated to provide unobstructed facial views they must not be positioned too high, and specialist advice should be sought on technical requirements.

(up to nine frequency bands). In contrast to induction systems, the frequency coverage is wide ranging between 55 and 300 kHz, allowing large channel separation and high transmission quality. In a room with normal lighting, one power radiator with four channels active should cover an area of up to 50 m².

Typically four radiators are required in medium-sized conference rooms, and preferably one should be located across each corner of the room. The radiators may be temporarily mounted on microphone stands or permanently installed. Receivers are portable, battery powered and connected by plug-in leads to headphones. One of the advantages of infrared transmission is the effectiveness of screening by walls and partitions etc.

6.3.9 Interpreters' booths

Requirements for interpreters' booths are specified in ISO 2603, 1998 and ISO 4043, 1998 (Mobile booths). Booths must be located at the side or rear of the hall and elevated to ensure good visual contact between all booths (including the control booth) as well as with the proceedings in the hall (participants, chairman, lecturers, etc.) and all visual aids (screens, etc.). The largest distance to the rostrum or screen must not exceed 30 m (98 ft) and steep viewing angles should be avoided, but a clear space of at least 2 m (7 ft) should separate the booths from both the participants and audience to avoid disturbance.

Separate access (1.5 m wide) to the booths from outside the hall must be provided (free from outside noise disturbance), with a dedicated restroom and toilets.

Booth specifications cover lighting, air-conditioning, working conditions and sound equipment. Special requirements apply when the hall is equipped with sound reinforcement, which might affect interpretation clarity (see 2.9.5).

6.4 LIGHTING

6.4.1 Exterior lighting

Floodlighting, and other forms of exterior lighting, are important in promoting awareness and interest in the centre or hotel, in demonstrating the character and architectural form of the buildings and in extending the activities of the building into its surroundings. Good exterior lighting reduces the incidence of accidents, and facilitates, as an aspect of security, the surveillance of people entering and leaving.

Functional requirements of exterior lighting include the illumination of car parks, footways, access roads and forecourts, both for visitors and for service, delivery and maintenance requirements. Consideration must be given to the day-time appearance of the columns and lamps, as well as the design and compatibility of street furniture generally (signs, columns and brackets). Statutory regulations will usually apply.

Amongst the main applications are:

- upward illumination to emphasize vertical features; contrasting bands of brightness at different levels define specific elements of the structure, giving it form and shape;
- concealed illumination under arches, in window recesses and penetrating spaces;
- floodlighting of external facades – the intensity and colouring of illumination will depend on the type of surface and contrast with surroundings;
- screened floodlighting of trees, monuments and other features, preferably in contrast to that of the building;
- symmetrical lighting of walks, balconies, terraces and entrance drives, using pillar or column lamps or wall lanterns;
- downlighting below canopies, portes cocheres and entrance lobbies to distinguish entrances.

6.4.2 Interior lighting

Lighting is used both for decorative and functional purposes, although the distinction between these roles is tending to reduce as aesthetics are translated into precise technical standards of designed appearance lighting.

The level of luminosity and its pattern are important in setting the 'mood' of the interior and for directing attention to appropriate features. If the range of luminosity is small, the scene lacks attraction or focus and appears dull; if in addition the level is low, it will appear gloomy. A brightly lit interior with uniform lighting provides little emphasis or modelling. *Variations in illuminance* are used to provide interest and compel attention. The bright features should be those of most significance to the users; the darker ones those of less importance, or those from which attention may need to be distracted. By varying the relative luminance (of ceilings and walls, etc.), architectural features may be emphasized or visual faults in the space corrected.

Directional effects in lighting have a marked influence on the appearance of three-dimensional objects, producing different contrasts in light and shadow, depending on the direction of the illumination vector, the vector/scalar illuminance ratio and the directional strength.

Strong modelling contrasts may be deliberately employed in feature work (see 6.4.8), but in foyers, reception and circulation areas and similar spaces, the quality of lighting will be judged by the manner in which human faces are revealed and by the brightness of the vertical surfaces. For this purpose lighting giving a vector/scalar ratio in the range 1.2–1.8 is generally considered to give a pleasing effect, the lower ratio being more suitable for informal or close communication and the higher for more formal or distant communication.

The preferred vector direction for facial illumination is between 15° and 45° below the horizontal – showing the desirability of side windows and/or light-coloured decoration to modify the harsher modelling effects of downward light.

Intensity of lighting and decoration colour changes from room to room should not be excessive. Transient areas (corridors and foyers) must provide intermediary conditions to allow visual and psychological adjustments to be made.

To meet functional requirements, the service illuminance must be adequate for the particular degree of discrimination and accuracy required and adjustable for the different room functions likely to be involved. Service illuminance, measured at desk or table level and on vertical surfaces such as display boards and teaching walls, will depend on the installed luminaire luminous flux, the utilization factor and the maintenance factor.

Comprehensive lighting design requires a wider range of criteria to be taken into account (illuminance of the working plane, scalar illuminance, balance of brightness between surfaces, glare limitations, emphasis and directional qualities). One such approach by which the luminaires required to achieve several of these illuminance ratios can be selected is the Multiple Criterion Design (MCD) method.

Specific requirements will apply to stage lighting and the lighting of exhibitions and displays (see 6.4.8). In addition, special consideration must be given to safety lighting for emergency needs (maintained lighting, signs, warnings and directions etc.) to ensure compliance with legal standards.

6.4.3 Daylighting

Daylighting of congress and convention halls has many disadvantages. It varies in level and directional characteristics, involves greater heat loss and air-conditioning loading on services, adds to sound insulation difficulties, presents design limitations in flexibility of use and layout, provides possible distraction and adds to the complexities of operation, such as the need to use blackout blinds.

Complete dependence on artificial lighting involves greater costs of luminaire installation and operation; the standards of emergency lighting and of generating capacity also need to be increased. In either event, psychological relief from prolonged enclosure under artificial conditions must be provided for congress delegates. This can be achieved by the use of restaurants, promenades, reception lobbies and other supplementary areas which have windows or glazed or open balconies allowing visual contact with the exterior. It is also essential to provide intermediary areas (passage ways, halls and lobbies) which have stepped, controlled lighting and temperature variations to reduce excessive contrasts between the inside and outside conditions.

The acceptability of windowless rooms depends very much on the volume and levels of lighting provided. As a guide, in halls and auditoria of 200–300 capacity or more, lack of natural lighting is not a drawback, particularly if the ceiling is high. In rooms of less than 100 capacity, the threshold at which a sensation of enclosure and oppression begins to impair concentration depends very much on the level of illumination, the space allowed per person, the room ceiling height and ambient temperature. Generally a level of 400 lux or more (on the horizontal plane) is required if a windowless room is not to give the impression of a closed space. Other factors such as the duration of the meeting, the variety of changes in lighting and activities and the time and sociability of the occasion also play a strong part.

6.4.4 Decorative effects

Ceilings

Visual and photometric features of the ceiling become increasingly important as the room height reduces or the area increases (as in large halls), bringing a greater area of the ceiling into the normal field of vision.

In meeting rooms and halls a high ceiling reflectance is desirable, both to assist the diffusion of light and to avoid excessive contrasts with the luminaires. Generally a reflectance factor of not less than 0.6 (Munsell value 8) is called for, particularly if the ceiling receives no direct light. The ceiling decoration and fittings must be non-specular to avoid reflection of light from other sources (projection, stage lighting).

In very large exhibition halls, where ready access to the ceiling void is necessary, the ceiling cavity is usually deliberately darkened to obscure this background.

Walls

Wall surfaces have a more significant effect on lighting and atmosphere in small meeting rooms. In large halls and auditoria the greater viewing distance allows colours of high chroma to be employed without being obtrusive, or with much reduction in general illumination. Small, well-defined areas of strong colour can be used to provide visual stimulation and relief from the uniformity of colour and form in a large area. However, the possible distracting and irritating effects of strong colour contrasts grouped within the field of vision must be considered.

In small meeting and conference rooms, the colouring and reflection properties of the walls have a more marked effect on illuminance. A high chroma paintwork or wall covering can make the surface unduly dominant, apparently reducing the size of the room as well as affecting the distribution of light. This effect is less significant if the walls are panelled in wood veneer or patterned laminate, such as in partitioning. Colour decorations can be greatly affected by the spectral properties of the 'white' lights used in luminaires, particularly where the wall colouring is in pastels of low saturation.

Where wall surfaces are to provide a source of indirect light (such as through wall washes), a high reflectance is necessary to minimize shading contrast and glare. Illuminated surfaces must be non-specular and carefully finished, either uniformly smooth or deliberately textured to give relief shading effects.

For meeting rooms generally, wall reflectance should be above 0.4 (Munsell value 7) but below 0.8 (Munsell value 9.5). The high values are necessary for walls in which there are windows, and desirable in the smaller meeting/function rooms.

Floors and furniture

Floors are generally carpeted to reduce impact noise and variations in acoustics when the room seating occupancy and layout changes. Relatively dark colours and camouflaging patterns are necessary to conceal dirt and wear, but changes in light reflection can result from the fibres being laid to produce shade and sheen. In a large hall (ballroom or banquet hall etc.) a floor cavity reflection of 0.2 to 0.3 is desirable. The surfaces of desks and writing tablets should also provide reflectances of this order, to reduce contrasts with writing and reading materials.

6.4.5 Subjective impressions

By providing a series of lighting cues which people use to interpret space, such treatments as lighting patterns, variations and surface effects can be used to provide different impressions of a room. Typical applications in hotels and congress centres are summarized below. To provide for multiple activities and variations in use (day-time, evening, formal, social) adjustment control of both peripheral and ceiling lighting is necessary.

Arrangements	Effects, uses
Longitudinal lines of ceiling luminaires in uniform array, with illumination of end walls	Reinforces sense of direction and spatial perspective. Used in circulation areas such as corridors, end-wall illumination helps to define and apparently shorten the corridor length
Uniform patterns of light with transverse array of the luminaires. Usually combined with peripheral lighting	Emphasizes width, and appears to bring subject (stage, person speaking or display) nearer to the audience. Peripheral lighting may be reduced during lectures etc. and increased between sessions
Uniform peripheral (wall) lighting, reinforced by the brightness of the space	Gives impression of spaciousnessing, reinforced by the brightness. Used in banquet halls and ballrooms and in large auditoria
Bright uniform lighting with some peripheral emphasis, such as with high reflectance walls or wall lighting	Impression of perceptual clarity, used for most workplaces, studios, offices, display areas, conference and seminar rooms
Non-uniform lighting, with luminance from periphery rather than overhead. Visual emphasis focused on the peripheral surfaces remote from the occupants with vertical illumination of walls and drapes etc. Horizontal to background vertical brightness ratios are reduced to between 1 : 20 and 1 : 100	Induces a sense of detached privacy, introspective behaviour and relaxed movement. May be used in formal congress halls as well as in lounges and other areas intended for relaxation
Non-uniform lighting with brightness of near horizontal surfaces (desks, tables etc.) increased in comparison with background vertical illumination, giving brightness ratios of between 1 : 1 and 100 : 1	Creates conditions for gregarious behaviour and group social activity such as in restaurants, coffee shops and bars. Table lights and downlighters over tables are used to emphasize this effect
Punctuation of lighting by direct illumination of features. Use of myriad reflections from multi-lamp fittings, chandeliers, mirrors and brightwork	Provides vitality, sparkle, animation and spectacle; heightens sense of occasion and excitement. Used in ballrooms, banquet halls, cocktail bars and nightclubs
Emphasized plane of illumination below darkened ceiling cavity	Apparently lowers visual ceiling, creating a more intimate scale. Used in multipurpose exhibition and congress halls to conceal engineering services and structural framework

Source: Lawson, F.R. (1994). *Restaurants, Clubs and Bars: Planning, Design and Investment for Food Service Facilities* (2nd edn). Architectural Press.

6.4.6 Illumination standards

Maintained service illumination standards based on the CIBSE Code for Interior Lighting 1994 are summarized below. For most situations, the illuminance stated is that required on the working plane. In circulation areas, a scalar illuminance at a height of 1.2 m is taken. These standards generally agree with CIE requirements.

Building area	Maintained service illumination (lux)	Notes
Circulation		
Entrance halls, lobbies	200	Increased to 300 lux in resort areas to reduce contrast with exterior daylight. Signs separately illuminated
Enquiry desks	500	Screening essential
Hotel reception and cashier desks	300	Downlighters usually built into canopy
Passages, corridors	100	Increased to 150 lux for day-time use
Lifts, stairs and escalators	150	At tread level
Foyers	100	Increased to 200 lux where entered direct from the street during
Cloakrooms	150	day-time
Meeting areas		
Auditoria, theatres and concert halls	100–150	At seating height, luminaire dimming must be provided
Congress halls, lecture theatres	300	500 lux on vertical plane of chalkboards and displayed information
Multipurpose halls	100–300	Allowing wide variation of luminance
Exhibition halls	300	On vertical plane, with reduction to 150 lux or below for light-sensitive exhibits
Conference and seminar rooms	500	Adjustable
Stage and platforms		Special lighting requirement
Cinemas	50	Minimum; increased for multiple use
Support areas		
Projection rooms, control rooms	150	Increased to 300 for servicing, editing etc.
Service lobbies	150	
Kitchens; working areas	500	Limiting glare index 22; controlled by Food Hygiene Regulations
Stores and workshops	150	
Restaurants	100–200	Depending on character
Lounges	100	
Bars, coffee bars	150	300 lux or more over bar counter
Function rooms	100–150	Allowing for variations in use
Other functions		
Staged sporting events and boxing ring	2000	Screened spotlights required
Billiards, snooker, table tennis	500	
Ballroom dancing		Special lighting effects
Outdoor		
Main entrance and exits	20	
Car parks, pedestrian precincts	20	Increasing to 50 lux for enclosed areas and high risk areas
Entrance gates and control, loading bays	100	

Minimum level at the time maintenance has to be carried out
Source: *CSIBE Guide A (1986)* and *Code for Interior Lighting* (1994). Chartered Institute of Building Services Engineers.

6.4.7 Light sources

Incandescent lamps

These include standard and low-voltage lamps, pear-shaped general light service and linear tungsten halogen types, blown bulb and pressed glass reflector lamps and crown-silvered (bowl reflector) bulbs for use with external reflectors.

Incandescent lamps are used to give warmth and intimacy to a room such as a lounge or restaurant, particularly when the lamps are in close proximity to the occupants (wall lighting, table lighting) They are also used in multi-lamp fittings for feature lighting in large ballrooms and foyers.

Downlighters giving a relatively concentrated beam are used in auditoria and over reception desks, tables and work areas. Reflector lamps have many applications in display lighting, and can have spot, wide arc or floodlit characteristics. Luminaires designed with screening may be used as wall washers or to illuminate features.

The efficacy of incandescent lamps increases with wattage, but the utilization will depend greatly on the construction and position of the luminaire. With high wattage lamps, provision must be made for heat dissipation.

Tubular fluorescent lamps

The colour spectrum and quantity of light emitted by low-pressure mercury discharge lamps depends on the composition of the phosphor coating, but they give higher efficacy than incandescent lamps. The tubes may be used in display cases (small diameter), in low wattage emergency lamps, and in circular lamps for compact fittings; they may be recessed into the ceiling or surface-mounted.

In exhibition halls, the tubes are often mounted on a suspended framework of battens below the ceiling void. For display areas, the background level is kept low to complement the strongly directional lighting of exhibits.

Gas discharge lamps

Gas or arc discharge lamps include low- and high-pressure sodium vapour, mercury vapour and metal halide types. The spectral energy distribution tends to be discontinuous, giving intense light in specific frequencies, but usually with high efficacy and long life emission. Applications include external lighting, lighting in large exhibition halls and some projection equipment.

6.4.8 Specific areas

Variations in lighting levels

Illumination requirements for meeting rooms generally involve a combination of direct and indirect lighting with extensive circuit switching and dimming controls. An illumination of 300 lux on the horizontal plane at seat or desk level should normally be provided, but for a windowless room this should be increased to 400 lux, and for a multipurpose hall it should be adjustable to 500 lux.

Dimming facilities (with synchronized blackout blinds over any windows) must be provided for cine and slide viewing, and emergency lighting installed to local requirements. Levels of emergency lighting should be related to the normal illuminance of the room. For lecture theatres and auditoria the minimum required level is 0.2 lux, increasing to 0.5 lux in halls and rooms normally lit to 500 lux. The illuminance need not be uniform, but may be increased (up to a ratio of 4 : 1) over escape routes. Luminaires should be mounted as high as possible or screened to prevent glare.

Lighting installed in the ceilings of auditoria and large conference halls is mainly direct and near vertical. To avoid risk of glare a cut-off angle of view for any light source must be above 40°, and direct luminaires are usually of the recessed (partly or fully) type to provide screening.

Indirect luminaires are also used for perimeter lighting, either as washes or wedges of light over specific areas. Perimeter lighting reduces strong contrasts as well as providing a brighter and more relaxing environment, but it must not be so pronounced as to create visual distraction from the stage or speaker. A visual cut-off of at least 45° is required.

Auditorium and meeting room lighting design

General requirements are as follows:

- the spatial illumination must be at a sufficient level to avoid strong contrasts and possible claustrophobic effects, whilst allowing concentration over long periods; it must also be capable of being dimmed (screen projection) and increased (discussions, intervals, social events, etc.);
- for practical requirements (note taking, viewing etc.) the planar illuminance horizontally at desk level and vertically on displays must be at an appropriate level;
- possible glare from luminaires, windows and high reflectance from surfaces must be avoided;
- a balance must be maintained between the relative brightness of surfaces in view and also colour harmonization;
- separate emergency lighting must be provided, giving a hall illumination of at least 0.5 lux;
- special stage lighting together with controls may need to be installed to allow multipurpose use of the hall or theatre;
- Provision should be made for energy reclaim from light fittings: some 50–75 per cent of lighting heat may be removed by using air-handling luminaires.

Lighting installations in large halls and function rooms

Lighting requirements in halls and function rooms need to be flexible to allow a wide range of use; although these will vary with the hall design, a typical installation would provide:

- at least three separate lighting circuits for general space lighting (including a combination of downlights and diffusing lights);
- separate lighting circuit(s) for perimeter lighting (wall lighting, pelmet lighting of drapes etc.);
- a separate circuit to spotlights, minimum three, for illumination of the speaker, displays and exhibits etc.;
- separate lighting control of the main feature lights (usually each is composed of a large number of small shielded light sources, as in chandeliers, giving a soft diffused light over the central area);
- an emergency lighting circuit giving 0.5 lux minimum illumination;
- as far as possible, all lighting circuits with balanced dimmer controls to provide lower levels of illuminance (5–30 lux) for screen projection, dancing etc.;

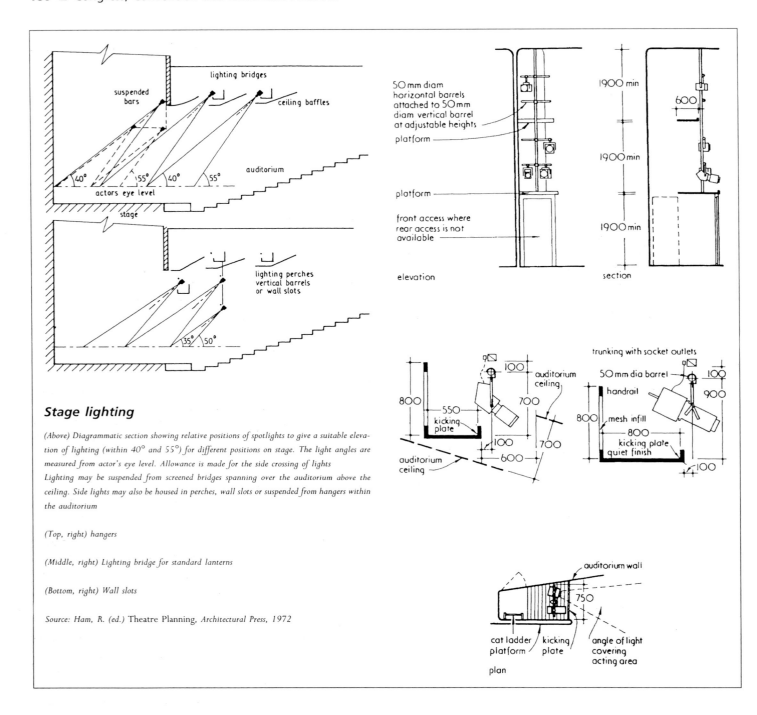

Stage lighting

(Above) Diagrammatic section showing relative positions of spotlights to give a suitable elevation of lighting (within 40° and 55°) for different positions on stage. The light angles are measured from actor's eye level. Allowance is made for the side crossing of lights

Lighting may be suspended from screened bridges spanning over the auditorium above the ceiling. Side lights may also be housed in perches, wall slots or suspended from hangers within the auditorium

(Top, right) hangers

(Middle, right) Lighting bridge for standard lanterns

(Bottom, right) Wall slots

Source: Ham, R. (ed.) Theatre Planning, Architectural Press, 1972

- multi-way floor ducts or cableways installed to allow separated wiring for extensions to power supplies, to socket outlets or receptacles (for projectors, motors, etc.), low-voltage relays (controls, signals) and microphone cables (screened as necessary); the positions of floor boxes and connections must be carefully determined;
- co-ordinated control circuits to motorized blinds, dimmers and equipment for slide and screen presentations.

The systems must be duplicated or triplicated if the room is to be divided into two or three parts for different groups.

Stage lighting requirements for auditoria involve more complex installations, including sound control equipment, as detailed in section 2.6.8.

Small conference and meeting rooms

Depending on the size and flexibility of use required, conference rooms usually have four to six lighting circuits covering:

- general room lighting, with a combination of soft downlights and wall washers with dimming facilities (usually set levels);

- task lighting of teaching walls and other writing surfaces;
- lighting of speaker and of other accent features (displays);
- separate lighting and power for the projection booth (if installed);
- power and control cabling outlets at various strategic positions;
- controls located behind the speaker's desk, plus room light switches at the entrance (duplicated controls in the booth).

Lighting of foyer and entrance hall

The foyer serves as a meeting and assembly place, a circulation area with information and directions and a common area giving access to bars, refreshments and cloakrooms. In an hotel this function may be an extension of the lobby but a specific foyer, with or without its own separate entrance, is usually necessary for congress and banquet functions.

Use	Examples
To emphasize building design, e.g. structural features	Floor troughs for upward lighting of columns; edge illumination of open staircases; underlighting of arches and recesses; wall washes of panels
Features, signs	Upward directional spot lights; luminaires in concealed recesses or canopies
Functional purposes: bookstalls, enquiry desks etc.	Higher local service intensities – 500 lux – with downward spotlights or floodlights at vertical angle of 60–80°
General lighting	With a relatively low ceiling, downlighters recessed into ceiling construction or surface-mounted in exposed coffers. For a high ceiling, suspended multi-lamp luminaires are generally used
Exhibition and display	Directional lighting at about 40° vertical angle, either using swivel fittings or trackline fixed parallel 2–3 m from wall (depending on height)
Safety	Emergency luminaires at steps, stairways and exits giving at least 0.25 lux, and across foyer and along corridors at least 0.2 lux (see regulations) Signs separately illuminated

Specialized requirements and lighting controls

Specialized requirements are involved in stage lighting for congress and multipurpose use (see 2.6.8), as well as in permanent and semi-permanent displays of works of art and other displays (see 3.3.9). In exhibition halls, stand illumination of exhibits varies with individual requirements but incorporates the principles outlined above.

Lighting grids for conference rooms and multi-use display areas are usually provided by electrically continuous tracks fitted on or in the ceiling. Lighting tracks provide both support for the lamps and direct electrical connections, but the track positions must allow for:

- changes in the furniture layouts (conference groups, banquets);
- possible room division and alternative uses;
- correct angle of illumination for wall pictures and illustrations.

Lighting controls vary with the scale and complexity of each area, ranging from purpose-built lighting control rooms (see 2.9.3) and portable lighting consoles stationed within the hall to local control panels in small conference rooms with extensions to allow control by the speaker when required. In function rooms and ballrooms the latter are often mounted in service lobbies adjacent to the room, but switches operating some of the lights must be provided at each entrance.

6.4.9 Display and exhibition lighting

In display work, the lighting must be used to create visual variety and stimulation. Whilst direct lighting is generally more emphasized, giving higher illuminances, extreme contrasts of brightness must be balanced by some diffused and background light to avoid discomfort glare.

Quantity of light:
The average brightness of the display and the masking of light sources must be considered from the different positions in which it will be viewed, and against the general level of lighting in the vicinity. For most displays an illuminance of 500 lux (50 lumens/ft^2) should be provided on the vertical or horizontal plane as appropriate, but this may need to be increased to 1000 lux in exhibition work.

Contrast with background:
Natural shadows formed under a clear blue sky have a reduction from one-third to one-tenth of the illumination of the direct sunlight beams. Similar ranges of contrast may be reproduced in display lighting (for example if general fluorescent light of, say, 200 lux is punctuated by beams from spot sources producing (at typical display distances) an illumination of particular items at around 1000 lux. Greater contrasts produce more dramatic and striking effects, but these are in a sense exaggerated. Background contrasts will also be affected by the darkness of drapes and surface finishes. A background reflection factor of 30–50 per cent provides a good range of contrast variation.

Modelling:
To provide modelling, directional light on displayed items is generally made up of three components – key, fill and backlight, although the last may be omitted. The spotlighting

fittings are usually mounted both overhead and in the footlight positions, with individual or lighting track connections. For a three-dimensional impression, with correctly angled light beams, a display depth of about 1.2 m is required.

Viewing angles for a single-aspect display extend over about 120° and may approach 180°. Multi-aspect displays, seen from all sides, require careful positioning of luminaires with precise cut-off angles (shutters, louvres or baffles) to prevent glare.

Colour:

The colour spectra of 'white' light sources may be critical in providing correct reflectance and 'warmth' of impression. As a rule, strong coloured light should not be used on the displayed items (except, perhaps, for small parts of the whole), but may be used to change background colouring contrasts.

Luminaires:

A wide range of incandescent lamps can be used, and some rationalization is needed to provide an orderly array. For key lighting, high-intensity spotlights of 100–150 W, with internal and external reflectors, are commonly used, whilst fill lighting is usually with reflector flood-lights (100–150 W). Low-voltage lamps may be installed to give highly concentrated beams.

The lamps may be partly or fully recessed into the surface, or mounted on brackets to provide the required offset for correctly angled illumination. Lighting tracks are also extensively used to facilitate repositioning.

For backlighting and general illumination (for example, of show cases), tubular fluorescent lamps are usually most suitable to provide a wide spread of luminance.

Direction of light

Directional lighting for display and exhibition work, television and photography requirements and for illuminating the persons speaking from a stage or platform, is ideally made up from three sources to provide a good balance of luminance and modelling.

Key light:

This is the main source, usually concentrated and intense, illuminating the face from above (optimum 45° vertical angle) and from one side (30–60° to the axis).

The position of the key lighting is fixed first. As its angle from the direct frontal view increases (from high to low-key) the effect is more dramatic, but less revealing. Higher grazing light (up to 50°) will emphasize shadow, whereas low-angled light (below 35°) may shine into the eyes of persons on the stage.

Fill light:

Softer and less intense, fill light is directed from above and from the other side, crossing roughly at right angles to the key light in order to soften shadows.

Back light:

Backlighting is usually from the same side as key light, but may be closer to the axis. Back light is used to separate the subject from the background, for example in modelling, stage, television and photography work, but may be omitted in platform lighting if the contrasts are not excessive. The light source must be screened from view and have a steep angle of incidence.

For stage use, many directional light sources – arranged in grids – will be required to cover the numbers of people who may occupy the stage at any time, allow for movement whilst keeping within the vertical angle limits (35°–50°), illuminate stage sets and other features, blend colours and produce varied lighting effects.

The higher lighting levels and directional control necessary for television and photographic work may involve the installation of special lighting circuits (total load 120 kW or more) to which projection lamps may be connected along the front of the stage.

Optimum acuity is achieved when the difference between the general brightness of the subject (foveal vision) and the immediate spatial background (peripheral vision) is from 1 : 1 to 4 : 1. For more distinctive contrast, the ratio of subject to background brightness should be increased to 10 : 1.

Significant reductions in visual acuity occur if the subject is seen silhouetted against a more highly illuminated background (window, illuminated backcloth or reflective screen etc.). Even moderate subject to background brightness ratios of 1 : 20 reduce visual acuity to about 20 per cent, and these reductions multiply as the background brightness increases.

6.5 AUDIO-VISUAL AID EQUIPMENT AND PROJECTION SYSTEMS

6.5.1 Video technology

Video and other technologies employed in producing and presenting information have many applications in congresses, presentations, training programmes, executive meetings and all types of exhibitions. At the same time, the rapid development of new equipment, costs of increasing sophistication, the need for skilled operators, expensive maintenance and obsolescence necessitate careful consideration of the wide range of choices available.

The following summary indicates the main types of equipment in use in the year 2000, and may be of help to the non-specialist in describing the technology and terminology used.

For further details, reference may be made to specialist publications as that by Simpson (1997).

Cathode ray tube (CRT)

The CRT emits a fine beam of modulated electrons scanning in lines across a face-plate coated with a phosphor, which fluoresces and produces changing pictures made up of illuminated spots (pixels). CRT has wide applications in television monitors.

Colour standards	Main countries[1]	System[2]
National Television Standards Committee (NTSC)	USA, Japan	525/30
Phase Alternating Line (PAL)	Europe	625/25
Seqquentiel Couleur à Memoire (SECAM)	France, Russia	625/25

[1] Also other influenced countries
[2] Lines per frame/frames per second.

CRT projectors use three monochrome tubes emitting red, green and blue (RGB) beams, which are adjusted to converge to produce a superimposed image on a screen. The projector may be for video only or have higher resolution suitable for multimedia data and graphics. Digital-to-analogue converters (DAC) are used to increase resolution, represented by SVGA 800 × 600, XGA 1024 × 768, SXGA 1280 × 024, UXGA 1600 × 1200 (pixels × lines).

Large CRT projectors require liquid face-cooling systems and the position in relation to the screen is critical, involving careful setting up. CRT projectors are usually ceiling mounted for front projection, and can be used with back projection screens and in video wall monitors. They are widely used in congress and exhibition halls for large screen presentations and enlarged video images of the speakers and proceedings.

Specifications for CRT projectors cover such aspects as:

- general – type (video/video, data, graphics), dimensions, weight, input voltage, power consumption, operating environment, cooling, heat emission, mounting;
- projection – CRT type, lenses, brightness (ANSI lumens), focusing, resolution, horizontal and vertical scan frequencies, RGB band width, colour systems;
- display – image size, colour temperature adjustment, electronic geometry and keystone circuitry correction, convergence (automatic);
- others – control features, inputs and memory, outputs, accessories, contrast modulation, image shifter, regulatory approvals, warranty.

Liquid crystal display (LCD)

LCD technology uses polarizing filters together with panels of liquid crystal material to control the transmission of light. In LCD projectors, the light – usually from a metal halide source – is separated into RGB components by dichroic mirrors to illuminate a composite polycrystalline silicon panel, and then combined for projection through a single zoom lens system. As with CRT, high resolution is required for computer graphics and data.

The position of the projector in relation to the screen is critical, but LCD is suitable for portable equipment, front and back projection, video walls and high-end applications using larger screens.

Specifications include system, lenses, lamp source, resolution, brightness, scanning frequencies, contrast ratio, picture sizes, colour systems, inputs, outputs, controls, dimensions, weight, voltage, power consumption, warranties and accessories.

Digital light processing (DLP)

Developed by Texas Instruments, DLP is a system that uses reflective light valves with a digital mirror device (DMD) to separate and divert the required light to a projection lens. DLP is particularly suitable for ultra-light portable equipment.

Specifications cover similar aspects to those for LCD projectors.

Plasma screens

Plasma displays employ the same principle as fluorescent lamps, using electrode discharges to ionize gas molecules, which excite a mixture of surface phosphors to emit full colour visible light. Plasma screens are currently limited in size to about 150 cm (60 in) in diagonal, but are thin, free from flicker and allow a wide viewing angle (160°). They have applications in computer-generated interactive displays (touch screen), exhibitions and information presentation.

Video walls

Video walls are made up from multiple video monitors arranged to present multiple images, a single enlarged image or other combinations, the combined images being produced by the use of digitized image processors to split the standard analogue pixel array between individual screens. Video walls mainly use CRT back projectors, but can incorporate LCD or DMP technologies. They are used in arenas, product launches, exhibitions and entertainment events.

Eidophor system

One of the first methods used to deliver large screen images, the Eidophor uses light from a xenon source, split by a dichroic mirror system, which is reflected onto a spherical mirror covered by thin viscous oil. The film is modulated by an electrical beam and scanned to project the image onto a large screen. The Eidophor process requires a large vacuum chamber and temperature control, necessitating a large projection room, but has been used for long throw screen images such as in magnified views of the speaker at a congress.

Laser projection

Light amplification by stimulated emission of radiation (laser) methods can be used in video projectors, but high power requirements and water cooling generally limit the applications to special entertainment and presentation events.

Video visualizers

Also called video overhead projectors, video presenters and visual system presenters, these consist of a video camera, optical system, lighting source and working surface. They can be used to project overhead transparencies, printed material, 35 mm slides and displayed objects, including microscopic specimens. In some models the motorized camera can rotate, pan and tilt and be used for video conferencing.

Electronic whiteboards

These can be used as standard whiteboards with dry markers, but can save anything written on the board on a personal computer (PC), print copies in four colours and transfer images to other sites. Interactive whiteboards include a touch screen facility, and enable information to be annotated over projected images in addition to copying.

Video cameras and camcorders

Cameras and camcorders are used for a wide range of applications:

- live transmission – instant transfer of proceedings to video projectors for enlarged screen viewing on stage, to other rooms for extended audiences, and to distant sites via ISDN lines and business satellite systems;
- recording of events – for subsequent review, editing, and use in seminars;
- production of presentation and training programmes – studio and live shooting, recording, editing, graphics, music and copying for in-house, intranet and internet information;
- video-conferencing – installed studios, carrels or portable equipment for live two-way or network transmission.

Images and associated audio-tracks can be stored in analogue or digital form using professional quality tape (such as Betacam) or disc format. The current trend is towards digital versatile disc (DVD) systems, which give increased capacity and high resolution.

Video conferencing

Video-, data and networked conferencing involves transmission via telephone and/or satellite systems between stations. Links to compatible high-speed digital transmission lines such as the integrated services digital network (ISDN) are normally required, and the system includes a terminal with multiple audio, video and multimedia interface connections, a set-top camera, microphone handset, speaker and monitor.

Portable systems hook up to a television monitor and ISDN lines. Large sets utilize a single anamorphic wide-angled lens, obviating the need for pan, tilt and zoom, together with large screen output devices (monitor, plasma panel or projection screen).

Video-conferencing can be offered by hotels, congress centres, executive conference centres and universities as an

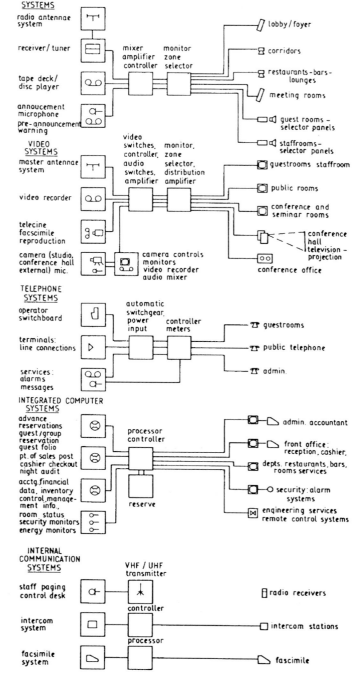

Audio-video and integrated systems

extension of a business services centre and/or as an extension to the meeting facilities. It may range from a fully equipped studio to a small fitted carrel.

Further developments

A number of technologies offer potential for future development, including flat panel displays using phosphors in a thin film electroluminescent device (TFEL), or light-emitting polymer (LEP) displays. Micro laser scanning techniques for projection systems are also under examination.

6.5.2 Slide and cine projection

Slide and overhead projectors

Slide and overhead projectors (OHP) are standard requirements for all conference and training programmes, and may be supplied by the venue or client or hired.

Overhead projectors enable images to be projected on to a screen behind the speaker from transparent sheets or rolls of acetate, which can be prepared in advance or used as a writing surface – normally 250 mm (10 in) square. Two main types of OHP are used:

- transmissive, with the fan cooled internal lamp source concentrated by an ellipsoidal mirror or fresnel lens on to the transparency platform;
- reflective, using a focusing reflective surface with the projector lamp housed besides the objective lens and requiring no cooling fan; this is portable and suitable for confined spaces.

Overhead projectors are normally mounted on the speaker's table at a distance from the screen of $1.0 \times$ screen width (10 in lens) to $1.6 \times$ screen width (14 in lens). This may be shortened to some extent by tilting the screen forward. In a small seminar room the screen may need to be set back across a corner to give the required projection distance.

A slide projector uses a cooled halogen lamp source (250–400 W) and is normally designed to take standard 24×35 mm slides held in a carousel or slide holder. The lens system is related to distance and should be interchangeable.

An example of specifications is:

- twin carousel slide projector with 250 W halogen lamp source and interchangeable 85 mm or 180 mm front projection lens and 60 mm lens for back projection; each carousel should have a capacity of 80 slides and be supplied with a remote control lead (with forward-reverse movement and focusing);
- stand for mounting equipment at an appropriate height with locking or fixing devices for stability;
- fast or slow speed dissolve unit plus snap change facility controlled by pulsed tape or remote hand control;
- cassette replay unit fitted with A/V head for pulsed tape presentation and with a public address facility which can also be used for background music;
- 1.8 m or 2.0 m fully supported screen (unless permanent screen is available).

All portable equipment must be simple, rugged and capable of high performance, and able to withstand frequent transportation and handling with varying conditions of use and inexperienced operators.

Cine projection

Equipment for cine projection ranges from specialist requirements for permanently installed cinemas to portable cine projectors, which may be required for meetings. Depending on the type of film and nature of use, safety regulations and licensing requirements may apply. For conference and training purposes cine film has practically been replaced by video, which offers greater versatility.

Where cine projection is required, 16 m film with optical or magnetic sound track is the standard for conference and lecture theatre use. Portable projection equipment may be set up in the room – leaving 900 mm (3 ft) space around – but in larger halls it is normally sited in a projection booth with other equipment. 35 mm film is more common for permanently installed equipment with xenon arc light sources, such as in large congress auditoriums.

For portable equipment screen sizes are generally 2 m square (6 ft 6 in) and range up to 3 m square (10 ft) in lecture theatres, corresponding to projection distances with a 50 mm lens of about 9 m and 16 m (31 ft and 53 ft) respectively.

6.5.3 Projection systems

Front projection:

This is the standard method using a projector located at the rear of the hall. The light projected through the space occupied by the audience requires clearance above head level or within the aisle width, and below ceiling obstructions (lamps, beams etc.). The projection axis should be as near normal to the screen as possible to avoid distortion, and screens may be partly tilted. Viewing requirements for screens affect both the seating plan and sectional elevations. Limits to the acuteness of extreme side seats, sight line clearances, and vertical angles of view are outlined in section 2.4.2, and details of booths in 2.9.2.

Back projection:

Back projection requires space behind the screen and the use of short throw (wide-angled) lenses. Mirror-lens assemblies may be required for restricted areas. Screen edge masking and the sealing (light and sound) of the projection are important. The illuminance of the hall must be lowered to provide contrast, and consideration must be given to the screen reflectance factor and gain (see below). Projection distances behind the screen are 1.5 to $2 \times$ screen width for short throw lenses, reducing to about $1 \times$ width for mirror assemblies.

Back projection offers a number of advantages compared to other methods:

- the use of a shielded translucent screen permits higher room illuminances (provided light is not directed at the screen);
- projection equipment is separated from the hall;
- multiple projection and slide screen presentations can be made together;

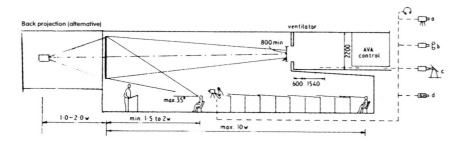

Television projection systems

Projectors may also be suspended from the ceiling within limits to the angle of axis and distance from the screen

• a central projection room can serve conference rooms backing on more than one side.

6.5.4 Screens

Projection screens may be portable or housed permanently in the room, the latter being rolled up, retracted or folded away when not required, or a permanent surface. The type of screen must be related to the system of projection (front or back), the size of the room (viewing distances) and the seating plan (viewing angles).

For front projection, both the comparative luminosity or gain and the optimum viewing angle depend on the screen surface. As a rule, surfaces providing a high gain tend to be more directional, limiting the angle of view, but allow higher ambient levels of light.

Surface	Gain	Viewing angle (•••)[1]
White matt	1	45–50°
Pearlized	1.5–2	30°
Glass beaded and lenticular	2.5–4	30–15°[2]
High gain aluminized	5+	10°[3]

Source: Simpson (1997)
[1] Angle of reflection relative to normal
[2] Reducing as the gain increases
[3] Highly directional; curved screens required for short distance CRT projectors allow higher levels of ambient light.

In all cases, front projection requires control of the light in the room or hall with dimming levels down to 5–10 lux. Shielded local lighting, 30–50 lux, should be provided at the lecturer's desk for note reading.

Back projection screens

In back projection screens, gain depends on the transmission of light. To minimize reflection of ambient light and improve contrast, front surfaces are usually grey matt. The short focal lengths used in projection are liable to produce 'hot spots', and this influences screen construction.

Transportable screens of translucent flexible PVC stretched on a frame can be used for both front and back projection, the latter having gain of about two with viewing angles up to 45°.

However, for permanent installations, to provide acoustic separation and avoid movement, it is necessary to use rigid screens of coated glass – normally up to 3.0 m × 7.6 m (10 ft × 25 ft) – or acrylic sheets, limited to 3.0 m × 7.6 m (7 × 10 ft).

Standard rigid screens have gains of one to two with maximum viewing angles 60°–45° respectively. Higher gain screens combine lenticular and/or fresnel finishes with matt black stripes, and have more directional viewing angles of about 30°.

6.5.5 Multi-vision presentations

Multiple screens arranged side by side can be used to present images from several projectors simultaneously; for example, from different views or with supporting technical details. Multi-screen productions are widely used in visitor centres and museums for tourist information and orientation, and for backgrounds to presentations, exhibitions and discotheques. Similar arrangements are used in lecture theatres and conference rooms to present overall and supplementary details using video, slide and overhead projectors.

The system may range from a three-screen, six-projector arrangement (either temporary or permanent) suitable for a conference room to an extended screen array or video wall for presentations. Side screens must be set at an angle to increase the viewing angle, and in large arrays are often curved. In planning multi-screen arrangements consideration must be given to the viewing requirements for screens generally, the size and condition of projected images, the space and the sound system.

Viewing requirements for screens generally include:

• maximum distance – 5–6 times width of projected image;
• minimum distance – 2 × width of projected image;
• maximum vertical angle – 30° above horizontal;
• Maximum edge angle to any image – usually 35°.

The size and definition of projected images will depend on the original format (slide, video, film), lens focus, position and lumen output of projectors.

The space taken up and conflict with other requirements (furniture, white board, lectern position, speaker) must be considered.

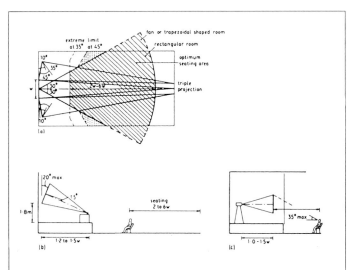

Multi-screen presentations

(a) Typical arrangement with side screens inclined at 10°. Alternatviely the screen may be curved to 3.5 W radius where W = width of individual screens. Optimum and limiting positions for seating are shown.

(b) Overhead projector details. To reduce keystoning the screen may be tilted to half the angle of projection (maximum 20°). A viewing angle of ± 5° from the normal is acceptable.

The projection distance is between 1.2 and 1.6 W (1.25 W for f = 12½").

Screens should be at least 1.8 m (6 ft) high to avoid light dazzling the speaker. Preferably two overhead projectors with screens should be provided to allow setting up in advance and dual projection

(c) Back projection using 35 mm or 50 mm lens for distances of 1.0 W or 1.5 W (W = width of screen). Screen height is two-thirds the width for normal format. The viewing distance from the screen may need to be increased for perforated screens. Back projection can be used with projection television.

The sound system should be integrated with speakers behind each screen to distinguish between different sources of sound.

6.5.6 Controls

A programmable control system is required to co-ordinate the operation of the various audio-video presentation media and associated equipment. In a purpose-built auditorium or lecture theatre this is located in the projection booth and more specialized lighting/sound control booths (see 2.9.2–2.9.4), but control equipment is also required for other conference and meeting rooms.

Room controllers are optimized for controlling the presentation equipment (slide and video projectors, screen, sound, etc.), room lighting, blinds, curtains and other requirements. Operated by the presenter, this may have a simplified touch screen or push buttons and be linked by hard wiring or cordless infrared or radio frequency (RF) signals. RF can be used, with a central processor sited elsewhere in the building controlling more than one room.

A 'state of the art' conference or training room installation will usually provide:

- video/data projection facilities;
- video-conferencing capability;
- a visualizer;
- a projection screen, curtains, blinds, lighting and sound control.

6.5.7 Room furniture and fittings

In hotels and other multi-use rooms, loose furniture with portable or removable equipment is normally set up to meet client specifications. Where a room or suite of rooms is regularly used for meetings or training programmes, the rooms may be fitted out with:

- teaching walls with removable/changeable panels for whiteboard, flip chart and screen;
- rail tracks for suspended white- and pinboards, one or two screens and shelf units which can be moved to the side when not required.

In each case, outlets for power microphone and control and an overhead lighting track will be provided.

6.5.8 Specific cases

Convention hall up to 150 delegates – equipment specifications

Stage set	Including back and side panels of adjustable height to about 2.5 m (8 ft 6 in) to form a backcloth with optional displays (company logo, theme of congress, information etc.)
Lectern	To be adjustable to the height of the speaker. Fitted with a flexible, vibration-free, mounted microphone and a jackpoint for a miniature lapel microphone. Other equipment includes a digital clock (actual or lapsed time); remote cueing; adjustable screened light for note reading, desk top for two A4 sheets 450 × 300 mm (18 × 12 in), plus storage for pencils, water glass, ashtray and a shelf for briefcases
Rostrum or platform	300 mm (12 in) high for use with the lectern or to provide a platform for a panel of speakers
Slide and film projection	A fully-supported 1.8 m or 2.0 m screen; a twin carousel slide projector dissolve unit; a cassette replay and a 16 mm cine projector, with appropriate adjustable stands

Sound system	Sound mixer with four microphones and inputs from cine track, tape cassette and record player. Two 50 or 60 W cabinet loudspeakers may also be required
Overhead projector	This should be provided with an acetate roll and installed on a desk or stand suitably located in relation to the screen
Aids	These could include a white board and flip chart on a stable stand, adjustable in height and tilt. The stand should be fitted with a pen channel. Display boards for information are also required inside and outside the hall
Light dimming and blackout	Synchronized control of light dimming and motorized blinds. A separate lighting control over the platform area is preferable.
Public-address system	Paging and background music with separate zoned controls to foyer, hall, reception lobby, exhibition areas, restaurants, lounges and guest rooms. The equipment should include broadcast receivers (fixed band and tunable); a long tape replay (cassette or 4-track cartridge) for background music; a disc turntable with single play or automatic change (33–45 rpm); microphone inputs; mixing equipment to allow over-riding for announcements (including oscillators, pre-announcement chimes, pre-recorded messages, automatic time switches, etc.) and distribution panels for mains and output terminals

Larger halls (300–1000) and more specialized facilities

Where congress markets (particularly at international level) form a major user of the hotel facilities and in municipal halls, additional facilities are likely to be required. These will take the following form:

Projection booth	A separate room or booth for video cine and slide projection. It enables larger screens to be used plus an operator's services to provide greater control over conditions. It is used for both front and rear projection
Multi-screen	To allow the presentation of slides and film side by side
Television projection	With cameras and video recording facilities for CCTV. Even if this equipment is not installed now, provision must be made for future need
Simultaneous interpretation	Usually direct wired or infra-red systems: the latter to allow loose furniture to be used in the hall. These should be installed together with facilities for chairing meetings, transmitting questions from delegates and permanent interpreters' booths

Speech reinforcement	Permanent loudspeakers should be installed and balanced acoustically. A 10–channel sound mixer may be required
Television recording	Cable ductwork and connections should be installed for additional lighting and television relays
Sound control room	Separate from the projection booth with control facilities for sound adjustment, recording and editing
Lighting control room	This may be combined with projection facilities or separate (for multipurpose use – see below)
Reception and waiting area	For the use of guest speakers. Should be provided with CCTV link to hall area or sound relay. It should be furnished with a desk and seats, have a cloakroom and toilet provided adjacently and have a separate entrance
Preparation rooms, technician workrooms, stores	Equipped for prerecording demonstrations, carrying out minor repairs to equipment and the storage of large mobile units as well as racked and shelved items.
Studios	These may be required for television, cine and still photography and audio recording. Other specialized facilities may be provided requiring individual access and design with sophisticated lighting

Multipurpose halls used for staged performances

Apart from providing for congress needs, halls used for concerts, live theatre and other entertainment purposes will require much more sophisticated sound and lighting control and stage-management facilities. Modification of acoustics may also be necessary. Facilities should include the following.

Stage management control systems	Rehearsal and performance control will be required from several positions on and off stage. These will consist of visual cueing; talk-back; ring or radial inter-communication networks to backstage and control areas; show relays; paging and interval warning messages or signals
Room acoustics:	Extended reverberation or assisted resonance will be necessary
Discotheques, dances, fashion shows, displays	A sound–lighting control console should be provided with tape-recorder and editing facilities, tape deck; two compact disc players of transcription quality with accurate location (cueing scale); a high-quality microphone on a swivel boom with additional microphone jackpoint; switch and fading controls, zoning unit; audio mixer with tone control and visual monitoring; multi-channel sound–light and chaser controllers; strobe controller;

dimming controls; headphones for operator and indexed storage racks for records and cassettes.

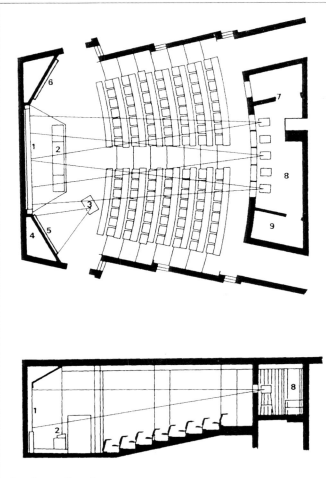

Lecture theatre

Layout for a lecture theatre seating 106 showing the arrangement of projection equipment and a sound control room which can be separated if required.

Key

1 Whiteboard/screen unit	*5 Tilting screen*
2 Lecturers' bench	*6 Chart rail*
3 Overhead projector	*7 Sound control room*
4 Overhead projector	*8 Projection room*
* storage*	*9 Equipment store*

6.6 ELECTRICAL SERVICES

6.6.1 Regulations

Electrical installations are normally subject to codes and regulations which lay down standards in the interests of safety. In addition to local mandatory requirements, reference is often made to the National Electrical Code (NEC) of the National Fire Protection Association of America and to equipment approved by the Underwriters' Laboratories (UL). In the UK, compliance with the Institution of Electrical Engineers (IEE) Regulations is normally specified. Conditions for connection to mains supplies, including the testing of installations, will also be laid down by the utility undertakings concerned.

6.6.2 Primary supplies

Mains supplies to premises are generally three-phase four-wire AC, with a cycle frequency of 50 or 60 Hz. Supply voltages vary from one country to another, and will also depend on the load requirements of the building. For large developments, such as a congress or exhibition complex, the supply will usually need to be brought in from medium or high-voltage distribution lines to one or more sub-stations or transformers on site, each serving a supply zone. In other buildings, transformer equipment may be located internally in a transformer room (dry-type or askarel transformers) or vault, meeting the necessary access, drainage, ventilation and protection requirements (fire, smoke, explosion, noise, transmission). As a rule switchgear must be housed in a separate room and metal clad in an arrangement to facilitate access, control and servicing. Mains terminals, transformers and main secondary distribution systems should be duplicated where necessary to avoid the failure of any part affecting the whole system. The main panel boards for sub-circuit distribution must also be located in equipment rooms (or ducts) that will allow working access independent from public circulation.

Self-generation of all or, more commonly, part of the electricity requirements may be feasible using combined heat and power generation (CHP) systems, which also provide space heating and/or domestic hot water through energy reclaim. This is usually practicable in large hotels in temperate zones in which surplus energy in winter can be sold back to the supply grid network. Local generation of 100 per cent requirements (see emergency supplies) is also warranted where the public supply is unreliable.

6.6.3 Emergency supplies

Automatic changeover to emergency battery supplies in the event of failure must be provided. In larger installations this will be automatically supplemented by generating equipment. Emergency supplies must maintain the following services:

- lighting – all exit signs, and 50 per cent of stairway lighting, 20 per cent of corridor lighting and 10–20 per cent of lighting in public areas;
- telephones, fire alarms and warning devices;
- fire-fighting apparatus (pumps, compressors);
- all sewage pumps and water pumps where necessary to maintain hot and cold water supplies;

- passenger elevators (with selector switch to operate each elevator in turn);
- food refrigerators and cold rooms;
- limited services to kitchen.

Battery rooms must comply with specific requirements for separate ventilation, fire resistance, drainage and water supplies, storage and operating space. The batteries must be kept constantly charged (usually by trickle charging).

6.6.4 List of supply requirements

	Service	Coverage: equipment, systems
Lighting	General purpose	Lighting installations, control and switching systems
	Safety lighting	Batteries, chargers, generators
	Stage lighting	Equipment, controls, dimmers
	External lighting	Facade, external circulation
	Visual signs	Directions, information, emergency
	Socket outlets	Floor and wall receptacles
Power	Motive power	Plant, equipment, controls
	Automation	Monitoring, regulation, servo systems, energy management
	Services	Kitchen and bar equipment
	Utilities	Sprinklers, pumps, fans
	Refrigeration	Compressors, pumps, fans
	Thermo-electric	Water heating, cooking
	Transportation	Elevators, hoists, conveyors
Safety	Protection	Earthing, overload and lightning protection systems
	Security	Cameras, monitors, alarms
	Fire detection	Sensors, signals, alarms
	Fire fighting	Activation, elevators, pumping and smoke extraction
Communication	Telephone	Exchange, installation services
	Transmittance	Receiving and transmitting systems, videoconferencing
	Television	Closed-circuit, broadcast, cable and videoprojection
	Public address	Reproduction, mixing, relay and speaker systems
	Reinforcement	Electro-acoustical, audio-visual and amplification
	Interpretation	Direct and radiant systems
Electronic data	Electricity	Stabilization, control, standby
	Computer	Central, sub-stations, links
	Peripherals	Terminals, printers, sensors, controllers, recorders
Administration	Reception	Terminals, printers, card readers, security monitors, telephones
	Reprographic	Photoprinters, binders
	Postal	Franking, addressing, stamping
	Accounting	Registers, printers, terminals
	Central services	Meters, clocks, indicators

6.6.5 Demand loads

Equipment loading and phase distribution requirements are often difficult to assess in premises such as multipurpose arts centres, which need to provide stage facilities. Maximum demand conditions must be assumed, and no diversity factor can be allowed. Branch circuit and feeder requirements must be determined from the full-load current ratings of the specific equipment connected (with ampacity factors of 1.25 for motor or combined loads).

However, general lighting loads in other areas (including socket or receptable outlets of 15 amp or less rating for lamps and portable appliances) can usually be assessed on an average unit rating:

General lighting load	W/m²	W/ft²	Notes
Congress halls, banquet halls	40–55	4–5	To allow flexibility in use and layout
Function rooms, conference rooms	30–55	3–5	Lower ceiling heights
Restaurants	20–30	2–3	The lower figure is based on NEC minimum load conditions and 100 per cent power factor
Shops, coffee shops, cafeteria	30–55	3–5	Servery counter and bar separately assessed. The lower figure is based on NEC minimum load conditions and 100 per cent power factor
Lecture theatres	30–55	3–5	
Auditoria (multipurpose)	10–45	1–4	Excluding stage lighting. The lower figure is based on NEC minimum load conditions and 100 per cent power factor
Reception areas	55	5	Frontdesk area
Circulation halls, corridors	6	0.5	Socket outlets (receptacles) at intervals, based on NEC minimum load conditions and 100 per cent power factor
Storage spaces	3	0.25	Increased for refrigerated stores and working areas, based on NEC minimum load conditions and 100 per cent power factor
Hotel rooms, hospitality suites	20	2	The lower figure is based on NEC minimum load condition and 100 per cent power factor
Offices	55	5	Allows for normal office equipment, based on NEC minimum load conditions and 100 per cent power factor
Exhibition halls	220–270	20–25	For equipment connection

Source: *National Electrical Code*. NFPA

| Surface trunking (metal) | In skirting and at bench level in offices (telephones, computer terminals, portable machines) Above stages and auditoria (stage lighting) At bench level in stores, workshops (equipment) |

6.6.6 Protection of installations

Separation:

The separation of different voltage supplies is essential unless specifically permitted (for certain control equipment) or insulated to the maximum voltage. The extent to which cables may fill the cross-sectional area of ducts and trays is limited.

Temperature:

Protection must be provided from excessive heat (which can cause damage to insulation and derating), such as from stage lighting, rear heating equipment and motors. Protection is also required from excessive cold (condensation) or temperature variation (condensation, expansion). Wiring voids in cold areas (refrigeration rooms, cold pipes, air-conditioning ducts) must be sealed.

Fire risk:

Ducts and risers must be fire-stopped wherever passing through separated compartments (e.g. from one floor to the next). Combustible material must not be used within the enclosure. Electrical wiring is not permitted within ventilation extracts from kitchens or conveying inflammable vapours (garages, fuel stores etc.). In areas of high risk, special apparatus must be used (sealed, non-sparking etc.) and mineral-insulated metal-sheathed cables may be installed.

Protection:

Protection must be given by:

- overload devices against excessive current (fuses, circuit breakers);
- correct rating of conductors;
- effective electrical insulation;
- mechanical protection;
- grounding or earth leakage circuit provision.

Enclosure:

Provisions for enclosure and protection of conductors include:

Type	Main locations and uses
Rigid conduit (metal)	Cast in floors, built or chased into walls – to individual socket or receptacle outlets in small rooms and offices. Suspended in roof space – to light fittings
Rigid conduit (non-metal)	Covered by wall plaster – to light switches, low-voltage circuits
Flexible conduit	In hollow partitions of demountable walls for machine connections
Exposed metal raceways (trays)	Service areas and plantrooms. In ceiling voids, high-level stage lighting (MICC)
Ducts	Cast in floors at one or more levels for meeting rooms (simultaneous interpretation systems, projection equipment, lectern controls); offices (portable and fixed equipment, telephones); exhibition halls (equipment and stand connections); foyers, snack bars (service counters, equipment)

6.6.7 Stage wiring

Where a stage or platform is installed separate wiring will be required for stage lighting (footlights, borderlights, proscenium sidelights etc.). As far as practicable, the cabling should be permanently installed to reduce the extent of trailing connections. Each branch circuit loading is limited to 20 amp unless heavy duty lamp-holders (non-interchangeable) are provided. Sub-circuit connections, fuses and controls should be centralized in protected distribution boards (fixed or portable) accessible to the stage operator.

For protection (against fire and damage) whilst allowing access for extension or alteration, stage wiring may be installed in metal trunking or clipped into metal trays or raceways. In the latter case, mineral-insulated metal-sheathed cabling should be used. All switchgear and distribution boards must be clearly labelled to indicate the circuits controlled (with wiring diagrams).

6.6.8 Television broadcasting

For colour television outside-broadcasting, high levels of lighting (about 700 lux) are generally required. The lighting system must be adaptable for other circumstances. Other operational requirements include:

- vehicle access and parking near to the hall (and stage) – minimum parking areas of 14 m × 4 m are required with 4 m height clearance, together with access and manoeuvring space; public circulation and essential services must not be obstructed;
- cable entry routes to the auditorium (and stage) with a wall access aperture about 0.2 m² (2 ft²) or 0.3 m (1 ft) above ground level leading to a service corridor or accessible duct; holes through fire-division walls must be fitted with fire-resistant shutters;
- power supplies to the mobile control van (up to 100 amp 240v single phase) from the main switchroom, allowing about 150 cm² (24 in²) cross-section for cable runs;
- supplementary lighting to the televised area may also be required (with temporary rigging); provision should also be made for similar cable access from the switchroom to this area;
- controls within the hall for technical direction together with cable routes to back-stage etc.

6.7 AIR-CONDITIONING, VENTILATION AND HEATING

6.7.1 Interior design conditions for comfort

Sensitivity to distracting conditions is particularly critical in situations that require long periods of concentrated attention. Internal design requirements in congress auditoria and halls need to take account of a number of variables.

Climatic conditions:
Higher internal temperatures of 23–25°C (73–77°F) are typical in hot climates, compared with the 20–23°C normally specified in temperate areas. Design conditions also allow seasonal variations; internal heating temperatures in winter, taking account of heavier clothing and acclimatization, are often 1–3°C below summer cooling requirements. Transient zones such as entrance lobbies and some foyers and corridors entered from outside are usually intermediary in temperature, 1–3°C above or below those of areas continuously occupied, to allow adjustment (CIBSE, 1999).

Surface temperatures:
This is an important consideration when meeting or function rooms are use intermittently and there is a time-lag before the temperatures of the surfaces adjust to that of the warmed or cooled air. The same condition applies when the building fabric (glass, windows, light cladding) has a high thermal transmittance value, producing a fall or rise in surface radiant temperature relative to the ambient air temperature.

In these cases, the effective temperature of the room should be raised or lowered by 1°C for each 1°C the mean radiant temperature falls or rises above 20°C.

Air movement:
The motion of air has a significant effect on comfort and tolerance of temperature variations, and is taken into account in determining 'effective temperature scales'.

Air velocities at head level below 0.1 m/s (20 fpm) give a feeling of stagnation. However, the extent to which the air velocity can be increased without discomfort (draughts) will depend on the temperature difference between the air stream and ambient air, the activity of the occupants, the part of the body feeling the air movement and the sensitivity of the individual concerned. Occupants are more sensitive to temperature differences and higher velocities on the neck than on the ankle.

BSEN ISO 7730 recommends that, for light and sedentary activities, mean air velocities should be less than 0.25 m/s (50 fpm) during cooling and less than 0.15 m/s (30 fpm) in winter.

Relative humidity:
A relative humidity of 45 per cent or more is considered significant in contributing to the 'freshness' of the air; air with less than 35 per cent RH is liable to cause dryness of the serous membranes and discomfort, whilst an increase much above 65 per cent may produce excessive perspiration and condensation, particularly in the absence of higher air velocities.

For auditoria and conference rooms, an optimum condition of 50±5 per cent RH is generally used for design purposes. Humidity control, based on dew point, is maintained by determining the absolute humidity in the return air lines, outside conditions and treatment plant.

In areas used for exhibitions of works of art and delicate objects, strict control of relative humidity is critical. Special considerations also apply in areas housing equipment sensitive to condensation damage.

Recommended comfort criteria (UK)

Area type	Dry resultant temperatures		Noise rating (NR)
	Winter (°C)	Summer (°C)	
Auditoria	22–23	24–25	20–30
Conference rooms	22–23	23–25	25–30
Training rooms	19–21	21–23	25–35
Exhibition halls	19–21	21–23	40
Museums/art galleries	19–21	21–23	30–35
Entrance lobbies/foyers	19–21	21–23	35–40
Restaurants/dining rooms	22–24	24–25	35–40
Bars/lounges	20–22	22–24	30–40
Offices (executive)	21–23	22–24	30
Hotel bedrooms	19–21	21–23	20–30
Hotel bathrooms	26–27	25–27	40
Television studios	19–21	21–23	25

Source: CIBSE (1999). *Environmental Criteria for Design*. Chartered Institution of Building Services Engineers.
Note: With temperature adjustment facilities.

6.7.2 Fresh air requirements

Supply rates of fresh air are determined by several criteria, namely:

- human respiration – increase in CO_2 level;
- dilution of airborne contaminants produced within the space;
- thermal comfort of occupants;
- smoke clearance in the event of fire;
- combustion appliance requirements.

The necessary ventilation rate to prevent CO_2 concentration rising beyond a limit of 0.25 per cent by volume (2500 ppm) is 1.8 l/s per person (3.8 cfm) seated quietly, rising up to 5.8 l/s per person (12.3 cfm) for light work. Acceptable dilution of body odours requires a higher rate of 8 l/s per person (17 cfm), and it is this that this determines the minimum fresh air requirements for sedentary occupants although CO_2 concentration is related and can be monitored to control the rate of air supply to match changing requirements.

Tobacco smoke also produces undesirable odours and may introduce risks from 'passive smoking'. Ventilation rates must be increased significantly as indicated below.

Outdoor air-supply rates may be described by the volumetric rates of air change per hour or, in more complex situations, by rates of air-flow per person or per unit floor area.

Ventilation standards for halls, theatres and other places of public assembly are laid down in local codes, and usually recommend a minimum fresh air supply of 8 l/s or 28 m³/h (17 cfm). This may need to be increased for multi-use activities, and many congress centres adopt 12 l/s (25 cfm) per person as the standard with higher rates in rooms in which smoking is allowed. Recommended outdoor air supply rates for air-conditioned spaces take account of the likely density of occupation and the amount of smoking.

Type of space	Smoking[1]	Recommended outdoor air supply	
		per person l/s (cfm)	per unit floor area[2] l/s/m² (cfm/ft2)
Theatre, concert hall[3]	None	8 (17)	
Multi-use congress hall[3]	Some	12 (25)	
Entrance lobbies[4], shops	Some	8 (17)	3.0 (0.59)
Ballrooms[3]	Some	12 (25)	
Hotel bedrooms	Heavy	12 (25)	1.7 (0.33)
Cafeteria[5]	Some	12 (25)	
Conference/meeting rooms[6]	Some	18 (38)	
Restaurants, bars[5]	Heavy	18 (38)	
Board rooms and conference rooms	Very heavy	25 (53)	6.0 (1.18)
Corridors			1.3 (0.25)
Restaurant kitchens			20.0 (4.00)
Toilets			10.0 (2.00)

Source: After CIBSE A1–9 Guide (1986). *Environmental Criteria for Design.* Chartered Institution of Building Services Engineers
[1] Maximum percentages of occupants who are smokers: some smoking, 25 per cent; heavy smoking, 45 per cent; very heavy, over 45 per cent. Ventilation rates for heavy and very heavy smoking areas may need to be increased, particularly for freshening rooms between changes in occupancy.
[2] If larger than the occupancy requirements or where occupancy varies widely
[3] Local codes may stipulate higher requirements
[4] Allowing for high infiltration of air
[5] Rate of extraction may be over-riding factor
[6] Average for larger meeting rooms with limited smoking.

Filtration grades range from 7–8 for museums and art galleries and 5–7 for auditoria, conference and hotel rooms to 4–5 for circulation areas.

Plant requirements for auditoria, ballrooms and other assembly areas are calculated on 100 per cent fresh air requirements, with provision for recirculating a proportion of recycled fully conditioned air from the room. Ratios of cleaned recycled air to fresh air may range from 100 : 0 for preheating or pre-

cooling to a maximum 25 : 75 during periods of occupation. Exceptionally, local codes may allow 50 : 50 ratios, provided the relative humidity is kept below 55 per cent.

In halls with very high ceilings, such as those used for banqueting or exhibitions where volumetric standards may not be appropriate, an alternative standard of 16 l/s/m² of floor area (3 cfm/sq ft) may be adopted. This is also used for areas with variable occupancy.

6.7.3 Determination of heat gain or loss

The heating and air-conditioning requirements of a building are determined by the interactive effects of its internal activities, insulation standards and external conditions. As a basis for calculating maximum heat loss or gain, the extreme conditions likely to be experienced from time to time in the locality must be determined. For design purposes, these are usually based on a 2.5 per cent probability occurrence (summer) and 97.5 per cent probability in winter, although in the latter case the median of extremes may be taken.

Heat losses are affected by the site and degree of exposure (surface resistance, infiltration), planning of buildings (ratio of volume to external envelope and height), constructional features (thermal transmittance values and edge losses) and operational considerations. The last factor will vary from room to room, taking into account daylighting and ventilation requirements.

Heat gains result both from external conditions (air temperature and direct solar radiation) and incidental uses of the building. Particular areas of large heat gain, such as plant rooms, kitchens, stage lighting, dimming equipment and projection rooms, require separate calculation of ventilation requirements.

In most meeting rooms and associated areas, the principal sources of heat are the lighting loads and the occupants themselves.

Average heat generated per average adult[1] for design purposes

Conditions	Watts	BThU/h
Auditorium – quiet seated	110	375
Conference/boardroom	115	390
Foyer/assembly/corridors	145	495
Restaurant/bar[2]	135	460
Dancing (social)	150–460	510–1570

Sources: Adapted from ISO 7730, ASHRAE 55, ISO 8996
[1] Based on average metabolic rates, heat generation per 1.8 m² from an adult body
[2] Allowing 9 W sensible heat and 9 W latent heat for food.

Solar radiation requires particular consideration, both in resort areas where hotels are usually oriented and designed to benefit from direct exposure to the sun and in urban situations in which meeting rooms often need to be sealed (to control external noise, pollution, climatic variation) and fully air-conditioned.

Transmission of solar heat through the building fabric depends on the exposure time, absorptivity of the surface, thermal capacity of the structure and its thermal transmittance value – these building features also affect heat loss in cold weather. Rapid fluctuations due to the effects of moving solar radiation on lightweight structures and large areas of cladding and glazing also present difficulties in balancing air-conditioning loads within the building, requiring automatic sensing/adjustment of conditions.

Alternative methods of reducing the effects of solar radiation through windows and glazed areas of a lobby, restaurant or lounge include:

* recessing windows to provide screening in the form of construction;
* provision of venetian blinds, awnings or vertically moving screens (e.g. between dual panes of glass);
* installation of jet cooling or heating air curtains along widow perimeters to counteract temperature variation.

Utilization of solar energy is also an important component of energy conservation and systems include:

* recovery and storage of solar energy for intermittent space heating and domestic hot water (vacuum glass solar collectors);
* photovoltaics using crystallized silicon solar cells to generate electrical power via inverters and storage batteries.

6.7.4 Air-conditioning systems

The choice of air-conditioning systems for individual meeting rooms and their associated areas depends largely on the volume of space and number of occupants, the range of functions and the extent to which conditions need to be controlled generally or locally. In most cases this involves central station plant.

Unitary equipment

For small, dispersed buildings, as in resort villages, some hotels and extensions, packaged unitary equipment provides the advantages of lower cost, simplicity of installation and individual control. Split-packaged and variable refrigerant flow (VRF) systems with individual units served by remote air cooled/condenser equipment may be used for guest room accommodation, small function and meeting rooms, restaurants and offices.

Central station systems

To some extent, central station systems overlap with packaged equipment. In the former, air is conditioned in a central plant and ducted to the various rooms in which it is required. For public areas, plant may be zoned to serve individual spaces such as auditoria and large ballrooms (mono-zone systems) or more variable requirements (multi-zone systems). Central systems may be extended to serve other areas, including guest rooms and small meeting rooms, using fan coil or induction units to allow local control.

Central systems facilitate maintenance and operation independent of the areas supplied, enable sophisticated control (temperature, humidity, air-flow rate, fine filtration, sterilization, automatic change-over to fire mode requirements) to be incorporated and allow energy savings to be introduced as a result of monitoring, recycling and integrated engineering design.

Mono-zone systems, with low-pressure variable air volume (VAV) supplies, involve large section ducts with airflow velocities typically 5.0 m/s (1000 fpm) reducing to 2.5 m/s (500 fpm) in noise-sensitive situations.

Multi-zone systems employ high-velocity primary airflow distribution in the order of 10–20 m/s (2000–4000 fpm), often using circular or oval ductwork with flexible connections to induction units or fan coil terminals which recirculate secondary air from the room with filtration and chilling/heating (two- or four-pipe connections) as required.

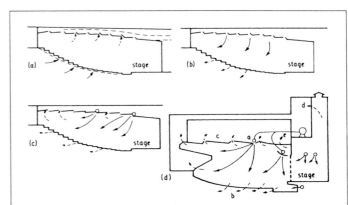

Ventilation systems with (a) upward flow, (b) downward flow, (c) front-to-rear flows and (d) theatre ventilation showing a typical arrangement to ensure minimum noise and to meet most legal requirements.* The diagram shows, at point a, high level input (capacity equal to 133 per cent of combined extract); at points b and c extract from auditorium (60 per cent of capacity) mainly from low level; at point d extract from stage (40 per cent of capacity) with direct discharge to open air; at point e emergency extract operated when stage isolated (with automatic dampers or emergency fan). Capacity 60 per cent of total

*Local requirements must be checked

6.7.5 Considerations affecting choice of system

Sophistication: High standards of air quality, control, distribution and safety provisions are required in auditoria and large halls with high-density occupation. Flexibility to enable rapid preheating/cooling (recycling), monitoring and adjustment to suit changing requirements are essential in an auditorium or hall used intermittently.

Noise levels: Acoustic treatment (including attenuation, directional flow streamlining and appropriate support) is necessary to achieve design criteria NR25 for congress halls; NR30 for smaller multipurpose halls. Acceptable noise levels affect outlet velocities, which usually range from 4 m/s (800 fpm) with high ceiling diffusers to 1.5 m/s (300 fpm) for low level discharges.

Distribution: In large volume, high ceiling halls, difficulties tend to arise from air stratification, pronounced temperature gradients, short circuiting and uneven distribution of airflows. Auditoria with fixed seating may employ downward, upward and/or cross-flow distribution (see 2.6.2). Large ballrooms and exhibition halls with variable layouts require cross- or reverse airflow arrangements (see 4.4.3).

Energy reclaim: Where possible, exhaust flows are ducted over the main lighting systems to remove heat at the source. Plant design usually incorporates recuperative or regenerative equipment for energy transfer to incoming air.

Separation: Systems (separate from that in the hall) are required for stage areas, projection and other booths, foyers and service lobbies. In halls that are divisible, both the whole and each separate area must have its own balanced system.

Plant: Air-conditioning plant is limited in unit capacity to about 50 000 m^3/hr, and normally at least two sets (each 60–70 per cent of total) will be installed for flexibility of operation and maintenance. Equipment is located as near as practicable to the supply zone, grouped with chilling and heating plant, and may be roof-mounted or housed in plant rooms (energy centres) adjacent, allowing access for maintenance and eventual replacement.

6.7.6 Heating

Space heating is mainly combined with air-conditioning, supplemented by local heating in entrance and perimeter zones (air curtains, fan convectors), work stations (particularly where there is a high exhaust rate), dressing and changing rooms and in individual offices and guest rooms having natural ventilation.

In addition, domestic hot water must be provided to various draw-off points (toilets, kitchens, service bars, dishwashing machines, employee changing areas and, in hotels, guest rooms and laundries).

Heat transference is usually by low-pressure hot water circulated at 82–72°C (180–160°F), but medium-pressure systems at 120°C (248°F) may be used in larger buildings, necessitating enclosure of the pipework and equipment. Boilers are usually installed at ground or basement level, but need to be closely associated with the air-conditioning plant.

Domestic hot water for kitchens, toilets and changing rooms is generally supplied from calorifiers located near the place of use.

6.7.7 Specific areas

Entrance lobbies

High rates of ventilation are likely due to the infiltration and stack effect, and air exhaust may not be required. Cooling is provided by equipment which has a high output in relation to its air-handling capacity (such as fan coil units), enabling space and duct size to be kept to a minimum. Primary air supply can normally be reduced to less than one change per hour.

For extensive areas of glazing, air curtains using recirculated air may be installed along the perimeter. Air-conditioning is also required to be concentrated over the main areas of activity in a lobby or foyer (reception desks, coffee bars etc.), together with balanced exhaust.

Restaurants, cocktail lounges, coffee shops

Air may be supplied from separate air-conditioning units or from primary plant with local heating/cooling to provide variable control. Ceiling diffusers are usually installed: a flow of 290–380 l/s (600–800 cfm) per diffuser and a temperature differential about 8°C (15°F) cooling and 10°C (18°F) heating is usually suitable for ceilings of average height.

Airflows may be concentrated over or under windows to counteract heat loss/gain, and also within the area of the food servery or cocktail bar. Balancing exhaust grilles in the front of these areas will be required to draw off cigarette smoke and fumes. High rates of extraction must be provided over displayed cooking equipment, and this may be balanced by supplying tempered air around the perimeter of the hood.

Negative pressures should be maintained in any adjacent kitchen to which ventilating air from the dining room may be partly exhausted. It is, however, important to avoid excessive draughts being created through service doors and across service counters.

Auditoria

Mono-zone systems are normally used with plant exclusive to this area. In a large hall, two or three separate air-conditioning units may be installed to meet the operational requirements. Alternative air distribution arrangements are summarized in 6.7.4.

Air supply, exhaust and emergency requirements will normally be subject to legislation.

Up to 75 per cent of the air admitted can be mechanically exhausted, of which about 40 per cent is usually extracted from the stage and 60 per cent from the auditorium. If the latter is through floor extracts, an additional high-level extract fan above the proscenium arch will usually be required with automatic change-over from floor to high-level extract when the safety curtain is lowered.

In addition to the occupancy load, much of the heat gain will result from the lighting installation. Many of the spotlights and other equipment used for stage lighting will be suspended over the auditorium (in an arena theatre with all the lighting in the auditorium this can represent a load of 200 kW or more), and in many cases this heat can be ducted away and recovered for space heating.

Stage ventilation must be separate (with safety curtain), and presents specific problems because of the height, heat load from equipment and the variable space occupied by the stage equipment. One solution is to install a low-pressure system using fresh air discharged through ducting around the walls at above one-third height. Used air is exhausted through the roof (with noise suppression) to give a slight negative pressure. During the winter supplementary heating (at several levels) will usually be required.

Provision must be made for escape of smoke in the event of fire, with automatically opening roof ventilators – such as haystack ventilators.

Orchestral areas below the stage will need to be provided with separate air-conditioning, preferably independent from that of the hall. A low-pressure system is normally used, supplied with fresh air only and exhausted through the stage. The inlet temperature should be controllable from the orchestra area.

Small meeting rooms, private dining rooms

Because of intermittent use in these areas, the air-conditioning system must have a wide range of adjustment. Multi-zone systems are generally installed with induction or fan coil units to provide terminal cooling/heating of air recycled from the room. Cross flow of air should be provided, with exhaust to service lobbies or corridors.

Ballrooms, banquet halls, congress halls

Function spaces of this type in hotels and other premises are usually designed to allow division into separate areas.

If a mono-zone system is installed, air supply and exhaust branches to each division must be suitably balanced with pre-set dampers for isolation when necessary. In hotels this is often a self-contained system independent from the air-conditioning of other parts of the premises.

With multi-zone systems, dual duct or terminal cooling/heating may be provided to allow individual adjustment to suit different requirements. Limits to noise levels (NR25) must be specified. Sound carry-over from one section to another via ductwork must also be considered. A slight positive pressure should be maintained to ensure directional flow towards service lobbies and kitchens.

Foyers, concourses and bars

Assembly areas associated with halls and auditoria are generally occupied for short periods, and precise standards of control may not be practicable. To meet the peak loadings of high-density occupation and smoking it is an advantage to provide two-speed ventilating fans giving at maximum speed a high rate of air change (say 30 to 50 changes/hour), and air movements of up to 0.25 to 0.4 m/s (50-80 fpm) in the occupied zone.

Operational areas

Requirements for the heating and ventilation of operational areas are generally dictated by exhaust conditions (removal of heat and impurities). Special considerations apply in the following areas.

Kitchens

High rates of extraction over cooking equipment will be necessary giving rise to large ventilation flows:

Zone	Air changes/hour
Over kitchen	20
Over general cooking zone	40
Over banquet cooking zone	60

Easily-removable grease filters (for frequent cleaning) and sealed access points must be provided, and automatic fire dampers installed. Some 60–80 per cent of the extraction flow should be made up by tempered air (warmed or cooled as required) supplied to the kitchen, with the remainder entering from the restaurant or service lobbies. Special ventilation, with cooling, is required in food and wine stores and butchery sections.

Public toilets

Approximately eight to ten air changes per hour are usually provided through a separate exhaust system balanced by air inflow from cloakrooms and adjacent corridors. The extraction fans must be duplicated, with automatic change-over in event of failure. Exhaust air cannot be recirculated. Legal minimum is three changes per hour.

Enclosed car parks

Special requirements apply to avoid risk of fire and exhausted smoke being discharged to other areas. These include separation, fire dampers, discharge outlets and spark-proof machinery etc.

6.8 SECURITY, SAFETY AND RISK MANAGEMENT

6.8.1 Security and business continuity planning

By bringing together groups of people who may represent valuable business interests, professional expertise, political authority and other sectors of influence, congresses and meetings and exhibitions present a degree of risk. Security must be provided for delegates, speakers and other visitors, valuable items of equipment (including exhibits), information and for the premises generally.

The assessment of threats or hazards will depend to a large extent on the subjects of the meeting, the host organization, attendees, publicity, extent of press and public entry (including other events at the same time) and access for vehicles. Recommendations by the AIPC cover the following procedures (AIPC, 1992):

- at time of booking – advice of police and security agencies on risks;
- pre-arrival – screening of delegate lists and press accreditations;
- access control – electronic screening, identification procedures, delegate badging;
- personal protection – hotel, transport, building and entry points, security arrangements and support, contingency plans;
- property and information protection – access control, safekeeping of classified material and valuable material, security vetting of staff and contractors, surveillance;
- contingency plans – to deal with emergencies arising from fire, medical, non-violent intrusion, violent intrusion, bomb threat and other causes.

Threat or risk assessment should be part of a wider provision to deal with all types of hazards that may arise, such as computer crimes/hacking, failure of IT or essential systems, industrial action by staff or external services, failure of suppliers to meet deadlines, terrorism, sabotage, accidents, fire, and natural disasters.

A business continuity plan to deal with these risks should cover such aspects as:

- **threat/risk surveys** – critical business functions; risks and probability of occurrence, impacts of disruption;
- **deterrent and preventative measures** – steps to identify early signs (breakdowns, defects), organized training, inspection, surveillance and monitoring;
- **strategies to deal with crises** – key teams, crisis managers, insurance and legal representatives, procedure for dealing with media, management training and roles;
- **recovery strategies for business resumption** – review of action, corrective procedures and measures to correct adverse publicity and to restore confidence.

6.8.2 Surveillance and protective systems

Remote observation and monitoring of areas inside and outside the building is an essential part of security and management operations. Closed-circuit television systems used for this purpose are made up from a number of cameras strategically located and linked to junction boxes (for transmission and power supply), then relayed to monitor screens with adjustment and switch-over controls housed in the security office.

CCTV cameras fall into several categories, depending on the location (indoors or outdoors, light conditions, angles of view), lens requirements (remote iris adjustment, focusing and

zooming) and head operation (pan and tilt). Positions of nearby lamps that could shine into the lens, causing glare, must be considered. For night vision, silicon-vidicon cameras used in parallel with infrared beams may be installed.

Typical locations for cameras:
- vehicle entrance/exit;
- staff entrance, including security check;
- inside lobby towards main entrance and above reception desk;
- foyers – towards entrance doors;
- emergency and secondary exits (operated on opening).

Other anti-intrusion systems include:
- infrared beams across specific paths;
- microwave fences to detect crossing;
- electrical continuity – to indicate opening of doors, etc.;
- ultrasonic and microwave wave pattern disturbance;
- security lighting – with illumination of car parks, paths, grounds and buildings.

6.8.3 Detection systems and identity checks

Concealed articles can also represent a threat to security and control. Guests' luggage, visitors' bags and posted or deposited parcels may conceal weapons, explosives or items stolen from the premises. Theft by staff and service personnel is also a matter for concern. Search operations must be carried out quickly and as discreetly as possible to avoid causing innocent people inconvenience and invasion of privacy and to minimize delay and congestion on arrival or departure.

Portable equipment used for search and detection includes:

- low dosage X-ray inspection of hand luggage etc. placed in an inspection chamber;
- a walk-through screening unit with remote electronics console to detect metal objects;
- fluoroscopic cabinets for inspection of unopened letters, packages and luggage.

Stringent safety requirements apply to the use of such equipment, and security services are normally hired for particular situations that could involve security risks. Identification systems are commonly installed in the staff entrance area, together with time-recording equipment. Similar identity badges may be issued to visitors and delegates.

6.8.4 Safety

Safety is a major consideration in all aspects of meeting, exhibition and hotel operations. Specific legal obligations apply, and the assembly of large numbers of people in unfamiliar surroundings imposes obligations on both the owners and organizers of venues.

Statutory obligations for safety cover fire protection and means of escape (see below) as well as workplaces, hygiene, engineering equipment and the premises generally. A system of regular inspection, reporting, recorded attention to defects and planned maintenance and replacements must be introduced (see 7.2.1–7.2.3).

Subject	Examples of safety checks
Property	Premises, furniture and equipment maintained in a safe condition
Workplaces	Space, equipment, protection of operators, conditions, supervision
Hygiene	Food and beverage services, water supplies, cleanliness
Engineering	Fresh air supplies, air treatment, electrical and gas installations
Circulation	Lifts, escalators, steps, stairs, landings, handrails, doors
Equipment	Secure fixing, emissions, ventilation, fire risks, potential dangers

Safety management organization includes:
- **safety manuals** – details of risks, precautions and actions to be taken in event of accidents and emergencies;
- **posted notices** – medical and emergency contacts, reporting procedures;
- **first aid training** – personnel responsibilities, duty schedules;
- **first aid facilities** – medical rooms and equipment requirements.

6.8.5 Fire protection

Protection against danger from fire in buildings is covered by legislation and includes:

- fire resistance of the walls, partitions, floors, staircases, lift shafts and doors to delay the spread of fire and retain structural integrity for specified periods (30 min, 1 h, 2 h or 4 h) to allow evacuation and fire control measures to be carried out;
- limitations on the use of combustible materials in areas of high risk and of lining materials which may create hazard to occupants from high rates of surface flame spread, smoke or toxic fume emission or by melting and shattering;
- installation of fire alarms, appropriate fire-fighting equipment and systems, emergency signs, lighting and ventilation of escape routes together with training of staff to deal with emergencies.

6.8.6 Means of escape in event of fire

Fire escape provisions are based on an evacuation time of 2–3 minutes from any occupied part of the building, and are subject to specific requirements in local Codes and Regulations. The size and number of exits from a room is determined by the maximum number of occupants, calculated from:

Type of room	m²/person
Close seating	0.5
Dance hall	0.6
Exhibition	1.5
Foyers, bars	0.3–0.5
Restaurants	1.0–1.5

Source: *GLC Code of Practice.*

As a rule, at least two alternative exits must be provided from a hall, sited more than 45° apart from any position in the room and within a direct distance of 30 m and maximum travel distance round furniture of 45 m (130 ft) – which may be increased in sprinkler-fitted rooms. Special requirements apply to auditoria with fixed seating (see 2.4.5).

Exit widths are calculated on the average width of a person, 559 mm (22 ins), the minimum clear exit width being for two persons or 1.12 m (44 in), increasing with numbers as follows:

Numbers of persons	Minimum exits	Minimum width, m (ft-in)
Up to 200	2	1.1 (3–7)
200–300	2	1.2 (3–11)
300–400	2	1.4 (4–7)
400–500	2	1.6 (5–3)

Plus an additional exit 1.6 m wide for every additional 250 persons or part thereof
Source: *GLC Code of Practice.*

Exit routes must be kept clear, protected from fire and smoke with self-closing doors opening in the directions of travel, fitted with emergency signs and lighting (12 lux) and must lead to a safe final exit and place of assembly in the open.

Where the hall is above or below ground level, the hall exits must allow for 10 per cent greater occupancy and lead to the final exits via fire-protected lobbies and staircases (with separate ventilation). Regular checking of appliances, exit routes and procedures (including fire drills) is essential.

6.9 OTHER REQUIREMENTS

6.9.1 Facilities for the disabled

Legislation and Codes of Practice in many countries stipulate that access and facilities must be provided for the disabled. To comply, it is necessary for owners and operators to:

- ensure that new work, alterations and adaptations comply;
- carry out access and facility audits;
- review operational and letting procedures.

Disability covers people with physical impairment (with limited mobility or wheelchair users) or sensory impairment (through limited sight and hearing difficulties).

To ensure that buildings can be used by everybody, audits should consider matters such as:

- designated car parking spaces/drop off points for the disabled;
- level or ramped access to the entrance;
- lifts designed for wheelchair users and people with visual disabilities;
- doors and corridors wide enough for wheelchairs users;
- accessible toilets equipped for wheelchair users;
- adequate access, spaces and sight lines for wheelchair users in auditoria;
- heights and colours of counters, handrails and reception points;
- positions of wall-mounted fittings; telephone points, fire alarms and call points;
- induction loops and other aids to improve communication;
- tactile indicators for the visually impaired;
- audible and visual fire alarms;
- a managed assisted escape strategy;
- adequately trained staff to help with questions and problems.

Source: Association of Building Engineers, 1999.

6.9.2 Energy conservation and environmental policies

As befits its role in representing the destination, a congress centre should take an active interest in safeguarding the environment. This calls for the preparation and implementation of an environmental programme to conserve the use of resources and avoid damage to the environment. Examples of audits may be summarized as follows.

Subject	Examples of steps required
Energy consumption	☐ Improved building insulation. ☐ Use of zone and time controls ☐ Regulation of ventilation ☐ Energy saving lighting ☐ Use of building management systems ☐ Specification of energy-saving kitchen equipment ☐ Location of cooling plant ☐ Energy recovery systems ☐ Use of solar energy ☐ Combined heat and power
Water consumption	☐ Water saving sprays and equipment ☐ Use of rainwater for irrigation ☐ Maintenance of plumbing systems ☐ Reduction of waste in domestic hot water circulation
Waste production	☐ Reduction of unnecessary printing ☐ Two-sided copying ☐ Use of e-mail ☐ Sorting and recycling of waste paper, metals, glass and plastics ☐ Separation and correct disposal of hazardous waste
Purchasing	☐ Use of eco-labelled products ☐ Specification of efficient, durable products which have long lives ☐ Purchase of products which do not cause waste problems ☐ Preference given to local goods
Staff	☐ Introduction of staff training and motivation programmes

Source: After Van Aerschot and Carney (1997).

7 Investment, maintenance, upgrading

7.1 DEVELOPMENT PROPOSALS

7.1.1 Development policies and goals

Policies and plans for future development fall into two main groups:

- development plans prepared by public authorities (state, municipal) in the interests of economic, environmental and social benefits for the community;
- business plans to achieve commercial objectives, which may include development proposals for new or improved facilities; these plans are normally drawn up by the owners and managers responsible.

Strategic planning must lay down the framework in which orderly development can take place to ensure the best use of resources to achieve the desired outcome. In the context of public investment in tourism projects – either directly or through financial assistance in the form of project loans or grant aid, infrastructure provision or fiscal incentives – the long-term objectives or goals for development must be considered.

Examples of planning goals:

- to revitalize a declining resort by introducing new markets – traditional seaside or spa resorts, for example, may develop new products combining recreation, sport and fitness improvement for medical insurance needs with management training programmes;
- to extend the tourist season in leisure and ski resorts, using conferences, special interest activities events and exhibitions to increase the take-up of accommodation in hotels and condominiums;
- to reconstruct large depressed downtown areas comprehensively rather than by piecemeal alterations, through the integrated development of public amenities, congress facilities, hotels, commercial offices, stores and other real estate programmes comprising whole blocks of property, open spaces and associated street works;
- to improve the competitiveness of the city or region by offering products as good as, if not better than, those in other destinations by enhancing the environment and image, providing attractive facilities tailored to the target market needs, upgrading hotel, restaurant and recreation standards and improving local services, training and infrastructures.

Planning goals may be achieved by a combination of incentives (specific financial and/or technical assistance) and restrictions (development and zoning controls and conditions). The investment invariably calls for both public and private participation.

Lingotto Conference Centre, Turin, Italy

Converted from the disused Fiat factory, the Lingotto complex contains a conference centre, a hotel (244 rooms), shopping arcades, halls for concerts and special events, gardens and underground car parks. The Conference Centre has a rectangular auditorium (60 × 26 m) seating up to 2099 in the centre of the building, surrounded by smaller conference rooms and business and press centres. It is also directly linked to the Lingotto Fiere, with a pavilion of 7950 m² for associated exhibitions.

Architect: Renzo Piano

7.1.2 Financial appraisal

Two levels of financial appraisal are involved for investments in meeting and exhibition space; project cost–feasibility analysis and cost–benefit analysis, the latter taking into account wider issues such as the social and economic benefits to the area as a whole. This may be broadened to evaluate alternative proposals and strategies, and the extent to which these will meet long-term planning objectives.

Project cost–feasibility analysis

This must consider the balance of capital financing costs, operating costs, depreciation allowances and other outgoings compared with the direct revenue generated. Costs include those that are:

- fixed regardless of sales (financing of loan, pre-opening costs, depreciation, rent, rates and taxes, administrative overheads);
- semi-fixed (power, lighting, maintenance and periodic costs of replacing equipment etc.);
- variable, increasing with the volume of sales (categories of labour, materials used and consumed, hired services).

Revenue generated by congresses and exhibitions will result from:

- hall hire (including supplementary rooms for smaller groups etc.);
- letting of exhibition space (to exhibition organizers or directly);
- sale of food, beverages, etc. (banquets, coffee, lunches, bar sales);
- letting of concessional space and services (car hire, tours, theatre bookings, florist, tobacco and newsagency shops etc.);
- sales of other services (stand design, secretarial services, telephone and other departmental charges).

In the case of a hotel, credit must be given to other sales generated as a direct consequence of meetings and functions:

- room sales (to delegates and accompanying persons);
- food and beverage income from extended stays.

Cost–feasibility appraisal of projects which are judged purely on the letting of meeting and exhibition space is unlikely to show a profitable return. However, the advantages to a hotel stem from the wider range of sales, particularly if this extends the seasonality of use (resort hotels) or use at weekends (city-centre hotels). Even for a hotel, there are intangible benefits which are not costed in accountancy terms. These are, for example, publicity, repeat business, justification for better guest facilities and contributions to costs of services which might otherwise not be viable.

Cost–benefit analysis

Much wider issues need to be considered when the overall benefit to the area (city, region or country) is evaluated. Such is the case where public investment in congress halls and exhibition facilities is involved. For such public investments, economic measurements must be made of:

- the revenue generated throughout the area as a direct effect of visitor spending, and local direct expenditure by congress and exhibition organizers (on hotels, catering, transport, distribution and other services);
- the employment created and the multiplier effect of these incomes inducing greater local consumption expenditure;
- the indirect effects of secondary and tertiary purchases by the hotels, etc. (on food, drink, construction, manufactured equipment and goods, gas, electricity, water, transport, distribution and other sectors);
- the direct and indirect contributions to local property taxes, tourist taxes, rates and value-added tax on purchases;
- intangible benefits (promotion, prestige, association with subject, commercial and trading contacts, public relations);
- community benefits, both direct and indirect (use of facilities for local entertainment and cultural interests), showing justification for local financing.

Planning is often on a large scale (of investment and time), involving changes in the character and use of the whole area as

---

Pennsylvania Convention Center, Philadelphia, USA

Located in the heart of Philadelphia, the main centre opened in 1993 and was extended by conversion of the adjacent historic Reading Terminal train shed in 1994, giving a total floor area of 120 770 m². The investment of US$523 million was funded by grants, sale of bonds and revenues from hotel occupancy taxes and the Convention Center operations.

Costs	%	Space allocation	%	Financing	%
Land	27.9	Exhibition halls	33.9	City grant	8.0
Construction	60.1	Ballroom	2.5	State grant	35.4
Reading market	2.3	Reading market	6.2	Bond proceeds	53.0
Financing	5.9	Meeting rooms	6.9	Hotel tax	3.6
Education and training	0.4	Grand Hall	3.6		100.0
		Public circulation	19.2		
Administration	2.5	Food and beverage	1.5		
	100.0	Storage and back of house	26.2		
			100.0		

A connected new 1200-room hotel opened in 1995, adding 41 meeting rooms and a second ballroom.

In the first 3 fiscal years, 1993–1996, the Center received many awards and achieved all its set goals (image of the city, share of convention and trade fair business, rejuvenation of neighbourhood, boost to tourism, hospitality industry, economy and employment, increase in the tax base). It has been projected that by 2003 there will be the need for a further 2000 hotel rooms.

Attendance at conventions, trade shows and local events		Spending impact ($M)
1993–1994	677 000	179
1994–1995	986 300	194
1995–1996	1 375 900	305
Totals	3 039 200	678

Analysis of 1996–1997 performance

Economic impact	$M	Tax revenue impact	$M	Operating budget	$M
Total spend of tradeshows and conventions		On state	15.9	Total operating revenues	8.9
New wages generated	119	On city	2.3	Total operating expenses	15.4
Spending by local events	10	Total	18.2		
Total	305				

Sources: Pennsylvania Economy League (1997). The Economic and Revenue Impact of the Convention Centre. Three-year report of the Pennsylvania Convention Authority, and press releases

---

access and communications are improved, as primary and secondary building takes place and existing property and land acquires escalating commercial value.

For these reasons, the planning of a large congress centre or exhibition complex cannot be considered in cost–benefit terms alone. It is necessary to look at the possible long-term impacts (both desirable and otherwise) and the extent to which these can be controlled by strategic planning and development regulation. This also has wide implications when the method of financing and level of public investment is considered.

7.1.3 Economics of operation: some case studies

Studies of congress centres over the last twenty years show that many incurred annual trading losses of between 22 and 26 per cent. Individual accounts depended on the days of occupancy achieved – which, for most centres, was between 55 and 70 per cent – and the ratio of conventions/exhibitions to entertainment use. The latter was usually in the order of 70 : 30 although some specialist centres operated with an 80 : 20 ratio and some resorts had a balance of 50 : 50. Median figures indicated that 42 per cent of costs could be attributed to the upkeep of the premises (maintenance, insurance, rates, utilities, energy, rents, licences, etc.), 35 per cent to employment, 15 per cent to supplies and services and 8 per cent to establishment and miscellaneous costs. These figures did not include capital and interest charges, which varied widely depending on building costs, grants and subsidies, interest rates and supplementary income or capital from associated developments. Compared with conventions, exhibitions often generated profitable revenues.

Direct local benefits from the operation of a centre included employment, taxes, purchases of supplies and services (15 per cent) and convention/exhibition visitor expenditure in the area (85 per cent). In most cases these benefits, even discounting any multiplier effects, were estimated to amount to between 3.5 and 4.0 times the total annual operating losses and financing costs.

In hotels operating convention facilities, the convention delegate generally uses more of the hotel services than other categories of guest. Detailed analysis of guest accounts in a number of hotels showed the average convention guest expenditure was 2.38 times that of the individual (rack rate) traveller, 1.92 times that from a corporate booking, 1.98 times that from a travel agent booking and 3.07 times that from a tour group contract.

Harrogate International Centre, UK

The Harrogate International Centre complex includes a 2000-seat conference auditorium linked to an adjacent hotel and 11 720 m² of exhibition space in seven halls, one of which is also used for banquets. Situated in the centre of the town with high quality shops and hotels nearby, the site includes an Edwardian theatre.

As part of a programme of continuous investment to improve the facilities, over £12 million (US$19 million) was spent in 1998–2000. Third (after London and Birmingham) in the number of conferences and exhibitions held in the UK, the Harrogate Centre attracted almost 370 000 delegates and business visitors in 1997, bringing £100 million (US$15 million) into the local economy which, together with £64 million (US$102 million) spent by holiday visitors, supported some 7000 jobs. Bookings for the year 1998–1999 included 56 trade fairs and exhibitions (179 event-days) plus 33 major conferences (107 event days).

Programmes will vary with the particular circumstances of each case. The following is an indication of the steps involved in planning and providing new or improved facilities. Financial, legal, development, marketing and operational aspects need to be taken into account at every step. Decisions should be taken before each main stage of expenditure or legal commitment.

Finance/legal	Development/control	Marketing/operations
Economic review	Preliminary examination	Initial market appraisal
↓	↓	↓
Economic objectives & goals	Development opportunities	Review of facilities & sites
	↓	
	Formulation of proposals	
	↓	
	Decision	
	↓	
Sources of finance	Study framework	Market analysis
↓	↓	↓
Terms & conditions	Recommendations	Facility requirements
	↓	
	Decision	
	↓	
	Appointment of consultants	
	↓	
Financial & legal advisers	Architect, planner, engineers	Operation
↓	↓	↓
Budget guidance	Conceptual design	Facility details
↓	↓	↓
Financial appraisal	Building cost estimates	Revenue & cost estimates
	↓	
	Decision	
	↓	
Cost–benefit analysis	Detailed design	Operational requirements
	↓	
	Decision	
	↓	
Conditions of contract	Specifications	Technical inputs
↓	↓	↓
Financial plan	Bidding procedure	Consultation
↓	↓	↓
Financial procedures	Approval of tenders	Project management
↓	↓	↓
Staged payments	Construction	Appointment key staff	Market promotion
↓	↓	↓	↓
Review of progress	Fitting out	Management policies	Site visits
↓	↓	↓	↓
Final payments	Furnishings	Operational procedures	Bookings
↓	↓	↓	↓
Review of finance	Completion	Staff training	Organization
↓	↓	↓	↓
Financial plan	Opening	Supplies	Ceremony
↓	↓	↓	↓
Financial management	Event management	Additional staff	Extended markets
↓	↓	↓	↓
Review of accounts	Monitoring	Review of practices	Performance review

7.1.4 Planning programmes

Design and construction of a large congress or exhibition complex is likely to take 3–4 years, and hotel building programmes usually extend over 18 months to 2 years. Bookings need to be taken during this development period to ensure the facilities are put to use as soon as they are ready in order to offset accumulating loan charges and operating costs.

It is essential for the building programme to be carefully co-ordinated with other associated developments (access and transport infrastructures, support facilities). Planning processes have become increasingly sophisticated with the use of computer modelling and analysis techniques, which cover not only work programming but also financial implications of different courses of action and the sensitivity of a proposal to changes in conditions.

Development programmes will vary with particular circumstances and requirements. The following is an indication of the steps involved in planning and providing new or improved facilities. Financial, legal, development, marketing and operational aspects need to be taken into account at every step. Decisions should be made before each main stage of expenditure or legal commitment.

Washington State Convention and Trade Center, Seattle, Washington, USA

Plans for the expansion of the WSCTC in 1998–2002 in downtown Seattle involved the development of an adjacent block of property, provision of relocation services for the displaced businesses and replacement housing. Private partnerships were formed with two developers to incorporate a 20-storey hotel tower (460 rooms) and 22-storey office tower as part of the overall project. This expansion will add a 9750 m² exhibition floor and new loading docks at the same level as the existing halls, more than doubling the previous space. The main entrance and lobby are to be relocated adjacent to the extension, and the street separating the two blocks will be covered by bridging and a huge arched glass canopy as a signature.

WSCTC: Briefing book

Architects: Loschky Marquardt & Nesholm Architects – selected by public request for qualifications in September 1995

7.1.5 Direct investment

Direct investment in congress and exhibition facilities is usually at municipal level. The method of financing will depend on the statutory jurisdiction of the authority concerned, and will often involve some form of public enquiry or electorate approval of the financial commitment. The latter may be in the form of a local tax (or rate) levy or bond.

The **general rate precept or general obligation bond** is the most common method of financing projects, involves levying a rate or property tax on the whole community. In some authorities the electorate must approve the issue of such a bond, with a requisite majority in favour. A feasibility study for this purpose must show the benefits to the local economy (employment, direct revenues, increases in tax revenues, etc.).

In the case of an **area rate precept or special district tax bond**, the commitments are limited to those business areas that will directly benefit (from appreciation in land values and increased business). Statutory limitations may apply.

The third type bond is the **revenue bond**. Capital bonds may be underwritten by the bonding of future net revenues from the investment. Usually some form of supplementary funding will be required, such as special taxes (on tourists, hotels, restaurants and land development), to provide the necessary coverage ratio (net revenue to annual debt service). To attract investors and underwriters, the annual revenues and costs must be evaluated over the full maturity period.

7.1.6 Other sources of finance

Federal, state and central government: In most countries, particularly those with centrally planned economies, funds are provided for approved projects through loans (usually long-term low interest). Funding for this purpose may be administered through governmental departments, specific regional funds, state banks or/and joint stock-holding companies.

International agencies: Technical assistance with loan finance may be provided for approved development projects – primarily as a catalyst for further investments – by a number of agencies, such as the World Bank Group (IBRD, IDA, IEC) and the UN Development Programme. Bilateral loans and grants are also offered by the governments of individual countries to assist other developing countries.

Semi-public bodies, joint public-private companies: These are usually established to finance projects on a commercial basis. They may include national banks and institutions acting jointly with external investment agencies. Investment in exhibition facilities is often sponsored, with minority shareholding, by the local Chamber of Commerce and Trade Associations.

Commercial investors: Property investment may be supported by development companies, property holdings and investment agencies acting on behalf of institutional and private investors. Hotel companies may also fully own property or have a minority interest, as well as contributing management and technical expertise. Hotel and other properties may also be operated under franchised arrangements.

Other sources: Finance for important public buildings may be provided by sponsorship, endowment and national lottery funds.

Indirect support: Federal or state funds for development projects are usually specifically designed to encourage commercial investment and generate employment. For this reason they are normally limited in availability (to particular regions, specific types of projects, periods of time) and subject to conditions. Amongst the methods of aiding hotel and tourism development projects are:

- grants, loans and subventions for hotel building, extension and improvement;
- special guarantees to foreign investors and assistance in securing loans from other sources;
- fiscal measures such as relief from direct or indirect taxes for specified periods or/and assistance in training and promotion.

The European Development Fund also provides grants to aid the development of tourism projects in designated regions, which are financed wholly or in part by public authorities (usually up to 20 per cent of investment costs and 30 per cent of direct infrastructure costs).

7.1.7 Costs

Capital costs of development need to be estimated at an early stage of planning and continuously adjusted as data become available. Decisions on feasibility and funding are invariably taken on the basis of the initial figures, and it is essential these are based on adequate allowances to cover all the work required.

Overall development	Items to be included
Site acquisition and development	Legal costs, relocation of existing businesses, infrastructure, ground works, leases
Construction of building	Preliminaries, insurances, site works, restrictions
Special equipment and systems	Stage equipment, elevators, kitchen equipment Communication, security and fire protection systems
Furniture, fittings and equipment	Stage, seating, furniture, furnishings, fittings Operating equipment, AVA requirements
Fees, licences and expenses	Professional consultants, legal, finance negotiation
Project management	Supervision and organization of work
Working capital	Interim and other incidental payments
Pre-opening costs	Staff appointments, training, purchases
Loan charges during construction	Interest payments and expenses (may be deferred by agreement)

Construction cost analysis

The range of costs/m² and percentages of the total for construction works vary widely depending on the size, requirements and conditions which apply to each project. Whilst the following analysis of building costs is based on a number of studies and indicates the main components involved, the totals and percentages of costs may vary widely with the nature of the work as outlined below in 7.1.8.

Analysis of work	Median figures (rounded) Cost/m²			Per cent of total
	£/m²	US$/m²	(US$/sq ft)	
Preliminaries and insurance	262.5	430.0		12.5
Work below lowest floor finish	73.5	120.4		3.5
	336.0	550.4	(51.13)	16.0
Structural elements				
Structural frame and upper floors	275.1	450.6		13.1
Roof and roof lights	90.3	147.9		4.3
Staircases	8.4	13.8		0.4
External walls	63.0	103.2		3.0
Windows, screens and external doors	58.8	96.3		2.8
Internal walls, partitions and doors (including moveable partitions)	81.9	134.2		3.9
Ironmongery, signage	10.5	17.2		0.5
Total	588.0	963.2	(89.48)	28.0
Finishes and fittings				
Wall and staircase finishes	107.1	175.4		5.1
Floor finishes	105.0	172.0		5.0
Ceiling finishes	67.2	110.1		3.2
Fittings and features	(included in above)			
Kitchen and bar fittings	63.0	103.2		3.0
Furniture	94.5	154.8		4.5
Total	436.8	715.5	(70.14)	20.8
Technical services and equipment				
Sanitary appliances and plumbing (including hot and cold water supplies, waste and soil pipes and drainage)	77.7	127.3		3.7
Air-conditioning and heating	277.2	454.0		13.2
Electrical services	180.6	295.8		8.6
Elevator and life installations	35.7	58.5		1.7
Stage equipment	75.6	123.8		5.3
Communication and sound equipment	50.4	82.6		2.4
Other special services and equipment	42.0	68.8		2.0
Total	739.2	1210.8	(112.48)	35.2
Total per built area	2100.0	3439.8	(319.56)	100.0

Note: Based on costs adjusted to 1998 prices.
Depending on sophistication, costs mainly ranged from £1700–£2400/m² ($2950–$3930/m²) but higher costs were incurred in very large projects.

7.1.8 Construction summary

Work below lowest floor finish: This usually involves a waterproofed reinforced concrete ground bed and retaining walls over pile foundations or isolated concrete pads to the main structural columns. Overall costs and percentages are affected by the extent of basement construction and by abnormal site conditions.

Structural framework: A major cost is incurred in constructing the large-span framework required to clear the auditorium of the hall. Most construction is in the form of reinforced concrete columns supporting ring or crossbeams at floor and roof levels. The stepped auditorium floors of fan-shaped design are usually supported by radial raked beams. Costs are increased by stage tower requirements.

Roof: In addition to weatherproofing, roof construction must allow for differential movement over the large spans, sound damping, heat insulation, support to roof-mounted plant and access for services and maintenance. For weight reduction, the auditorium roof may be metal surfaced on decking supported by steel trusses. In other areas, roofs are generally asphalted and surfaced with paving for access.

External walls: Depending on the architectural form, external walls may be brick-faced cavity walls, *in situ* reinforced concrete with formed or treated surfaces or panel claddings. Solar screened glass panels, double glazed for thermal and sound insulation, may be used in vertical or inclined facades.

Internal structural walls: Structural walls are invariably constructed *in situ* of reinforced concrete, and usually serve as fire and sound divisions as well as providing structural support. Staircases generally are also constructed *in situ* of suspended reinforced concrete to meet fire requirements.

Partitions: Fixed partitions separating rooms, corridors and ducts, etc., dictated by fire resistance and noise insulation standards, are usually a minimum of 100 mm brick or block plastered although stud partitions may be used in party walls to offices. Moveable partitions dividing halls and auditoria into small areas are usually top hung, and may vertically fold and slide into wall recesses or fold horizontally into ceiling recesses. Large complex moveable division of areas affects structural design and costs.

Windows and doors: Windows or glazed walls are required for lobbies and transitional zones, restaurants, lounges and the smaller meeting rooms. Promenade and balcony areas enjoying a view are deliberately designed to increase contact with the outside environment. Provision must be made for solar screening and for cleaning windows and fixed glazed panels. Main entrance doors and draught lobbies are usually armour-plated glass, providing a clear view of the interior. Doors may be automatically opening or simply self-closing with weight-balanced action and provision for disabled access. To meet security requirements, all doors (including inner and outer lobby doors) must be securely lockable and fitted with entry detecting devices and CCTV monitors.

Wall finishes: In lobby and circulation areas the options usually fall between moulded or plastered structural concrete, faced brickwork or linings such as marble or other types of durable panelling which meet fire requirements. The textured surfaces are often emphasized by spotlighting or illuminating wall washes. Finishes to the main halls and auditoria are greatly influenced by acoustic requirements. In some situations the surface configuration may be deliberately faceted to provide diffusion; in others, sound absorptive panels may be required.

Floors: The main reception hall, lobby and staircases often have high quality durable surfaces of marble or terrazzo combined with carpeted areas and noise absorbing surfaces.

Elsewhere, floors are screeded and directly covered with underlay and carpet, although thermoplastic flooring may be used in areas subject to concentrated damage such as service entrances and bar surrounds. Ballroom flooring may be constructed of sprung maple boarding, secured and covered by carpet when used for meetings.

Ceilings: Suspended acoustic tile or panel ceilings are extensively used in public areas and meeting rooms. In larger auditoria plaster may be applied *in situ* to suspended mesh, frame-shaped to the required ceiling contours. In other cases the ceiling may be designed in the form of suspended panels, which can be raised or lowered and tilted to alter their reflection properties.

Staircases: The design and finishes of main staircases are important because of their prominence, extent of use and fire and safety requirements. Ballustrading often consists of a metal frame with glass panels to maintain the open appearance. High quality and durability of handrails and metalwork finishes are important considerations. The installation of an automatic sprinkler system and fire mode ventilation is usually compulsory.

Fittings: The percentage costs of fittings is high, covering high-expenditure items such as built-in reception and service counters, bars, kitchens, cloakroom and changing room fittings, auditorium seating and some stage fixtures.

Engineering services: In total, engineering installations, plant and special services amount to around 35 per cent of the total construction costs (more where elaborate stage equipment and lift systems are required), with major items like air-conditioning accounting for some 12 per cent.

Special services include stage equipment, lifts, acoustic systems, security installations, communications and kitchen equipment.

7.2 MAINTENANCE AND OPERATION

7.2.1 Importance

Future maintenance and operational requirements must be considered at every stage of the planning and design process. Not only will these items represent a large and increasing expense during the life of the building, but the success of a design will also be judged largely on the satisfaction of its performance. Losses will be incurred by breakdowns, closures and inefficiencies, affecting the financial balance and also the goodwill of the customers and staff alike.

The sensitivity and reaction of a user to discomfort and failings in expected standards is heightened by the importance of the event, and this strong subjective effect must be taken into account in life-cycle cost analyses. Efficiency in conversion, including cleaning and freshening, is often a crucial factor in permitting multipurpose use of halls and auditoria.

7.2.2 Costs of maintenance

Real costs of maintenance are often difficult to assess, since this work overlaps with other budgets. The tendency is to hire equipment and purchase items on a contract hire basis which includes supply and maintenance costs. Property leasing arrangements also vary in their coverage. The rent of a building such as hotel or hall may include the maintenance of the building shell, or this may be a separately assessed charge.

Interior design is often covered by life-cycle planning, with depreciation allowances to enable reinvestment in complete refurbishing and renovation after a set period of use.

7.2.3 Life-cycle costing

To allow for depreciation costing and the future renewal or replacement of equipment, fittings and furniture estimates must be made of the life expectancy of each major item or group. Life-cycles depend on many factors:

Factor	Considerations
Extent of wear and tear	Related to the types of materials which are acceptable: carpets, wallcoverings, drapes, upholstery
Location	Conspicuousness, impression created
Standards of premises	Image, grading, prices charged, market competition
Operational importance	Effects and extent of failure (interruption of use, damage, loss of service)
Relative costs	Compared with replacement, relative costs and difficulties of cleaning, maintenance and repair
Obsolescence	Pace of developments in performance, service and efficiency
Legal and insurance requirements	Governing safety, security, employment, hygiene and environmental conditions
Changes in use	Progressive changes in market conditions, changes in fashion and attitude. Changes in competition and new market opportunities
Degree of permanency	In terms of construction or plant. Difficulties of replacement (access, disturbance, cost). Extent to which flexibility has been allowed for in the design and construction

Investment decisions must take account of forseeable changes in both market conditions and operating requirements. In design, provision must be made for the replacements and changes likely to be involved. As far as possible these must be phased to coincide with other work, so that comprehensive modernization and refurbishing can be carried out at the same time to maximize the benefits.

7.2.4 Life-cycle periods

Typical life-cycle periods for major renovation or renewal in convention hotels and congress halls are:

Renewals	Period (years)
Decorations, furnishing fabrics	2–4
Carpets, fittings and furniture	
Bars, cocktail lounges	5–7
Coffee shops	5–7
Restaurants	6–8
Conference and seminar rooms	6–8
Capitalized leased equipment	4–7
Electronic equipment – control, communication, accounting	4–6
Office equipment, photographic and reprographic equipment	4–6
Food service and catering equipment	7–10
Major engineering plant (HVAC, sanitary, electrical)	10–15
Buildings: large-scale renovations	15–25

Source: Lawson, F. R. (1995). *Hotels and Resorts*. The Architectural Press, London.

These are typical planned schedules for accounting purposes. The range of years allows for variations in individual items and standards of premises (highest–lowest). It also indicates the latest periods for planning and budgeting as well as for replacement. Kitchen equipment, for example, should be planned for a seven year life and should be replaced within seven to ten years.

7.2.5 Planned maintenance

Ongoing maintenance is necessary to ensure that standards of performance are kept to an acceptable level of efficiency and satisfaction. The maintenance must be planned in advance so that the work can be organized at the most convenient time, replacements and equipment obtained and accurate records and costings kept.

Planning covers *preventive maintenance* to minimize the risk of failure or breakdown by giving regular attention to servicing of plant and equipment, and *corrective maintenance* to restore an area or system to an appropriate standard at the end of its design life-cycle.

Provision must also be made for *breakdown maintenance* to ensure that minor items are replaced or repaired as and when they become defective. This requires an efficient system of reporting and recording defects. It also requires good storage and updating of spares and records, and prior arrangements for work to be carried out without delay when required (by direct staff or contractors).

Maintenance efficiency necessitates some degree of rationalization in purchasing. A greater variety in items that may need to be replaced means more capital tied up in spares, more storage, specifications, records and instructions. This is even more complex when items are manufactured specially to order.

7.2.6 Planned maintenance organization

In introducing a system of maintenance it is necessary to prepare a detailed inventory of all the items (or groups) within each area of the premises, categorized according to the nature of maintenance work required. Procedures must be drawn up for:

- routine inspection (staff involved, items to be checked, procedures for reporting faults);
- routine preventive maintenance (cleaning, lubricating, servicing of plant and equipment);
- periodic re-decoration and renovation work (schedules for decorating rooms, dry-cleaning and laundering, repolishing, re-surfacing and re-covering of furniture etc.);
- long-term replacement programmes (furniture, equipment);
- emergency requirements;
- staffing requirements based on job specifications related to the work listed;
- contracting-out of work where this can be arranged in advance, including contract hire agreements;
- administration (direction and instruction of staff, records of equipment and work, costing of jobs, budgeting for future requirements);
- workshop and storage requirements and practices.

7.2.7 Advantages of planning maintenance

Planned maintenance enables defects to be remedied without delay and replacements to be introduced progressively, whilst drawing on experience of operations and designing out previous shortcomings.

By planning work ahead this can be fitted into the calendar of use of the premises, thereby creating minimum disruption and loss of revenue. Cost planning can be employed and budgets prepared for future programmes.

7.3 UPGRADING AND IMPROVING POTENTIAL

7.3.1 Comprehensive schemes

Modernization of existing halls generally calls for closedown and complete renovation, including replacement of furniture and fittings. In most cases, part rebuilding will be involved to provide additional space to improve visitor facilities and operational efficiency. Usually, new air-conditioning, lighting and sound systems will need to be installed.

Improvements in auditoria and other purpose-designed areas rely on an analysis of faults and deficiencies for which remedies can be identified. A comprehensive scheme of works may be limited to interior fitting work by structural constraints.

Modernization of banquet halls and outmoded ballrooms will usually involve the redivision of space into more flexible areas suitable for the types of events indicated by market studies.

7.3.2 Costs

The retrofitting costs involved in major conversion work can be as high as the equivalent newly built space. There may be some justification for demolition and rebuilding, particularly where more profitable use can be made of the site by adding to floor ratios (basements, additional storeys) or relocation in another area.

Against this must be weighed the value of history and association, both of which are major factors of uniqueness in promoting interest amongst international markets.

The debate for and against investment in the renovation of important buildings is often protracted, necessitating public enquiries and consideration of counterproposals.

7.3.3 Investigation and appraisal

As a preliminary to carrying out any major scheme of improvement or alteration, the following aspects must be considered.

Timing

Alterations should be phased to coincide with the life-cycle maintenance/replacement programmes to avoid unnecessary expenditure or a decline in standards resulting from deferment of work.

Disruptive work will need to be concentrated in the low season to minimize loss of revenue. Other commitments must be considered and contingency plans arranged (including temporary relocation).

Planning must start well in advance (2 years or more) to allow time for consultation, briefing, planning, detailed design, statutory approval, estimation of cost, negotiations for finance, organization of work and rearrangement of user programmes. The timing of re-opening or extension should be arranged to coincide with an event, to maximize publicity and impact.

Potential

The potential of the space must be investigated. This will involve market feasibility studies and cost appraisal of possible alternative benefits arising from:

- higher utilization of the hall or lecture theatre as a result of greater flexibility, easier setting-up and cleaning;
- better performance and quality, providing greater user satisfaction, market scope and competitiveness;
- savings in use and reductions in operating costs and maintenance, giving greater profitability, economies in energy consumption, plus savings in staff and administrative costs;
- safety and security (which may be mandatory), such as improvements in fire safety, visitor security, hygiene and sanitary facilities.

Palais des Congres de Paris

Paris has been the world's leading conference city for international association meetings for 18 years, with the Paris Conference Centre hosting over 1000 events per year, 50 per cent of them international. Since its opening in 1974 the Centre has undergone progressive improvements, and is being entirely restructured for the new millenium with an additional 41 000m² of floor space — nearly doubling the capacity — and a new avant garde facade, all without hindering the existing activities.

Current facilities include: Main auditorium seating 3723 (1813 in front half)
Stage area: 220 m² (2365 sq ft) with 14.5 × 9.5 m screen
Salle Bleue, seating 720
Conference rooms for 380, 280, 210, 112, and 22–30
Exhibition areas totalling 8000 m² (86 000 sq ft).

The centre is linked to the Hotel Concorde La Fayette, a soaring elliptical-shaped tower that creates a landmark for the complex.

Architects for original project: G. Gillet, H. Guibout, S. Makoletenkov

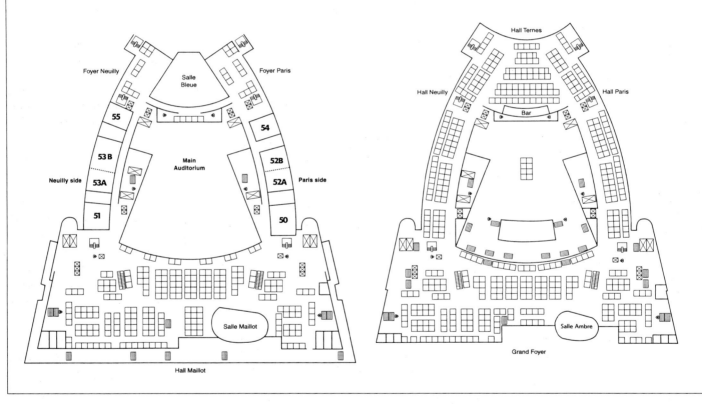

The required work may be extended to allow easier access and circulation or management control. To some extent, the potential for improvement, particularly on a moderate scale, will be revealed by monitoring the existing users' impressions and reactions. It is, however, also necessary to look beyond the existing use in order to ensure maximum benefit is obtained from the alterations. Most halls and function rooms in hotels also serve for banquets, dances, receptions and other purposes, and the optunum size and facilities provided are likely to be determined by these uses rather than by meeting requirements alone.

Similarly, municipal congress centres are invariably multipurpose in function, providing facilities for staged performances, shows, entertainment and/or spectator sports for which the audience numbers may be critical in terms of feasibility.

7.3.4 Market feasibility

In the case of existing facilities, the market strategy will very much depend on the following:

Location: There may be restrictions to extending use, problems of access and parking and constraints due to the character of the locality.

Present product mix: An evaluation must be made of the range of facilities offered, the frequency of each use, types of meals provided, the scale of charges, relative profitability, overnight stays and repeat business.

Changes and trends: Possible changes in use over time, in market structures and requirements, in technical developments, in competition and in legal requirements should be considered.

Company/institutional policy: This will depend on the type of establishment and its standards, compatibility with other users, image and degree of specialization.

Extension of use: This involves the scope for introducing new products (see below) or greater specialization, for increasing quality (grade of hotel, status of establishment) and for market development by direct or indirect promotion.

Market feasibility will involve an analysis both of the demand and supply, including an evaluation of trends and possible future patterns.

Demand analysis:
- Quantitative – extent of catchment area, population; numbers of existing users, origins, mode of travel, length of stay, average spend;
- Qualitative – customer profiles, socio-economic groupings, expenditure breakdowns;
- Motivational – reasons for attraction, repeat use, levels of satisfaction, impressions.

Supply analysis:
- Quantitative – competitive facilities, capacities, costs, accessibility;
- Qualitative – comparative standards, charges, range of products and services, new developments;
- Alternative – costs of providing and operating alternative proposals; potential increase in numbers or/and increase in charges; break-even and profitability ratios; effects on other operations (additional costs/losses and benefits).

7.3.5 Other influences

Without life-cycle improvements, the earning capacity of a hotel or centre will progressively reduce and the value of the property as an investment decline. The option of sliding into a lower grade and less discriminating market is often an uneconomic use of the site or building.

Refurbishing involves high reinvestment of capital, and it is at this time that hotel companies experiencing cash-flow problems may be obliged to sell off properties. In the case of publicly owned properties, the authorities may have to sell other assets or commit further public finance for which other uses and priorities may be in contention.

Modernization and maintenance needs tend to accumulate during difficult years of low profitability and uncertainty and be brought forward in cycles of economic growth. The impacts of taxation allowances and grant aid can often be dramatic.

7.3.6 Briefing and programming

Formal briefing of specialists is usually in two stages:

- predesign – outlines of proposals for sketch design, technical appraisal and cost estimates;
- design – details of requirements, priorities, programmes, limitations.

For alteration/improvement work, the brief establishes both instructions and parameters within which the project will need to be carried out. A well-defined brief is important not only to establish the working relationship between client and adviser, but also to provide a framework for co-ordinating other activities and inputs (staff, other departments involved, suppliers and event organizers). Essential components of the brief must include:

- terms of appointment – the extent of responsibility, approval of fees;
- purpose of project – the aims, range of activities to be accommodated;
- scope – the extent of coverage, other areas involved and inter-disciplinary relationships;
- design requirements – the standards for interior design, the accommodation to be provided, arrangements for access, layout and extension, the degree of flexibility required, the equipment to be included, the standard of environmental control;
- operational requirements – the operations to be covered, the specific equipment and connections required, staff circulation and support services, the desired savings in operation;
- legal requirements – the legislation applicable to premises and to work, conditions for approval, legal responsibilities;
- financial constraints – capital allocation, cost limits for particular areas, arrangements for approval of accounts and stage/terminal payments;
- programme – priorities in work, critical dates for entry and completion, restrictions, responsibilities for supervision;
- contract conditions – the type of contract, method of selecting contractor and suppliers, requirements of programme, means of enforcement, warranties.

The type of specialist appointed will depend very much on the resources of the establishment and on the nature of the work involved.

> ### Shanghai International Convention Centre
>
> *Completed in 1999, the Shanghai International Conventional Centre forms part of a massive redevelopment project on the East side of the Huangpu river, which has transformed a featureless suburb, within relatively few years, into a new city of skyscrapers, multi-lane highways, and high-tech business and industry. The centre offers a total of 40 meeting rooms (the largest for up to 800 delegates), two convention halls, a 4500 m² banquet hall seating 3000 and a 4000 m² media centre/exhibition hall. Facilities include a 10-language simultaneous interpretation system and advanced telecommunications networks. Nearby is a new exhibition centre, extended in two phases, to 200,000 m² of display space.*
>
> *Reference: Meeting Planner: Vol 2 No 10, Autumn 1999*

7.3.7 Monitoring

It is essential to obtain reactions from the users of the premises in order to develop future marketing strategies and, when appropriate, arrange the improvements required to make the facilities more effective. The views of users are often quite different from those of people long familiar with the situation.

Data collection is expensive in administration and often intrusive unless carefully integrated into the programme, such as in review and evaluation sessions. Monitoring must distinguish between matters that affect the group and those that are individual.

Quantitative factors: for future marketing and promotion:

Group factors:
☐ Classification ☐ Size ☐ Type of meeting or function
☐ Duration ☐ Accommodation nights ☐ Total budget
☐ Reasons for choice ☐ Contact for future

Individual data:
☐ Client profile ☐ Origin ☐ Personal expenditure
☐ Motivation for attendance

Qualitative factors: for guidance on future improvements:

Group responses: degree of satisfaction with facilities and services:

☐ Information/assistance ☐ Registration ☐ Meeting rooms
☐ Guestrooms ☐ Other facilities ☐ Audio-visual aids
☐ Attention to requests ☐ Food services ☐ General amenities and standards ☐ Overall assessment

Individual views:
☐ Personal expectancy ☐ Complaints
☐ Evaluation of experience

A typical example of grading (5 high to 1 low) and comparing the importance of relevant factors is illustrated below. None of these *ad hoc* procedures is of long-term value without an organized system of recording particulars, response action and changes over time.

Comparative grading of importance (hypothetical)

Factors	By client (post experience)					By management (pre-experience)				
	5	4	3	2	1	5	4	3	2	1
Easy location and access		×							×	
Efficiency of registration	×							×		
Quietness/comfort of bedrooms			×							×
Quality of food			×					×		
Efficiency of food service	×						×			
Pleasantness of staff				×				×		
Comfortable seating in hall			×				×			
Easy viewing of speaker/slides				×					×	
Clarity of speakers/interpreters	×									×
Adequacy of coffee service				×					×	
Attention to requests	×					×				

8 Organization of events: checklists

8.1 PLANNING MEETINGS

8.1.1 Work plans

Planning programmes for major meetings usually encompass three ranges of activity – long, medium and short-range planning – and, because of the long time-scales involved, programmes will often overlap. Although individual situations and requirements will vary, work plans usually involve the following steps:

Long-term	In advance
Site analyses prepared	4–6 years*
Guidelines determined by board/committee	4–6 years
Inquiries to convention bureaux, hotels: file established	4–6 years
Inspection visit to site	3–5 years
Site confirmed by board/committee	3–5 years
City and hotels formally notified, proposals considered	3–5 years
Detailed requirements prepared	3–5 years
Inspection visit for hotel and/or venue selection	2–4 years
Hotel etc. confirmed, reservation dates confirmed	2 years
Information updated	1–4 years

Medium-term

Draft programme prepared and exhibitors notified

Meeting requirements determined, rooms assigned

Quotations obtained from suppliers and services

Menu prices, room rates confirmed

Detailed recommendations for programme and events prepared

} 12 months

Meeting and function schedules finalized

Tours, special programmes and events confirmed

Local services arranged – security, transport, photography, signs, plaques, flowers

Budget reviewed in light of revised costs

Programme confirmed and printed details prepared

Mailing and promotion organized.

Trade press notified

Exhibition requirements finalized

} 6–9 months

Short-term

Pre-registrations and other changes monitored

Staffing schedules and itineraries prepared

Room set-ups, equipment and services listed

Exhibit handling and security arranged

Daily programmes and checklists prepared

Public relations, photography, press releases organized

Reception and registration facilities set up

} 3–0 months

*Typical for large national–international association meetings. Lead times for other meetings are much shorter:

Association committees etc.	6 months
Corporate meetings involving incentive travel or national sales/promotion	8–12 months
Management/training meetings	4 months

8.1.2 Contracts

Formal contracts must be drawn up between the company or association arranging the meeting and the management of hotels, congress halls and other facilities and services that are to be supplied. This is usually in the form of a letter setting out (or confirming arrangements for) the terms and conditions of engagement, together with a written reply of acceptance. In preliminary negotiations many of the bookings are provisional, and the right to make changes (subject to limitations and conditions) must be stipulated in the initial agreement. This also applies to exhibition needs, which will require entry in advance of the event and possibly special facilities including advance storage and security.

Agreements will also be drawn up between organizers and intermediaries, and the advice of bodies such as the American Society of Association Executives should be sought for collective recommendations. Amongst the matters which should be specified in an agreement are:

- **names of parties** to the agreement (the association or company and the facility supplier);
- **agreement to engage** the facility and its staff and to furnish the same under the terms specified;
- **scheduled dates** and days of meeting/convention, plus the date and time for entry to set up exhibitions;
- **rates to be charged** for sleeping rooms, the categories of rooms and the range of prices or flat rates;

- **estimated number of rooms** required, the categories of rooms and minimum and maximum numbers;
- **guarantees** by the facility to provide at least the maximum number of rooms requested and by the company or association to provide occupancy for at least the minimum number of rooms allocated;
- **changes in numbers** – the procedure for notifying changes in numbers, for review dates and times, for releasing rooms by either party and the cut-off dates for final agreements; no change in the guaranteed maximum or minimum should be made without the written agreement of both parties;
- **room allocations** – the arrangements for requesting room deposits, the assignment of reserved suites and specified rooms and reporting daily occupancies;
- **improvements** – the contract may include clauses requiring improvement or addition of certain rooms, areas or services prior to the event, failing which the agreement may be cancelled;
- **meeting room requirements** – a tentative schedule of the meeting rooms required, the intended period of use, the type of function and the rental charge, to be followed by a confirmed schedule setting out details by the agreed cutoff date; the rights to use public space in the facility (exclusively or in part) should be stated;
- **exhibit space requirements** – tentative reservations followed by firm details by the agreed date;
- **services to be provided** – a full specification of items to be provided in the hall and exhibition areas (cleaning, extra lighting and power supplies, carpeting, security, advance storage, audio-visual equipment and operator rates, etc.);
- **special needs** and agreed charges;
- **union regulations** – conditions to be observed;
- **food and beverage functions** – the guaranteed numbers are to be notified in advance of each function with an agreed percentage over the guarantee; agreements on·food costs per meal per person and beverage charges with provision for a review of prices up to the agreed date;
- **complimentary accommodation**, details to be agreed;
- **changes and penalties:** in the event of any changes in the facility (repairs or alterations) which might interfere with the event or if the maximum number of rooms specified in the contract cannot be met, equal alternative accommodation must be secured by the facility at its own expense; if the minimum number of rooms is not occupied but held available, the company or association must reimburse the facility (less food costs);
- **liability coverage** – exclusions and arbitration, the provisions for liability insurance, exclusions making it necessary to terminate the agreement and the establishment of an arbitration procedure for settling disputes;
- **signatures** of authorized parties.

8.1.3 Meeting planners' checklists

Checklists are essential to ensure that all the required facilities are provided, services arranged in advance, details given atten-

tion and relevant contracts drawn up. Checklists must be prepared at an early stage by the meeting planners in consultation with the client representatives. In the case of an association this is usually the secretariat or an organizing committee, whilst corporate events are often arranged through the sales, training or other department involved (see 1.5.3, 1.5.4).

General:
☐Title ☐Dates ☐Destination ☐Target attendance
☐Theme ☐Topics ☐Patronage

Organization:
☐International organization ☐National organization
☐President ☐Secretary ☐Contact details
☐Organizing committee ☐Staff ☐Division of responsibilities
☐Professional organizer's services ☐Exhibition organizer
☐Official language ☐Other languages ☐Interpreter
requirements ☐Timetable
☐Financial plan and budgets ☐Monitoring system

Facility requirements:
☐Venue selection ☐Capacity – largest hall
☐Other conference rooms ☐Break-out rooms
☐Offices ☐Exhibition halls ☐Banquet facilities ☐Services
☐Equipment requirements ☐Agreements

Advance programme:
☐Special invitations ☐Speakers ☐Chairpersons
☐Opening and closing sessions ☐Ceremonies
☐Papers ☐Abstracts ☐Translations ☐Printing

Marketing and promotion:
☐Marketing plan ☐Advertisements ☐Mailing lists
☐Conference brochure ☐Information ☐Public Relations

Conference services:
☐Accommodation lists ☐Locations of hotels ☐Negotiations
☐Transport to venue ☐Services in locality
☐Transport to destination ☐Airlines ☐Ground services
☐Other public transport ☐Negotiations

Contracts and insurance:
☐Tasks and responsibilities ☐Terms and conditions
☐Agreements ☐Dates for bookings and cancellations ☐Legal
aspects ☐Insurance provisions ☐Cancellation ☐Changes in
programme ☐Third party insurance ☐Staff insurance
☐Property insurance

Congress programme
☐Timetable ☐Schedule of events ☐Co-ordination
☐Registration ☐Opening and closing ceremonies
☐Presentations ☐Plenary meetings ☐Main lectures
☐Parallel lectures ☐Seminars and panels ☐Working groups
☐Executive meetings ☐Expected numbers ☐Equipment
requirements ☐Interpreters ☐Attendants ☐Chairpersons
☐Speakers ☐Restrooms
☐Exhibitions ☐Posters ☐Satellite meetings

Free time programmes:
☐Receptions ☐Banquets ☐Other evening events

☐Sightseeing tours ☐Excursions ☐Visits ☐Transportation ☐Meals and refreshments ☐Guides

Accompanying persons:
☐Participation in functions ☐Organized events ☐Assembly ☐Sightseeing ☐Tours ☐Visits ☐Hostesses ☐Meals ☐Refreshments ☐Gifts

Miscellaneous:
☐Pre- and post-meeting tours ☐Theatre bookings ☐Special needs – disabled, dietary ☐Seating plans ☐Flowers ☐Photographs ☐Flags, insignia ☐Mementoes

Printing:
☐Programmes ☐Invitations ☐Papers ☐Enrolment forms ☐Lists of participants ☐Badges ☐Labels ☐Folders ☐Press releases ☐Signs ☐Publication of proceedings

Accounting – expenses
☐Rentals ☐Equipment hire ☐Interpreters ☐Insurances ☐Printing ☐Advertisements ☐Telephones ☐Postage ☐Staff costs ☐Organizer services ☐Visits/tours ☐Functions

Receipts:
☐Fees – attendees ☐Accompanying persons ☐Meals and beverages ☐Sponsorships ☐Advertisements ☐Subsidies ☐Interest ☐Exhibitors ☐Other sales ☐Cancellations

8.1.4 Service providers' checklists

Service providers such as congress centres, hotels and suppliers have to ensure that:

- the requirements of the meetings and other events can be fully satisfied (for reputation and repeat business);
- their facilities and services will be efficiently and profitably utilized (to achieve business plans and performance targets);
- overlaps and conflicts of use are avoided (to meet contractual obligations and other business needs).

Detailed lists of dates, session times, room allocations and particular requirements are essential in planning each event, and these must be drawn up in consultation with the event organizer, food and beverage management and other key staff.

Each room allocation and set-up must take account of numbers, seating plans, platform arrangements, audio-visual aid equipment and services required – including client supplied and hired items.

Food and beverage requirements involve more specific details such as dates, times, rooms, numbers, seating plans, menus, style of service, table decorations, dietary needs, after-dinner speeches and presentations.

Exhibitions involve other considerations, such as access and handling needs, including size and weight limitations (see 8.2).

Organization and work plans must be prepared indicating staffing requirements, work schedules, responsibilities and arrangements for liaison with the client.

Summary charts are used to show proposed room usage over a period and the gaps available for other in-filling events.

8.1.5 Post-congress/convention reports

A review and evaluation of each event is an essential part of the monitoring process to assess the success and value of the programme, adjust future marketing and organizational strategies and determine additional facility or service needs.

Details of monitoring procedures for operators are outlined in 7.3.7.

8.2 EXHIBITION ORGANIZATION

8.2.1 Participation

Participants in exhibitions and trade shows can be grouped into organizers of events, venues, exhibitors, technical sub-contractors and visitors. Each group is motivated by different objectives, and will apply specific sets of criteria in deciding if and how to proceed. Although established shows are relatively stable and often booked well in advance, in other cases the investment involved can be high and requires careful budgeting and planning.

Risks may arise from economic changes (recession, currency changes, non-feasibility), competition (poaching of ideas and markets, overcrowding of calendars), disputes (strikes, changes in government support) or indirect factors.

8.2.2 Exhibitors

Benefits

The reasons for taking part in exhibitions and trade shows may be to:

☐Increase direct sales ☐Meet clients, suppliers and new contacts ☐Build/maintain customer relationships ☐Generate leads ☐Obtain market intelligence ☐Gauge the response to new products and services ☐Penetrate new markets ☐Change the image of the company ☐Recruit new dealers and agents ☐Build databases ☐Study the activities of competitors.

Specific objectives

Prior to participation, exhibitors need to precisely define, quantify and prioritize:

☐ Their objectives
☐ The key markets to be targeted

☐ The way information should be presented and communicated

☐ Goals and budgets and their control.

Exhibitor costs Examples

Space rental	☐Space only ☐Shell stand
Stand design	☐Design ☐Construction ☐Fittings ☐Refurbishing ☐Rentals ☐Graphics
Freight	☐Transportation ☐Storage ☐Customs ☐Handling
Show services	☐Utilities (electricity, telephones) ☐Cleaning ☐Florist ☐Photography
Staff	☐Attendance ☐Accommodation ☐Meals ☐Training
Related	☐Brochures ☐Printing ☐Advertising ☐Promotions ☐Hospitality

Evaluation of costs and benefits

Following each event, an evaluation must be made of aspects such as the:

☐Value of sales achieved ☐Number of qualified leads ☐Cost per useful contact ☐New contacts made ☐Numbers of brochures issued ☐Media coverage generated ☐Increase in levels of awareness ☐Value of market intelligence.

8.2.3 Technical sub-contractors

Amongst the sub-contractors providing exhibition services and equipment are:

☐Freight forwarders ☐Graphic artists and set designers ☐Stand fitters ☐Electricians ☐Plumbers ☐Furniture hirers ☐Printers ☐Florists ☐Cleaning agencies ☐Entertainers.

The companies concerned may be fully dependent on exhibitions or have wide ranging interests. In many cases specialist knowledge and equipment is involved, such as in erecting shell schemes or in forwarding exhibits, and some venues nominate (tied) contractors for the technical connections. Work is usually commissioned well in advance and largely undertaken in the short build-up and break-down periods.

8.2.4 Organizers' checklists

Exhibition organizers have more specific requirements covering aspects such as:

☐Preliminary research ☐Negotiation of contracts for the venue ☐Contracts for services ☐Preparation of plans ☐Promotional literature ☐Contacts with potential sponsors ☐Contacts with target exhibitors ☐Sales of space and services ☐Production of catalogues ☐Sales of advertising space ☐Settlement of accounts.

8.2.5 Venue particulars

Organization:
☐Name of show ☐Last held ☐Space rented ☐Attendance ☐Organizer ☐Contact(s)
☐Dates ☐Build-up ☐Open days ☐Break-down

Exhibition space:
☐Hall(s) ☐Total area ☐Booth area ☐Floor plans ☐Entrances ☐Aisle widths ☐Clear height ☐Restrictions ☐Floor loading ☐Floor covering

Access:
☐Separate access ☐Parking ☐Waiting areas ☐Unloading bays ☐Location ☐Dimensions ☐Limitations – ☐(height) ☐(width) ☐(weight) ☐Levels ☐Transfers to halls ☐Handling

Exhibits:
☐Main dimensions ☐Weight ☐Concentrated loading ☐Special requirements

Utility services:
☐Locations ☐Connections ☐Electrical supplies ☐Voltages ☐Communications ☐Compressed air ☐Vacuum ☐Water supplies ☐Drainage ☐Gas ☐Spot lighting ☐Special lighting

Booths:
☐Shell schemes ☐Dimensions ☐Rentals ☐Construction ☐Standard fittings ☐Extra fittings ☐Furniture ☐Floor covering ☐Decoration

Free-standing exhibits:
☐Locations ☐Areas ☐Rentals ☐Stand design ☐Construction ☐Fitting out ☐Equipment ☐Displays

Security:
☐Pre-exhibition ☐During exhibition ☐Storage ☐Checking

Facilities:
☐Registration ☐Information ☐Services ☐Cloakrooms ☐Toilets ☐First aid ☐Bank ☐Tourist bureau ☐Shop(s) ☐Organizer's offices ☐Business services ☐Press centre ☐Refreshment stands ☐Bars ☐Cafeteria ☐Restaurants ☐Exhibitors' cafeteria ☐Hospitality rooms ☐Staff numbers ☐Toilets ☐Changing rooms ☐Stand services ☐Cleaning ☐Other requirements

8.2.6 Model of the exhibition process

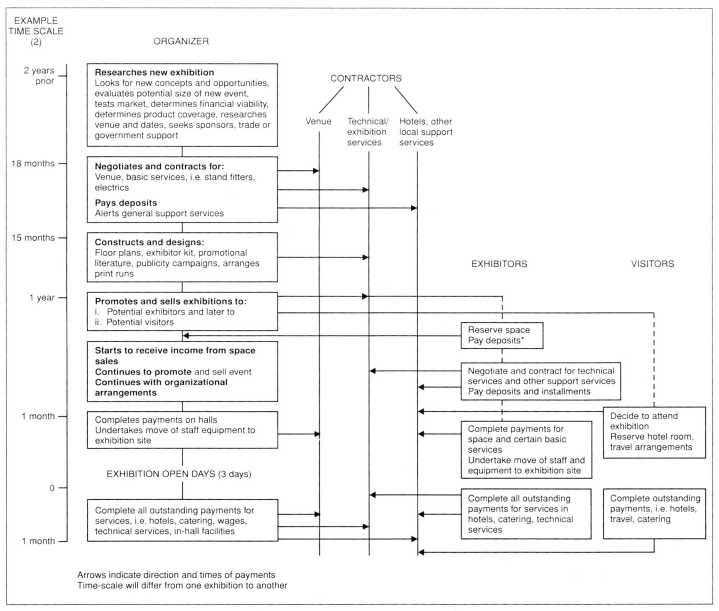

EXAMPLE
TIME SCALE
(2)

ORGANIZER

2 years prior — **Researches new exhibition** Looks for new concepts and opportunities, evaluates potential size of new event, tests market, determines financial viability, determines product coverage, researches venue and dates, seeks sponsors, trade or government support

CONTRACTORS

Venue   Technical/ exhibition services   Hotels, other local support services

18 months — **Negotiates and contracts for:** Venue, basic services, i.e. stand fitters, electrics

Pays deposits Alerts general support services

15 months — **Constructs and designs:** Floor plans, exhibitor kit, promotional literature, publicity campaigns, arranges print runs

EXHIBITORS   VISITORS

1 year — **Promotes and sells exhibitions to:**
i.   Potential exhibitors and later to
ii. Potential visitors

Reserve space
Pay deposits*

Starts to receive income from space sales
Continues to promote and sell event
Continues with organizational arrangements

Negotiate and contract for technical services and other support services
Pay deposits and installments

1 month — Completes payments on halls Undertakes move of staff equipment to exhibition site

Complete payments for space and certain basic services
Undertake move of staff and equipment to exhibition site

Decide to attend exhibition
Reserve hotel room, travel arrangements

EXHIBITION OPEN DAYS (3 days)

0 —

Complete all outstanding payments for services, i.e. hotels, catering, wages, technical services, in-hall facilities

Complete all outstanding payments for services in hotels, catering, technical services

Complete outstanding payments, i.e. hotels, travel, catering

1 month —

Arrows indicate direction and times of payments
Time-scale will differ from one exhibition to another

*Note: Exhibitor payments for space continue, with penalties for cancellation

8.3 ORGANIZATIONS

Many of the leading organizations publish valuable marketing data as well as guidelines on practice and standards (see 1.7). At international and regional level, the following play a prominent role:

AACVB   Asian Association of Convention and Visitor Bureaus
Secretariat, c/o Macau Tourist Office. 2/F Tourism Activities and Conference Centre,
Rua Luis Gonzaga Gomes, Macau, China.

AIIC   L'Association Internationale des Interprètes de Conférence.
Head Office: 10 Avenue de Secheron, CH - 1202, Geneva, Switzerland

AIPC   L'Association Internationale des Palais de Congrès
Secretary General, rue du Musée 6, B-1000, Brussels, Belgium

ASAE   American Society of Association Executives
1575 I Street NW, Washington DC., 20005-1168, USA

CIC   Convention Industry Council (formerly Convention Liaison Council)
Headquarters: 8201 Greensboro Drive, Suite 300, McLean, VA 22102, USA

EFTC   European Federation of Conference Towns
BP 182, B-1040 Brussels, Belgium

EMILG   European Meetings Industry Liaison Group
Secretary General, Kieweg 12, B-1730, Asse, Belgium

IACC   International Association of Conference Centers
243 North Lindburgh Boulevard, St Louis, MO 63141, USA

IACVB   International Association of Convention and Visitor Bureaus
2000 L Street, Suite 702, Washington DC, 20036-4990, USA

IAPCO   International Association of Professional Congress Organisers
rue Washington 40, B-1050, Brussels, Belgium

IATA   International Air Transport Association
PO Box 160, CH-1216 Cointrin, Geneva, Switzerland

ICCA   International Congress and Convention Association
Head Office: Entrada 121, NL-1096, EB., Amsterdam, The Netherlands

IH& RA   International Hotel and Restaurant Association
251 rue du Faubourg, Saint Martin, 75010 Paris, France

MPI   Meeting Professionals International
Headquarters: 4455 LBJ Freeway, Suite 1200, Dallas, Texas 75244-5309
European Bureau: Blvd St- Michel 15, B-1040 Brussels, Belgium

PCMA   Professional Convention Management Association
100 Vestavia Parkway, Suite 220, Birmingham, Alabama 35216, USA

SITE   Society of Incentive Travel Executives
21 West 38th Street, 10th Floor, New York, NY 10018 -5584, USA

UFI   L'Union des Foires Internationales
35 bis, rue Jouffroy - d'Abbans, 575017, Paris, France

UFTAA   Universal Federation of Travel Agents Association
Ave Marnix 30, Bte 1050, Brussels, Belgium

UIA   Union of International Associations
Congress Department, rue Washington 40, 1050 Brussels, Belgium

WTO   World Tourism Organization
Capitan Haya 42, Madrid 20, Spain

WTTC   World Travel & Tourism Council
20 Grosvenor Place, London SW1X 7TT, UK

Every major destination is represented by the national and regional tourism authorities, the local convention and visitor bureau and individual companies and groups offering venues and services. Most service suppliers are also represented through their professional and trade associations. In Great Britain, for example, these include the tourist authorities BTA, ETB, STB, WTB and associations such as ABPCO., ABTA., ACE., AEO., BACD., BECA., BEVA., BUAC., GBTA., HCIMA., H&RA., ITMA., MIA., SAE., SEO. as well as branches of international bodies like the AIIC. There are similar organizational structures in most other countries involved in the MICE industry.

ExCel, Royal Victoria Docks, London

The case for a new exhibition centre for London was first presented in 1985 (BTA 1985) but the initial project was frustrated by lack of suitable infrastructure. Now the 40 ha (100 acre) site is served by main highway links with London and the motorways, an extension of the London Underground (5000 persons/hr), 3 DLR stations and nearby main rail interchange as well as the City Airport and moorings for ships.

Excel is a £250 million (US$360 million) exhibition centre which is being developed in three phases. Phase 1 in 2000 provides 90,000 m² of column free space, phase 2 will add 50,000 m² and the final phase will bring the total to 155,000 m². When complete this will be the largest single building for the events industry in the UK. On site developments include 5 hotels (1150 rooms) of 3 to 5-star standard, 400 serviced apartments, and over 20,000 m² of cafes, restaurants and bars in restored waterfront warehouses. Over 14,000 jobs are expected to be generated.

The main building comprises two 375 × 87 m (120 × 285 ft) clear span halls with a central boulevard 20 m (66 ft) wide. The halls can be divided by acoustic discreet partitions 10 m (32.8 ft) high to accommodate exhibitions from 4000 to 65,000 m². No stand is more than 87 m (285 ft) from an entry point. There are 65 seminar rooms, conference suites for 1000, banquet areas for 1200 and catering modules all within short distance of the exhibit areas. Conventions for 4500 can be accommodated in the halls.

Marshalling areas for 800 commercial vehicles with 3-lane roadways give direct access to the halls through 30 separate entries, each 7 m × 5.3 m. There are 5000 car parking spaces on site. ExCel provides a totally integrated communications system, with smart card technology, internet and intranet servcies, interactive web sites, intelligent signage and touch screens. Stand services are distributed in under floor ducts and all hall modules have food and beverage outlets and toilets — the latter, being designed with movable walls to allow for changes in male:female ratios of occupancy.

Ten months before opening over 150 events had been booked for the first year of operation.

Architects: Moxley Architects
Civil Engineers: McAlpine Design Group
Structural Engineers: Buro Happold
Servcies Engineers: Hoare Lee & Partners

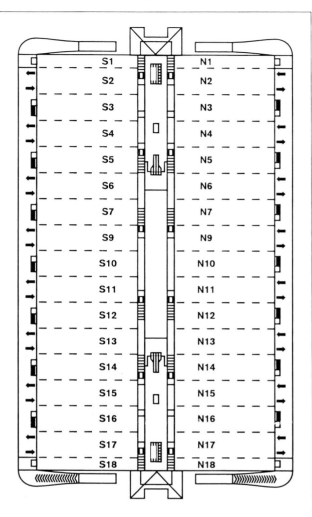

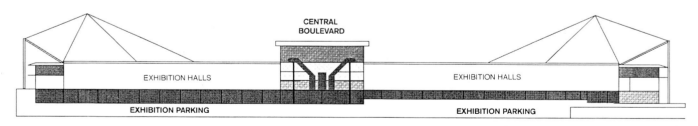

Construction January 2000 (Bridge design: Litschutz/Davidson)

International Convention Centre, Durban, South Africa

Centrally located between the business district and beachfront hotels, the new ICC Durban is only 15 minutes from the airport. It is planned around three inter-linked halls providing 7000 m² of flat-floor column-free space, which can be divided with operable walls into 11 smaller venues and can serve as a vast banquet hall, exhibition venue, sports arena, ballroom, concert hall or convention theatre. With extensive glass facades, the shimmering steel roof is shaped like an undulating wave; an echo of the sand dunes and ocean.

The layout is functional, with four loading entrances and service areas along one side. Visitor access is through the main foyer and extended concourse, which also leads to 23 smaller rooms (on two floors) with adjacent open courtyards. Registration and organizers' offices are located off the foyer. The Plenary Hall has raked seating for 1800 – divisible into two halls of 840 seats – which can be elevated up into the ceiling to leave a flat banquet floor.

Catering is supplied from a central kitchen to 12 satellite kitchens, serving up to 3500 meals at one sitting. Halal and kosher catering is accommodated. Interpretation booths for five languages are provided in the Plenary Hall, and other halls have infrared radiators installed.

Architects: *Stauch Vorster (KZN) in association with Hallen Custers Smith and Johnson Murray Architects*
Client: *City of Durban (Kwazulu Natal, South Africa)*
Project and Development Managers: *Andrew & Bouille (PTY) Ltd*
Consulting Engineers: *Young & Satharia (Structural) in association with Lawrence & Boorsma*

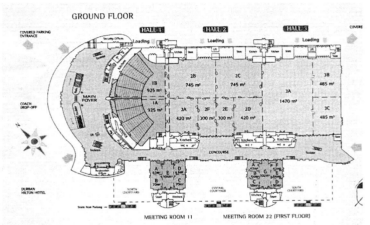

International Convention Centre, Durban, South Africa

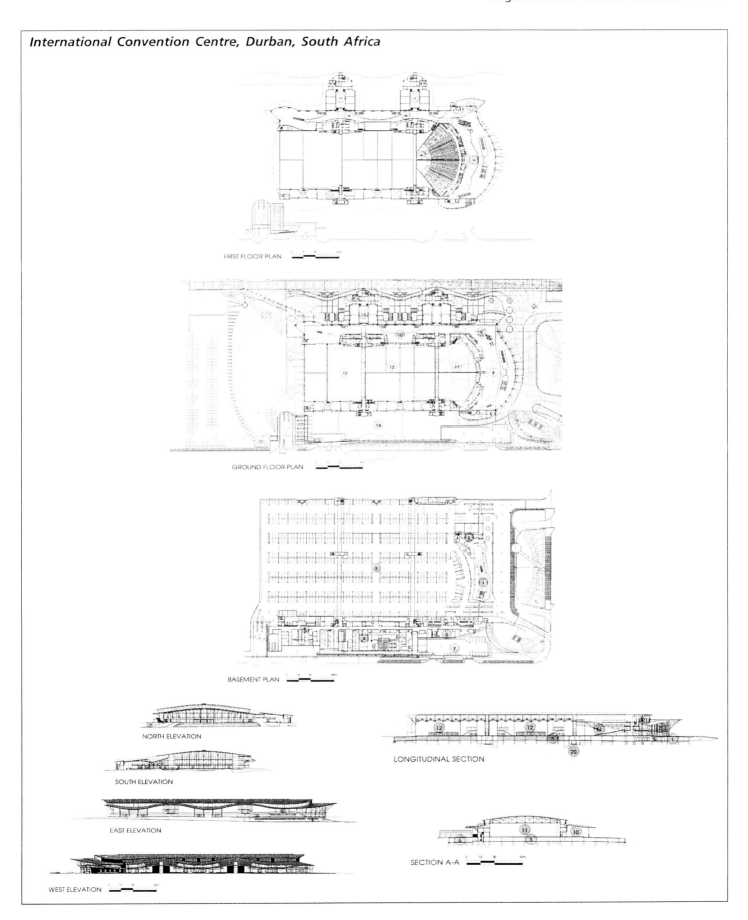

FIRST FLOOR PLAN

GROUND FLOOR PLAN

BASEMENT PLAN

NORTH ELEVATION

SOUTH ELEVATION

EAST ELEVATION

WEST ELEVATION

LONGITUDINAL SECTION

SECTION A-A

9 Trends and future developments

9.1 OPPORTUNITIES AND THREATS

Meetings, incentive travel, conventions and exhibition (MICE) activities, like other sectors of the service industry, tend to mirror the cycles of economic progress and development, although the lead times involved in organizing events can have a delaying effect and, even in times of recession, these activities are often seen as an investment to secure improvements in positioning, trade and performance.

As in leisure tourism, the MICE industry is highly competitive and relies heavily on the effectiveness of organization and promotion. However, compared with mass tourism, the success of MICE events are determined not so much by price, but by their value in achieving the desired objectives.

Arguably the greatest challenges facing the industry in the next decade and beyond are likely to be concerned with maintaining growth and sustaining the benefits of investment, particularly in light of the intensive development of new facilities.

Whilst teleconferencing and other advances in communications are likely to have some impact on business travel, this should also stimulate a need for actual contact and the interactive exchange of ideas and information through group meetings and incentive travel.

Growth and structural changes in intergovernmental organizations, international corporations, professional institutions and national bodies involving wide representation all point towards a continuing demand for congresses, conventions and exhibitions.

Many of the latest developments in technology have been outlined in the relevant chapters of this book, and the examples illustrate new developments in facilities, including a number that will be completed in 2000 and beyond. The following summary is the author's view of some of the major changes that are taking place and trends that are likely to affect the future of this industry.

9.2 MARKETING

Buyer's market: The opening of over 30 new purpose-built congress centres world-wide at the beginning of the millennium will inevitably generate further interest and demand, whilst also leading to greater competition in the medium term.

Value analysis: With increasing pressures on time, choice and accountability, companies and individuals are likely to take greater account of cost-effectiveness (opportunity cost) and personal goal achievement in evaluating events.

Market channels: Direct marketing is extending rapidly with the use of internet sales and centralized databases. Training programmes may be organized for both direct presentations and intranet distribution.

Major market subjects such as medicine, technology, business and financial services and law will inevitably continue to grow with developments in these fields. Emergent subjects that reflect changes in societies, employment and lifestyles are also likely to increase.

Niche markets The market coverage is widening to include out-of-season adult study programmes, special interest groups and social activities with demographic shifts towards more mature participants.

Distant learning: Extension of requirements for continued professional development, postgraduate courses and company training programmes is giving rise to the need for periodic seminars combined with intranet and other distant learning arrangements.

Video conferencing: The installation of video conferencing links provides an opportunity for venues to market this facility as a supplement to meetings or as a studio hire facility for local businesses and organizations.

International exhibitions: Large trade shows are increasingly becoming polarized into relatively few major centres able to accommodate their requirements, and a number of specialist sections with parallel seminar programmes.

Regional trade shows will continue to have a role in maintaining and extending customer contacts. General consumer exhibitions are tending to become more subject-focused and orientated around specific themes.

Market analysis: Increasing sophistication in analysing markets and their requirements includes the use of auditing techniques, individual encoders and continuously revised databases.

9.3 FACILITIES

Communications: Rapid developments in integrated services digital networks (ISDN) and similar high speed, high capacity transmission systems for data, voice mail and video communications will have an increasing impact on conference and exhibition services.

Video projection: Video is becoming the standard means of presenting audio-visual information, offering wide versatility in recording events on or off site, transmitting and projecting material (instantly or from prepared presentations) in one or several locations. Rapid developments are taking place in the portability of equipment and increasing size and scope for presentation of images.

Video-conferencing: Communication and production facilities in the form of studios and smaller self-contained carrels with sophisticated equipment (microphones, cameras, projectors, plasma screens) are expected to be offered as an extension of the roles of modern congress and exhibition centres.

Back projection: New and converted centres increasingly provide back-projection facilities for slides and video, together with the latest equipment, control systems and trained staff.

Integrated management systems: Integrated systems, widely used in hotel operations, are being extended and applied to congress and exhibition management, covering for example reservations, travel/accommodation requirements, registration, billing, accounting, monitoring, building services operations, employee organization, personnel records, maintenance and security requirements.

Co-ordination: To facilitate overall operational arrangements and convenience, smart card technology will be increasingly used in organizing events and personalizing requirements.

Environmental management: Increasing concern in safeguarding the environment is prompting venues to adopt defined policies to reduce energy consumption (below) and waste of other resources by prudent use, recovery and recycling and/or improved efficiencies.

Energy reduction: Energy savings being introduced include building management systems of monitoring and control, optimization, load shedding, demand prediction, combined heat and power systems, regenerative/recuperative recovery of waste heat and the use of solar energy for powering communications and domestic hot water.

Risk management: Organized risk management assessment and business continuity procedures, together with specific training, are essential in all major meeting and exhibition venues and hotels.

Security: To ensure the security and safety of visitors, information and equipment, as well as the property generally, venues are increasingly installing sophisticated surveillance, locking and detection systems. Fire safety and measures to deal with accidents and emergencies are also an essential feature of management policies.

Disabled facilities: All centres and hotels are required to provide access and facilities to enable disabled visitors to participate in events. This calls for an audit of requirements, detailed planning and conversion work in many existing venues.

9.4 VENUES

Executive conference centres: The development of purpose-designed conference centres is expected to continue and extend into resort hotels offering dedicated blocks of rooms for out-of-season conference use. Company-owned executive and training facilities are increasingly using facility management services.

Hotels: Potential developments include the introduction of designed suites of meeting rooms equipped with high technology services and operated as a franchised package.

Congress centres: Venues in major market destinations tend to expand to meet the demands for larger plenary auditoria and banquet halls, more small meeting rooms and extended exhibition space. In other cases, rationalization may be more feasible.

Integration: To attract a wider range of marketing activities and facilitate organization, new and expanded congress centres will increasingly create a focus for tourism development and be linked to associated hotels.

Attractions: Competition between destinations will demand increasing attention to the importance of good access, integrated transport, highly efficient services and attractive, safe environments for relaxation.

Organization: Liaison and collaboration between the numerous associations and organizations representing the MICE industry is expected to increase in the interests of improving statistics and standards, as well as promoting greater awareness of the value and benefits of these activities.

Professionalism: The needs of operational management and services in the industry call for greater professional recognition and the development of organized training at all levels.

Projects illustrated

BY LOCATION

Harrahs Sky City, Aukland, New Zealand
Bali International Convention Centre, Bali, Indonesia
Waterfront Hall, Belfast Northern Ireland
International Congress Centrum, Berlin, Germany
International Convention Centre, Birmingham, England
National Exhibition Centre, Birmingham, England
Brisbane Convention and Exhibition Centre, Brisbane,
   Queensland, Australia
Cairns Convention Centre, Cairns, Australia
Cairns International Hotel, Cairns, Queensland, Australia
Robinson College, Cambridge, England
Techniquest Science Discovery Centre, Cardiff, Wales
Bella Center, Copenhagen, Denmark
Corfu Grecotel Congress Centre and Resort
Disneyland, Paris
Dover Heritage Centre, The White Cliffs Experience, Dover,
   England
Edinburgh International Conference Centre, Scotland
Scanticon Denver, Colorado, USA
Palcio de Congresos, Kursaal, Donostia – San Sebastian,
   Spain
Jumeirah Beach Hotel and Conference Centre, Dubai, United
   Arab Emirates
International Convention Centre, Durban, South Africa
Congress Centre Messe, Frankfurt, Germany
Hawaii Convention Center, Honolulu, Hawaii, USA
Hong Kong Convention and Exhibition Centre, Hong Kong
Tampere Hall, Tampere, Finland
Congress Centre Messe, Frankfurt, Germany
Scottish Exhibition and Conference Centre, Glasgow,
   Scotland
Telecom World, Hong Kong, China
Istanbul Convention and Exhibition Centre, Istanbul, Turkey
Jyvaskla International Congress and Fair Centre, Jyvaskla,
   Finland
Kunibiki Messe, Shimane Prefecture, Japan

Scanticon Borupgard, Helsingor, Denmark
La Grand Motte Palais des Congres, La Grand Motte, France
Leipziger Messe, Leipzig, Germany
Lille Grand Palais, France
ExCel Exhibition Centre, Royal Victoria Docks, London,
   England
Palais des Congres de Lyon, Lyon, France
Palcio Municipal de Congresos de Madrid, Madrid, Spain
Bridgewater Hall, Manchester, England
G.Mex, Manchester, England
Forum Grimaldi, Monaco
International Congress Centre, Munich, Germany
Palais des Congres de Paris, Paris, France
Europarque Convention Centre, Porto, Portugal
Congress Centre, Salzburg
San Diego Convention Center, California, USA
Singapore International Convention and Exhibition Centre
De Vere Grand Harbour Hotel, Southampton, England
Le Palais de la Musique et des Congres, Strasbourg, France
Sydney Harbour Casino, Sydney, New South Wales, Australia
Sydney Convention and Exhibition Centre, Darling Harbour,
   Sydney, Australia
Four Seasons Hotel, Chinzan-so, Tokyo, Japan
Tokyo International Forum, Tokyo, Japan
Valencia Congress, Valencia, Spain
Pacifico Yokohama, Yokohama, Japan
Messe Zurich, Zurich, Switzerland

CASE STUDIES

Harrogate International Centre, England
The New Munich Trade Fair, Munich, Germany
Pennysylvania Convention Center, Philadelphia
Washington Convention and Trade Center, Seattle
Shanghai International Convention Complex, China
Lingotto Conference Centre, Turin

References and Bibliography

Marketing and Overview of the Industry

(Text reference)

ASAE 1992 American Society of Association Executives Report, Washington DC   1.5.3

Auma (1998) *German Trade Fair Industry, 1998* Association of the German Fair Industry, Cologne   1.8.1

British Tourist Authority/English Tourist Board (1997) *International Passenger Surveys, 1996*, London   1.6.1

CLC (1998) Convention Liaison Council, (Now the Convention Industry Council, CIC), *Meetings Industry Glossary* McClean, VA, USA   1.1.5

Convention Liaison Council (1995) *Value of Convention and Meeting Business in the USA.* (Reported in Convene Magazine), McLean, VA, USA   1.6.2

German Convention Bureau, Infratset Study (1994–5) *The German Meetings Market, 1996*, Frankfurt/Maine   1.5.1

Harrison, R., (ed.) (1994) *Manual of Heritage Management*, Butterworth-Heinemann, Oxford

IACVB (1999) *Analysis of Delegate Expenditures*, International Association of Convention and Visitors Bureaus, Annual report 1998   1.6.4.

ICCA (1997) *The International Meetings Market* ICCA in association with International Meetings Association, Amsterdam (Annual reports)   1.4.2

Lawson (1985) *Exhibition Facilities in London: Providing for the Future*, British Tourist Authority, London   1.8.4

Lawson (1982) 'Trends in Business Management', *Journal of Tourism Management*, 3 (4) December, 1982, pp. 208–302, Oxford   1.7.3

London Visitor and Convention Bureau (1998) *Overseas Visitors to London, 1997.* International Passenger Survey, London   1.6.3

Meetings Industry Association (1997) The Right Solution, *The UK Conference Market, 1995–6*, MIA, Broadway, UK   1.5.4

Rogers, T. (1998) *Conferences: A Twenty-first Century Industry*, Addison, Wesley Longman, Harlow

Singapore Tourist Office, *Foreign Convention and Exhibition Expenditures*, Singapore   1.6.3

SITE (1998) Society of Incentive Travel Executives, New York, USA   1.1.4

Sixsmith, M., (ed.) (1995) *Touring Exhibitions: The Touring Exhibitions Group's Manual of Good Practice*, Butterworth-Heinemann, Oxford

Tourism Vancouver, Greater Vancouver (1997) *Economic Impacts of Conventions, 1997* Vancouver, Canada   1.6.2

UIA (1997) *International Meetings, Comparative tables on their development, geographical distribution and number of participants*, UIA, Brussels (Annual reports)   1.4.2

UIA (1995) *Analysis of International Meetings:* Research by the Congress Department, UIA., Brussels   1.4.2

US Travel Service (1975) *The Markets for International Congresses*, Washington DC   1.6.2

Vienna Convention Bureau (1977) *Conference data*, Vienna, Austria   1.6.2

Washington DC, Convention and Visitors Association (1997) *Annual Report: Conventions and Meetings, Washington, 1997*   1.6.2

W.T.O., Annual, *Yearbook of Tourism Statistics, Tourism Highlights* World Tourism Organization, Madrid

WTO (1997) *Tourism Market Trends, Tourism Global Forecasts*, World Tourism Organization, Madrid

WTO (1998) *Travel and Tourism Fairs: Guidelines for Exhibitors*, World Tourism Organization (in association with European Tourism and Trade Fair Agencies, ETTFA), Madrid

Wilkie (1987) *UK Exhibitions and their Evaluation*, MPhil thesis, University of Surrey   1.7.8

Facility Planning and Design

(Text reference)

Appleton, L. (1996) *Buildings for the Performing Arts: A Design and Development Guide*, Architectural Press, Oxford

Baud-Bovy, M. and Lawson, F.R. (1998) *Tourism and Recreation Handbook of PLanning and Design*, Architectural Press, Oxford

Davies, T.D. and Beasley, K.A. (1988) *Design for Hospitality: Planning for Accessible Hotels and Motels*, Nichols Publishing, New York

Ham R. (1988) *Theatres: Planning Guide for Design and Adaptation.* Architectural Press, Oxford

Holmes-Siedle, J. (1996) *Barrier-Free Design: A Manual for Building Designers and Managers*, Architectural Press, Oxford

Inskeep, E. (1991) *Tourism Planning*, Von Nostrand Reinhold, New York

Lawson, F.R. (1981) *Conference, Convention and Exhibition Facilities: Planning, Design and Management*, Architectural Press, Oxford

Lawson, F.R. (1985) *Hotels and Resorts: Planning, Design and Refurbishment*, Architectural Press, Oxford

Lawson, F.R. (1994) *Restaurants, Clubs and Bars: Planning, Design and Investment for Food services*, Architectural Press, Oxford

Matthews, G. (1991) *Museums and Art Galleries: Design and Development Guide*, Architectural Press, Oxford

Penner, R.H. (1991) *Conference Center Planning and Design*, Architectural Design and Technology Press, London 1.1.5

Rutes, W.A. and Penner, R.H. (1985) *Hotel Planning and Design*, Whitney Library of Design, New York

Sheard, J.G. (1997) *Stadia: A Design and Development Guide*, 2nd edn., Architectural Press, Oxford

Wilkinson, C. (1995) *Supersheds: The Architecture of Long Span, Large Volume Buildings* 2nd edn., Architectural Press, Oxford

Technical Aspects

(Text reference)

AIPC (1992) *Conference Safety Handbook*, Association Internationale des Palais de Congres, Paris 6.8.1

ANSI Standard Z24 19 (1957) *Laboratory Measurement of Airborne Sound Transmission Loss of Building Floors and Walls*. American National Standards Institute, Washington, DC. 6.2.5

ASHRAE (1997) *Handbook of Fundamentals*, & ASHRAE 1997 *Pocket Guide* American Society of Heating, Refrigeration and Air conditioning Engineers, New York, USA

ASHRAE, 1996, *Handbook: HVAC Systems and equipment*, American Society of Heating, Refrigeration and Air conditioning Engineers

Association of Building Engineers (1999) *Access for all: an Explanatory Leaflet* Weston Favell, UK 6.9.1

Bains, A. (1973) *Environment 1. Acoustic factors. AJ Handbook of Office Buildings*, Architects Journal 1973, pp. 1329–1332, London 6.1.3

BIFM (1999) *Best Practice Guide: Business Continuity Planning*, British Institution of Facility Management, Saffron Walden, UK

CIBSE (1994) *Code for Interior Lighting* Guide LG4 (1991) *The visual environment in lecture, teaching and conference rooms* and Guide LG8 (1994) *Museums and Art Galleries*. Chartered Institution of Building Services Engineers, London

CIBSE, Guide D (1997) *Fire Engineering* and Guide F (1998) *Energy efficiency in buildings*. Institution of Building Services Engineers, London

CIBSE (1999) *Environmental Criteria for Design*, Chartered Institute of Building Services Engineers, London 6.7.1

CIE Publications, *Guide to Interior Lighting*, Commission International de l'Eclairage, Paris

Croome, D.J. (1977) *Noise, Building and People*, Pergamon Press, Oxford 6.2.4

GLC Code of Practice: *Places of Public Entertainment: Technical Regulations*, Greater London Council (Basis for subsequent standards)

Ham, R. (1972) *Theatre Planning*, Architectural Press, Oxford 6.3.8

Ham, R. (1988) *Theatres: Planning Guidance for Design and Adaptation*, Architectural Press, Oxford

Izenour, G.C. (1977) *Theatre Design*. McGraw-Hill, New York

Knudsen, V.O. and Harris, C.M. (1962) *Designing in Architecture*, Wiley

Lord, P. and Templeton, D. (1986) *The Architecture of Sound: Planning and Designing Auditoria*. Architectural Press, Oxford

MacDonald, L.W. and Lowe, A.C. (ed.) (1977) *Display Systems: Design and Application*, John Wiley & Sons

Miller, G.A. (1973) *Language and Communicating*, McGraw-Hill, New York

National Electrical Code, National Fire Protection Association, Boston, USA

Pank, B. (1996) *The Digital Fact Book*. Quantel Ltd., 8th Edition

Parkin, P.H. and Humphries, H.R. (1969) *Acoustics, Noise and Buildings*, (3rd edn), Faber and Faber, London 6.1.5, 6.1.8

Phillips, D. (1999) *Lighting Modern Buildings*, Architectural Press, Oxford

Simpson, R.S. (1997) *Video Walls: The book of the big electronic image*, Focal Press, Oxford

Simpson, R.S. (1996) *Effective Audio Visual*, (3rd edn), Focal Press, Oxford

Templeton, D., Mappe, P., Saunders, D. (1997) *Acoustics in the Built Environment: Advice for the Design Team*, Architectural Press, Oxford

Thomson, G. (1986) *The Museum Environment*, (2nd edn), Butterworth-Heinemann (in association with The International Institute for Conservation of Historic and Artistic Works), Oxford

Turner, N. (1974) *Acoustic performance standards for offices*, Building Services Engineering, **41**, 223–30, London 6.1.3

Van Aerschot, A. and Carney, A. (1997) *Environmental Guidelines for Congress Centres*. AIPC Annual Conference and 39th General Assembly, Moscow, 1997 6.9.2

Watkinson, J. (1994) *An Introduction to Digital Video*, Focal Press, Oxford

Whitaker, J.C. (1994) *Electronics Displays*, McGraw-Hill, New York

Magazines

The Arup Journal, Brown, D.J. (ed.) 1/96: Edinburgh International Conference Centre, 2/96: Brisbane Convention and Exhibition Centre, 1/97: Bridgewater Hall, 2/98: Scottish Exhibition and Conference Centre Ove Arup Partnership, 13 Fitzroy St, London W1P 6BQ

Architect's Journal: 6 June, 1996: Leipzig Glass Hall, 6 March 1997: Belfast in Concert, The Architects Journal, London (weekly)

Building Services Journal, Bunn, R. (ed.), Engineering equipment and services, Chartered Institute of Building Services Engineers, Delta House, 222 Balham High Rd, London SW12 9BS   (monthly)

AV Magazine, Lloyd, P. (ed.), Audio Visual Information for Business Communications, Quantum Publications, Quantum House, 19 Scarbrook Rd, Croydon, Surrey CR9 1LX   (monthly)

Some Leading Magazines: Meetings Conventions and Exhibitions

Europe

Association Meetings International:
   CAT publications, Ashdown Court, Lewes Rd, Forest Row, E. Sussex RH18 5EZ

Conference & Exhibition Fact Finder
   Pembroke House, Campsbourne Rd, Hornsey, London N8 7PE

Conference and Incentive Travel:
   Haymarket Publishing, 174 Hammersmith Rd, London W6 7JP

Congresos, Convenciones e Incentivos:
   C/Princesa, 1, Torre de Madrid, Planta 27a Of. 1, 28008 Madrid, Spain

Exhibition Bulletin:
   131 Southlands Rd, Bromley, Kent, BR2 9QT

Expo News:
   Groupe Expo News, 5 rue de Chazelles, 75017, Paris, France

Hotels:
   Cahners Publishing Netherlands, Postbus 9001, 2130 DB Hoofddorp, The Netherlands

Meeting & Congressi:
   Corso S Gottardo, 39, 20136 Milano, Italy

Meetings & Incentive Travel:
   CAT publications, Ashdown Court, Lewes Rd, Forest Row, E. Sussex RH18 5EZ

Meeting Planner International:
   Hallmark Communications, Unit B-5, Enterprise Point, Melbourne St, Brighton, E. Sussex BN2 3LH

Successful Meetings:
   Corso Porta Romana, 20122, Milano, Italy

TW, Tagungs-Wirtschaft:
   Mainzer Landstrasse 251, D-60326 Frankfurt-am-Main, Germany

United States

Association Management:
   ASAE, 1575 I Street, NM., Washington D.C., 20005-1168

Association Meetings:
   63 Greta Road, Maynard, MA 07154

Convene:
   100 Vetsavia Parkway, Suite 220, Birmingham, Alabama, AL 35216

Corporate and Incentive Travel:
   Coastal Communications Corp., 488 Madison Ave, New York, NY 10022

Hotels:
   Cahners Business Information, 1350 East Touhy Avenue, Des Plaines Illinois, 60018, USA

Meeting News:
   Gralla Publications, 1515 Broadway, New York, NY 10036

Meetings and Conventions:
   Reed/Cahners Travel Group, 500 Plaza Drive, Secaucus, NJ 07094-3626

Restaurant/Hotel Design International:
   Bill Communications, 633 Third Ave, New York, NY 10017

Successful Meetings:
   Bill Communications, 633 Third Ave, New York, NY 10017

Index